# *Teach Yourself* VISUALLY™

## Windows® Home Server

Visual

by Paul McFedries

Wiley Publishing, Inc.

## Teach Yourself VISUALLY™ Windows® Home Server

Published by
**Wiley Publishing, Inc.**
10475 Crosspoint Boulevard
Indianapolis, IN 46256

Published simultaneously in Canada



*Library of Congress Control Number: 2007941557*

ISBN: 978-0-470-22639-1

Manufactured in the United States of America

10 9 8 7 6 5 4 3 2 1

### Trademark Acknowledgments



### Contact Us

For general information on our other products and services please contact our Customer Care Department within the U.S. at 800-762-2974, outside the U.S. at 317-572-3993 or fax 317-572-4002.

For technical support please visit www.wiley.com/techsupport.

Wiley Publishing, Inc.

**Sales**

Contact Wiley
at (800) 762-2974 or
fax (317) 572-4002.

# Praise for Visual Books

***"Like a lot of other people, I understand things best when I see them visually. Your books really make learning easy and life more fun."***

John T. Frey (Cadillac, MI)

***"I have quite a few of your Visual books and have been very pleased with all of them. I love the way the lessons are presented!"***

Mary Jane Newman (Yorba Linda, CA)

***"I just purchased my third Visual book (my first two are dog-eared now!), and, once again, your product has surpassed my expectations.***

Tracey Moore (Memphis, TN)

***"I am an avid fan of your Visual books. If I need to learn anything, I just buy one of your books and learn the topic in no time. Wonders! I have even trained my friends to give me Visual books as gifts."***

Illona Bergstrom (Aventura, FL)

***"Thank you for making it so clear. I appreciate it. I will buy many more Visual books."***

J.P. Sangdong (North York, Ontario, Canada)

***"I have several books from the Visual series and have always found them to be valuable resources."***

Stephen P. Miller (Ballston Spa, NY)

***"Thank you for the wonderful books you produce. It wasn't until I was an adult that I discovered how I learn – visually. Nothing compares to Visual books. I love the simple layout. I can just grab a book and use it at my computer, lesson by lesson. And I understand the material! You really know the way I think and learn. Thanks so much!"***

Stacey Han (Avondale, AZ)

***"I absolutely admire your company's work. Your books are terrific. The format is perfect, especially for visual learners like me. Keep them coming!"***

Frederick A. Taylor, Jr. (New Port Richey, FL)

***"I have several of your Visual books and they are the best I have ever used."***

Stanley Clark (Crawfordville, FL)

***"I bought my first Teach Yourself VISUALLY book last month. Wow. Now I want to learn everything in this easy format!"***

Tom Vial (New York, NY)

***"Thank you, thank you, thank you...for making it so easy for me to break into this high-tech world. I now own four of your books. I recommend them to anyone who is a beginner like myself."***

Gay O'Donnell (Calgary, Alberta, Canada)

***"I write to extend my thanks and appreciation for your books. They are clear, easy to follow, and straight to the point. Keep up the good work! I bought several of your books and they are just right! No regrets! I will always buy your books because they are the best."***

Seward Kollie (Dakar, Senegal)

***"Compliments to the chef!! Your books are extraordinary! Or, simply put, extra-ordinary, meaning way above the rest! THANK YOU THANK YOU THANK YOU! I buy them for friends, family, and colleagues."***

Christine J. Manfrin (Castle Rock, CO)

***"What fantastic teaching books you have produced! Congratulations to you and your staff. You deserve the Nobel Prize in Education in the Software category. Thanks for helping me understand computers."***

Bruno Tonon (Melbourne, Australia)

***"Over time, I have bought a number of your 'Read Less - Learn More' books. For me, they are THE way to learn anything easily. I learn easiest using your method of teaching."***

José A. Mazón (Cuba, NY)

***"I am an avid purchaser and reader of the Visual series, and they are the greatest computer books I've seen. The Visual books are perfect for people like myself who enjoy the computer, but want to know how to use it more efficiently. Your books have definitely given me a greater understanding of my computer, and have taught me to use it more effectively. Thank you very much for the hard work, effort, and dedication that you put into this series."***

Alex Diaz (Las Vegas, NV)

# Credits

**Project Editor**
Alissa Birkel

**Acquisitions Editor**
Jody Lefevere

**Copy Editor**
Marylouise Wiack

**Technical Editor**
Jim Kelly

**Editorial Manager**
Robyn Siesky

**Business Manager**
Amy Knies

**Sr. Marketing Manager**
Sandy Smith

**Manufacturing**
Allan Conley
Linda Cook
Paul Gilchrist
Jennifer Guynn

**Book Design**
Kathie Rickard

**Production Coordinator**
Kristie Rees

**Layout**
Carrie A. Cesavice
Andrea Hornberger
Jennifer Mayberry
Christine Williams

**Screen Artist**
Jill A. Proll

**Illustrators**
Ronda David-Burroughs
Cheryl Grubbs

**Proofreader**
Laura Bowman

**Quality Control**
David Faust
Susan Moritz

**Indexer**
Broccoli Information Management

**Special Help**
Cricket Krengel

**Vice President and Executive Group Publisher**
Richard Swadley

**Vice President and Publisher**
Barry Pruett

**Composition Director**
Debbie Stailey

## About the Author

**Paul McFedries** is a Windows expert and full-time technical writer. Paul has been authoring computer books since 1991 and he has more than 50 books to his credit. Paul's books have sold more than three million copies worldwide. These books include the Wiley titles *Teach Yourself VISUALLY Windows Vista*, *Windows Vista: Top 100 Simplified Tips & Tricks*, *Teach Yourself VISUALLY Computers*, 5th Edition, and *The Unofficial Guide to Microsoft Office 2007*. Paul is also the proprietor of Word Spy (www.wordspy.com), a Web site that tracks new words and phrases as they enter the language.

## Author's Acknowledgments

It goes without saying that writers focus on text, and I certainly enjoyed focusing on the text that you'll read in this book. However, this book is more than just the usual collection of words and phrases. A quick thumb through the pages will show you that this book is also chock-full of images, from sharp screen shots to fun and informative illustrations. Those colorful images sure make for a beautiful book, and that beauty comes from a lot of hard work by Wiley's immensely talented group of illustrators, designers, and layout artists. They are all listed in the credits on the facing page, and I thank them for creating another gem. Of course, what you read in this book must also be accurate, logically presented, and free of errors. Ensuring all of this was an excellent group of editors that included project editor Alissa Birkel, copy editor Marylouise Wiack, and technical editor Jim Kelly. Thanks to all of you for your exceptional competence and hard work. Thanks, as well, to acquistitions editor Jody Lefevere for asking me to write this book.

# Table of Contents

## Windows Home Server Basics

Understanding Windows Home Server Basics . . . . 4
Learn About Windows Home Server's Features . . . . 6
Discover What You Can Do with Windows Home Server . . . . 8
Learn About Windows Home Server's Benefits . . . . 10
Learn About Advanced Uses for Windows Home Server . . . . 12

chapter 2

## Networking Computers

Understanding Networking . . . . 16
Survey Networking Hardware . . . . 18
Discover Network Configurations . . . . 20
Examine Network Security . . . . 22
Discover Wireless Networking . . . . 24
Learn About Wireless Networking Devices . . . . 26
Configure a Wireless Gateway . . . . 28
Connect to a Wireless Network . . . . 30
Implement Wireless Network Security . . . . 32

## chapter 3 Configuring Windows Home Server


Connect Windows Home Server to Your Network . . . 36
View the Windows Home Server Network . . . 38
Install Windows Home Server Connector . . . 40
Run the Windows Home Server Console . . . 42
Create a Start Menu Shortcut for the Console . . . 44
Change the Workgroup Name . . . 46
Change the Computer Name . . . 48
Configure Windows Home Server with a Static Address . . . 50
Change the Windows Home Server Password . . . 52
Remove a Computer from Windows Home Server . . . 54
Rediscover Windows Home Server . . . 56
Customize the Windows Home Server Start Menu . . . 58
Customize the Windows Home Server Taskbar . . . 60


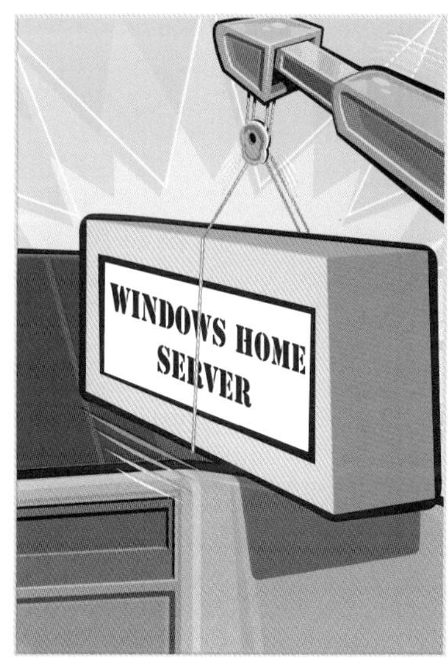


## chapter 4 Setting Up User Accounts


Understanding User Accounts . . . 64
Select a User Accounts Password Policy . . . 66
Change the Password on the Local Computer . . . 68
Add a User Account . . . 70
Synchronize the Local and Server Passwords . . . 72
Change a User's Display Name . . . 74
Change a User's Password . . . 76
Disable a User Account . . . 78
Enable a User Account . . . 80
Enable the Guest Account . . . 82
Remove a User Account . . . 86

# Table of Contents

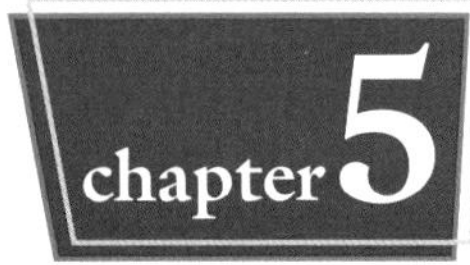


## Working with Windows Home Server Settings

Display the Windows Home Server Settings .......... 90
Change the Date and Time .......... 92
Choose a Different Region and Language .......... 94
Configure Windows Update .......... 95
Restart Windows Home Server .......... 96
Shut Down Windows Home Server .......... 98
Activate Automatic Windows Error Reporting .......... 100
Install a Windows Home Server Add-In .......... 102
Uninstall a Windows Home Server Add-In .......... 104

## Using Windows Home Server Storage

Understanding Windows Home Server Storage .......... 108
Learn About Hard Drive Types .......... 110
View Windows Home Server Storage .......... 112
Add Storage to Windows Home Server .......... 114
Remove Storage from Windows Home Server .......... 116
Replace Your Main Hard Drive .......... 118

## chapter 7 Sharing Files


Understanding Windows Home Server File Sharing . . . . . 126
Access the Windows Home Server Shared Folders . . . . . 128
Map a Shared Folder to a Drive Letter . . . . . 130
View the Shared Folders in the Console . . . . . 132
Rename a Shared Folder . . . . . 134
Turn Folder Duplication On and Off . . . . . 136
Apply User Permissions on a Shared Folder . . . . . 138
Apply User Permissions on All Shared Folders . . . . . 140
View Shared Folder History . . . . . 142
Create a New Shared Folder . . . . . 144
Delete a Shared Folder . . . . . 146
Work with a Shared Folder Offline . . . . . 148


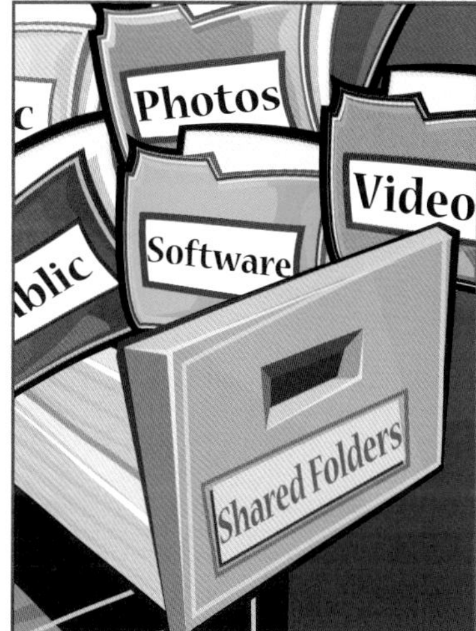


## chapter 8 Working with Digital Media


Understanding Digital Media . . . . . 152
Understanding Digital Media Streaming . . . . . 154
Turn On Media Sharing . . . . . 156
Play Streamed Media in Media Player . . . . . 158
Play Streamed Media in Media Center . . . . . 160
Set Up a Photos Slide Show . . . . . 162
Display Server Photos in the Vista Sidebar . . . . . 164
Add a Digital Media Folder to Media Player . . . . . 166
Rip Music to Windows Home Server . . . . . 168
Add a Digital Media Folder to Media Center . . . . . 170
Turn Off Media Sharing . . . . . 172

# Table of Contents

## Backing Up Your Computers

Understanding the Windows Home Server Backup Technology ........ 176
Configure the Backup Time ........ 178
Configure Automatic Backup Management ........ 180
Add a Disk Drive to a Computer's Backup ........ 182
Exclude a Folder from a Computer's Backup ........ 184
Back Up a Computer Manually ........ 188
Stop Backing Up a Computer ........ 190

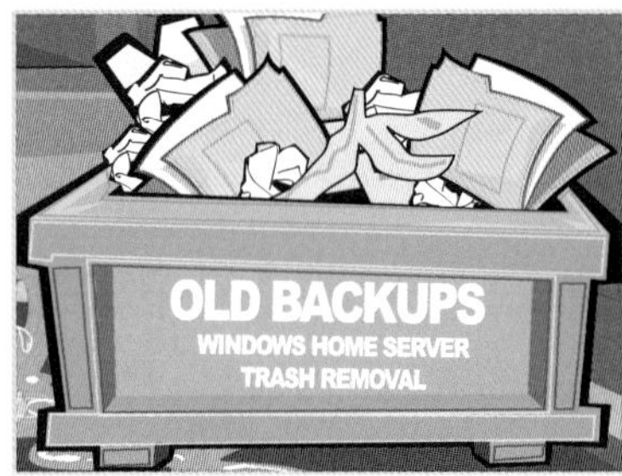


chapter 10

## Working with Computer Backups

Understanding Computer Backups ........ 194
View a Computer's Backups ........ 196
View Backup Details ........ 198
Prevent a Backup from Being Deleted ........ 200
Schedule a Backup for Deletion ........ 202
Delete Backups Manually ........ 204
View a Backup's Files ........ 206
Restore a Previous Version of a File ........ 208
Restore a Backed Up File ........ 210
Restore a Computer's Previous Configuration ........ 214

## chapter 11 Making a Remote Connection to Windows Home Server


Understanding Remote Desktop Connections . . . . 222
Make a Basic Connection . . . . 224
Work with the Connection Bar . . . . 226
Customize the Remote Desktop Window . . . . 228
Customize the Remote Desktop Sounds and Keystrokes . . . . 230
Start a Program Automatically When You Connect . . . . 232
Optimize the Connection Performance . . . . 234

## chapter 12 Connecting to Other Network Computers


Configure Windows Vista as a Remote Desktop Host . . . . 238
Configure Windows XP as a Remote Desktop Host . . . . 240
Install Remote Desktop Connection on Windows XP . . . . 242
Connect Using Remote Desktop Connection . . . . 244
Give a User Remote Access . . . . 246
Activate the Windows Home Server Web Site . . . . 248
Display the Remote Access Home Page . . . . 250
Connect Using the Remote Access Home Page . . . . 252
Disconnect from the Remote Computer . . . . 254
Customize the Remote Access Site Settings . . . . 256

# Table of Contents

## chapter 13 Connecting to Computers via the Internet


Understanding Remote Internet Access . . . . . 260
Configure the Router Automatically . . . . . 262
Get the Windows Home Server Address. . . . . 264
Configure the Router Manually . . . . . 266
View Router Details. . . . . 270
Set Up a Windows Home Server Domain Name . . . . . 272
Get the Router Internet Address to Configure Your Own Domain . . . . . 274
View the Domain Name Details. . . . . 276
Display the Remote Access Home Page Over the Internet . . . . . 278
Connect to a Computer Over the Internet . . . . . 280
Disconnect from the Remote Computer. . . . . 282
Work with Shared Folders Over the Internet . . . . . 284
Run the Windows Home Server Console Over the Internet . . . . . 286


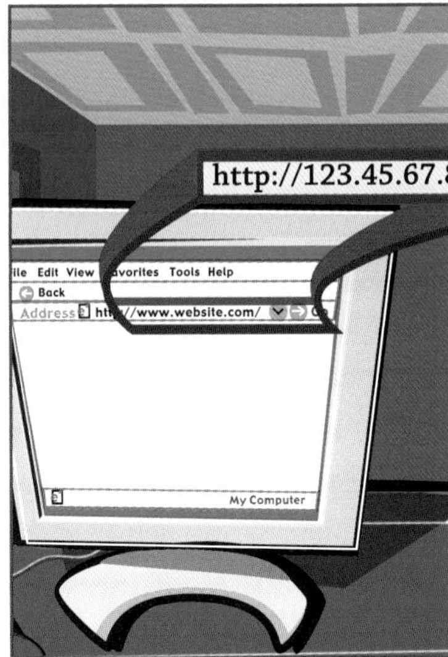

# Maintaining and Troubleshooting Windows Home Server

View Network Health . . . . . . . . . . 290
Understanding the Network Health Notifications . . . . . . . . . . 292
Check System Drive Free Space . . . . . . . . . . 294
Delete Unnecessary Files from the System Drive . . . . . . . . . . 296
Defragment the System Drive . . . . . . . . . . 298
Check the System Drive for Errors . . . . . . . . . . 300
Repair a Networking Problem . . . . . . . . . . 302
Reinstall Windows Home Server . . . . . . . . . . 304

# How to use this book

Do you look at the pictures in a book or newspaper before anything else on a page? Would you rather see an image instead of read about how to do something? Search no further. This book is for you. Opening *Teach Yourself VISUALLY Windows Home Server* allows you to read less and learn more about Windows Home Server.

### Who Needs This Book

This book is for a reader who has never used this particular technology or software application. It is also for more computer literate individuals who want to expand their knowledge of the different features that Windows Home Server has to offer.

### Book Organization

*Teach Yourself VISUALLY Windows Home Server* has 14 chapters.

### Chapter Organization

This book consists of sections, all listed in the book's table of contents. A *section* is a set of steps that show you how to complete a specific computer task.

Each section, usually contained on two facing pages, has an introduction to the task at hand, a set of full-color screen shots and steps that walk you through the task, and a set of tips. This format allows you to quickly look at a topic of interest and learn it instantly.

Chapters group together three or more sections with a common theme. A chapter may also contain pages that give you the background information needed to understand the sections in a chapter.

### What You Need to Use This Book

To perform the tasks in this book, you need the following:

- A computer with Windows Home Server installed.
- The equipment required to set up a network.
- A broadband Internet connection.

### Using the Mouse

This book uses the following conventions to describe the actions you perform when using the mouse:

#### Click

Press your left mouse button once. You generally click your mouse on something to select something on the screen.

#### Double-click

Quickly press your left mouse button twice. Double-clicking something on the computer screen generally opens whatever item you have double-clicked.

#### Right-click

Press your right mouse button. When you right-click anything on the computer screen, the program displays a shortcut menu containing commands specific to the selected item.

#### Click and Drag, and Release the Mouse

Move your mouse pointer and hover it over an item on the screen. Press and hold down the left mouse button. Now, move the mouse to where you want to place the item and then release the button. You use this method to move an item from one area of the computer screen to another.

## The Conventions in This Book

A number of typographic and layout styles have been used throughout *Teach Yourself VISUALLY Windows Home Server* to distinguish different types of information.

### Bold

Bold type represents the names of commands and options that you interact with. Bold type also indicates text and numbers that you must type into a dialog box or window.

### Italics

Italic words introduce a new term and are followed by a definition.

### Numbered Steps

You must perform the instructions in numbered steps in the order listed to successfully complete a section and achieve the final results.

### Bulleted Steps

These steps point out various optional features. You do not have to perform these steps; they simply give additional information about a feature.

### Indented Text

Indented text tells you what the program does in response to your following a numbered step. For example, if you click a certain menu command, a dialog box may appear, or a window may open. Indented text may also tell you what the final result is when you follow a set of numbered steps.

### Notes

Notes give additional information. They may describe special conditions that may occur during an operation. They may warn you of a situation that you want to avoid, for example the loss of data. A note may also cross-reference a related area of the book. A cross-reference may guide you to another chapter, or another section within the current chapter.

### Icons and Buttons

Icons and buttons are graphical representations within the text. They show you exactly what you need to click to perform a step.

You can easily identify the tips in any section by looking for the TIPS icon. Tips offer additional information, including tips, hints, and tricks. You can use the TIPS information to go beyond what you learn in the steps.

# CHAPTER

# Windows Home Server Basics

Are you ready to start learning about Windows Home Server? This chapter helps you get started by giving you an overview of Windows Home Server, including its features and benefits. You will also learn about what you can do with Windows Home Server.

Understanding Windows Home Server Basics ........................................................4

Learn About Windows Home Server's Features ................................................6

Discover What You Can Do with Windows Home Server......................................8

Learn About Windows Home Server's Benefits ..............................................10

Learn About Advanced Uses for Windows Home Server ..................................12

# Understanding Windows Home Server Basics

Windows Home Server is a computer operating system that is made for home networks. It is designed to make it easier to set up and manage a network.

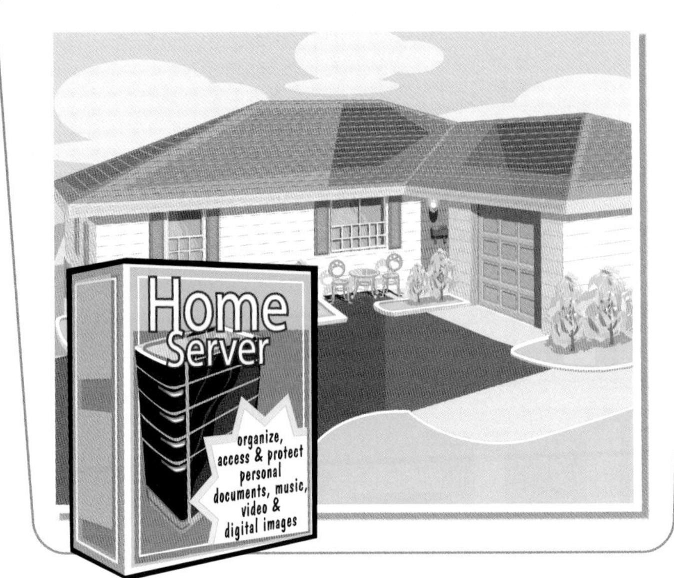


### Windows: The Operating System

Windows Home Server is a member of the Windows family of operating systems from Microsoft. An *operating system* is a software program that controls everything on a computer, including the installed devices, what you see on the display, and how your keystrokes and mouse clicks work.

### Home: Where Your Network Resides

Windows Home Server is designed for use with home networks that have up to ten computers attached to the network using either wired or wireless connections. If you do not yet have your network set up, see Chapter 2.

### Server: Providing Services

Windows Home Server is not meant to be used for day-to-day tasks. Instead, it is a *server* operating system, which means that it provides services, storage, security, and network management features for the other computers on the network, which are often called *clients*.

### Powerful Features

Windows Home Server comes with many powerful features, including scheduled backups of client computers, centralized storage, media streaming, simplified network management, and remote access to all of the network computers. You can find more detailed descriptions of these features in the next section.

### No Special Hardware

Although Windows Home Server offers powerful features, you do not need a powerful computer to run them. Almost any new or recent PC can run Windows Home Server. The minimum requirements are a 1 GHz Pentium III processor, 512MB of memory, an 80GB hard drive, a network card for a wired connection to the network, and a DVD drive.

### Headless Operation

Windows Home Server is not meant for everyday use; in fact, most computers that come with Windows Home Server installed do not even include a keyboard, mouse, or monitor. You turn on Windows Home Server and then access everything you need through the Console program. A computer without a keyboard, mouse, or monitor is said to be *headless*.

# Learn About Windows Home Server's Features

Windows Home Server comes with several key features that are designed to keep your data safe, give you easy access to digital media and data, make networking tasks easy to manage, and give you remote access to your computer.

**You can learn more about each of the following features elsewhere in this book.**

## Nightly Backups

When you connect a Windows Vista or Windows XP computer to the Windows Home Server network, the server automatically configures that computer for regular backups. This means that Windows Home Server backs up all of the computer's data – its documents, files, programs, and settings – every night.

## Centralized Storage

Adding multiple hard drives to Windows Home Server combines those drives into a single storage pool that you can use to store data from all of the network computers. Windows Home Server makes this easier by offering several built-in shared folders, including Photos, Music, Videos, Software, and Public, as well as a shared folder for each user account on the system.

### Streaming Media

*Streaming media* involves broadcasting a digital image, audio file, or video file so that other computers and devices on the network can pick up the broadcast and play it. You can configure Windows Home Server to stream the contents of its Photos, Music, and Videos folders.

### Data Redundancy

To help keep your data safe, you can configure the Windows Home Server shared folders with a feature called *folder duplication*. This means that if you have multiple hard drives on the server, Windows maintains a duplicate copy of each file. If a server hard drive should fail, you do not lose any data because copies exist on another hard drive.

### Windows Home Server Console

You can use the Windows Home Server Console program to easily manage the most important aspects of your network. The Console enables you to configure and work with computer backups, manage user accounts, configure the Windows Home Server shared folders, add and remove hard drives, and configure many other Windows Home Server settings.

### Remote Access

Windows Home Server comes with a Remote Access feature that enables you to log on to another network computer and operate that computer as though you were sitting in front of it. You can use the Remote Access feature either while you are logged on to your network or from outside your home through an Internet connection.

# Discover What You Can Do with Windows Home Server

With Windows Home Server added to your network, you can perform a number of tasks. The most common tasks are setting up user accounts, creating shared folders, storing data on the server, playing media, and adding more storage.

**You can learn more about each of these tasks in this section and elsewhere in this book.**

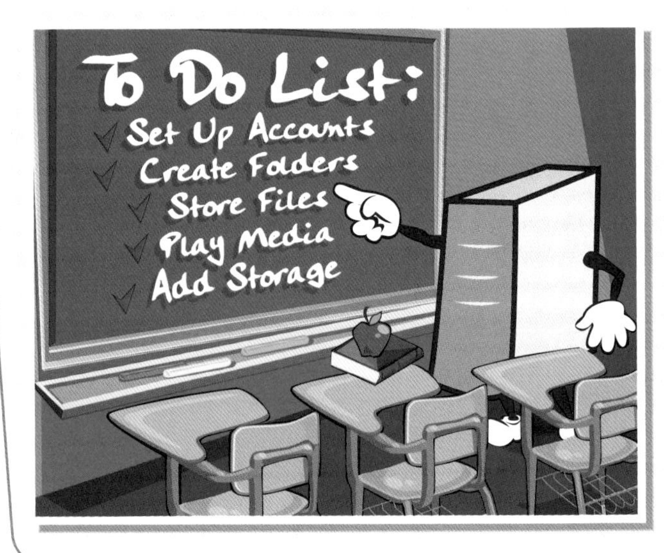


### Set Up Family Accounts

The Windows Home Server Console has a User Accounts tab that allows you to create user accounts. This enables you to create a separate account for each family member that you want to give access to the server's shared files. You can create up to ten accounts in Windows Home Server.

### Create Shared Folders

Windows Home Server comes with several predefined shared folders. However, you do not have to use just those folders. If you want, you can create your own shared folders on the server. This enables you to create different folders for different types of files, such as letters and recorded TV shows.

### Store Files

You can copy or move files from your computer to one of the Windows Home Server shared folders. This procedure is similar to copying or moving files from one part of your system to another. Copying a file to the server creates a second copy in case you need it, while moving a file to the server is useful for freeing up disk space on your computer.

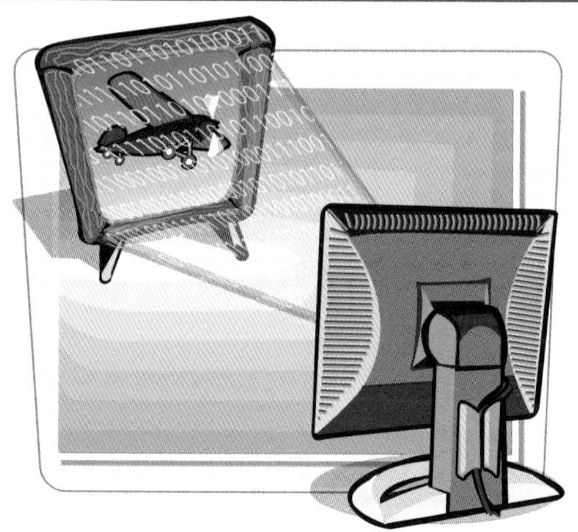

### Play Media

Once you configure the Photos, Music, or Videos shared folder to stream, you can then play those streams on a computer or device that is connected to the network. For a computer, you can display or play a stream by using Windows programs such as Media Player and Media Center. You can also access a stream using devices such as the Microsoft Xbox 360, a digital media player, or a digital picture frame.

### Increase Storage

Windows Home Server's storage consists of all of the hard drives attached to your system, minus a 20GB area for the Windows Home Server system files. If you attach another hard drive to the Windows Home Server computer – for example, an external hard drive plugged into a USB port – you can add that drive's capacity to the storage pool.

# Learn About Windows Home Server's Benefits

Windows Home Server offers you a number of benefits. These include the capability to restore both individual files and entire PCs, easy file sharing over the network, monitoring the health of home computers, and the capability to work with your own computer from remote locations.

**You can learn more about each of these benefits in this section and elsewhere in this book.**

### Restore Lost Data

Windows Home Server's nightly backups ensure that if you lose or damage an important file, you can open the backup and restore the file. Windows Home Server maintains several backups for each PC, so you can also restore a previous version of a file.

### Recover a PC

Windows Home Server backs up all of a computer's data, including the important system files that Windows uses to operate, and the files that run your programs. If a home computer crashes and cannot be started, you can use the Home Computer Restore CD to restore the entire computer from one of its backups on Windows Home Server.

### Share Files

You can use the Windows Home Server shared folders to collaborate with other people. You can store a file in a shared folder and then give other users permission to view and make changes to that folder. Those users can then access the folder and view or edit the file.

### Monitor Network Health

Windows Home Server uses an icon in the taskbar's notification area to let you know if a problem exists with the network, with the server, or with one of the computers. For example, if a Windows Vista user has their security settings lowered, the icon displays a message to let you know.

### Simple to Use

Networking can be very complex, but Windows Home Server avoids this complexity by requiring very little initial configuration, and by hiding the difficult parts of networking tasks so that you do not have to deal with them. Instead, you can accomplish most things by using the Windows Home Server Console.

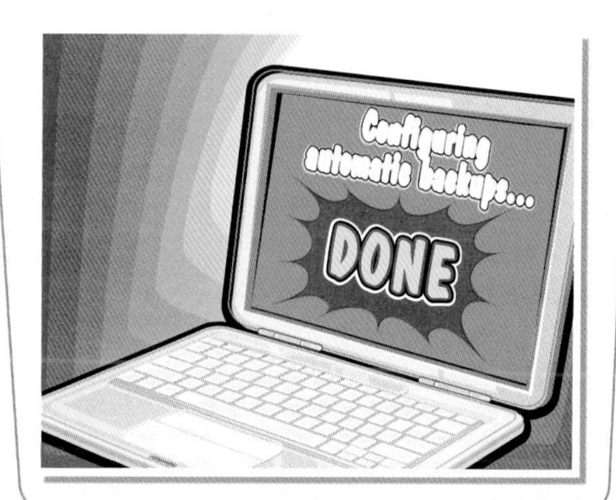

# Learn About Advanced Uses for Windows Home Server

The Windows Home Server Console makes it easy to perform a large number of basic tasks. However, Windows Home Server is also a powerful system that enables you to perform more advanced tasks, such as setting up folder security, installing add-ins, and making remote connections.

Advanced To-Do List
Set Up Security
Install Add-Ins
Connect to the Server
Work Anywhere
Connect Via the Internet
Get a Domain


**You can learn more about each of the following tasks elsewhere in this book.**

### Set Up Security

Windows Home Server enables you to specify which user accounts have access to which shared folders. In each case, you can specify whether the account can make changes in the folder, or only view the contents of the folder. You can even prevent a user from accessing a folder altogether.

### Extend Windows Home Server

Although Windows Home Server has several useful features, Microsoft has also made it easy for programmers to add new features to Windows Home Server. These features are called *add-ins* and they can add new tabs to the Windows Home Server Console, new Windows Home Server settings, and new Windows Home Server programs.

### Connect to Windows Home Server

Most of your interaction with the server occurs through the Windows Home Server Console program, particularly if you run the server as a headless device. However, you may sometimes need to use Windows Home Server, and not just the Console. In such cases, you can use a home computer to connect to Windows Home Server and operate it remotely.

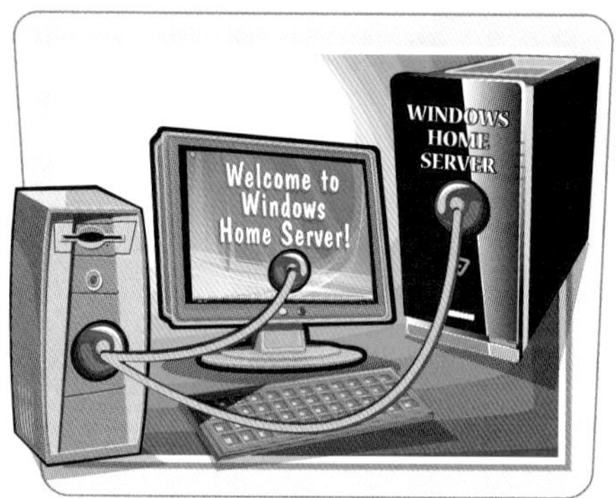


### Work Anywhere in Your Home

With Windows Home Server's Remote Access feature, you can connect to your own computer from anywhere else in your home. For example, if you have a computer in the den, you can use it to access the computer in your home office. Similarly, you could take a notebook computer outside and access your main computer using a wireless network connection.

### Connect through the Internet

With Windows Home Server's Remote Access feature, you can connect to your network through the Internet. For example, you could use your workplace Internet connection to run the Windows Home Server Console. Similarly, you could access a wireless hotspot in a coffee shop and use the Internet to log on to your network and then connect to your computer.

### Get a Custom Subdomain Name

A *domain name* is an Internet address, such as microsoft.com or google.com. A *subdomain* is a more specific address, such as support.microsoft.com. Windows Home Server enables you to create your own subdomain using the homeserver.com domain name – for example, smithfamily.homeserver.com. You can then use this address to connect to the Windows Home Server Remote Access pages.

CHAPTER

# Networking Computers

To use any of Windows Home Server's features, you must configure your home computers as a network. You can use cables to establish the connections, and with some extra wireless equipment, you can also network computers without cables.

Understanding Networking....16
Survey Networking Hardware....18
Discover Network Configurations....20
Examine Network Security....22
Discover Wireless Networking....24
Learn About Wireless Networking Devices....26
Configure a Wireless Gateway....28
Connect to a Wireless Network....30
Implement Wireless Network Security....32

# Understanding Networking

A *network* is a collection of computers that are connected by using either a cable hookup or a wireless hookup. A network gives you a number of advantages, such as being able to share files and equipment and being able to access Windows Home Server.

### Share Files

Networked computers are connected to each other, so they can exchange files with each other using the connection. This enables people to share information and to collaborate on projects. For example, Windows Home Server comes with predefined shared folders for files such as pictures, videos, and music.

### Share Equipment

Computers connected over a network can share some types of equipment. For example, one computer can share its printer, which enables other network users to send their documents to that printer. Networked computers can also share hard drives, CD or DVD drives, and document scanners.

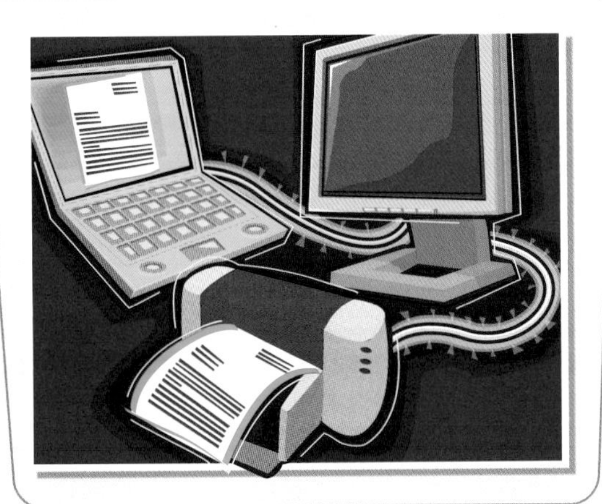

## Share the Internet

If a computer or other device has an Internet connection, it can share that connection with other network users. This enables other users to access the Internet without having to set up their own direct connection.

## Back Up Files

Many people use a network to back up important files to one of the connected computers. You do not need to worry about this with your Windows Home Server network because the server automatically backs up each connected computer every night.

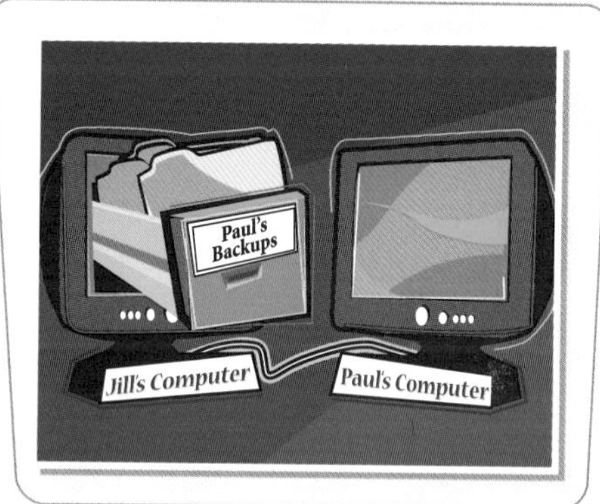


## Save Money

Networks can be costly to set up because you must purchase the necessary equipment. However, a network can save you money because you can share equipment such as printers, and you can share a single Internet connection. For more information, see the section "Survey Networking Hardware."

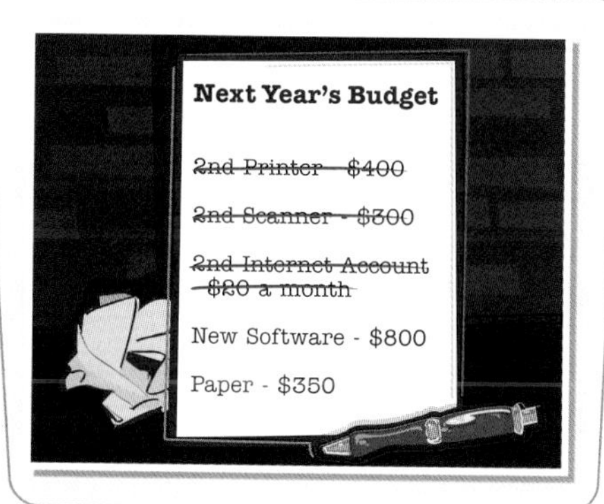


## Save Time

Although networks require some time to administer, this time is more than offset by the time that you save by not having to share files manually using disks, as well as the time required to do manual backups of your computers. You can also avoid having to set up other equipment and Internet connections.

# Survey Networking Hardware

Although Windows Home Server, Windows Vista, and Windows XP have built-in network capabilities, you still need a few hardware devices to connect your network.

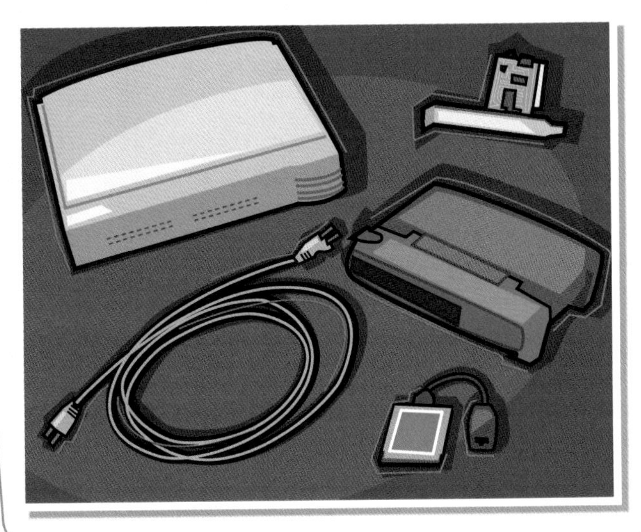

### Network Interface Card

Each computer on the network requires a *network interface card* (NIC), also called a *network adapter* or *network card*. An NIC can be a circuit board inside the computer, a USB device that you attach to a USB port, or a PC Card that you insert into a notebook computer.

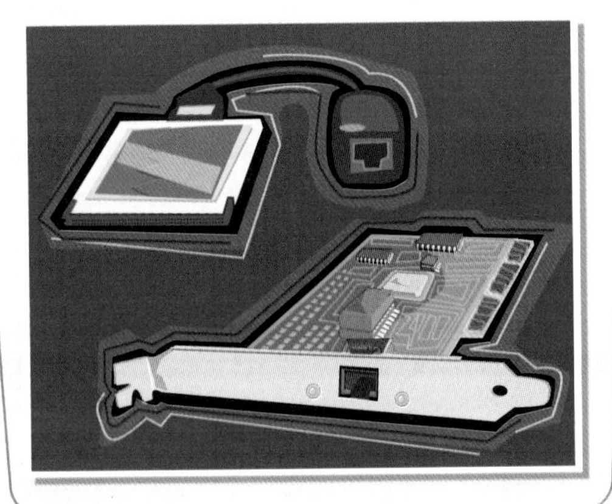

### Network Cable

A *network cable* plugs into the NIC in the back of each computer on the network. Information, shared files, and other network data travel through the network cables. Note that your Windows Home Server computer must use a wired connection to the network.

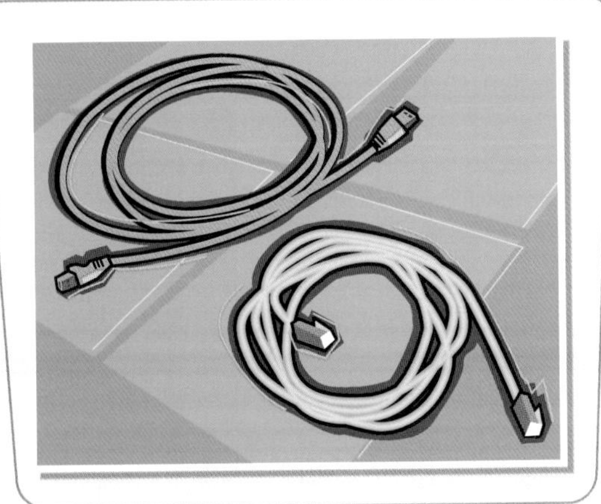

### Broadband Modem

A *broadband modem* is a device that gives you high-speed access to the Internet. In most cases, your Internet service provider (ISP) supplies you with a broadband modem. However, you can often purchase a broadband modem in a retail store and then use the information inside the box to sign up with an ISP.

### Switch

A *switch* is a central connection point for all of the computers on the network. For each computer using a wired connection, you run a network cable from the computer's NIC to a port in the back of the switch.

### Router

A *router* is similar to a switch, but it can route incoming data to a specific network address. This is useful when the computers share a high-speed Internet connection because the router ensures that the Internet data goes to the computer that requested it. On a home network, a router that connects to the Internet is called a *residential gateway*.

# Discover Network Configurations

The network configuration determines how the computers are physically connected, and how they share information with each other. These configurations range from small and simple, such as a peer-to-peer local area network, to large and complex, such as a client/server wide area network.

### Local Area Network

A *local area network* (LAN) is a group of networked computers that are relatively close together, such as in the same building. Home networks, in particular, are typically set up as LANs and are most often used to share an Internet connection or to run multiple-player computer games.

### Ethernet

The *network architecture* determines how data is sent along the network. Although the most popular architecture used to be *Ethernet*, which transmits data at 10 megabits per second (Mbps), most people now use *Fast Ethernet*, which transmits data at 100 Mbps. Many networks now use *Gigabit Ethernet*, which transmits at 1,000 Mbps.

### Configure Your Network

You must first connect your broadband modem to its data line. A digital subscriber line (DSL) Internet connection requires a telephone line connected to your modem, while a cable Internet connection requires a TV cable connected to the modem's cable port. Next, you plug your broadband modem directly into the router, and then plug your router into your switch.

### Peer-to-Peer Network

A *peer-to-peer network* is one in which each computer performs its own network tasks, such as storing files, sharing resources with the network, implementing network security. Peer-to-peer networks are inexpensive and simple to set up, so they are most suitable for small networks. Windows Vista and Windows XP come with built-in peer-to-peer networking capabilities.

### Client/Server Network

A *client/server network* is one in which the networking tasks are mostly handled by a large, powerful computer called a *server*. The computers in the network, called the *clients,* connect to the server and use it to store files, run programs, and implement security. The client/server model is designed for large, complex networks.

### Windows Home Server Network

A Windows Home Server network is a hybrid of a peer-to-peer network and a client/server network. Windows Vista and Windows XP computers can act as peers and share data with each other. However, they can also act as clients when they access Windows Home Server, for example, to use its shared folders or to play streaming media.

# Examine Network Security

Network security determines who has access to the network's resources — such as its computers, files, and printers — and what each authorized user is allowed to do with those resources. For example, some authorized users may be allowed to edit and delete files, while others may only be able to view files.

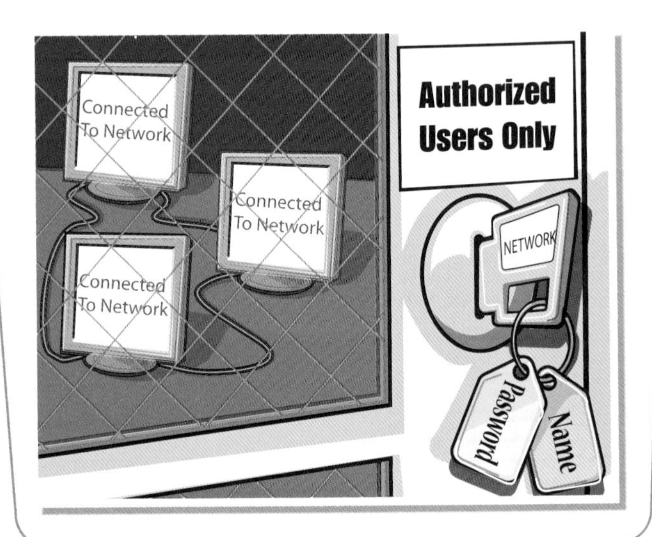


### Log On

To access a network's resources, you must first *log on* to the network by providing a username and password. With Windows Home Server, you must log on to the server separately if you want to use the Windows Home Server Connector program or access the network from a remote location.

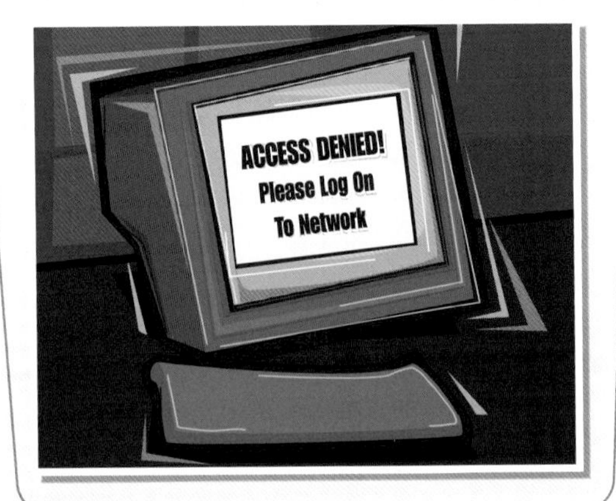


### Username

The first part of your network logon information is your username. This name uniquely identifies you on the network. Other network users can give you access to their files and other resources, based on your username. Your Windows Vista or Windows XP username is usually the same as your Windows Home Server username.

### Password

The second part of your network logon information is your password. This is a sequence of characters known only to you and, on a large network, the network Administrator. By typing your username and password during the logon, you establish yourself as an authorized network user.

### Permissions

*Permissions* determine what each authorized network user can and cannot do with the network's resources. For example, giving users *Read* permission enables them only to open a file for viewing. Giving users *Full* permission enables them to also make changes to a file, create new files, and delete files.

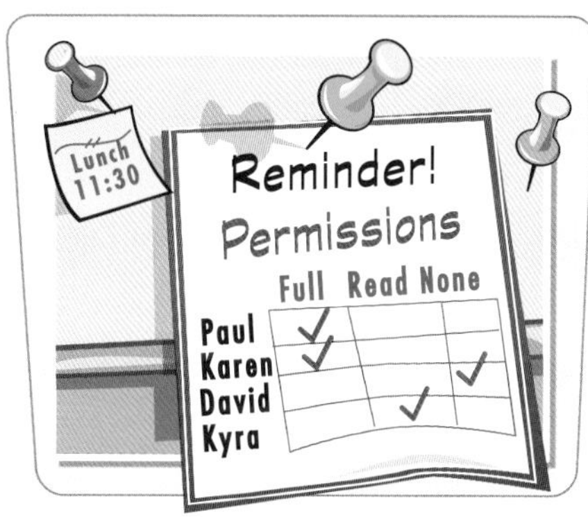


### Log Off

Just as it is important to log on to the network to gain authorized access, it is also important to log off the network when you no longer need it. If you remain logged on to the network and leave your computer unattended, another person could use your computer to access the network and possibly cause mischief or damage.

### Firewall

A *firewall* is a device or program that prevents unauthorized users from infiltrating a private network. You can use a hardware device, such as a router, as a firewall. Windows Home Server, Windows Vista, and Windows XP have built-in software firewalls. Many third-party firewall programs also exist, such as Windows Live OneCare from Microsoft and ZoneAlarm from Check Point.

# Discover Wireless Networking

A wireless network is a collection of two or more computers that communicate with each other using radio signals. A wireless network uses equipment that does not require cables, phone lines, or any other direct, physical connection.

**In an *ad hoc* wireless network, the computers connect directly to each other. In an *infrastructure* wireless network, the computers connect to each other through a common device, usually called an *access point*.**

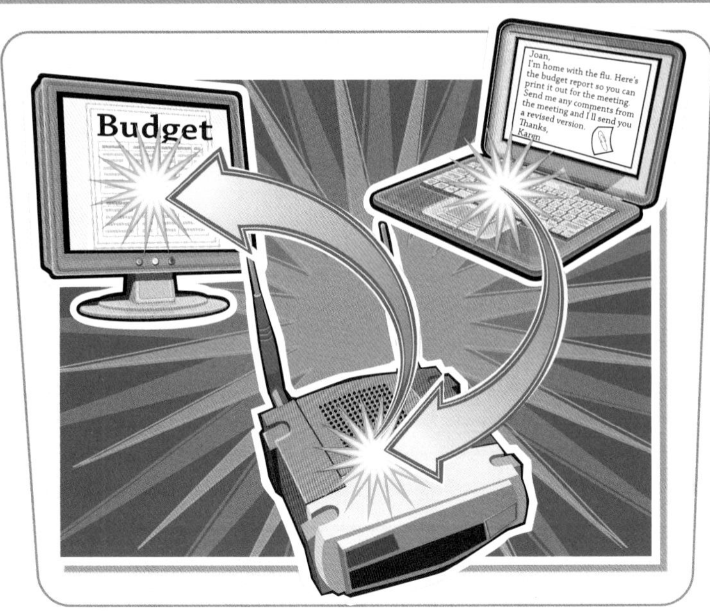

Budget
Joan,
I'm home with the flu. Here's
the budget report so you can
print it out for the meeting.
Send me any comments from
the meeting and I'll send you
a revised version.
Thanks,
Karen


### Radio Signals

Wireless devices transmit data and communicate with other devices using radio signals that are beamed from one device to another. Although these radio signals are similar to those used in commercial radio broadcasts, they operate on a different frequency.

### Radio Transceiver

A *radio transceiver* is a device that can act as both a transmitter and a receiver of radio signals. All wireless devices that require two-way communications use a transceiver. Devices that require only one-way communications — such as a wireless keyboard or mouse — have only a transmitter, and you attach a separate receiver to your computer.

## Wireless Technologies

The most common wireless technology is *Wireless Fidelity*, which is also called Wi-Fi or 802.11. There are four main types of Wi-Fi: 802.11, 802.11a, 802.11b, and 802.11g. Each type has its own range and speed limits. Another popular wireless technology is *Bluetooth*, which enables individual devices to automatically create *ad hoc* networks. Other examples of wireless technologies are cellular, microwave, and infrared.

## Wireless Ranges

All wireless devices have a maximum range beyond which they can no longer communicate with other devices. Peripherals such as keyboards have a range of only a few feet. In practice, Wi-Fi networking ranges span from 75 feet for 802.11a to about 150 feet for 802.11b and 802.11g.

## Wireless Speeds

Wireless transmission speed is an important factor to consider when you set up a wireless network or a wireless Internet connection. Less expensive wireless networks often use 802.11b, which has a theoretical top speed of 11 Mbps. The popular 802.11g standard has a theoretical speed limit of 54 Mbps. The new 802.11n standard has a theoretical speed limit of 540 Mbps.

# Learn About Wireless Networking Devices

Wireless networking requires devices that have wireless capabilities. Although wireless networking capabilities are built in to many of today's computers, in most cases you will need to purchase additional wireless devices.

## Wireless Network Adapters

To access a wireless network, your computer requires a wireless network adapter.

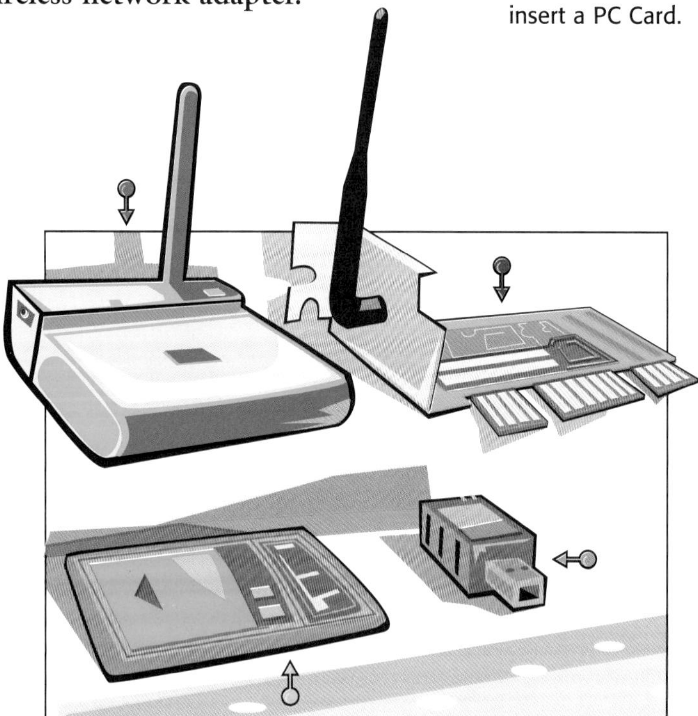

**PC Card**
For notebook computers that do not have built-in wireless capabilities, you can insert a PC Card.

**Network Interface Card**
You can insert a wireless network interface card (NIC) into your desktop computer.

**USB**
For easier installation on a desktop computer, you can plug a USB wireless network adapter into a free USB port.

**Bluetooth Adapter**
To set up an *ad hoc* network with any Bluetooth device, your computer requires a Bluetooth adapter, which usually plugs into a USB port.

### Wireless Access Point

A *wireless access point* (AP) is a device that receives and transmits signals from wireless computers to form a wireless network. Many APs also accept wired connections, and so both wired and wireless computers can form a network. If your network has a broadband modem, you can connect the modem to a type of AP called a *wireless gateway,* which extends Internet access to all of the computers on the network.

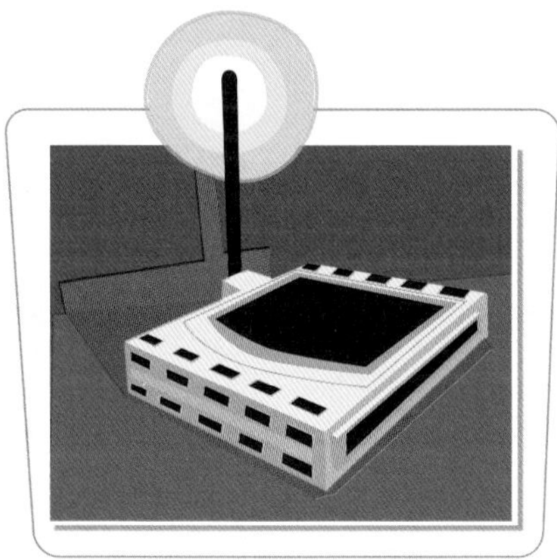

### Wireless Range Extender

If you find that your wireless access point is not reaching certain areas of your home or office, you can use a wireless range extender to boost the signal. Depending on the device and wireless access point, the extender can more than double the normal wireless range.

### Wireless Print Server

Another common wireless device is a wireless print server to which you attach a regular printer. This allows all of the wired and wireless computers on your network to access the printer.

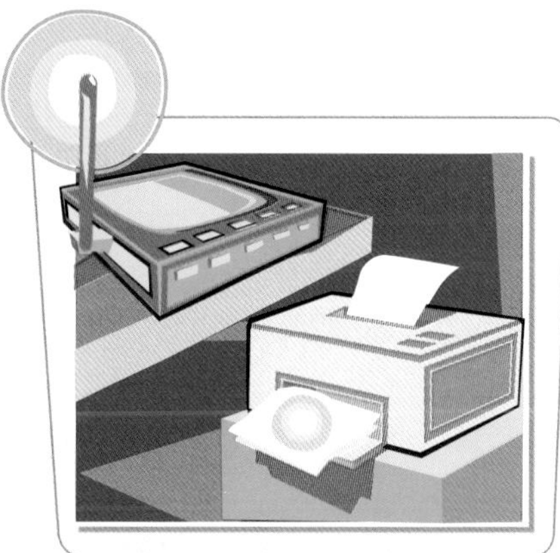

# Configure a Wireless Gateway

A wireless gateway is a type of wireless access point that connects to a broadband modem to give all of the computers on the network access to the Internet.

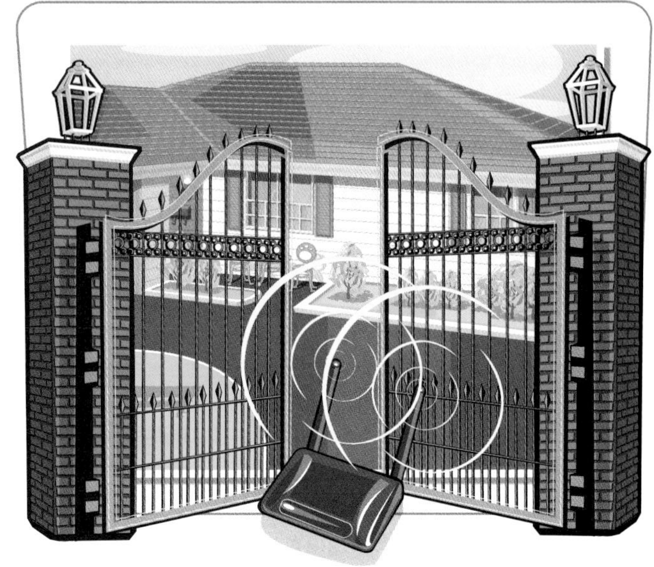

### Connect Cables

You should first turn off the gateway and the broadband modem, and then run a network cable from the modem to the WAN port on the back of the gateway. You then run another network cable from one of your computers to any LAN port on the back of the gateway, and then turn on the gateway and modem.

### Access the Gateway

On the computer connected to the gateway, you must start your Web browser, type the gateway address (usually either **http://192.168.1.1** or **http://192.168.0.1**), and press Enter. If required, you need to type the default username and password that is supplied by the gateway manufacturer. The gateway's setup page appears.

## Set the Connection Type

The wireless gateway establishes the Internet connection for your network, so you must specify the type of connection used by your ISP. There are three main types: Dynamic IP, Static IP, and PPPoE.

### Dynamic IP Address

An *Internet Protocol* (IP) address is a set of numbers that uniquely identifies a device that is connected to the Internet. Most ISPs assign IP addresses dynamically, or automatically, when you connect to their service. If your ISP does this, you can configure the gateway to obtain the address automatically.

### Static IP Address

If your ISP provided you with a static IP address, you must configure the gateway with this static IP address. You must also type the subnet mask, gateway address, and one or more Domain Name Server (DNS) addresses. Your ISP can provide you with all of this information.

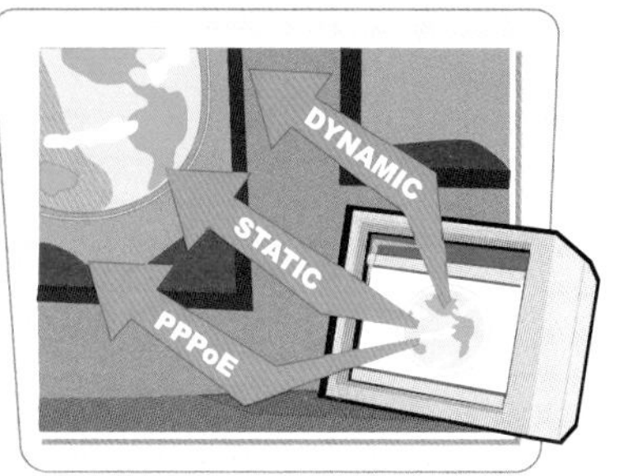


### PPPoE

If your ISP requires a *Point-to-Point Protocol over Ethernet* (PPPoE) connection, you can type the username and password that your ISP provided to you.

### Set the Network Name

Each wireless network has a public name – often called a *Service Set Identifier* (SSID) – that identifies the network to wireless devices. Your gateway comes with a default name, but you should change the name to something that you will remember and that uniquely identifies your network.

### Enable DHCP

Each computer on your network must also have an IP address. The easiest way to do this is to enable the gateway to generate addresses automatically using the *Dynamic Host Configuration Protocol* (DHCP).

You must first ensure that each computer is set up for DHCP. In Windows Vista, click **Start**, click **Connect To**, click **Open Network and Sharing Center**, and then click **Manage network connections**. Right-click **Wireless Network Connection**, click **Properties**, and then type your security credentials. Double-click **Internet Protocol Version 4** and ensure that the **Obtain an IP address automatically** option is activated.

# Connect to a Wireless Network

With your wireless network adapters installed and your wireless gateway or access point configured, you are ready to connect to your wireless network. This will give you access to the network's resources, as well as to the Internet if you have a wireless gateway.

### Connect for the First Time

After you initially set up a computer for wireless networking, or if you move your portable computer to a hotspot or other area with new networks in range, your computer displays a list of the available wireless networks. You can then connect to the network that you want to use.

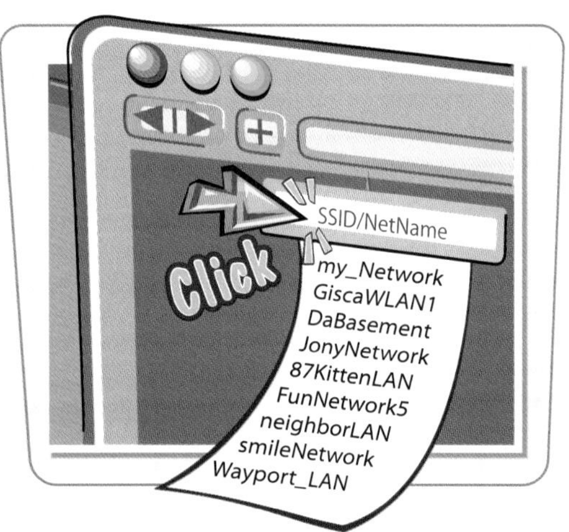


### Connect to a Secure Network

If the network that you want to use is unsecured – as many public hotspots are – then you can immediately access the network. However, most private wireless networks are secured against unauthorized access. In this case, the network asks you to type the appropriate security information.

## View Available Networks

If you take your portable computer to a public place, such as a hotel, airport, or coffee shop, there may be a nearby wireless network that offers Internet access. You can use your computer to display a list of available wireless networks. In Windows Vista, you can click **Start** and then click **Connect To**.

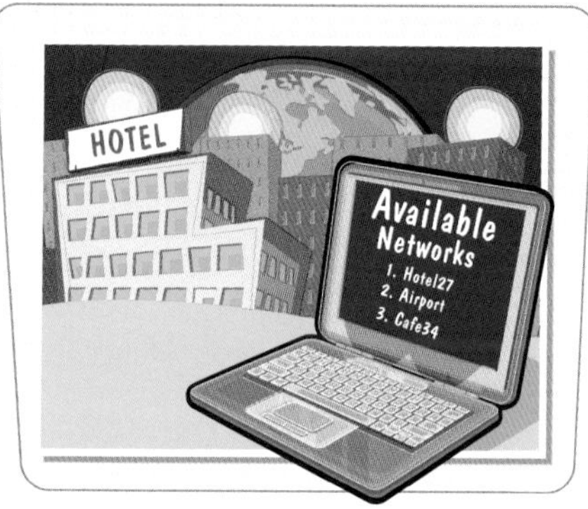


## Reconnect to a Wireless Network

If you lose your wireless network connection, you must reconnect to continue using it. One way to do this is to display the list of available wireless networks and then connect to the one that you want. Windows Vista also attempts to reconnect you to the network automatically as soon as it detects that the network is within range.

## View Signal Strength

If you are having problems with a wireless network connection, check the signal strength. In Windows Vista, position the mouse over the icon in the taskbar. Alternatively, you can right-click the icon and then click **Network and Sharing Center**.

## Disconnect from a Wireless Network

When you no longer need a wireless network connection, or if you want to try a different available network, you should disconnect from the current network. Display the list of available wireless networks, click the network to which you are connected, and then click **Disconnect**.

# Implement Wireless Network Security

Wireless network security involves implementing a few basic measures that prevent unauthorized users from accessing your Windows Home Server network.

## Wireless Security Issues

### Radio Signals

Wireless networks are inherently less secure than wired networks because radio signals are broadcast in all directions, including outside of your home or office. This enables a person within range to pick up those signals and access your network.

### Wardriving

*Wardriving* is an activity where a person drives through various neighborhoods with a portable computer or other device set up to look for available wireless networks. If the person finds a nonsecured network, they can use it for free Internet access or to cause mischief with shared network resources.

## Implement WPA

### Enable WPA

*Wi-Fi Protected Access* (WPA) is a wireless security feature that encrypts wireless network data so that unauthorized users cannot read it. You must enable WPA in your wireless gateway or access point. You can use the device's setup program to enable the WPA setting. Note that this setting may be called WPA Personal or WPA2 Personal.

### Enter a Security Key

To decrypt the data on a WPA-secured wireless network, users must type a *security key*, which is a series of characters that identifies the person as an authorized user. You can use your gateway or access point setup program to type the WPA security key that you want to use, and then store the key in a safe place.

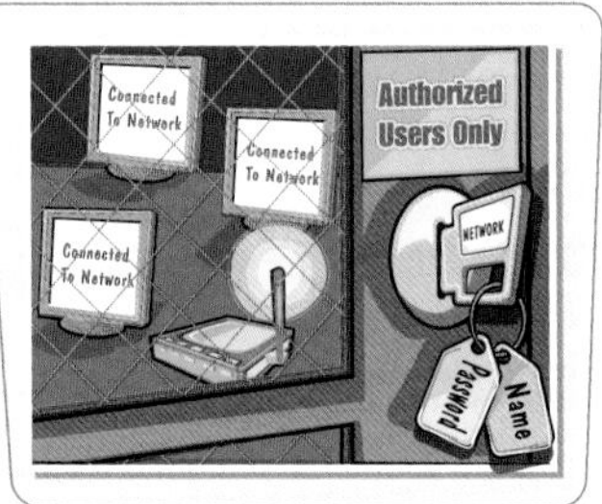

## Other Security Measures

### Disable Broadcasting

Your operating system remembers the wireless networks to which you have successfully connected. Therefore, when all of your computers have accessed the wireless network at least once, you no longer need to broadcast the network's SSID. As a result, you should use your AP setup program to disable broadcasting, and to prevent others from seeing your network.

### Change Default SSID

Even if you disable broadcasting of your network's SSID, users can still attempt to connect to your network by guessing the SSID. All APs come with predefined names, such as *linksys* or *default*, and a would-be intruder will probably attempt these standard names first. You can increase the security of your network by changing the SSID to something more difficult to guess.

### Change AP Password

Any person within range of your wireless access point can open the device's setup page by typing **http://192.168.1.1** or **http://192.168.0.1** into a Web browser. The person must log on with a username and password, but the default logon values (usually admin) are common knowledge among wardrivers. To prevent access to the setup program, be sure to change the AP's default username and password.

CHAPTER

3

# Configuring Windows Home Server

To ensure that Windows Home Server and your other computers can work together, there are a few configuration tasks that you need to perform.

Connect Windows Home Server to Your Network ....................................................36

View the Windows Home Server Network ................................................38

Install Windows Home Server Connector..............................................40

Run the Windows Home Server Console..................................................42

Create a Start Menu Shortcut for the Console ................................................44

Change the Workgroup Name ..........................46

Change the Computer Name ...........................48

Configure Windows Home Server with a Static Address......................................50

Change the Windows Home Server Password ..............................................52

Remove a Computer from Windows Home Server.......................................................54

Rediscover Windows Home Server .................56

Customize the Windows Home Server Start Menu .........................................................58

Customize the Windows Home Server Taskbar ..................................................60

# Connect Windows Home Server to Your Network

Are you ready to start using Windows Home Server? Your first task is to connect Windows Home Server to your home network so that other computers can see it.

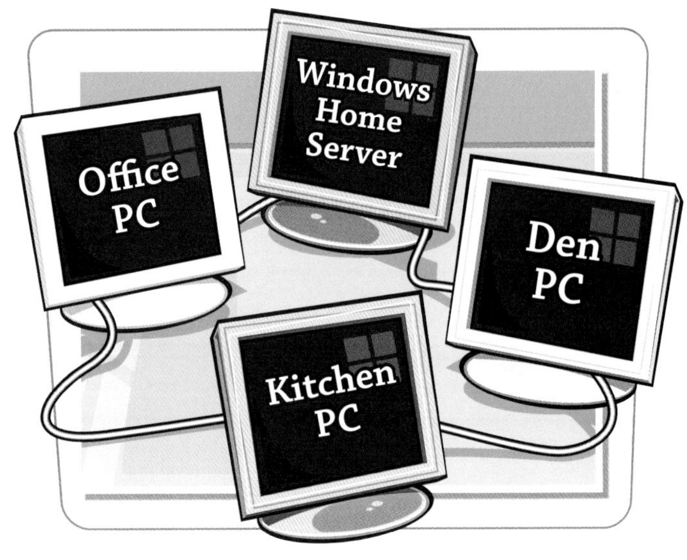


### Wired Connections Only

It is important to remember that Windows Home Server does not support wireless network connections. Other computers can connect to the network wirelessly, but Windows Home Server cannot. Backups, media streaming, and other Windows Home Server features require a lot of network bandwidth, and a wireless connection would be too slow.

### Make the Connection

To connect the Windows Home Server computer to your network, you need a network cable. You can attach one end of the network cable to the network port in the back of the Windows Home Server computer. You can then attach the other end of the cable to a free port in the back of your network's switch or router.

### Cable Considerations

When installing the Windows Home Server network cable, you must ensure that the cable is long enough to reach the switch or router without being overly taut, and avoid laying the cable in such a way that it becomes pinched or kinked. Be sure to lay the cable so that it is always at least a few inches away from telephones and other electromagnetic sources.

### Troubleshoot Problems

If you do not see Windows Home Server when you view your network, you should check your cable connections or reboot the server. You can also run the Windows Home Server network repair feature, described in Chapter 14. You may need to modify the Windows Home Server workgroup name (see the section "Change the Workgroup Name," later in this chapter).

### Run the Server Headless

If your server computer has a mouse, keyboard, and monitor connected, you can turn off the computer, disconnect the peripherals, and then restart the computer. You can manipulate the server with the Windows Home Server Connector program (see the section "Install Windows Home Server Connector") or by remote access, as described in Chapter 11.

# View the Windows Home Server Network

To ensure that Windows Home Server is properly connected to your network, you need to view the network using another computer.

**You can use either Windows Vista or Windows XP to view the network.**

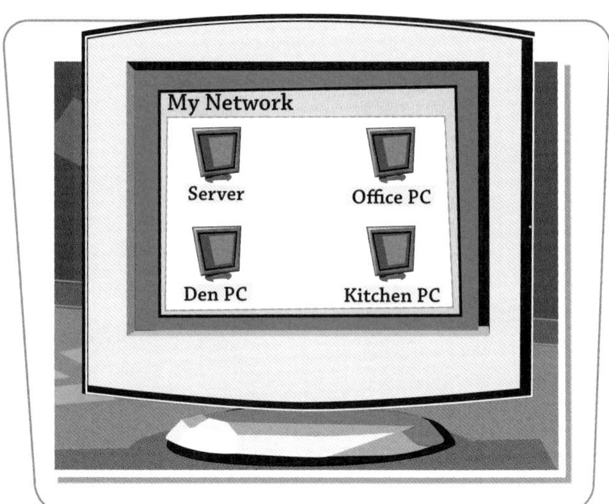


## View the Windows Home Server Network

### USING WINDOWS VISTA

1. Click **Start**.
2. Click **Network**.

The Network window appears.

- In the example network shown, this is the icon for Windows Home Server.

***Note:*** *The default name for the Windows Home Server computer is SERVER, so you should look for an icon with that name. If you want to change the server name, see the section "Change the Computer Name," later in this chapter.*

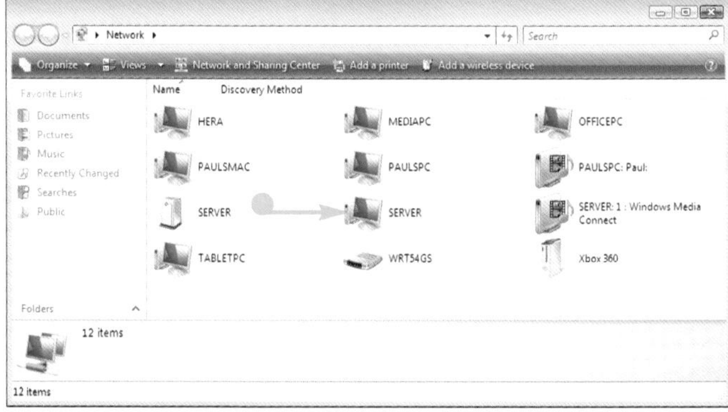

### USING WINDOWS XP

1. Click **Start**.
2. Click **My Network Places**.

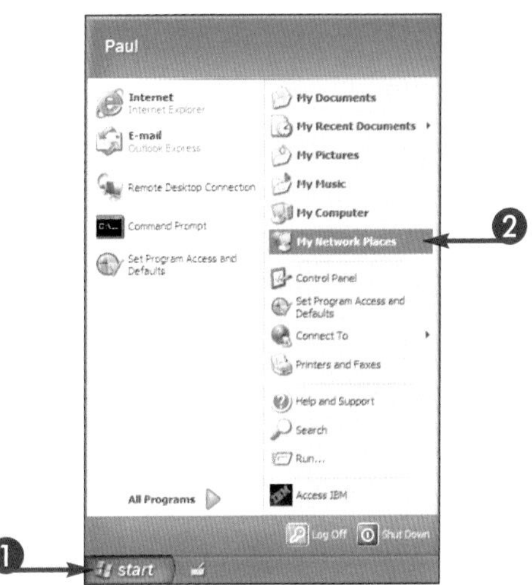

The My Network Places window appears.

3. Click **View workgroup computers**.

Windows XP displays icons for each computer in your workgroup, including Windows Home Server.

**Why does Windows Vista show more than one icon for Windows Home Server?**

Each icon represents a different aspect of Windows Home Server. One icon represents Windows Home Server as a network device; a second icon represents Windows Home Server's shared folders (this is the icon you use most often); and a third icon appears when Windows Home Server is sharing media with the network. Keep in mind that you may not see all three icons on your system.

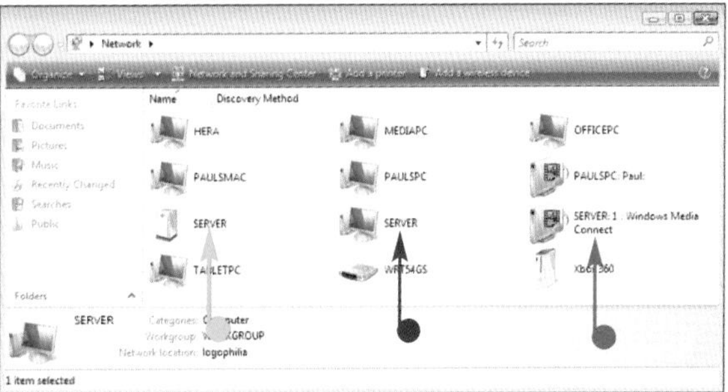

- Network device
- Shared folders
- Shared media

# Install Windows Home Server Connector

In order to use a home computer to configure the server, set up user accounts, access backups, and perform other Windows Home Server tasks, you must install the Windows Home Server Connector software on that computer.

**This task requires the Windows Home Server password, which was specified during the Windows Home Server installation.**

## Install Windows Home Server Connector

1. On the home computer, insert the Windows Home Server Connector CD.

   The AutoPlay window appears.

2. Click **Run setup.exe**.

*Note: If the User Account Control dialog box appears, you must either click* ***Continue*** *or type an Administrator's password and then click* ***Submit****.*

   The Windows Home Server Connector installation wizard appears.

3. Click **Next**.

   The End-User License Agreement screen appears.

4. Click **I accept the terms of the license agreement**.

5. Click **Next**.

   The wizard installs the programs and then locates your Windows Home Server computer.

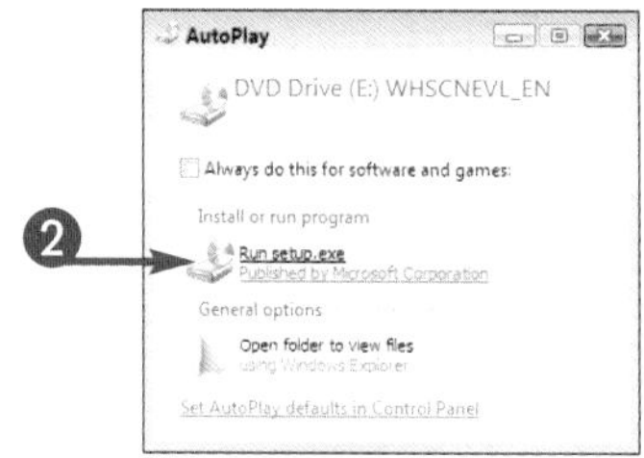

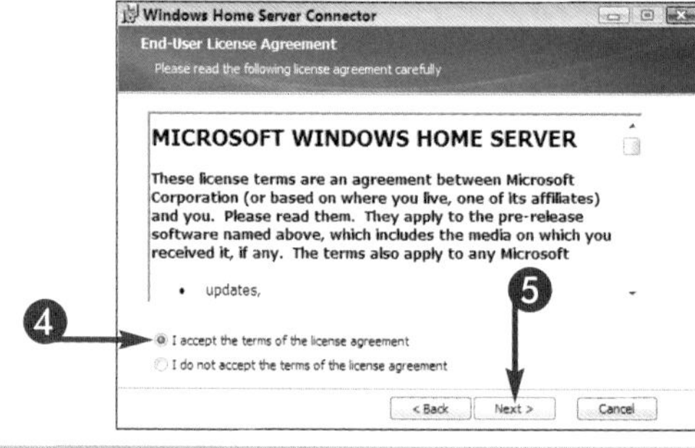

The Log On to Your Windows Home Server dialog box appears.

***Note:** If the wizard cannot find your home server, click **Find my home server manually**, click **Next**, and then click **Next** again.*

6 Type the Windows Home Server password.

7 Click **Next**.

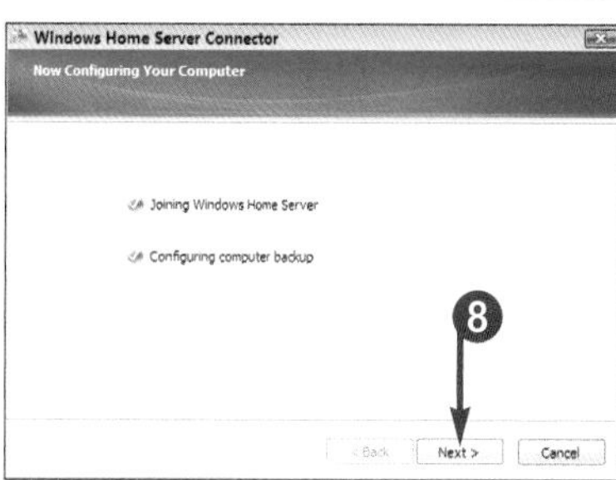

The wizard connects your computer to Windows Home Server and configures the computer for automatic backups.

8 Click **Next**.

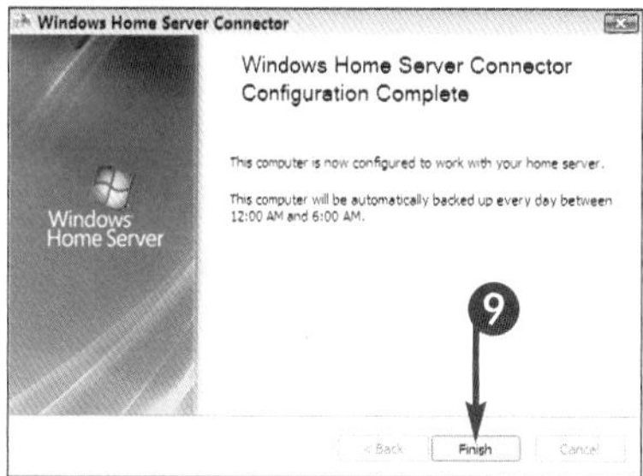

The final wizard dialog box appears.

9 Click **Finish**.

TIPS

### Can I install Windows Home Server Connector on any of my home computers?

Windows Home Server Connector
Compatible:
Windows Vista
Windows XP
Incompatible:
Windows Me
Windows 2000
Windows 98
Mac


No, unfortunately the Windows Home Server Connector software is not compatible with all versions of Windows. You can only install Windows Home Server Connector on PCs that are running either Windows Vista or Windows XP. Note, too, that Windows Home Server Connector does not support other operating systems, such as Macintosh or Linux.

### What can I do if I do not remember the Windows Home Server password?

What is your mother's maiden name?

The Windows Home Server password – the password for the Administrator account – was specified during the Windows Home Server installation. If you do not remember the password, follow steps **1** to **5** to display the Log On to Your Windows Home Server dialog box. Click **Password hint** to open the Password Hint dialog box, which displays a password reminder.

# Run the Windows Home Server Console

You can view backups, work with user accounts, shared folders, and server storage, and configure Windows Home Server settings, by running the Windows Home Server Console program.

**To open the Windows Home Server Console, you must know the password for the server's Administrator account.**

1. Click **Start**.
2. Click **All Programs**.

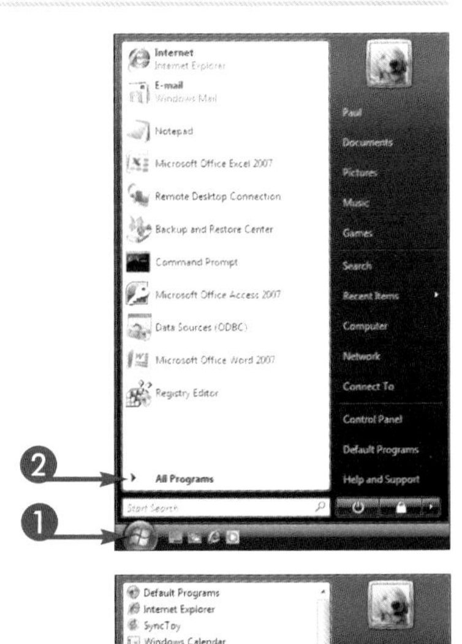


3. Click **Windows Home Server Console**.

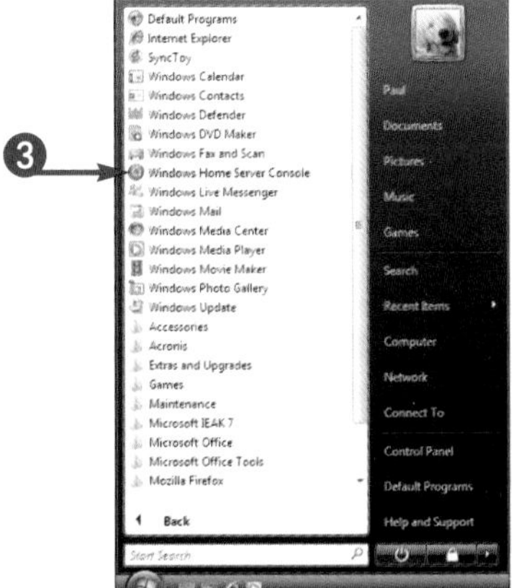

The Windows Home Server Console logon screen appears.

4. Type the Windows Home Server password.
5. Click **Go** (⊕).

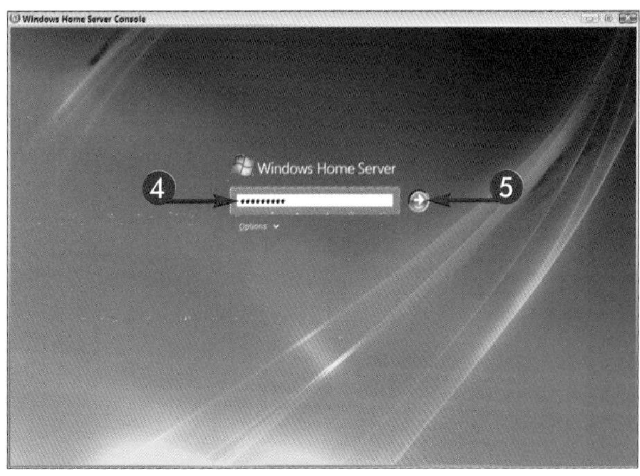


The Windows Home Server Console appears.

**Do I have to type the Windows Home Server password every time I use the Console?**

No, you can configure the logon screen to remember the password so that you no longer have to type it when you start the Console. Follow steps **1** to **4** to type the password, click **Options**, and then click **Remember the Windows Home Server password**.

**What can I do if I do not remember the Windows Home Server password?**

You must specify the Windows Home Server password to open the Console. If you do not remember the password, follow steps **1** to **3** to display the Windows Home Server Console logon screen. Click **Options** and then click **Password hint** to open the Password Hint dialog box, which displays a password reminder.

# Create a Start Menu Shortcut for the Console

In order to reduce the time and the number of mouse clicks that it takes to start the Windows Home Server Console program, you can add a shortcut for the Console program to the main Start menu.

## Create a Start Menu Shortcut for the Console

1. Click **Start**.
2. Click **All Programs**.
3. Right-click **Windows Home Server Console**.
4. Click **Pin to Start Menu**.

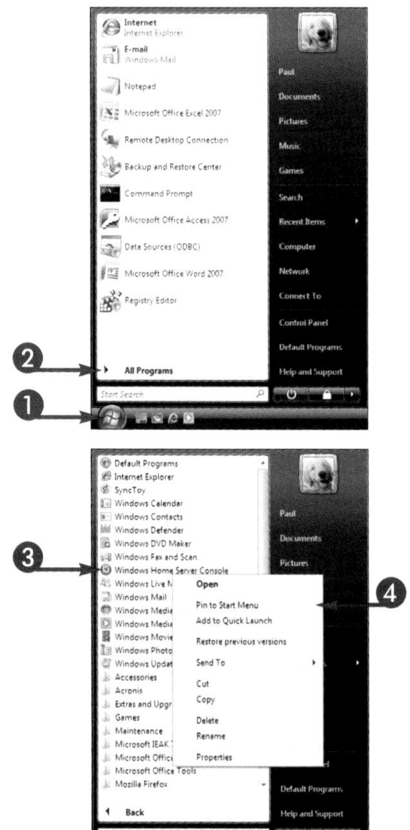

5 Click **Back**.

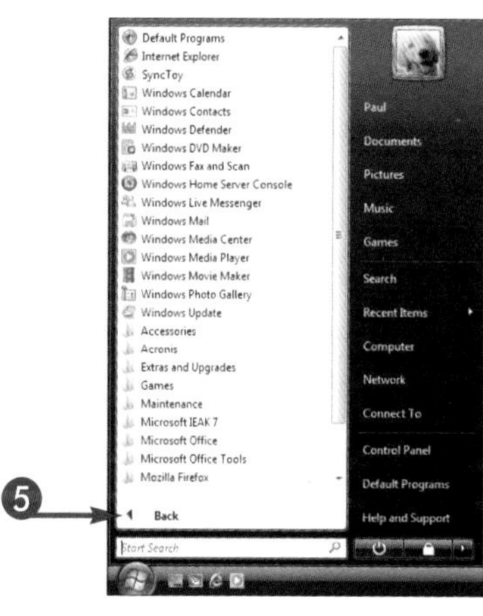

- A shortcut for the Windows Home Server Console appears in the Start menu.

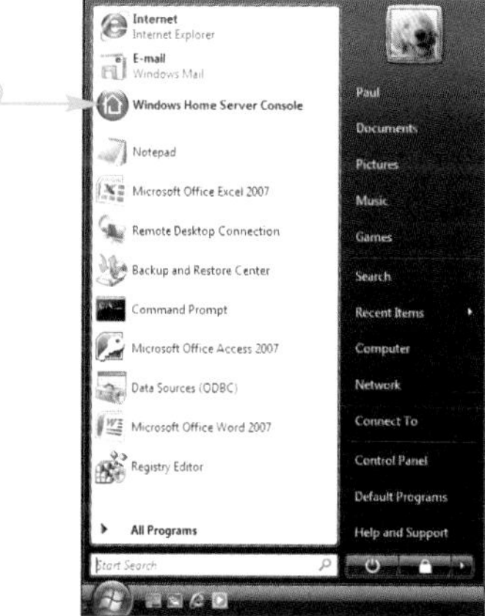

**Can I create a keyboard shortcut for the Windows Home Server Console?**

Yes. Follow these steps:

1 Click **Start**.

2 Right-click **Windows Home Server Console**.

3 Click **Properties** to open the Properties dialog box.

4 Click the **Shortcut** tab.

5 Click inside the Shortcut key box and type a letter, number, or symbol.

- Windows displays a shortcut that combines Ctrl, Alt, and the key that you pressed.

6 Click **OK**.

7 In Windows Vista, type your User Account Control credentials.

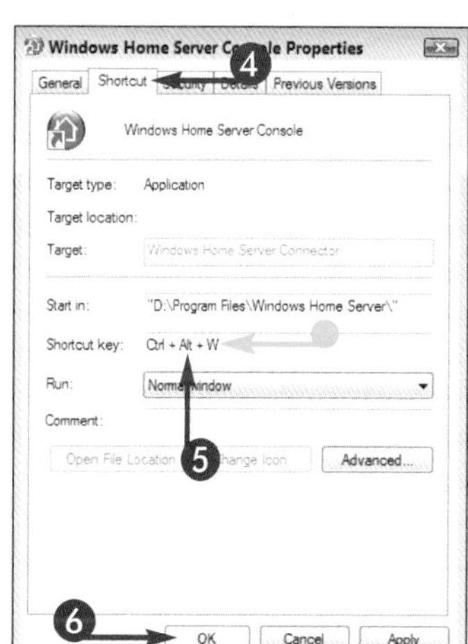

# Change the Workgroup Name

To make it easier to work with all of the computers on your network, each computer should use the same workgroup name. The default name used by Windows Home Server is usually Workgroup.

**To work directly with Windows Home Server, as shown in this section, you may need to connect to the server remotely. For more information, see Chapter 11.**

## Change the Workgroup Name

1. Click **Start**.
2. Right-click **My Computer**.
3. Click **Properties**.

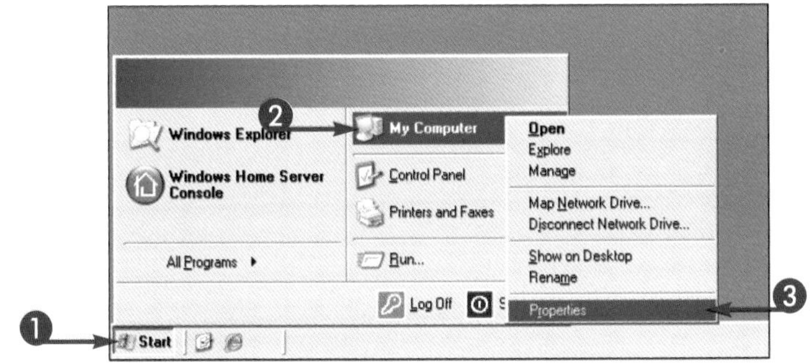


The System Properties dialog box appears.

4. Click the **Computer Name** tab.
5. Click **Change**.

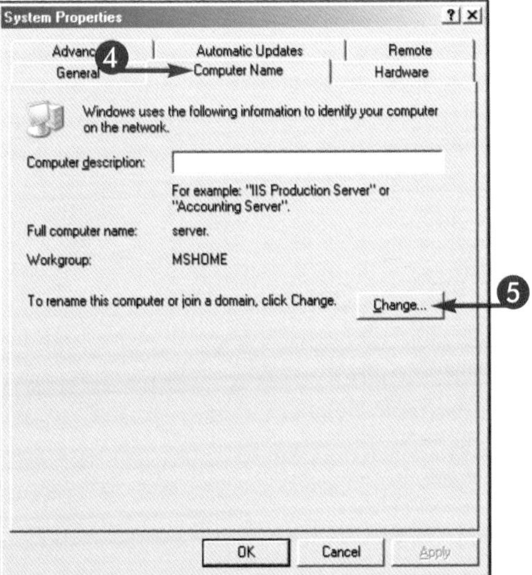

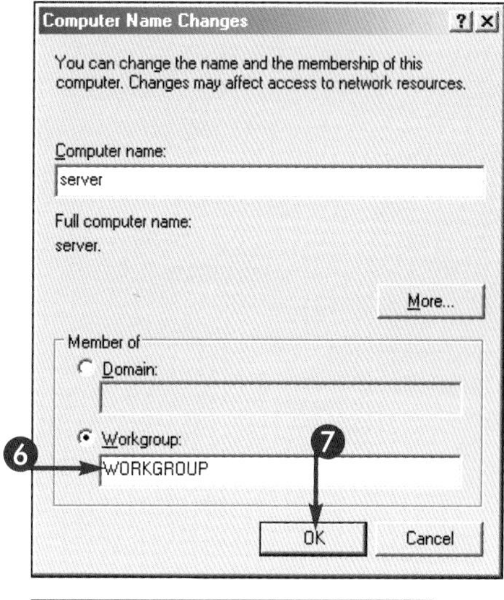


The Computer Name Changes dialog box appears.

6. Type your network's common workgroup name.

**Note:** *The name must be 15 characters or less, and it can only contain letters, numbers, and underscore characters (_).*

7. Click **OK**.

A welcome message appears.

8. Click **OK**.

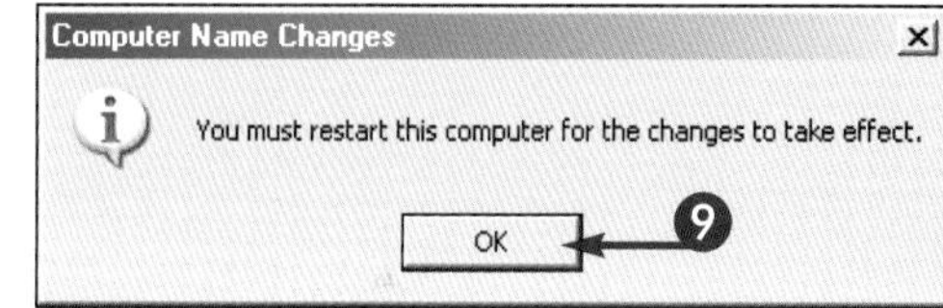


Windows warns you that you must restart your computer.

9. Click **OK**.
10. Click **OK** to close the System Properties dialog box.
11. Restart your computer.

Windows restarts and activates the new workgroup name.

### How do I change the workgroup name in Windows Vista?

Click **Start**, right-click **Computer**, and then click **Properties** to open the System window. Click **Change settings** and then type your User Account Control credentials to open the System Properties dialog box with the Computer Name tab already displayed. Follow steps **5** to **11** in this section to change the workgroup name.

### Is there a faster way to display the System Properties dialog box and its Computer Name tab?

Yes, you can use a keyboard shortcut. In Windows Vista or Windows XP, first press [Windows] + [R] to open the Run dialog box. In the Open text box, type **control sysdm.cpl,,1**. (In Windows Vista, you can also type **systempropertiescomputername**.) Click **OK**.

# Change the Computer Name

If you do not like the computer name that is assigned to Windows Home Server, you can change it. The default name used by Windows Home Server is usually Server, but you can change it to any other name that is not already used on your network.

**To work directly with Windows Home Server, as shown in this section, you may need to connect to the server remotely. For more information, see Chapter 11.**

## Change the Computer Name

1. Click **Start**.
2. Right-click **My Computer**.
3. Click **Properties**.

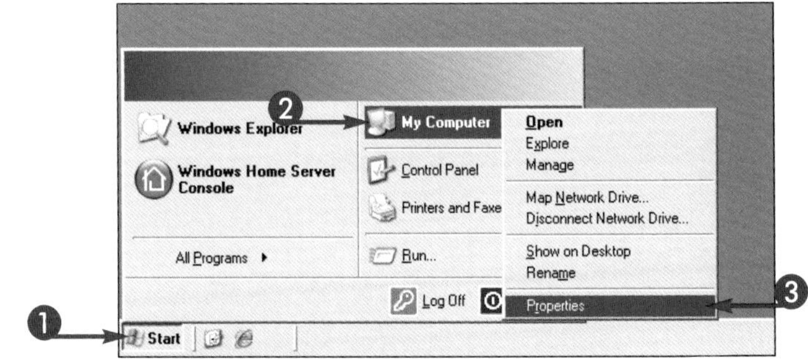


The System Properties dialog box appears.

4. Click the **Computer Name** tab.
5. Click **Change**.

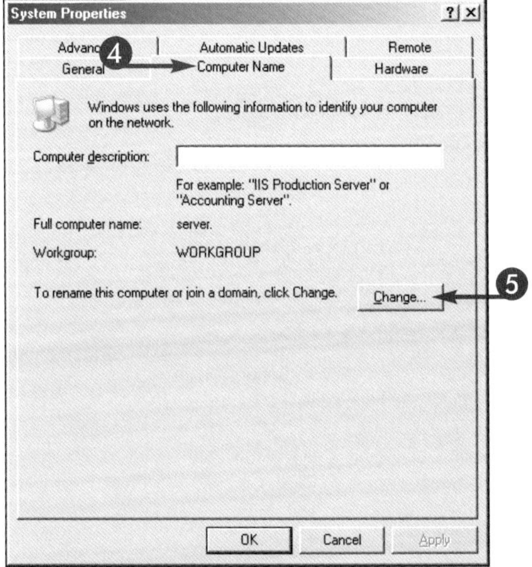

The Computer Name Changes dialog box appears.

6 Type the computer name that you want to use.

***Note:** The name must be 15 characters or less, and it can only contain letters, numbers, and underscore characters (_).*

7 Click **OK**.

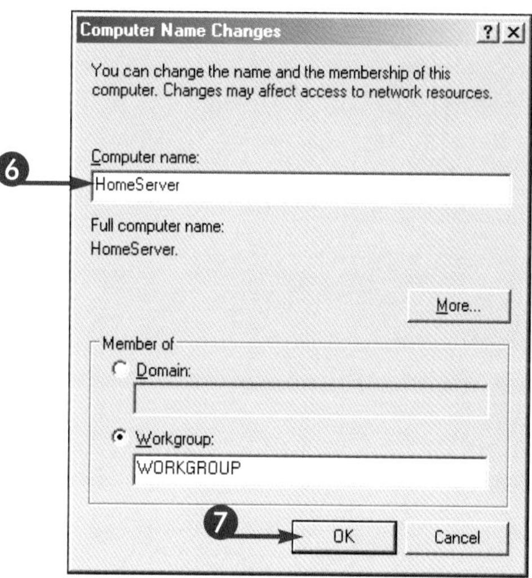


Windows warns you that you must restart your computer.

8 Click **OK**.

9 Click **OK** to close the System Properties dialog box.

Windows asks if you want to restart your computer.

10 Click **Yes**.

Windows restarts and activates the new computer name.

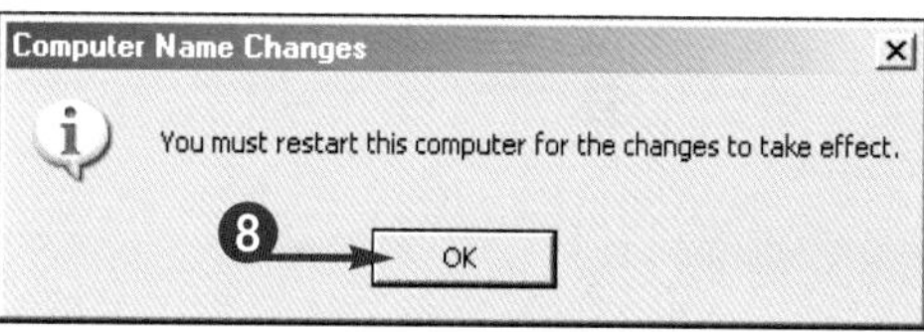


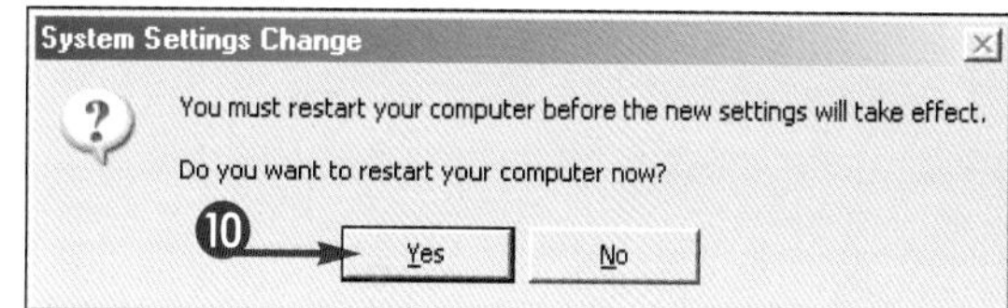

### How do I change the computer name in Windows Vista?

Click **Start**, right-click **Computer**, and then click **Properties** to open the System window. Click **Change settings** and then type your User Account Control credentials to open the System Properties dialog box with the Computer Name tab already displayed. Follow steps **5** to **10** in this section to change the computer name.

### After I change the Windows Home Server name, the Windows Home Server Console no longer works. What is the problem?

When you installed Windows Home Server Connector, it discovered the Windows Home Server computer on your network and made note of the computer's name for future reference. When you changed the name, the Windows Home Server Console could no longer find the server. To fix this problem, you must rediscover the server (see the section "Rediscover Windows Home Server," later in this chapter).

# Configure Windows Home Server with a Static Address

To make it easier to access Windows Home Server remotely, you can configure the server with a static IP address. By default, Windows Home Server is assigned a different address each time it reboots.

**To work directly with Windows Home Server, as shown in this section, you may need to connect to the server remotely. For more information, see Chapter 11.**

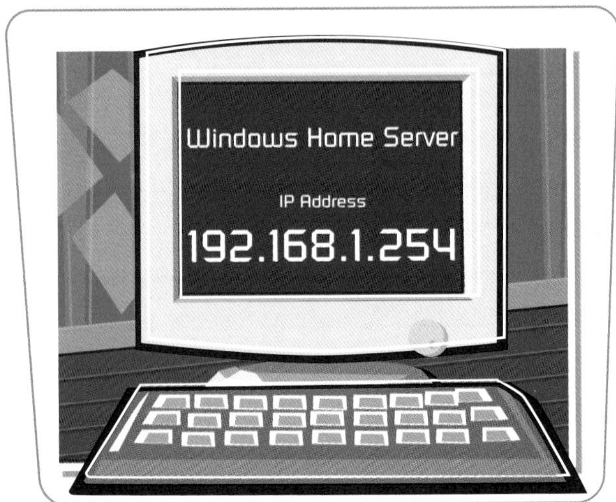


## Configure Windows Home Server with a Static Address

1. Click **Start**.
2. Click **Control Panel**.
3. Click **Network Connections**.
4. Right-click **Local Area Connection**.
5. Click **Properties**.

The Local Area Connection Properties dialog box appears.

6. Click the **General** tab.
7. Click **Internet Protocol (TCP/IP)**.
8. Click **Properties**.

The Internet Protocol (TCP/IP) Properties dialog box appears.

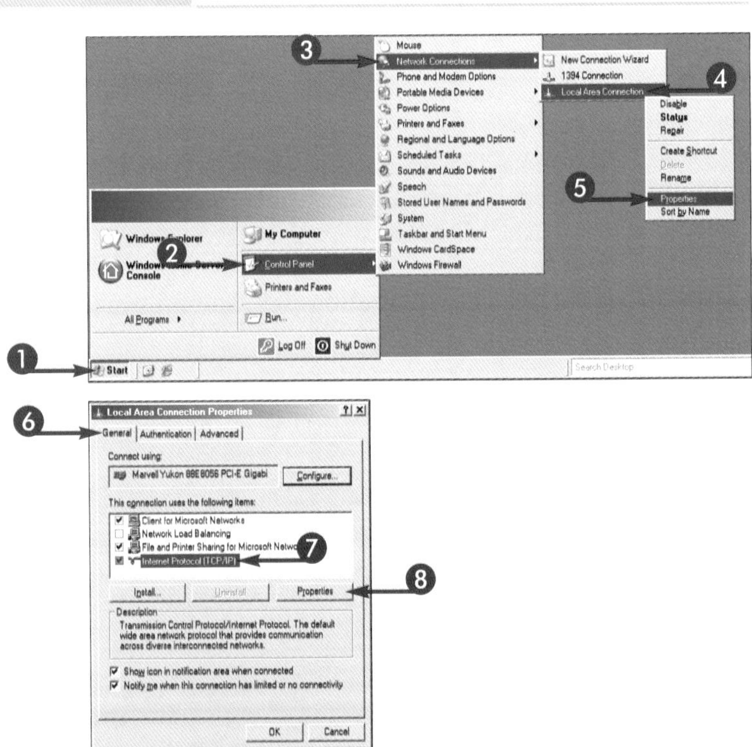

9. Click **Use the following IP address** (○ changes to ◉).
10. In the IP address box, type the static address you want to use, including the Subnet mask.
11. In the Default gateway box, type the address of your network's router or gateway device.
12. In these boxes, type the IP addresses of your ISP's DNS server.
13. Click **OK**.

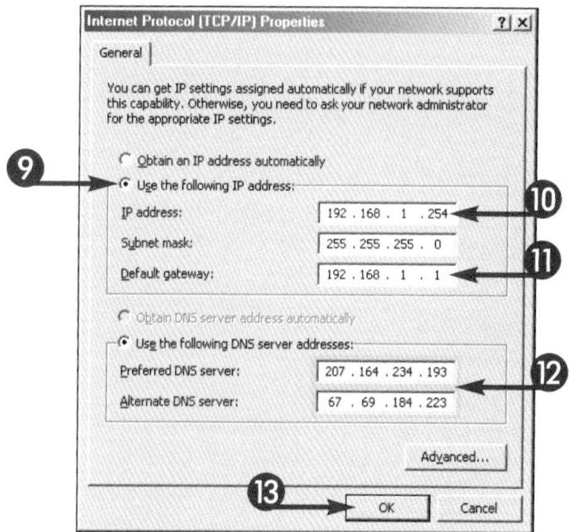


14. Click **Close**.

Windows Home Server activates the static IP address.

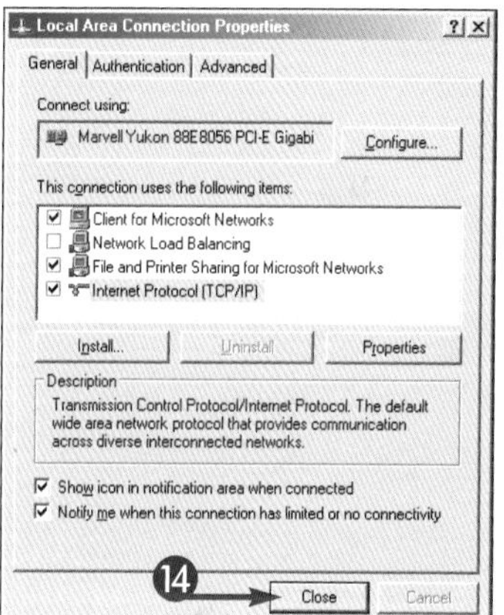

### Which IP address should I use?

You usually have a limited range of IP addresses that you can use. For example, if your router or gateway address is 192.168.1.1, then the range is from 192.168.1.2 to 192.168.1.254. Similarly, if your router or gateway address is 192.168.0.1, then the range is from 192.168.0.2 to 192.168.0.254. However, to avoid conflicts with other computers, you should use the highest address, such as 192.168.1.254.

### How do I know which DNS server addresses to use?

Click **Start** and then click **Run** to open the Run dialog box. Type **cmd** and click **OK** to open a Command Prompt window. Type **ipconfig /all** and press Enter. In the command results, look for DNS Servers and note the two IP addresses that appear; these are the server addresses that you can use.

```
IP Address. . . . . . . . . . . . : 192.168.1.105
Subnet Mask . . . . . . . . . . . : 255.255.255.0
Default Gateway . . . . . . . . . : 192.168.1.1
DHCP Server . . . . . . . . . . . : 192.168.1.1
DNS Servers . . . . . . . . . . . : 207.164.234.193
                                    67.69.184.223
```

# Change the Windows Home Server Password

You can increase Windows Home Server security by regularly changing the Windows Home Server password. This is the password associated with the server's Administrator account.

**To change the Windows Home Server password, you must know the existing password for the server's Administrator account.**

## Change the Windows Home Server Password

1. Start the Windows Home Server Console.

*Note: See the section "Run the Windows Home Server Console," earlier in this chapter.*

2. Click **Settings**.

The Windows Home Server Settings dialog box appears.

3. Click **Passwords**.
4. Click **Change Password**.

The Windows Home Server Password Change dialog box appears.

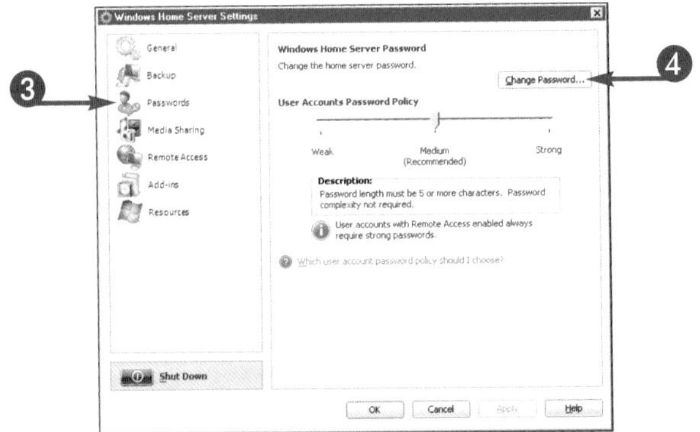

5. In the Password text box, type the new password.
6. In the Confirm password text box, retype the new password.

- A check mark appears here if the password is at least seven characters long.
- A check mark appears here if the password is complex.

7. In the Password Hint text box, type a hint for the password.
8. Click **OK**.

Windows Home Server tells you that it has changed the password.

9. Click **OK**.
10. Click **OK**.

The next time you run the Windows Home Server Console, you can use the new password.

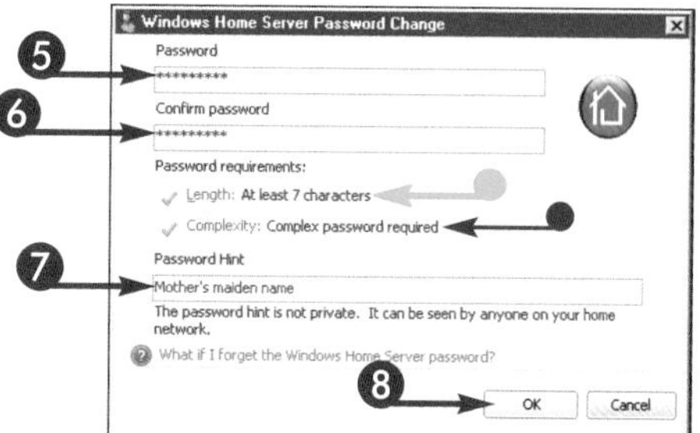


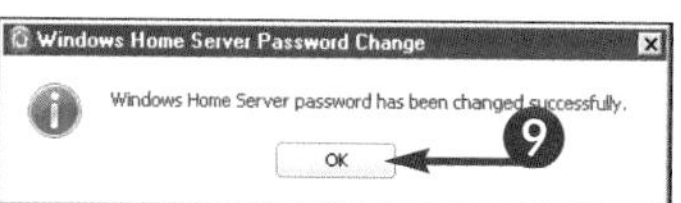


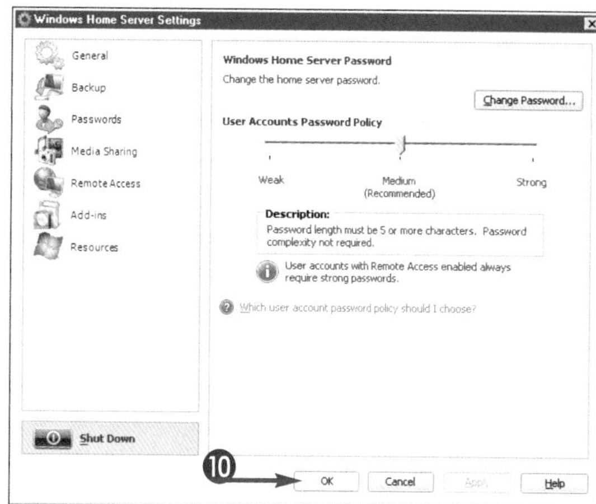

### What is a complex password?

A complex password is one that includes at least one character from at least three of the following four categories: lowercase letters, uppercase letters, numbers, and symbols (such as !, @, $, and _). A complex password is more secure because it is difficult to determine using software.

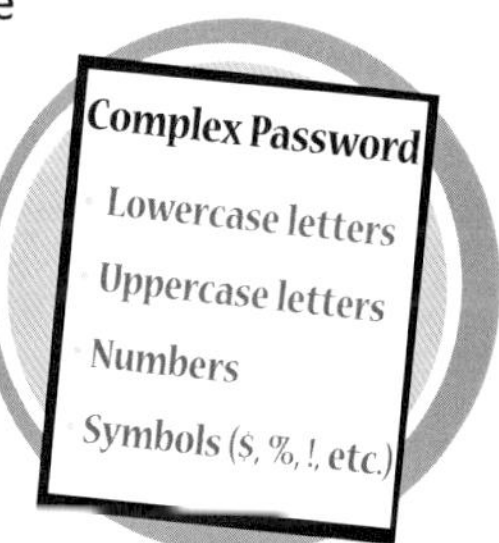


### Is it possible to change just the password hint?

Yes. You can change the password hint without also changing the password. Follow steps **1** to **4** to display the Windows Home Server Password Change dialog box. In the Password text box and the Confirm Password text box, type the existing Windows Home Server password. In the Password Hint text box, type the new hint, and then follow steps **8** to **10**.

# Remove a Computer from Windows Home Server

If you have a computer that you no longer use, you can shorten overall backup times and reduce the clutter in the Windows Home Server Console by removing that computer from Windows Home Server.

**To remove a computer from Windows Home Server, you must know the password for the server's Administrator account.**

## Remove a Computer from Windows Home Server

1. On the computer you want to remove, uninstall Windows Home Server Connector.
2. Start the Windows Home Server Console.

*Note:* *See the section "Run the Windows Home Server Console," earlier in this chapter.*

3. Click **Computers & Backup**.
4. Click the computer you want to remove (here, MediaPC).

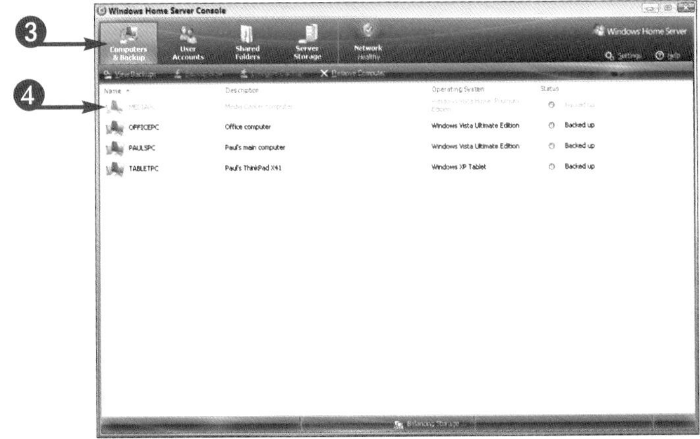


5. Click **Remove Computer**.

The Remove a Computer dialog box appears.

6 Click **I am sure I want to remove this computer** (☐ changes to ☑).

7 Click **Remove**.

Windows Home Server removes the computer from the Computers & Backup tab.

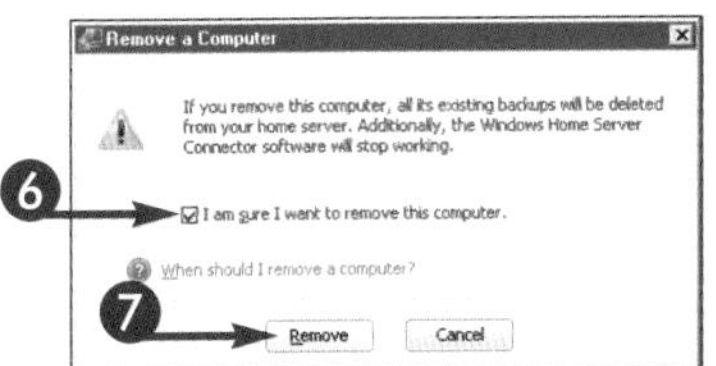

## How do I uninstall Windows Home Server Connector in Windows Vista?

1 Click **Start**.

2 Click **Control Panel**.

3 Click **Uninstall a program**.

The Programs and Features window appears.

4 Click **Windows Home Server Connector**.

5 Click **Uninstall**.

Windows Vista asks you to confirm that you want to uninstall the program.

6 Click **Yes**.

7 Type your User Account Control credentials.

Windows Vista uninstalls Windows Home Server Connector.

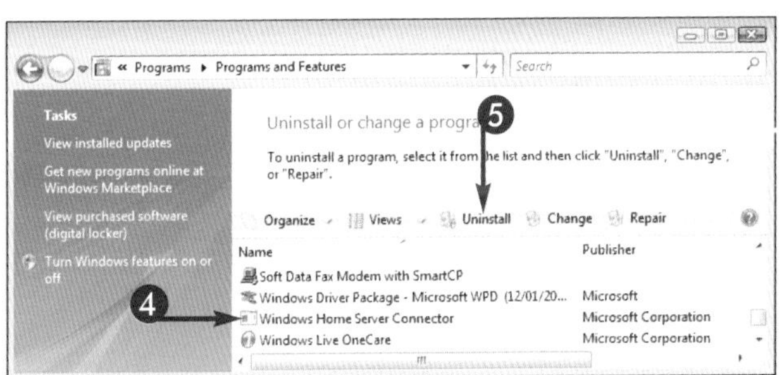

# Rediscover Windows Home Server

If you can no longer access Windows Home Server because you changed the server's address, name, or password, you can rediscover the server and restore the connection.

**To rediscover Windows Home Server, you must know the password for the server's Administrator account.**

## Rediscover Windows Home Server

❶ Click **Start**.

❷ Click **All Programs**.

Windows Vista changes the All Programs command to Back.

❸ Click **Accessories**.

❹ Click **Run**.

***Note:*** *You can also press* [Windows key] + [R] *to open the Run dialog box.*

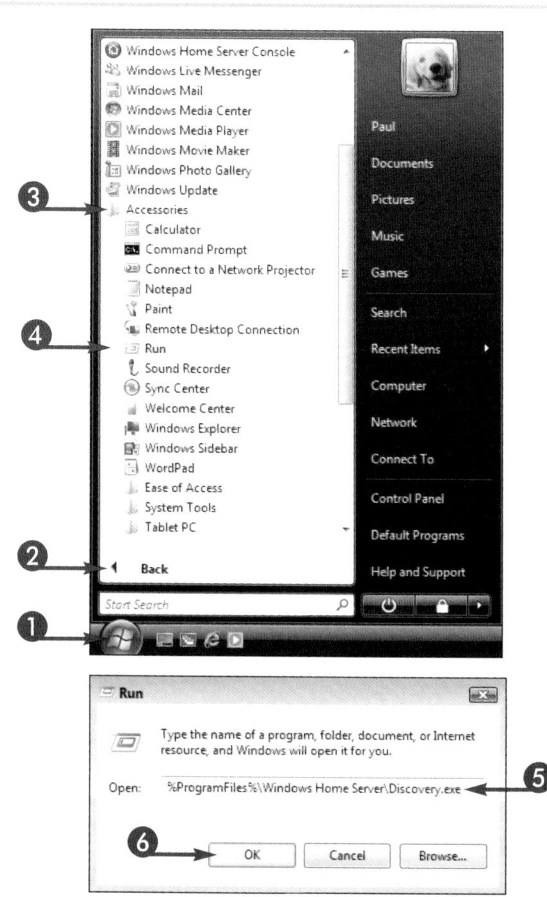


The Run dialog box appears.

❺ Type **%ProgramFiles%\Windows Home Server\Discovery.exe**.

❻ Click **OK**.

***Note:*** *If you see the User Account Control dialog box, type your credentials.*

Windows rediscovers the Windows Home Server computer.

The Log On to Your Windows Home Server dialog box appears.

7 Type the Windows Home Server password.

8 Click **Next**.

Windows Home Server Connector configures your computer.

9 Click **Next**.

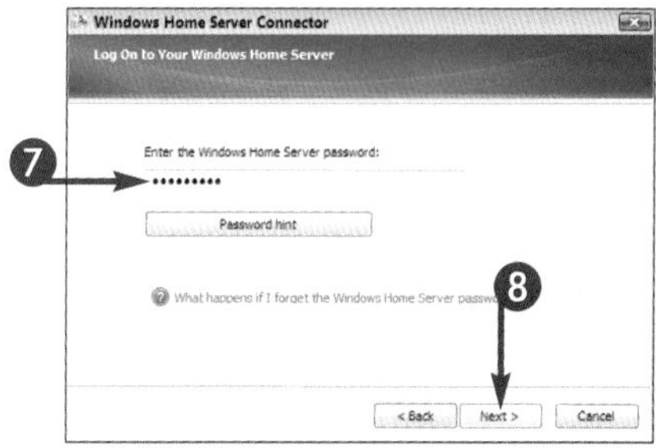


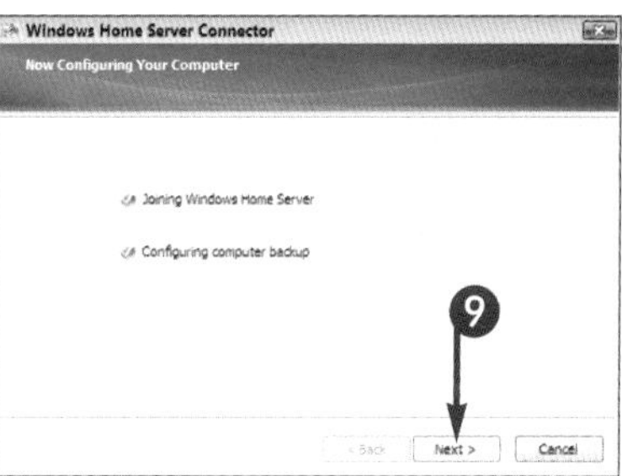


The final wizard dialog box appears.

10 Click **Finish**.

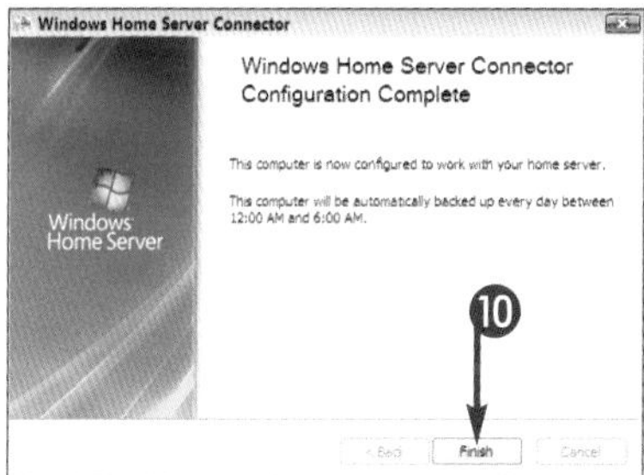

## TIPS

### Why do I sometimes lose the connection to Windows Home Server?

Your computer expects Windows Home Server's name, address, and password to be the same as when you installed the Windows Home Server Connector software. If one or more of those values change, your computer may lose the connection and you will need to rediscover Windows Home Server as described in this section.

### How do I know when I need to rediscover Windows Home Server?

One way to find out is when you try to run the Windows Home Server Console and Windows reports that it cannot connect to the server. However, the easiest way is to look at the Windows Home Server icon ( ) in the taskbar. If this icon is gray, then you have lost the connection to the server.

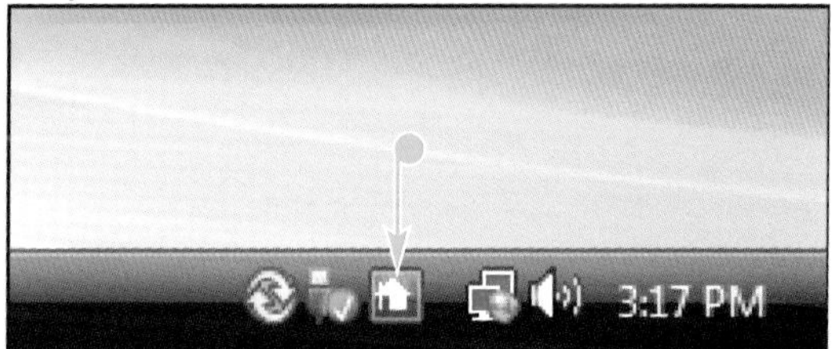

# Customize the Windows Home Server Start Menu

You can personalize how the Windows Home Server Start menu looks and operates to suit your style and the way you work.

**To work directly with Windows Home Server, as shown in this section, you may need to connect to the server remotely. For more information, see Chapter 11.**

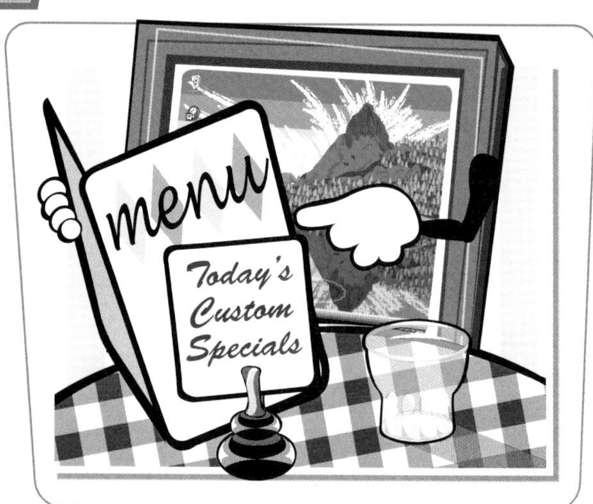


## Customize the Windows Home Server Start Menu

1. Right-click **Start**.
2. Click **Properties**.

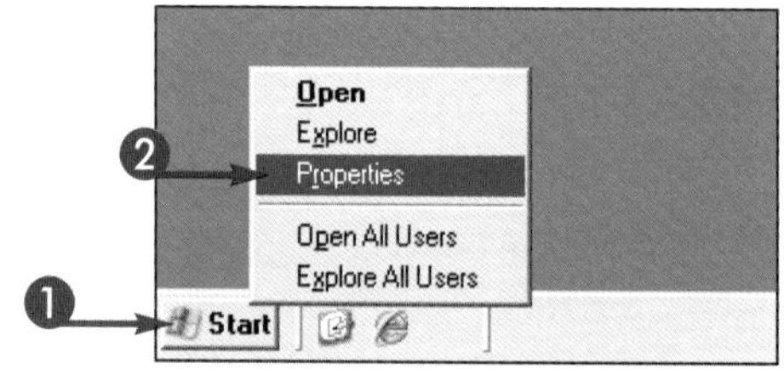


The Taskbar and Start Menu Properties dialog box appears.

3. Click the **Start Menu** tab.
4. Click **Start menu** (◯ changes to ◉).
5. Click **Customize**.

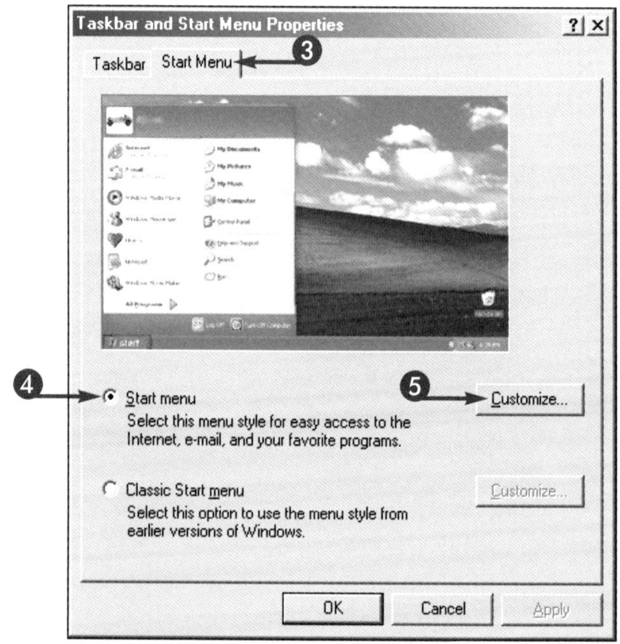

The Customize Start Menu dialog box appears.

- To switch to smaller icons, you can click **Small icons** (◯ changes to ◉).
- To display the Internet icon, you can click **Internet** (☐ changes to ☑).
- To display the E-mail icon, you can click **E-mail** (☐ changes to ☑).

6 Click **OK**.

7 Click **OK** to close the Taskbar and Start Menu Properties dialog box.

Windows Home Server activates the new Start menu settings.

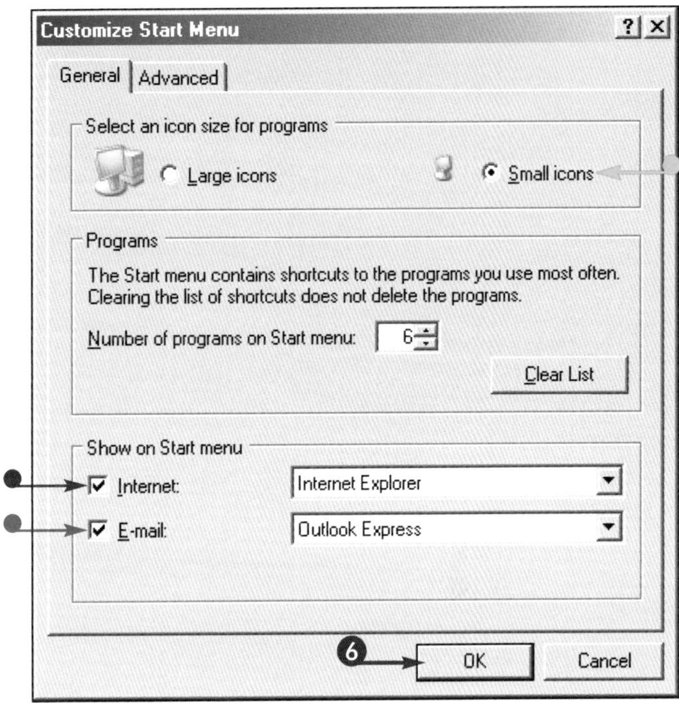


TIP

**My Start menu is missing icons such as My Documents, Favorites, and My Recent Document. How do I display these icons?**

Follow steps **1** to **5** in this section to display the Customize Start Menu dialog box. Now follow these steps:

1 Click the **Advanced** tab.

2 In the Start menu items list, click the check box for any item you want to display (☐ changes to ☑).

3 In the Start menu items list, click the **Display as a link** option for any item you want to display (◯ changes to ◉).

4 Click here to display the My Recent Documents icon (☐ changes to ☑).

5 Click **OK**.

Windows customizes the Start menu to show the icons you selected.

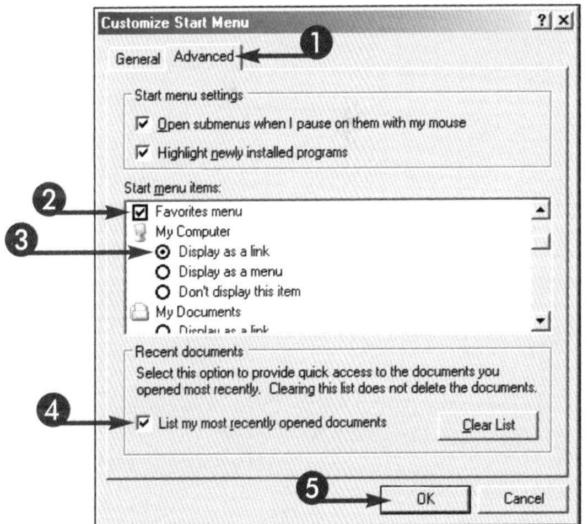

# Customize the Windows Home Server Taskbar

You can personalize how the taskbar looks and operates to make it more efficient and to suit your own working style.

**To work directly with Windows Home Server, as shown in this section, you may need to connect to the server remotely. For more information, see Chapter 11.**

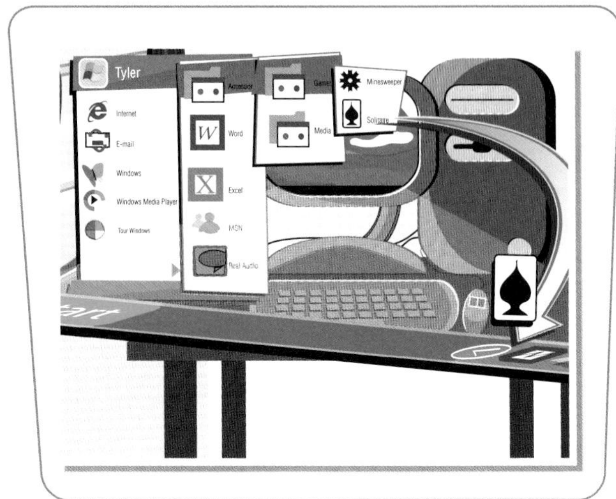

## Customize the Windows Home Server Taskbar

1. Right-click an empty section of the taskbar.
2. Click **Properties**.

   The Taskbar and Start Menu Properties dialog box appears.

- These areas show you the effect that your changes will have on the taskbar.

3. Click **Lock the taskbar** (☑ changes to ☐) to unlock the taskbar so that you can resize or move it.
4. Click **Auto-hide the taskbar** (☐ changes to ☑) to hide the taskbar when you are using a program.

***Note:*** *To display the hidden taskbar, move your mouse pointer to the bottom edge of the screen.*

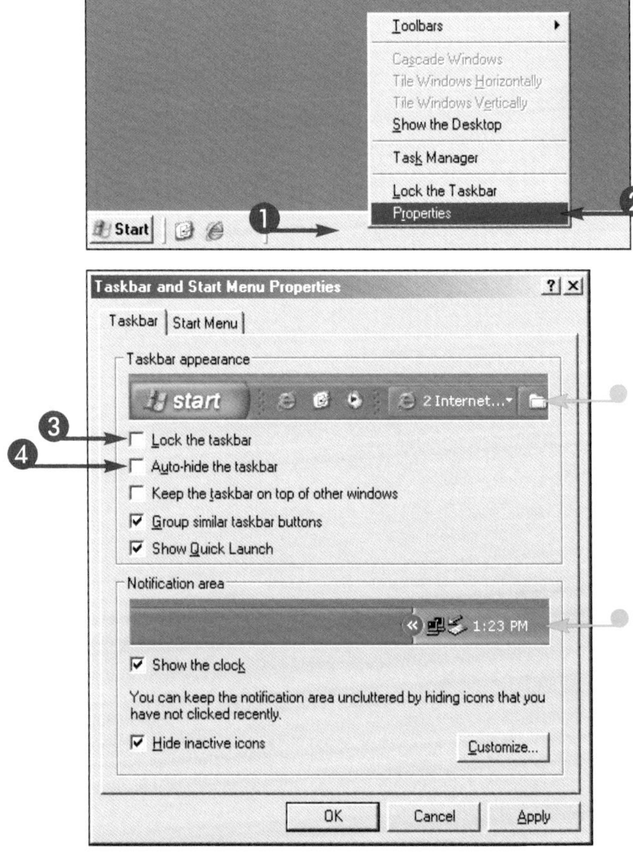

5 Click **Keep the taskbar on top of other windows** (☑ changes to ☐) to allow maximized windows to use the full screen.

6 Click **Group similar taskbar buttons** (☑ changes to ☐) to disable the grouping of taskbar buttons.

7 Click **Show Quick Launch** (☑ changes to ☐) to hide the Quick Launch toolbar.

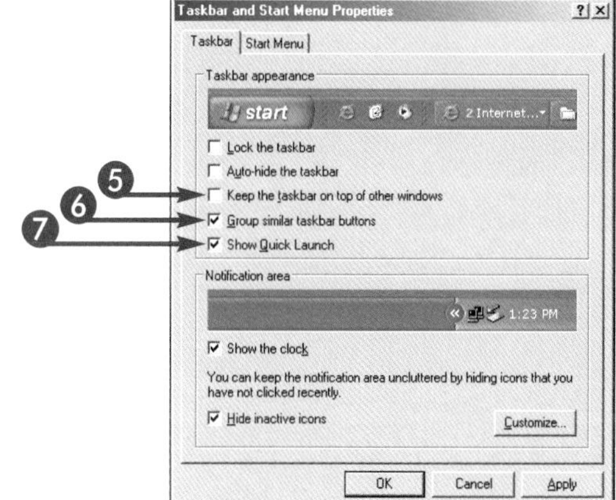


8 Click **Show the clock** (☑ changes to ☐) to hide the clock.

9 Click **Hide inactive icons** (☐ changes to ☑) to hide unused icons in the notification area.

***Note:*** *If you leave the Hide inactive icons option on, you can click « to display the hidden icons. Click « again to hide the icons.*

10 Click **OK**.

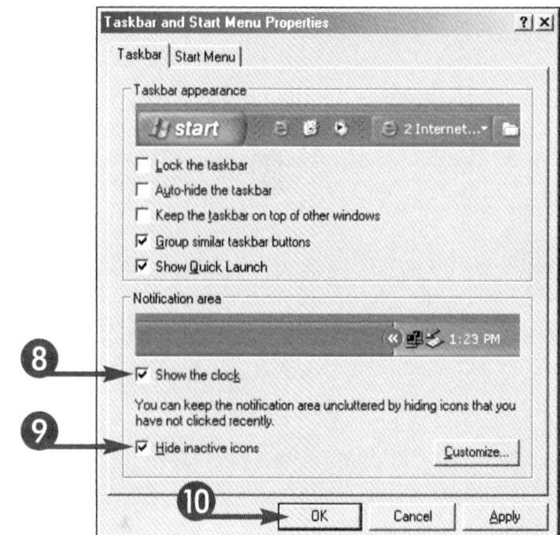

### How do I resize the taskbar?

To resize the taskbar, click and drag the top edge of the taskbar up (to display more taskbar rows) or down (to display fewer taskbar rows).

### How do I move the taskbar?

To move the taskbar, position the mouse over an empty section of the taskbar, and then click and drag the taskbar to another edge of the screen.

# CHAPTER 4

# Setting Up User Accounts

You can create user accounts for each person on your network. This allows them to access the Windows Home Server shared folders, log on to the network remotely, and have their own shared folder on Windows Home Server.

Understanding User Accounts ....................... 64
Select a User Accounts Password Policy ...... 66
Change the Password on the Local Computer ....................................... 68
Add a User Account ....................................... 70
Synchronize the Local and Server Passwords ....................................... 72
Change a User's Display Name ..................... 74
Change a User's Password ............................. 76
Disable a User Account ................................. 78
Enable a User Account ................................. 80
Enable the Guest Account ............................ 82
Remove a User Account ................................ 86

# Understanding User Accounts

To work effectively with user accounts, you need to understand a few key concepts such as the logon name and password, folder access permissions, and enabling remote access.

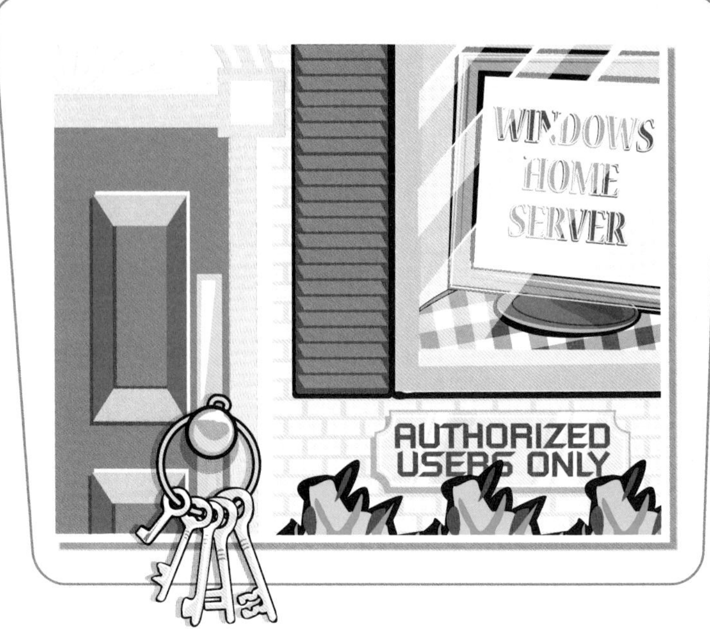


**Logon Name**

The first part of the user account information is the *username*. This name uniquely identifies a person on Windows Home Server. On a home network, the logon name is usually the same as the person's first name.

**Password**

The second part of the user account information is the *password*. This is a sequence of characters known only to the user and to the person acting as the Windows Home Server Administrator. By typing the correct password and logon name, you establish yourself as an authorized Windows Home Server user.

## Synchronize with Windows

Each network user also has a local user account on Windows Vista or Windows XP. To keep things simple, it is best to set up a person's Windows Home Server user account to have the same logon name and password as their Windows Vista or Windows XP user account.

## Folder Access

*Folder access* determines what each Windows Home Server user can and cannot do with the server's shared folders. For example, giving users *Read* access only enables them to open a file for viewing. Giving users *Full* access enables them to also make changes to a file. A user whose access is set to *None* cannot access shared folders.

## User Subfolder

When you set up a user account on Windows Home Server, that person is automatically assigned their own subfolder in the Users shared folder. This subfolder's name is the same as the user's logon name, and only that person has permission to use the folder. As a result, the user has Full access to the folder, while none of the other users have access.

## Remote Access

When you create a user account, you can specify whether the user can access the network through the Internet. Users to whom you grant remote access permission can use a Web browser to log on to the network over the Internet and access the Windows Home Server shared folders, as well as the desktops of some network computers.

# Select a User Accounts Password Policy

Before creating any user accounts, you need to select a user accounts password policy. This policy determines the types of passwords that you can assign to each account.

**To set the Windows Home Server password policy, you must know the password for the server's Administrator account.**

PASSWORD POLICY
THOU SHALT NOT CREATE
ANY PASSWORD OF LESS
THAN SEVEN CHARACTERS.


## Select a User Accounts Password Policy

1. Start the Windows Home Server Console.

***Note:** For more information, see Chapter 3.*

2. Click **Settings**.

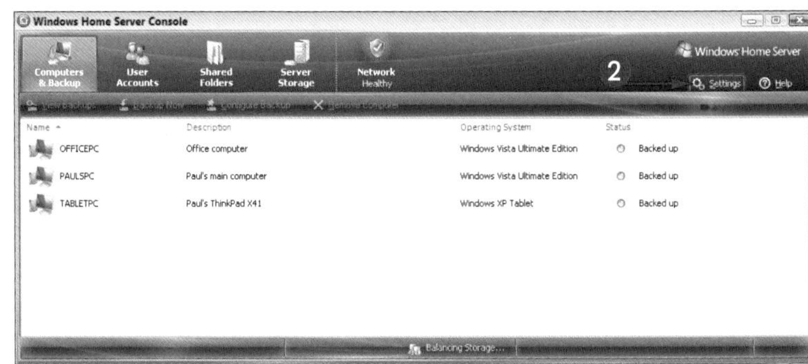


The Windows Home Server Settings dialog box appears.

3. Click the **Passwords** tab.

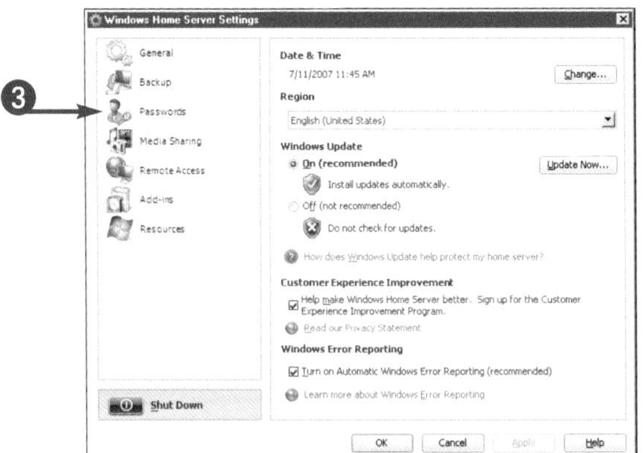

4 In the User Accounts Password Policy section, click and drag the slider to the policy you want to use.

- The Description box displays a brief explanation for the policy you select.

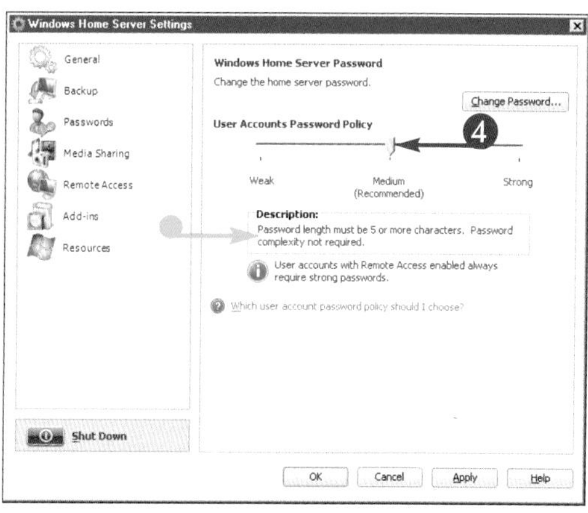

5 Click **OK**.

Windows Home Server activates the new password policy.

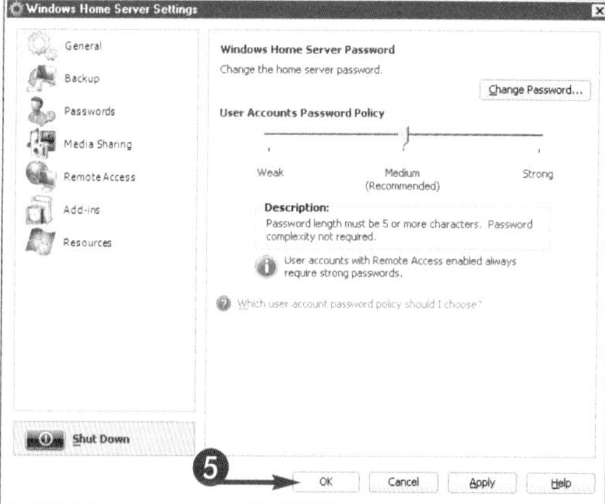

### What do the different password policies mean?

The three password policies have the following characteristics:

Weak. You can assign any password to an account — even no password at all.

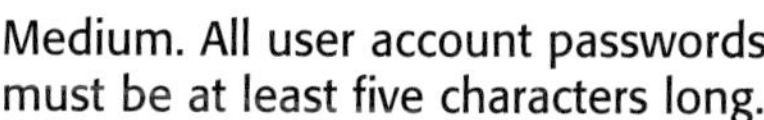

Medium. All user account passwords must be at least five characters long.

Strong. All user account passwords must be at least seven characters long and must include characters from at least three of the following categories: lowercase letters, uppercase letters, numbers, and symbols.

### Which password policy is best for a home network?

If your network does not include wireless connections, then the Medium password policy is probably secure enough, as long as you do not use an obvious password such as the person's name. If your network includes wireless connections, which are inherently less secure, then you should use the Strong password policy. The Weak policy is not secure, so you should not use it.

# Change the Password on the Local Computer

To make it easier to use Windows Home Server, the user account on the local computer needs the same password as the user account on Windows Home Server. If you want to use a particular password on the server, then you need to change the local password to match.

**The following steps show you how to change the password in Windows Vista. The Tip section shows you how to change the password in Windows XP.**

## Change the Password on the Local Computer

1. Click **Start**.
2. Click **Control Panel**.

The Control Panel window appears.

3. Click **Add or remove user accounts**.

***Note:*** *If you see the User Account Control dialog box, either click* ***Continue*** *or type an Administrator password and then click* ***Submit****.*

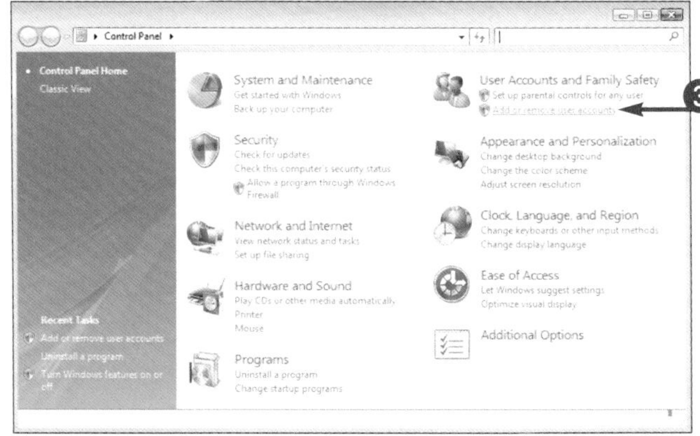

The Manage Accounts window appears.

4 Click the icon of the user you want to work with.

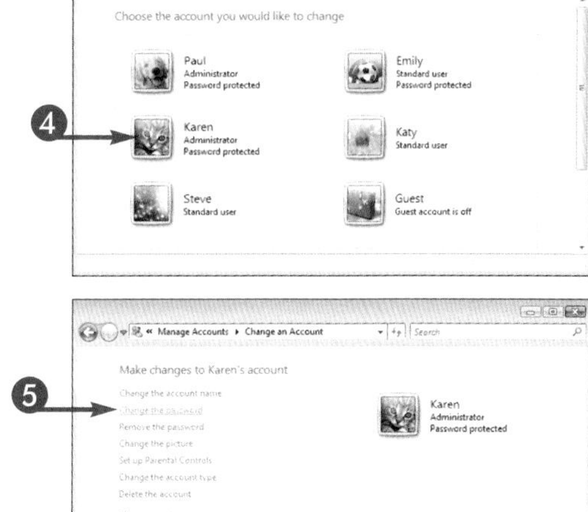


The Change an Account window appears.

5 Click **Change the password**.

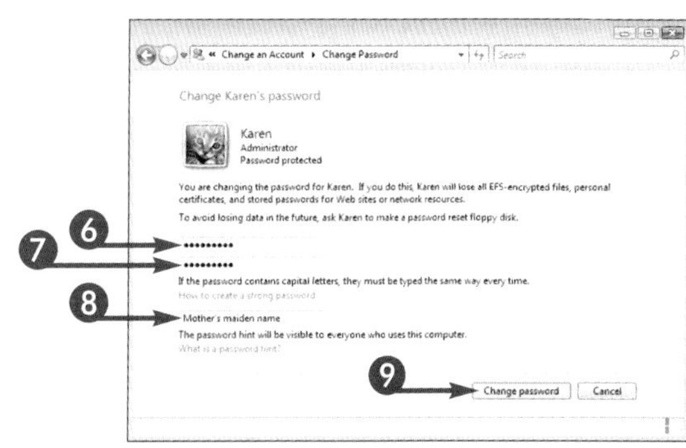


The Change Password window appears.

6 Type the new password.

7 Type the new password again.

8 Type a password hint.

9 Click **Change password**.

Windows Vista changes the user's password.

**How do I change the password in Windows XP?**

Follow these steps:

1 Click **Start**.

2 Click **Control Panel**.

3 Click **User Accounts**.

4 Click the account you want to change.

5 Click **Change the password**.

6 Type the new password.

7 Type the new password again.

8 Type a password hint.

9 Click **Change Password**.

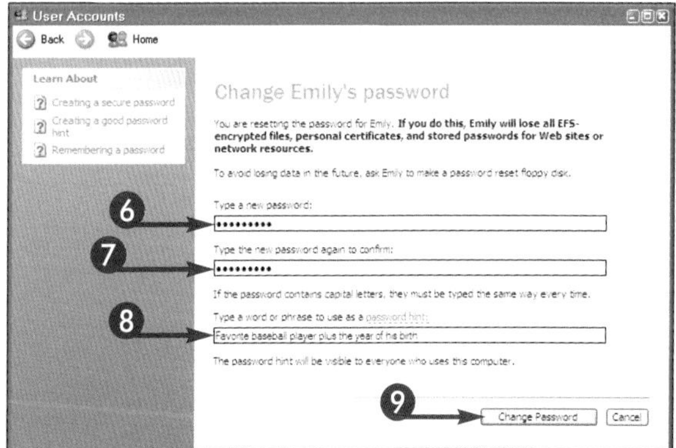

# Add a User Account

To enable a person to work with the Windows Home Server shared folders and to access the network remotely, you must provide that person with a user account on Windows Home Server.

**To add a user account to Windows Home Server, you must know the password for the server's Administrator account.**

## Add a User Account

1. Start the Windows Home Server Console.

***Note:*** *For more information, see Chapter 3.*

2. Click **User Accounts**.

***Note:*** *If you see the User Accounts Setup dialog box, click* ***OK****.*

3. Click **Add**.

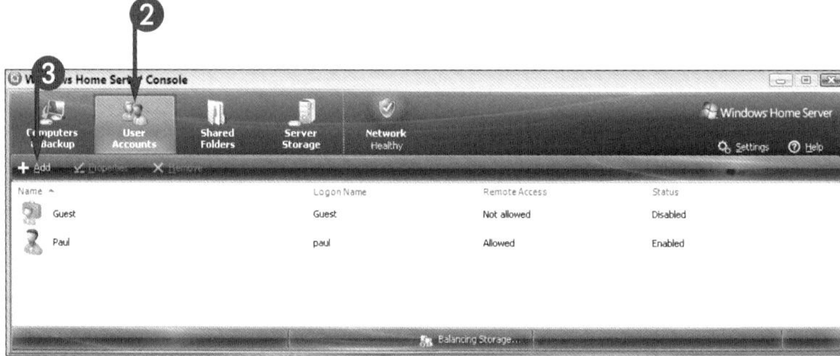

The Add User Account Wizard appears.

4. In the First name text box, type the user's given name.

- You can also type the user's surname in the Last name text box.

5. In the Logon name text box, type the user's logon name.
6. If you want to allow this user to access Windows Home Server remotely, click **Enable Remote Access for this user** (☐ changes to ☑).
7. Click **Next**.

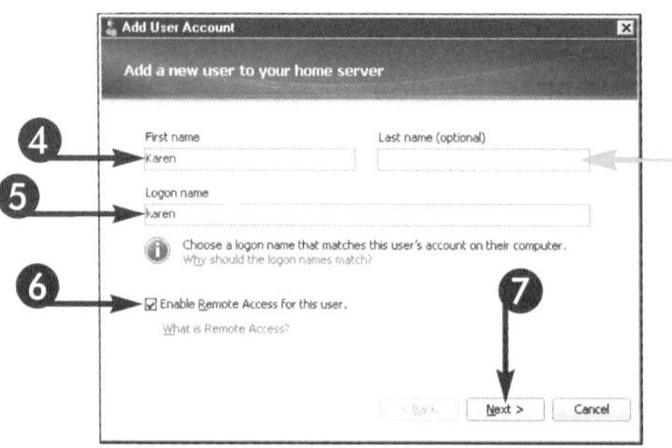

8. In the Password text box, type the user's password.
9. In the Confirm password text box, retype the password.
   - A check mark appears here if the password meets the length requirement of the password policy.
   - A check mark appears here if the password meets the complexity requirement of the password policy.
10. Click **Next**.
11. Set the user's access to the Music folder by clicking **Full**, **Read**, or **None** (○ changes to ◉).
12. Repeat step **11** for the other shared folders.
13. Click **Finish**.

    Windows Home Server creates and configures the new user account.
14. Click **Done**.

    Windows Home Server adds the user to the User Accounts list.

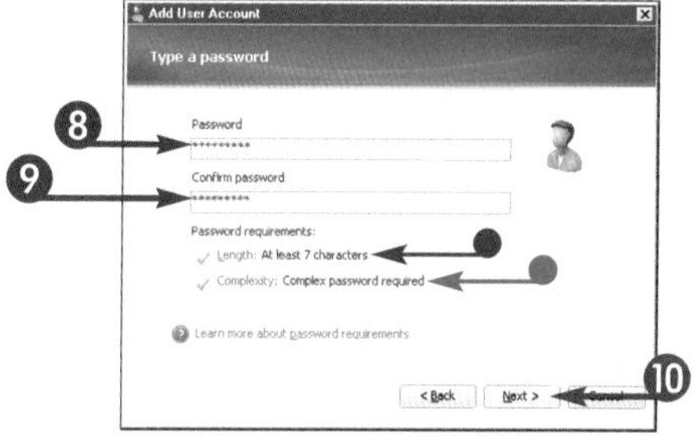


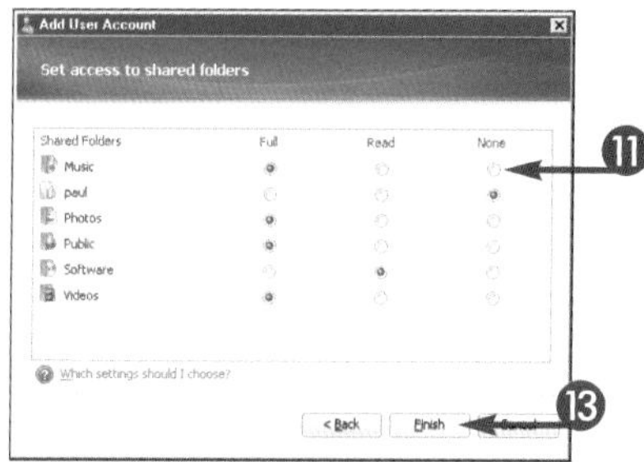


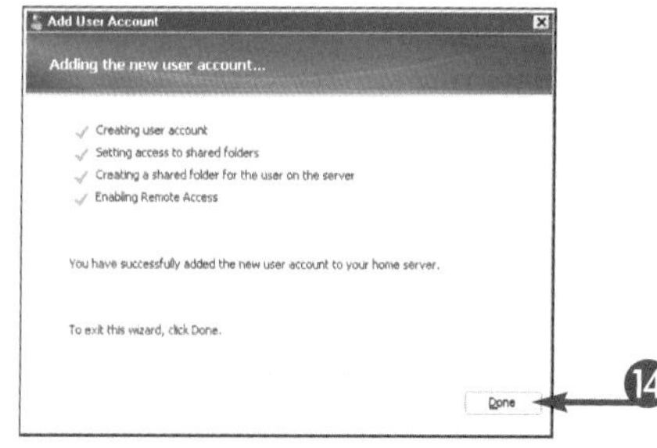

### I am using the Medium password policy, so why does Windows Home Server require a complex password for a particular user?

The Medium password policy normally does not have a complexity requirement. (For more information, see the section "Select a User Accounts Password Policy.") However, if you select **Enable Remote Access for this user** (☐ changes to ☑) in step **6**, Windows Home Server overrides the password policy and requires the user to have a strong password, which is much more secure.

### How many accounts can I add to Windows Home Server?

You can add up to ten accounts to Windows Home Server. Note that this total does not include the built-in Guest account. (For more information on the Guest user, see the section "Enable the Guest Account.") If you have ten accounts defined, the only way to add another one is to delete one or more existing accounts. (For more information, see the section "Remove a User Account.")

# Synchronize the Local and Server Passwords

To easily log on to Windows Home Server and use the shared folders and Remote Access feature, your local user account should have the same password as your Windows Home Server user account. To ensure this, you can synchronize the two account passwords.

## Synchronize the Local and Server Passwords

1. If you see the "Passwords do not match" notification, click the notification dialog box.

- If you do not see this notification, right-click the Windows Home Server icon and then click **Update Password**.

  The Update Password dialog box appears.

2. Click **Keep my password on the home server** (◯ changes to ◉).

- If you prefer to use the local password, you can click **Keep my password on this computer** (◯ changes to ◉).

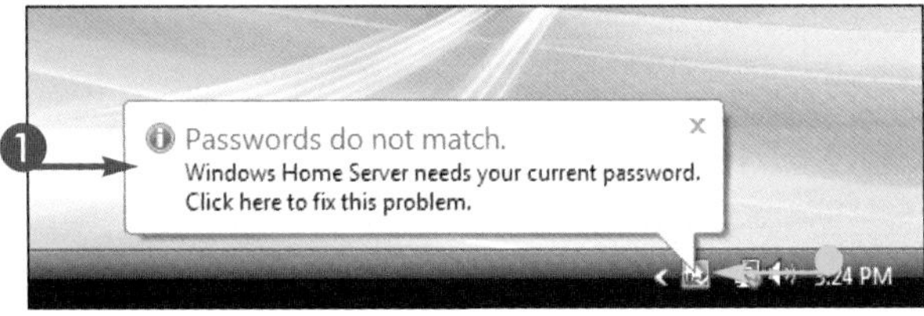


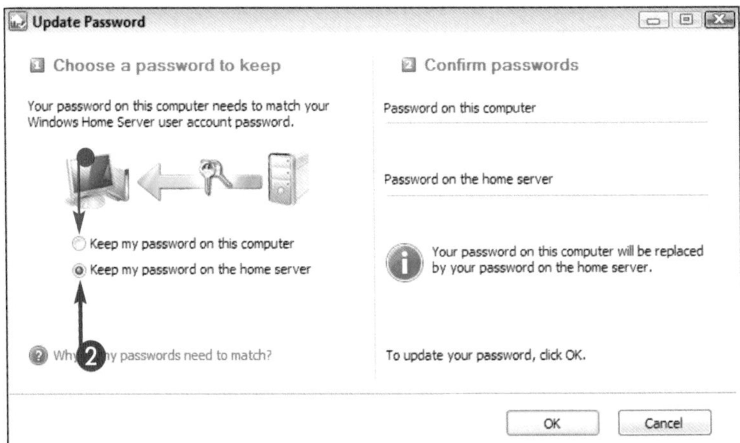

3. Type the password for the local user account.
4. Type the password for the Windows Home Server user account.
5. Click **OK**.

   Windows Home Server synchronizes the two passwords.
6. Click **Close**.

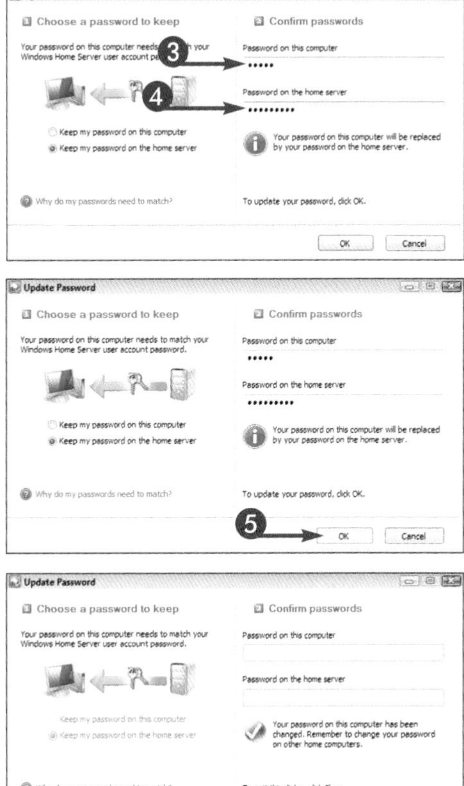

### Do I have to synchronize the local and server passwords?

No, it is not necessary that the two accounts use the same password. However, accessing Windows Home Server is much less convenient if the two passwords do not match. Without synchronized passwords, Windows Home Server prompts you for your logon information every time you try to work with a shared folder on the server or use the Remote Access feature.

### Should I keep the local password or the Windows Home Server password?

In almost all cases, you should keep the Windows Home Server password. This is because your Windows Home Server password is usually more secure than your local password. This is particularly true if you selected the Strong password policy (see the section "Select a User Accounts Password Policy"). Using the stronger Windows Home Server password also enhances the security of your computer.

# Change a User's Display Name

You can customize how a user account appears within Windows Home Server by changing the user's display name. For example, if you specified the first and last names of a family member when you set up the account, you may prefer to remove the last name.

**To change a user's display name in Windows Home Server, you must know the password for the server's Administrator account.**

## Change a User's Display Name

1. Start the Windows Home Server Console.

***Note:*** *For more information, see Chapter 3.*

2. Click **User Accounts**.

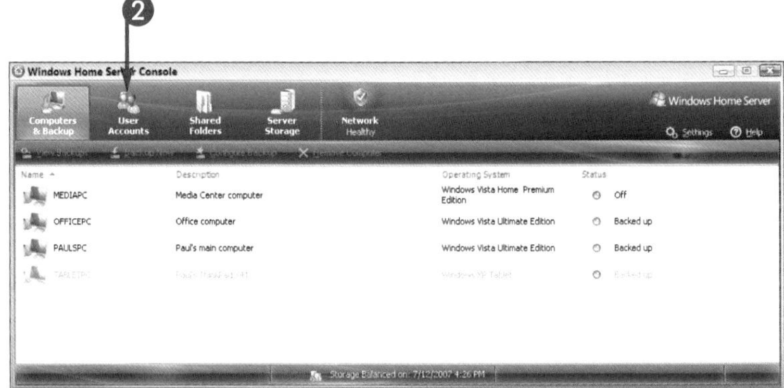


- This column shows the display name for each user.

3. Click the user you want to work with.
4. Click **Properties**.

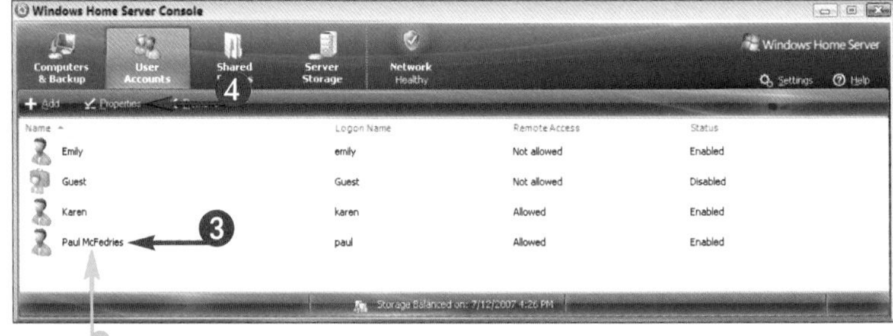

The user's Properties dialog box appears.

5. In the First name text box, edit the user's given name.
6. In the Last name text box, edit the user's surname.
7. Click **OK**.

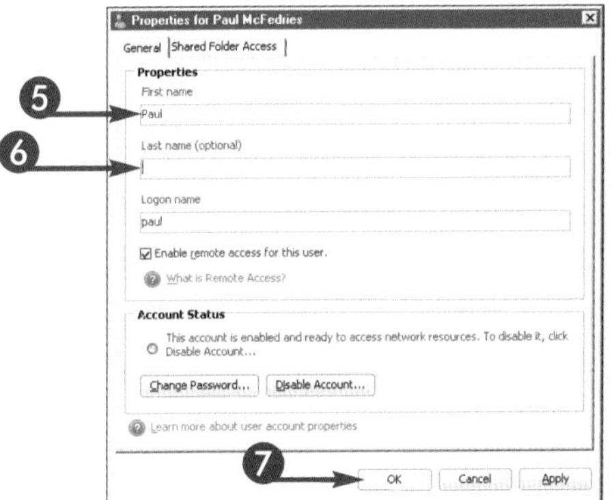


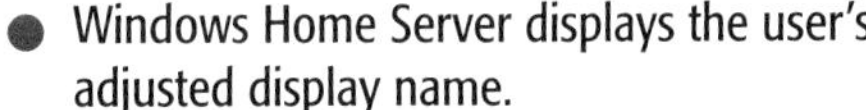

- Windows Home Server displays the user's adjusted display name.

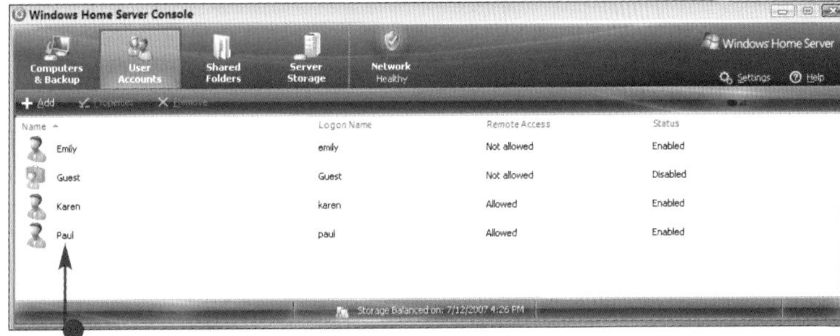

### Are there any restrictions on the display names?

There are only two restrictions that you need to be aware of: both the First name field and the Last name field accept a maximum of 31 characters. Other than these restrictions, you are free to type any text you like in those two text boxes.

### Are there faster methods that I can use to open a user's Properties dialog box?

Yes. The fastest method is to double-click the user in the User Accounts tab. Alternatively, right-click the user and then click **Properties**.

# Change a User's Password

For improved security, it is a good idea to regularly change each user's Windows Home Server account password. You may also need to change a user's password if you select a different password policy and you want to update the user's password to meet the policy requirements.

**To change a user's password in Windows Home Server, you must know the password for the server's Administrator account.**

## Change a User's Password

1. Start the Windows Home Server Console.

*Note: For more information, see Chapter 3.*

2. Click **User Accounts**.
3. Click the user you want to work with.
4. Click **Properties**.

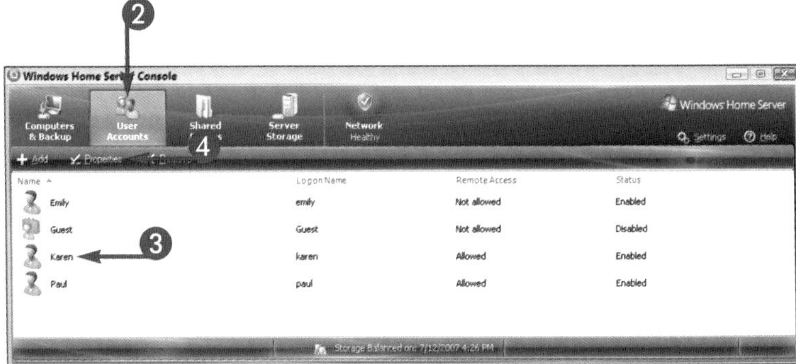

5. Click **Change Password**.

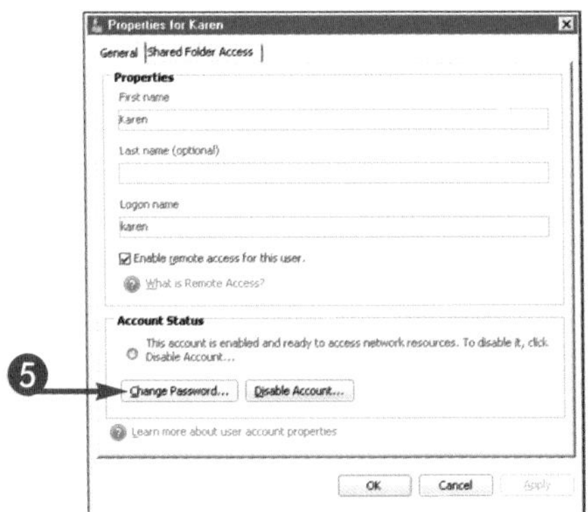

The Change Password dialog box appears for the user you selected.

6 In the Password text box, type the user's new password.

7 In the Confirm password text box, retype the new password.

- A check mark appears here if the password meets the length requirement of the password policy.
- A check mark appears here if the password meets the complexity requirement of the password policy.

8 Click **OK**.

Windows Home Server updates the user's password.

The Password Changed dialog box appears.

9 Click **OK**.

10 Click **OK**.

The user can now log on using the new password.

***Note:*** *Be sure to tell the user the new password.*

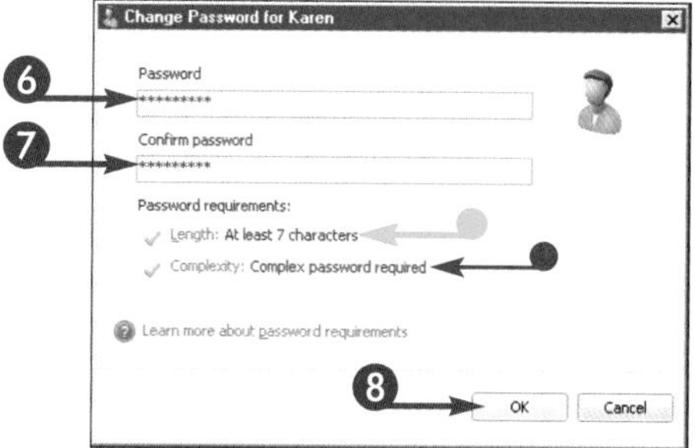


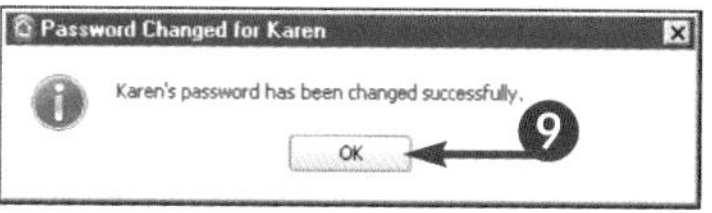


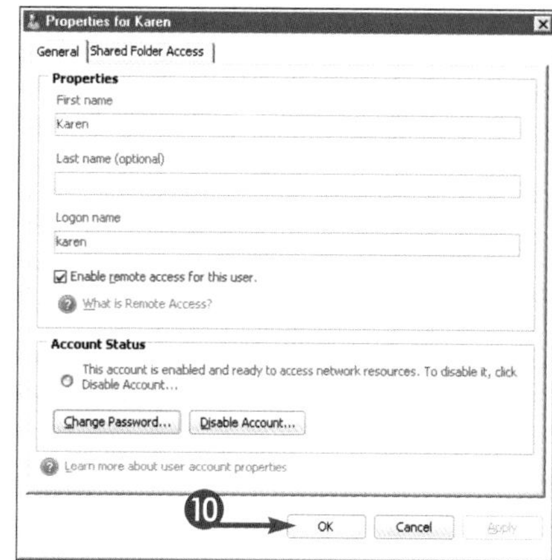

### If I change the password on the user's server account, do I also have to change the password on the user's local account?

Although you do not have to change the local user account password to match the new server account password, it is a good idea. The next time you log on to a home computer with that user account, you should see the "Passwords do not match" notification. Click the notification and then follow the steps shown earlier in the section "Synchronize the Local and Server Passwords."

### What do I do if a user forgets their password?

Strong passwords are inherently more secure, but they are also longer, and so it is easier for users to forget them. Fortunately, Windows Home Server makes it easy to restore the user's access to the server. Simply follow the steps outlined in this section. Because Windows Home Server does not ask you to supply the user's old password, you only need to create a new password for the user.

# Disable a User Account

You can temporarily prevent a person from accessing the Windows Home Server shared folders and from remotely accessing the network by disabling that person's user account.

**To disable a user account in Windows Home Server, you must know the password for the server's Administrator account.**

## Disable a User Account

1. Start the Windows Home Server Console.

*Note: For more information, see Chapter 3.*

2. Click **User Accounts**.
3. Click the user you want to disable.
4. Click **Properties**.

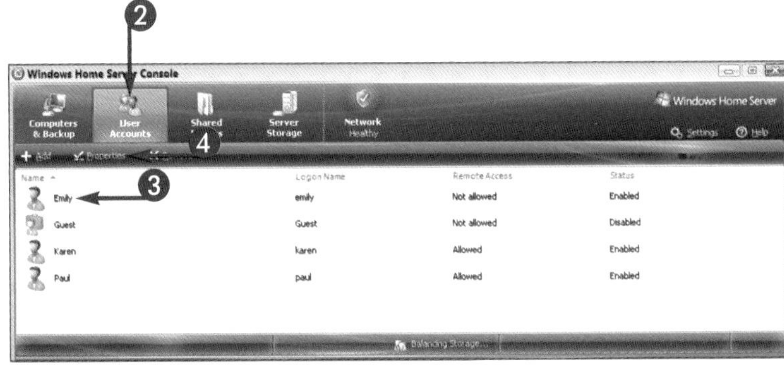


The user's Properties dialog box appears.

5. Click **Disable Account**.

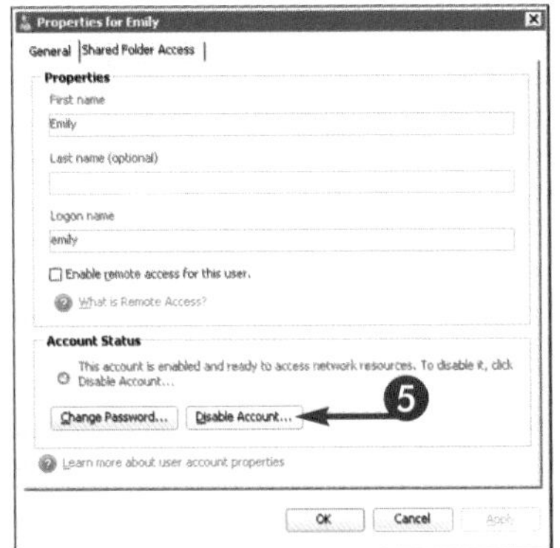

Windows Home Server asks you to confirm that you want to disable the user account.

6 Click **Yes**.

Windows Home Server disables the account.

7 Click **OK**.

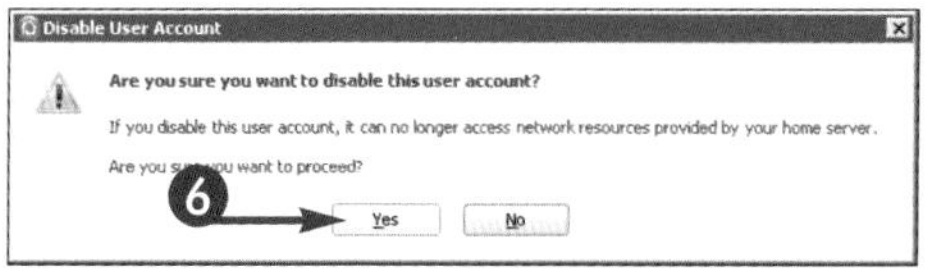


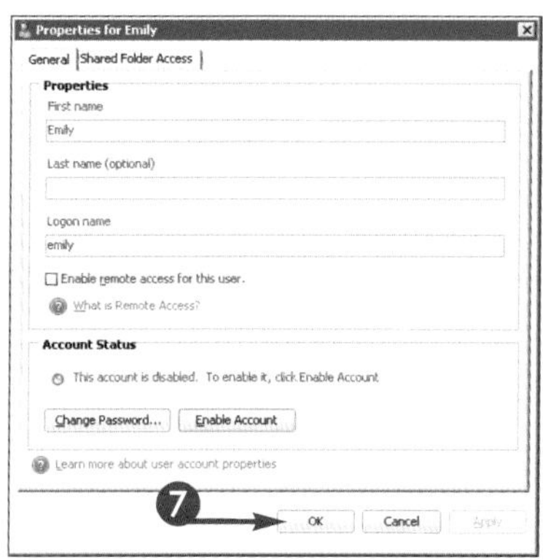


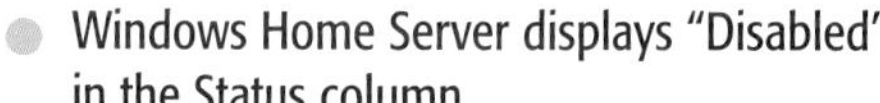

Windows Home Server displays "Disabled" in the Status column.

The user can no longer access the Windows Home Server shared folders or use the remote access feature.

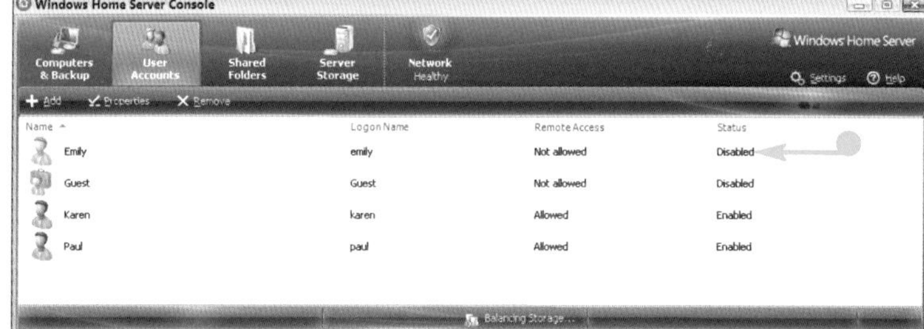

### Is there a faster way to disable an account?

Windows Home Server offers a slightly faster method that saves you a couple of steps:

1 Start the Windows Home Server Console.

2 Click **User Accounts**.

3 Right-click the user you want to disable.

4 Click **Disable Account**.

Windows Home Server asks you to confirm that you want to disable the user account.

5 Click **Yes**.

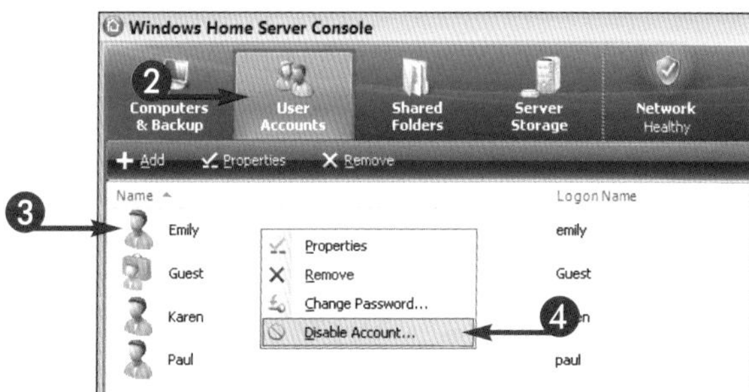

# Enable a User Account

If you have previously disabled a user account, you can allow that user to once again access the Windows Home Server shared folders and to remotely access the network by enabling that person's user account.

**To enable a user account in Windows Home Server, you must know the password for the server's Administrator account.**

## Enable a User Account

1. Start the Windows Home Server Console.

***Note:*** *For more information, see Chapter 3.*

2. Click **User Accounts**.
3. Click the user you want to enable.
4. Click **Properties**.

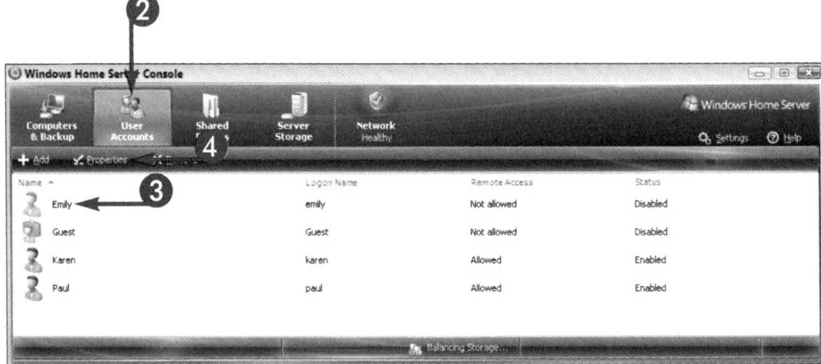


The user's Properties dialog box appears.

5. Click **Enable Account**.

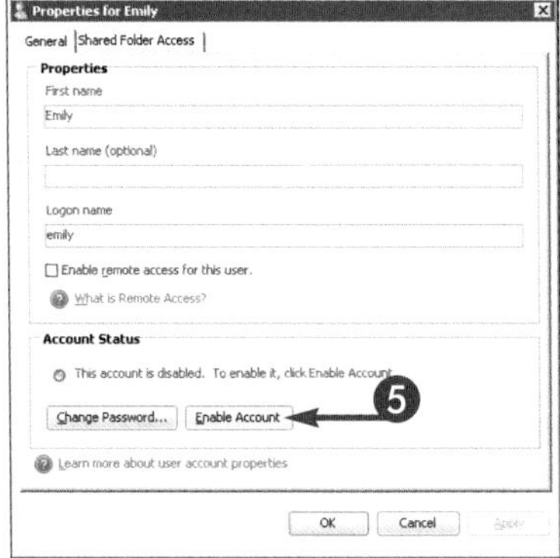

Windows Home Server enables the user account.

6 Click **OK**.

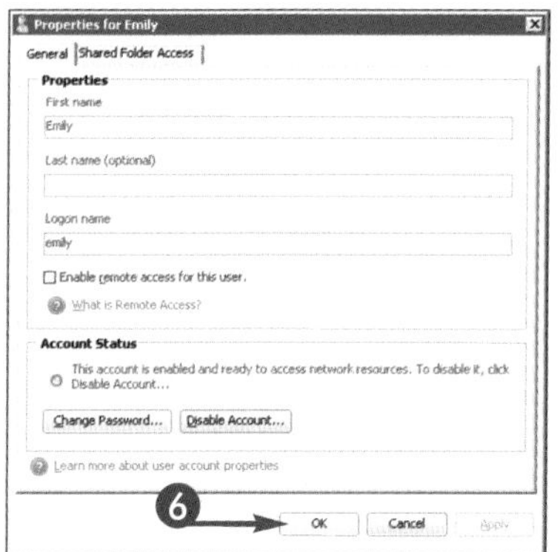

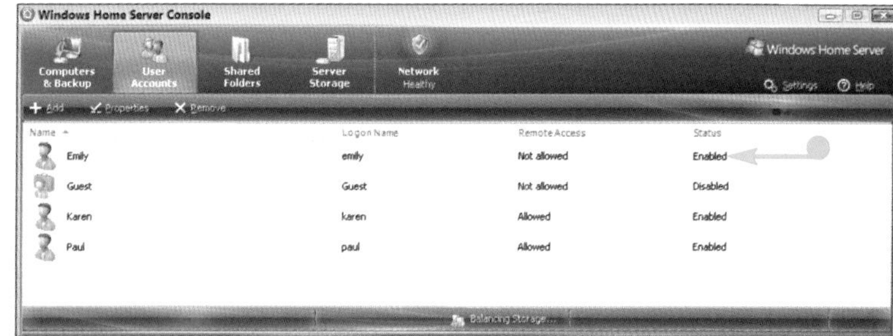

- Windows Home Server displays "Enabled" in the Status column.

The user can once again access the Windows Home Server shared folders and use the Remote Access feature.

### Is there a faster way to enable an account?

Windows Home Server offers a slightly faster method that saves you a couple of steps:

1. Start the Windows Home Server Console.
2. Click **User Accounts**.
3. Right-click the user you want to enable.
4. Click **Enable Account**.

Windows Home Server enables the account.

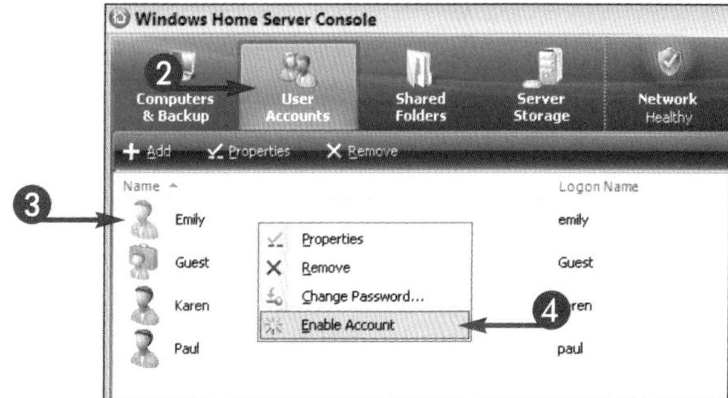

# Enable the Guest Account

You can give visitors and houseguests temporary access to the Windows Home Server shared folders by enabling the built-in Guest account, which is disabled by default.

**To enable the Guest account in Windows Home Server, you must know the password for the server's Administrator account.**

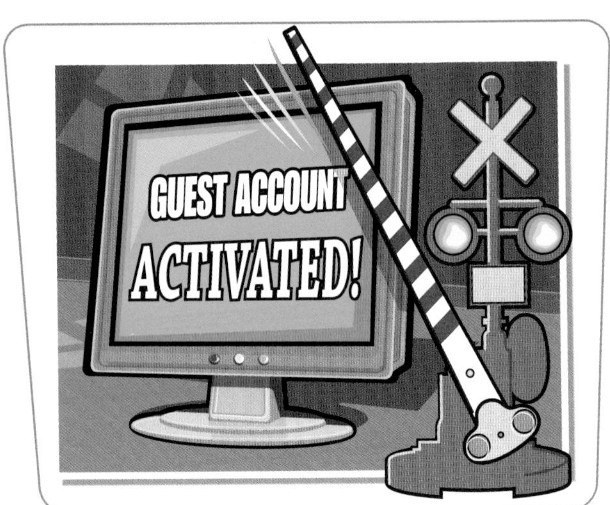


## Enable the Guest Account

1. Start the Windows Home Server Console.

**Note:** *For more information, see Chapter 3.*

2. Click **User Accounts**.
3. Click the **Guest** account.
4. Click **Properties**.

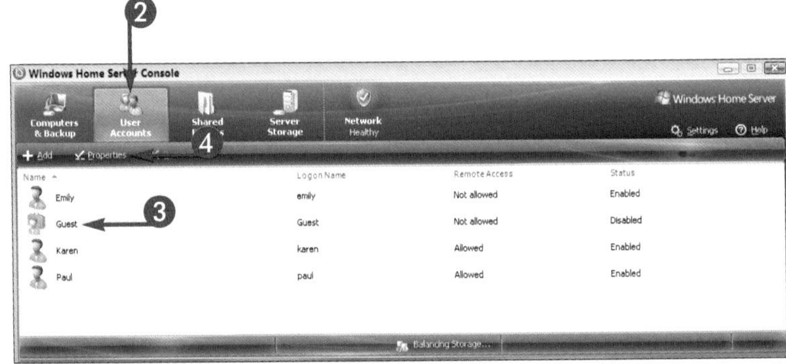


The Guest user's Properties dialog box appears.

5. Click **Enable Account**.

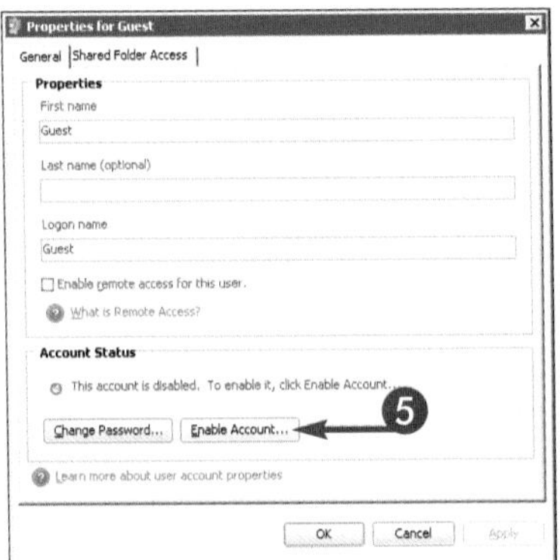

The Enable Guest Account Wizard appears.

6 Click **Next**.

The Choose a password dialog box appears.

7 Click **No Guest Password** (◯ changes to ◉).

- If you intend to leave the Guest account enabled for an extended time, you can click **Create a Guest Password** (◯ changes to ◉) and then type a password in the Password and Confirm password text boxes.

8 Click **Next**.

### Under what circumstances would I use the Guest account?

The Guest account is meant for users who need to access Windows Home Server temporarily. For example, you may have a visitor who needs to work with the server's shared folders. Rather than creating a new account or giving that person the logon name and password of an existing account, you can have that person log on using the Guest account, which has very limited privileges on Windows Home Server.

### Is there a quick way to launch the Enable Guest Account Wizard?

Yes. Follow these steps:

1 Start Windows Home Server Console.

2 Click **User Accounts**.

3 Right-click the **Guest** account.

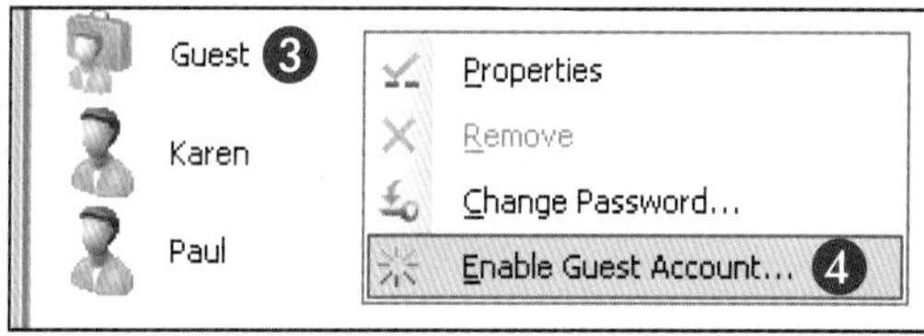


4 Click **Enable Guest Account**.

# Enable the Guest Account *(continued)*

If you do not supply a password for the Guest account, you can enhance your security by making sure that you do not give the Guest account Full access to any shared folder.

**Remember that people from outside of your home can pick up wireless network signals, and so someone you do not know could use the Guest account to access Windows Home Server.**

## Enable the Guest Account *(continued)*

The Set user's access to shared folders dialog box appears.

9 For each shared folder, click the type of access you want to allow for the Guest account (○ changes to ●).

10 Click **Finish**.

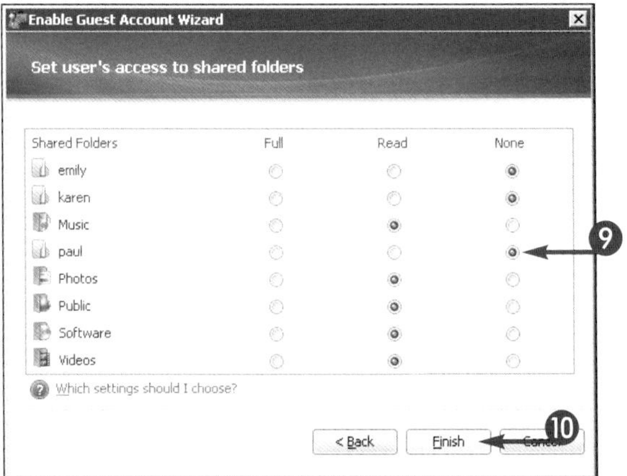


Windows Home Server enables the Guest account.

11 Click **Done**.

⓬ Click **OK**.

- Windows Home Server displays "Enabled" in the Status column.

A visitor can now use the Guest account to access the Windows Home Server shared folders.

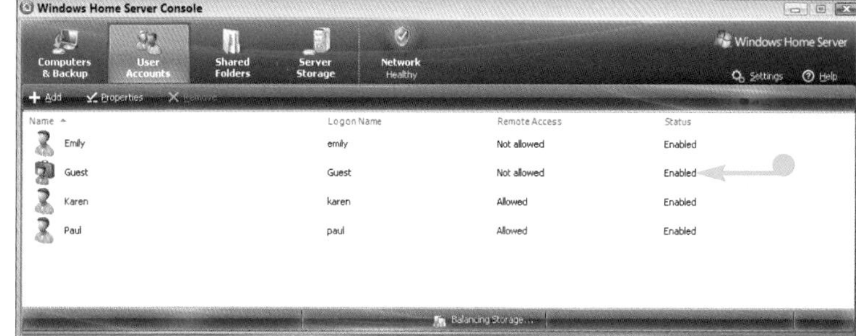

### How do I disable the Guest account after the visitor has finished using it?

You can quickly disable the Guest account by following these steps:

1. Start the Windows Home Server Console.
2. Click **User Accounts**.
3. Right-click the **Guest** account.
4. Click **Disable Account**.

   Windows Home Server asks you to confirm that you want to disable the account.
5. Click **Yes**.

   Windows Home Server disables the Guest account.

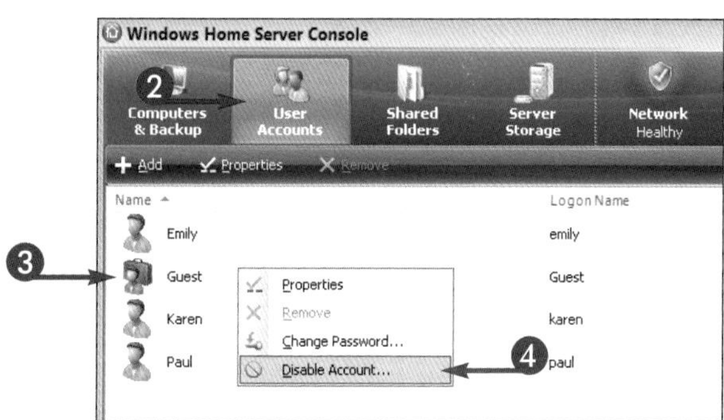

# Remove a User Account

You can delete a user's account when it is no longer needed. This reduces the number of users in the User Accounts tab of the Windows Home Server Console, and can free up some disk space.

**To remove a user account in Windows Home Server, you must know the password for the server's Administrator account.**

## Remove a User Account

1. Start the Windows Home Server Console.

*Note: For more information, see Chapter 3.*

2. Click **User Accounts**.
3. Click the user you want to remove.
4. Click **Remove**.

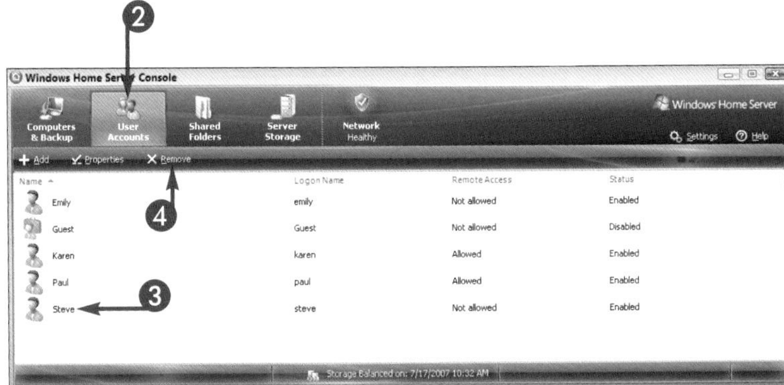


The Remove a User Account Wizard appears.

5. Click **Remove the shared folder** (◯ changes to ◉).

- If you prefer to keep the user's shared folder, you can instead click **Keep the shared folder** (◯ changes to ◉).

6. Click **Next**.

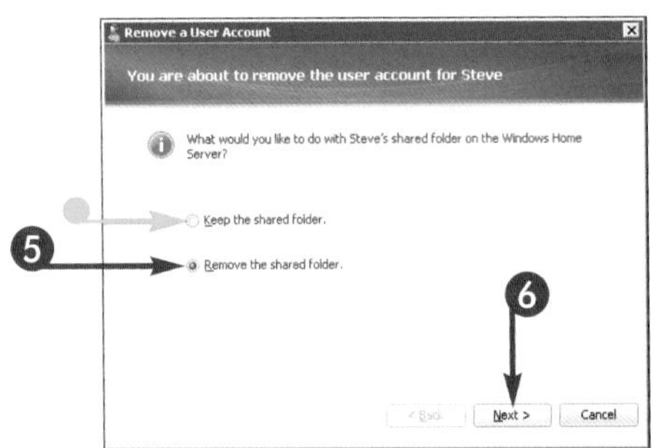

The Remove the user account dialog box appears.

7 Click **Finish**.

Windows Home Server removes the user account.

8 Click **Done**.

The user can no longer access Windows Home Server.

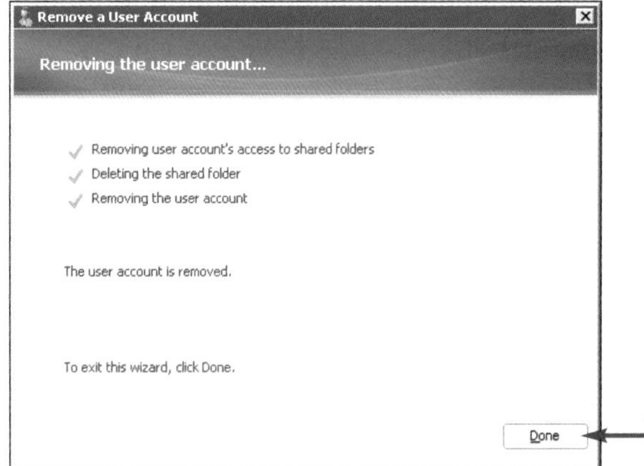

### When should I delete a user account?

You should always delete an account when it is no longer needed. For example, if you create a user account for a houseguest who is on an extended visit, you should delete the account when the guest leaves. Similarly, if you have ten user accounts, which is the Windows Home Server maximum, then the only way to add another account is delete an existing one.

### Should I always delete the user's shared folder?

Not necessarily. For example, the user may have stored important files on the shared folder and you may want to preserve those files. In this case, you can either keep the user's shared folder or you can first move the user's files to another folder – for example, the Public shared folder – and then delete the shared folder when you delete the account.

CHAPTER

# Working with Windows Home Server Settings

Windows Home Server comes with a number of built-in settings that you can configure. These settings control items such as the current date and time, the region and language, and Windows Update. You can also add new features to Windows Home Server by installing add-ins.

Display the Windows Home Server Settings ....90
Change the Date and Time ....92
Choose a Different Region and Language ....94
Configure Windows Update ....95
Restart Windows Home Server ....96
Shut Down Windows Home Server....98
Activate Automatic Windows Error Reporting ....100
Install a Windows Home Server Add-In ....102
Uninstall a Windows Home Server Add-In ....104

# Display the Windows Home Server Settings

You can view the current state or value of any Windows Home Server setting by using the Console program to display the Windows Home Server Settings dialog box.

**To display and work with the Windows Home Server Settings dialog box, you need to know the password for the server's Administrator account.**

## Display the Windows Home Server Settings

1. Start the Windows Home Server Console.

***Note:*** *For more information, see Chapter 3.*

2. Click **Settings**.

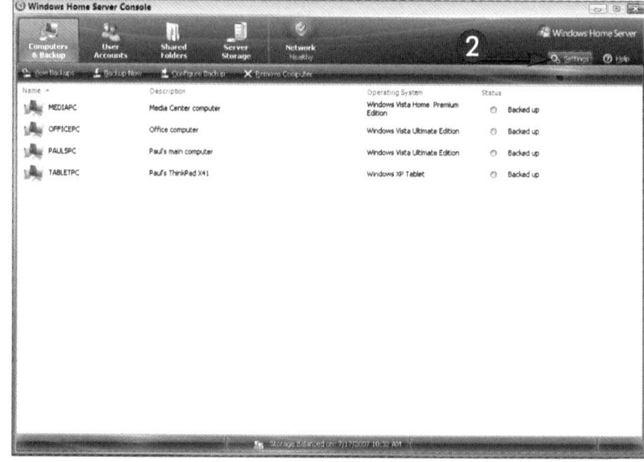

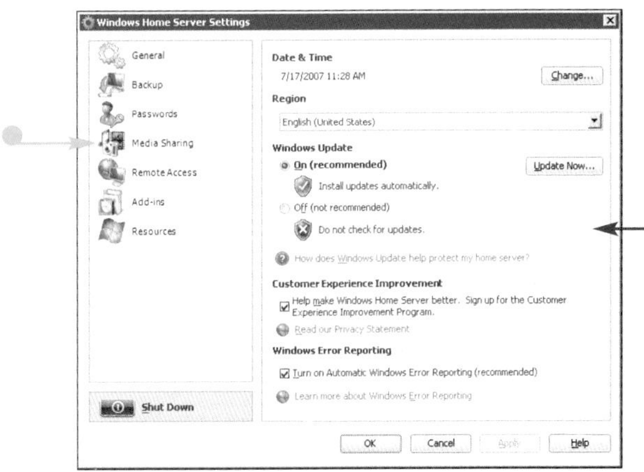


The Windows Home Server Settings dialog box appears.

- You can click these tabs to see the different settings.
- The settings and their current states or values appear here.

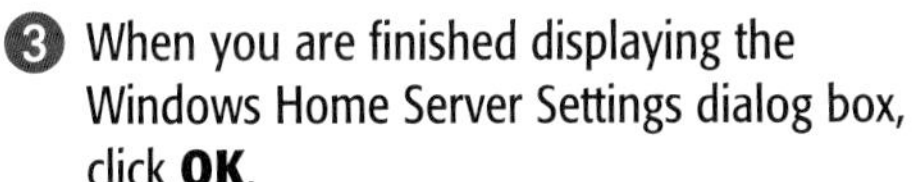

3. When you are finished displaying the Windows Home Server Settings dialog box, click **OK**.

   If you made changes to one or more settings, Windows Home Server activates the changes.

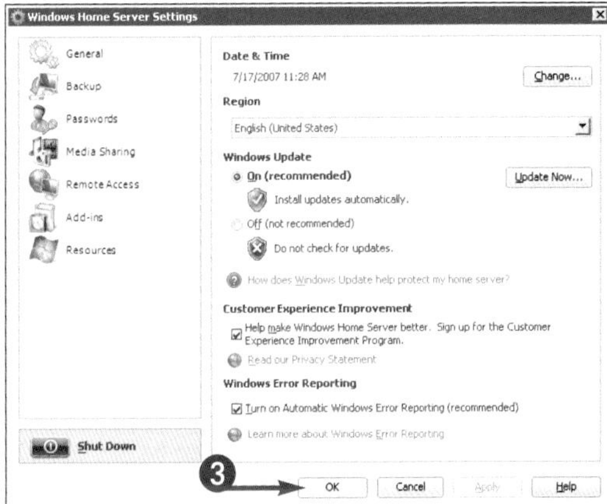

### What is on the Resources tab?

The Resources tab displays information about Windows Home Server and your server computer. The Learn More and Support sections offer a few links to Windows Home Server resources on the Internet. If you have not yet activated your copy of Windows Home Server, you can click the **Activate Windows** button (●) to start the process.

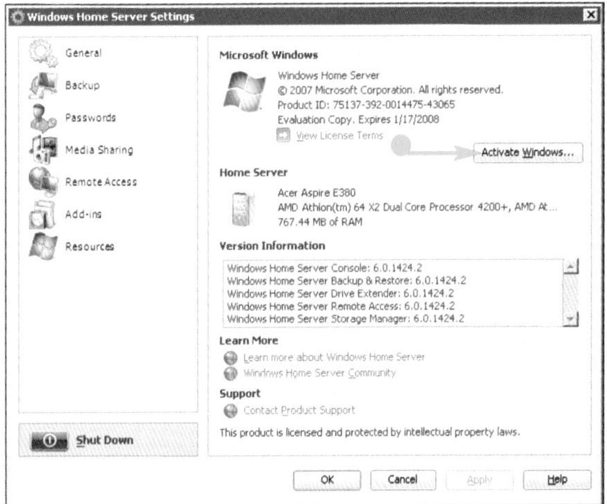

# Change the Date and Time

You can ensure that Windows Home Server applies dates and times accurately and performs certain tasks at the correct time by changing the date and time to the correct values for your area.

**A good example of a time-sensitive task is Windows Home Server's Backup feature, which runs every night at midnight.**

## Change the Date and Time

1. Start the Windows Home Server Console.

*Note:* *For more information, see Chapter 3.*

2. Click **Settings**.

The Windows Home Server Settings dialog box appears.

3. Click the **General** tab.

- The current Windows Home Server date and time appear here.

4. Click **Change**.

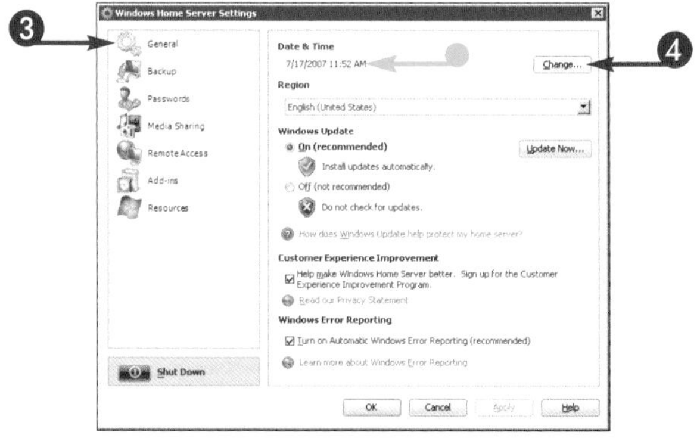

The Date and Time Properties dialog box appears.

5. Click ▼ and then click the month you want.
6. Click ⬍ to specify the year.
7. Click the day of the month.
8. Click ⬍ to set the correct hour, minute, second, and AM or PM.
9. Click **OK**.

Windows Home Server adjusts its internal clock to the new date and time.

- The updated date and time appear in the General tab.

10. Click **OK**.

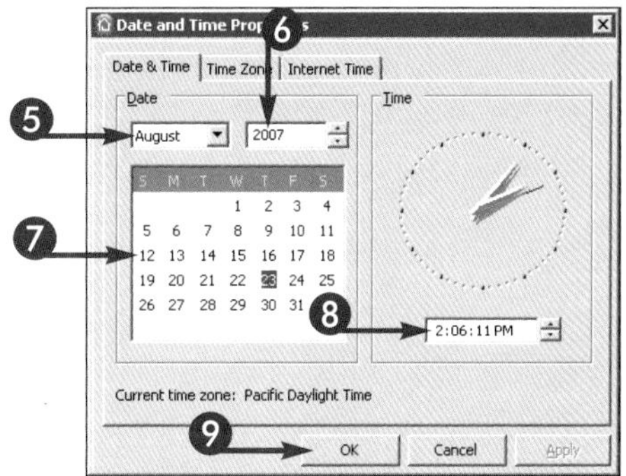


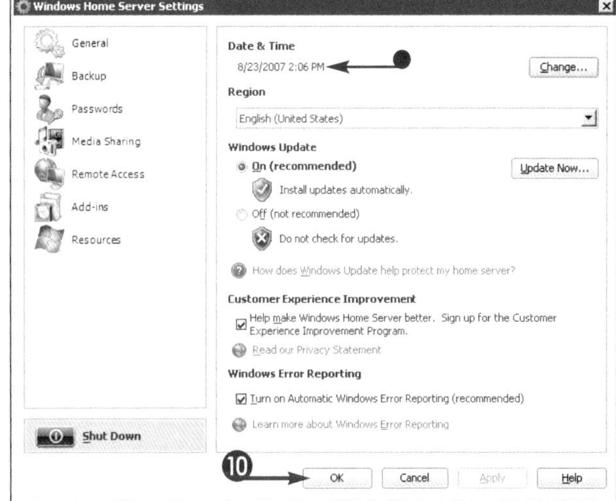

### How do I adjust the Windows Home Server time zone?

Windows Home Server uses the Pacific Time zone by default. To change this, follow these steps:

1. Follow steps **1** to **4** to open the Date and Time Properties dialog box.
2. Click the **Time Zone** tab.
3. In the drop-down list, click ▼ and then click the time zone you want to use.
4. Click **OK**.

***Note:** You may need to adjust the time after choosing a different time zone.*

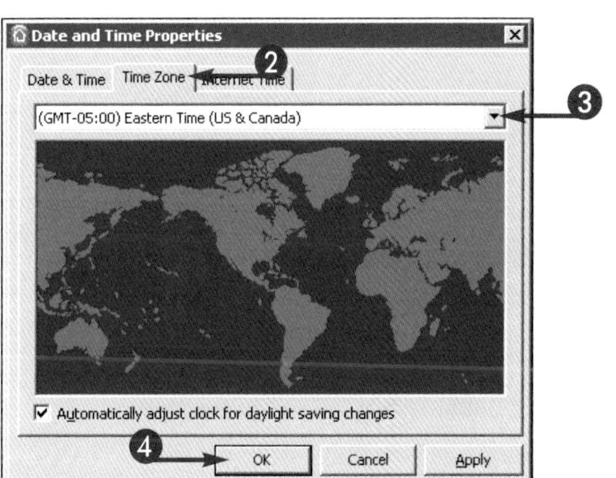

# Choose a Different Region and Language

You can customize Windows Home Server to display dates, times, currency values, and measurements according to the region where you live.

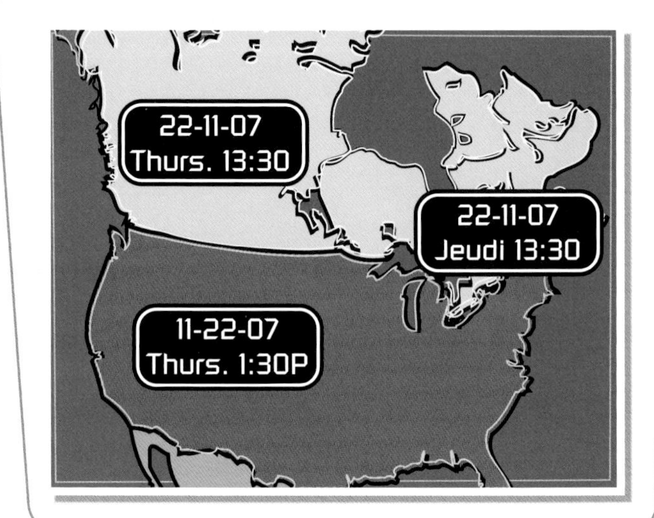


**For example, if you live in Canada and speak English, you can choose the English (Canada) region. This changes the default date format from month/day/year to day/month/year.**

## Choose a Different Region and Language

1. Start the Windows Home Server Console.

*Note:* *For more information,* *see Chapter 3.*

2. Click **Settings**.

The Windows Home Server Settings dialog box appears.

3. Click the **General** tab.
4. In the Region drop-down list, click ▾ and then click the region and language you want to use.
5. Click **OK**.

Windows Home Server begins using the new region and language.

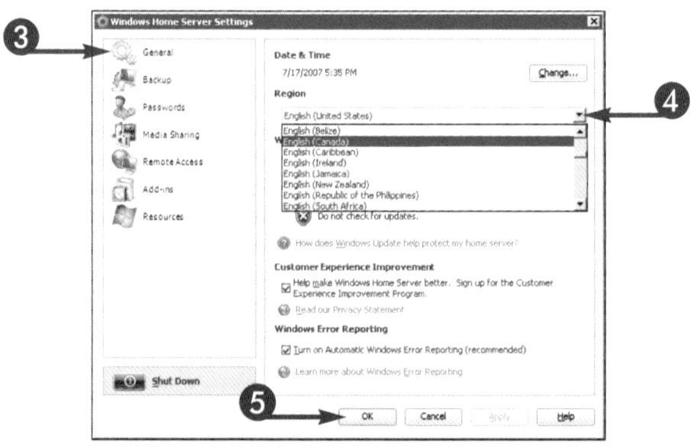

# Configure Windows Update

chapter 5

Microsoft makes Windows Home Server updates available from time to time. These updates fix problems and resolve security issues. You can reduce computer problems and maximize online safety by setting up Windows Home Server to download and install these updates automatically.

**By default, Windows Home Server uses automatic updates. However, it is worthwhile to confirm that this setting is activated.**

## Configure Windows Update

1. Start the Windows Home Server Console.

*Note: For more information, see Chapter 3.*

2. Click **Settings**.

The Windows Home Server Settings dialog box appears.

3. Click the **General** tab.
4. Click **On (recommended)**.

- If you prefer to update Windows Home Server yourself, you can click **Off (not recommended)**.
- If you are updating Windows Home Server manually, be sure to click **Update Now** at least once each week.

5. Click **OK**.

Windows Home Server will now automatically download and install updates.

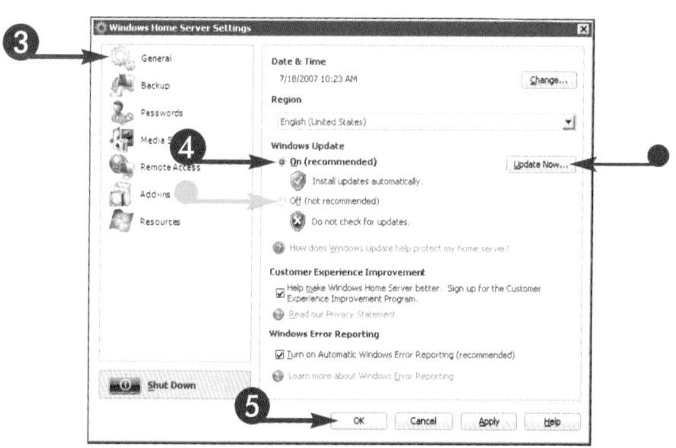

# Restart Windows Home Server

You can restart Windows Home Server, which means that it shuts down and starts up again immediately. This is useful if your computer is running slowly or acting peculiar. Sometimes a restart solves the problem.

**Knowing how to restart Windows Home Server is also useful when you install a program or device that requires a restart to function properly. If you are busy right now, you can always choose to restart your computer later, when it is more convenient.**

## Restart Windows Home Server

1. Start the Windows Home Server Console.

***Note:*** *For more information, see Chapter 3.*

2. Click **Settings**.

3. Click **Shut Down**.

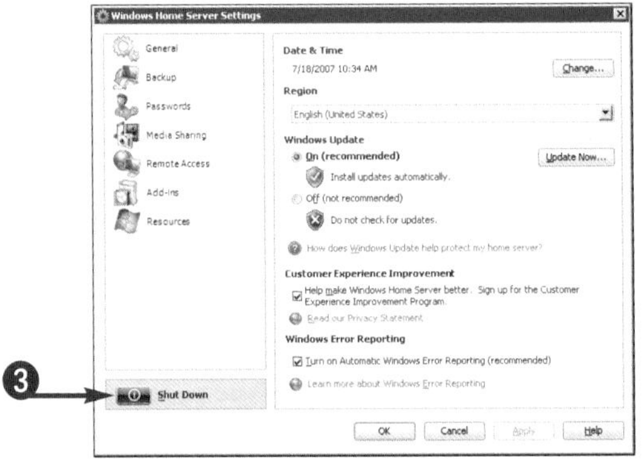

The Shut Down dialog box appears.

4 Click **Restart**.

Windows Home Server restarts.

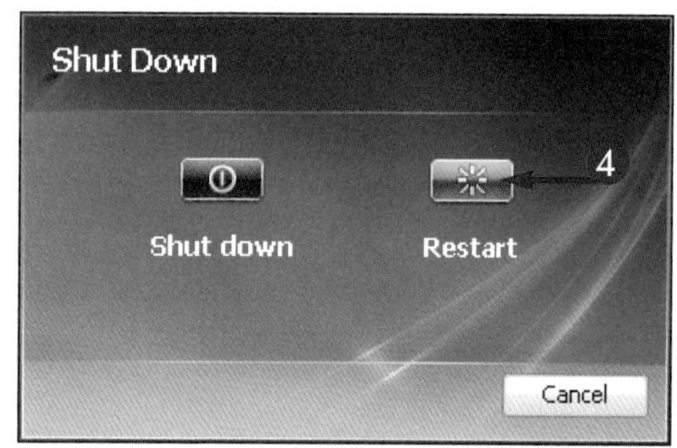


The Windows Home Server Console lets you know that it has lost the connection with the home server.

5 Click **OK**.

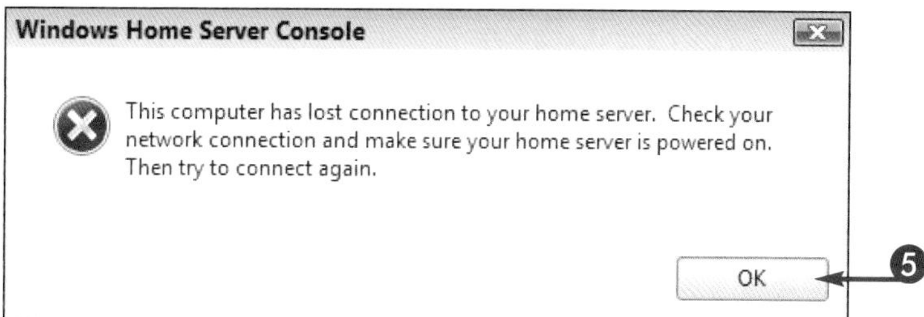

**How do I know when Windows Home Server has restarted?**

The easiest way to determine this is to watch the Windows Home Server Tray icon in the taskbar's notification area. When Windows Home Server shuts down, the icon turns gray to indicate that Windows no longer has a connection to the home server. When Windows Home Server restarts, the icon turns green to indicate that the connection has been reestablished.

- Windows has lost the connection to the home server.
- Windows has reconnected to the home server.

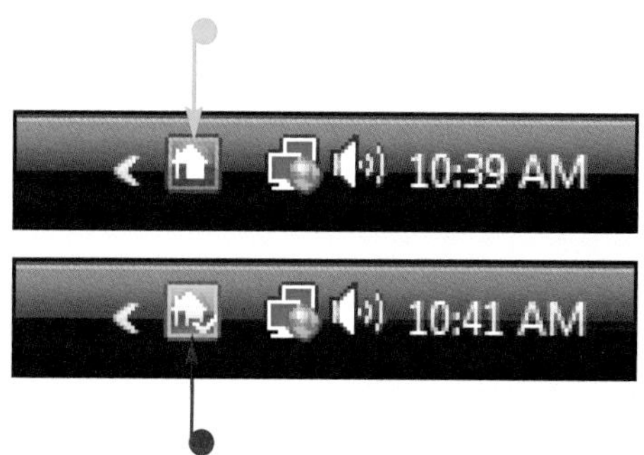

# Shut Down Windows Home Server

If you are going on a vacation or other extended trip, you should shut down Windows Home Server. However, do not just shut off your computer's power. Follow the proper steps to avoid damaging files on your system.

**Shutting off the computer's power without properly exiting Windows Home Server can cause two problems. First, if you have unsaved changes in some open documents, you will lose those changes. Second, you could damage one or more Windows Home Server system files, which could make your system unstable.**

## Shut Down Windows Home Server

1. Start the Windows Home Server Console.

**Note:** *For more information, see Chapter 3.*

2. Click **Settings**.

The Windows Home Server Settings dialog box appears.

3. Click **Shut Down**.

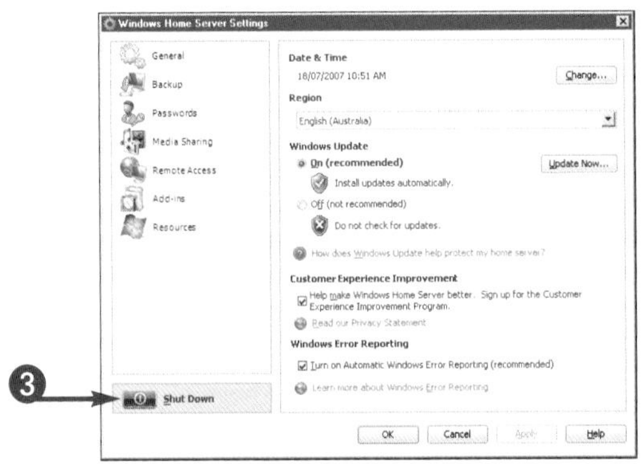

The Shut Down dialog box appears.

4 Click **Shut down**.

Windows Home Server shuts down.

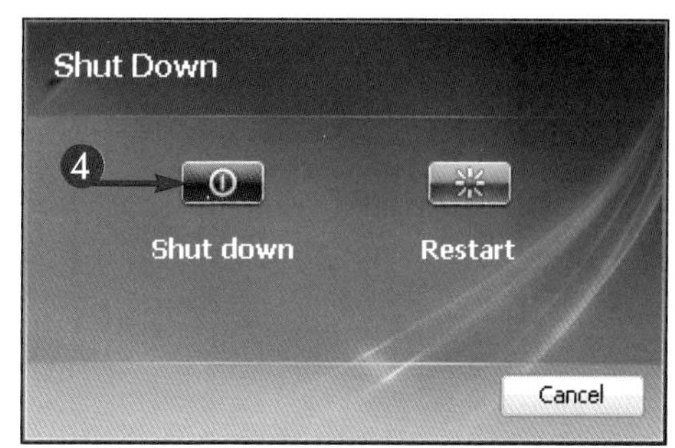


The Windows Home Server Console lets you know that it has lost the connection with the home server.

5 Click **OK**.

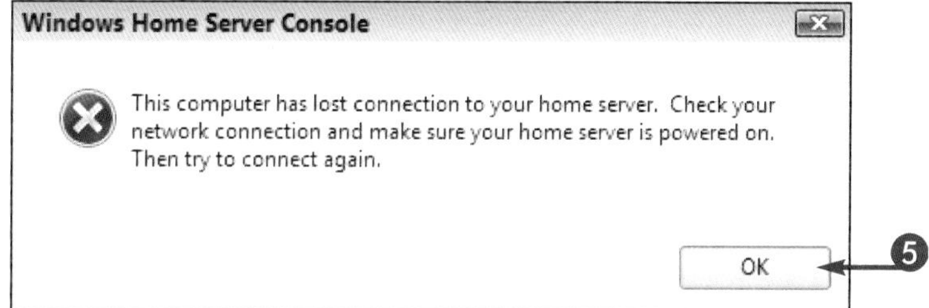

**How do I shut down Windows Home Server if I have direct access to the computer?**

If you have direct access to Windows Home Server either through a keyboard, mouse, and monitor connected to the system, or through a remote desktop connection, then follow these steps:

1 Click **Start**.

2 Click **Shut Down**.

The Shut Down Windows dialog box appears.

3 Click ▾ and then click **Shut down**.

4 Click **OK**.

Windows Home Server shuts down.

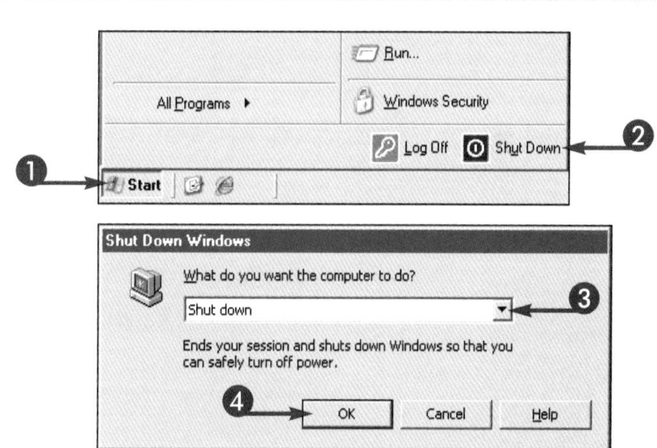

# Activate Automatic Windows Error Reporting

You can help Microsoft improve Windows Home Server by activating the Automatic Windows Error Reporting service. This feature sends information to Microsoft when a Windows Home Server error occurs.

**The report includes data that helps Microsoft to understand the problem and to create a solution.**

## Activate Automatic Windows Error Reporting

1. Start the Windows Home Server Console.

**Note:** *For more information, see Chapter 3.*

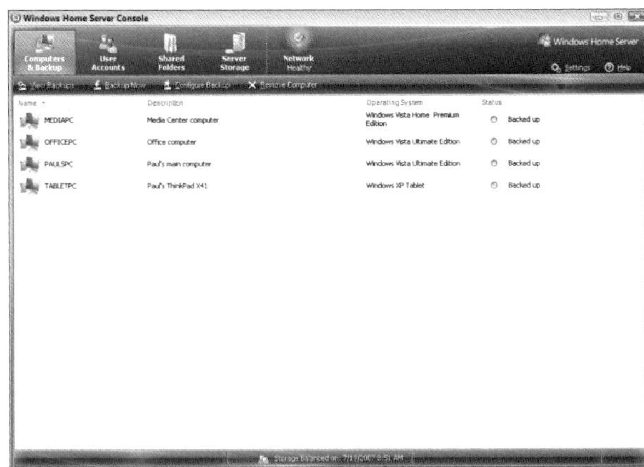

2. Click **Settings**.

The Windows Home Server Settings dialog box appears.

3. Click the **General** tab.

4. Click **Turn on Automatic Windows Error Reporting (recommended)** (☐ changes to ☑).

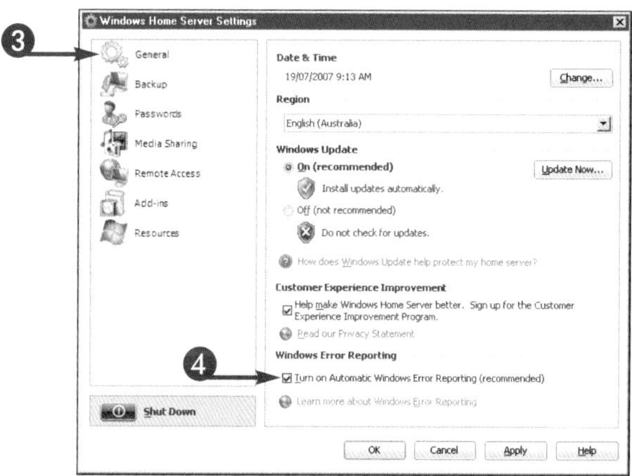

5. Click **OK**.

The next time an error occurs on the server computer, Windows Home Server will automatically send an error report to Microsoft.

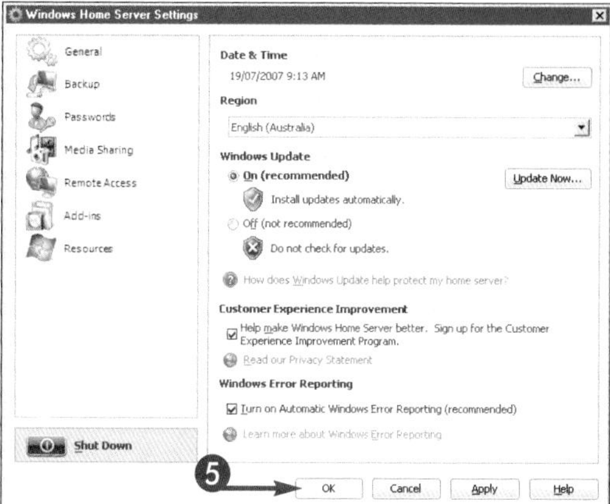

### What kind of information is sent to Microsoft?

The error report contains information that helps Microsoft engineers see where the problem occurred and to possibly discover the source of the problem. The report details where the problem occurred and what kind of problem it was, and contains information about the server, such as the installed devices and memory size. All of this may help Microsoft fix the problem, and the solution is then made available to you through Windows Update.



### Is any personal information sent with the report?

A small possibility exists that a report may contain some personal information. For example, most reports include the contents of the system memory at the time the problem occurred. If you were working on a file that contained personal data, that data may be included in the report. This is very unlikely with Windows Home Server, but if you do not feel comfortable that personal information could be sent, you can turn off this feature.

# Install a Windows Home Server Add-In

You can add new features to the Windows Home Server Console by installing an add-in program. Most add-in programs create either new tabs for the Windows Home Server Console or new tabs for the Windows Home Server Settings dialog box.

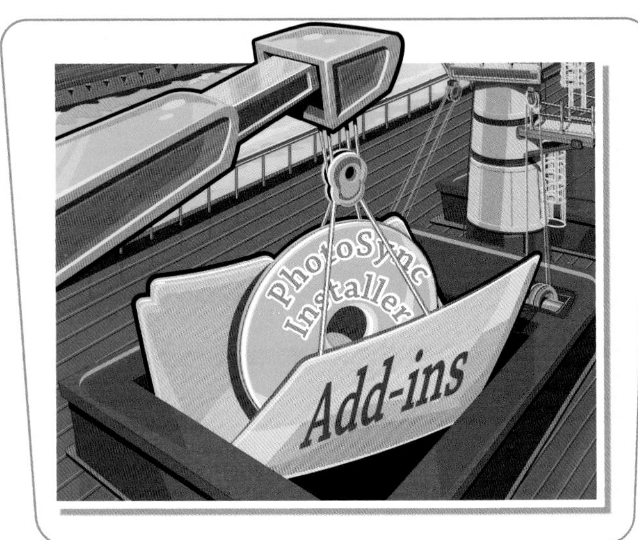


## Install a Windows Home Server Add-In

1. Start the Windows Home Server Console.

*Note: For more information, see Chapter 3.*

2. Click **Settings**.

The Windows Home Server Settings dialog box appears.

3. Click the **Add-ins** tab.
4. Click the **Available** tab.
5. Click **Install** for the add-in you want to install.

Windows Home Server installs the add-in.

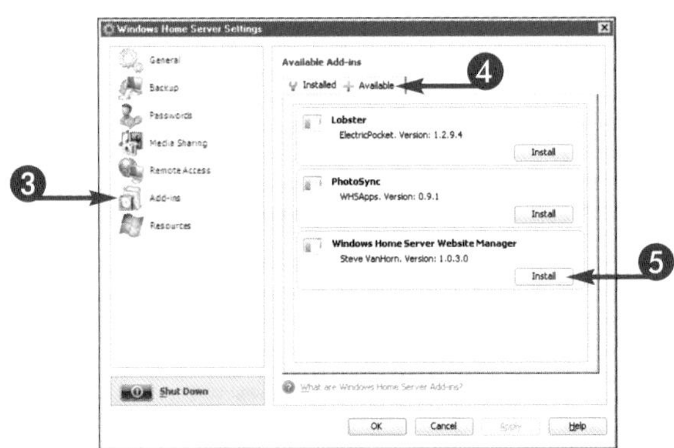

In most cases, the add-in prompts you to restart the Windows Home Server Console.

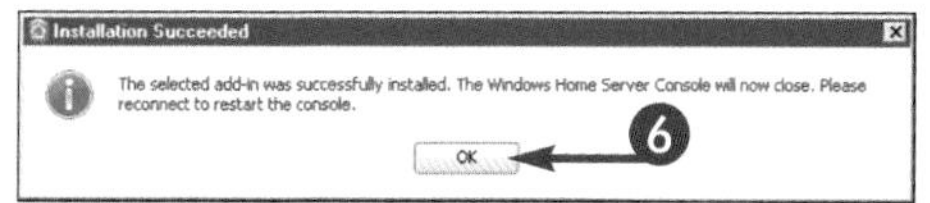


6. Click **OK**.

The Windows Home Server Console closes.

7. Restart the Windows Home Server Console.

- Depending on the add-in, you may see a new tab in the Console window.
- If the add-in customizes the Windows Home Server Settings dialog box, then you can click **Settings** to see the changes.

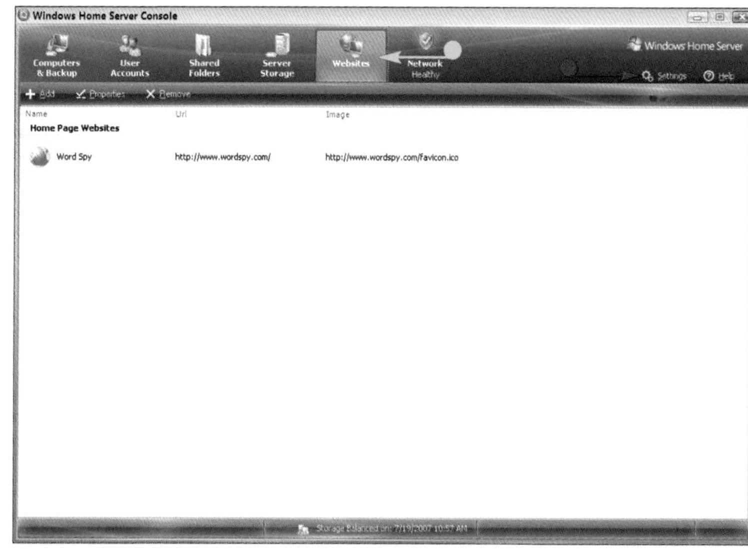

### Where can I find Windows Home Server add-ins?

As of this writing, a Web site named We Got Served, located at http://wegotserved.co.uk/, is maintaining a list of Windows Home Server add-ins. You can also use Google.com or some other Web search engine to search the phrase "Windows Home Server add-ins." Windows Home Server maintains a special shared folder to store add-in installation files, which use the .msi extension.

### How do I download Windows Home Server add-ins?

Look for a link to the installation file and then click that link. When the File Download - Security Warning dialog box appears, click **Save**. In the Save As dialog box, navigate to the Windows Home Server shared folder, double-click the **Software** folder, and then double-click the **Add-ins** folder (●). Click **Save** to copy the installation file to the Add-ins folder. The add-in automatically appears in the Available tab.

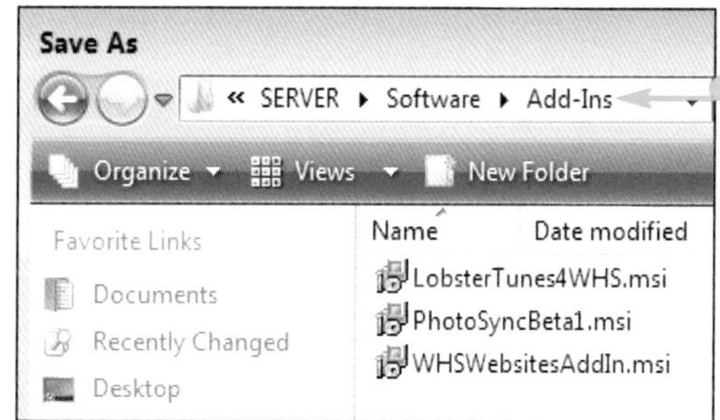

# Uninstall a Windows Home Server Add-In

If you installed a Windows Home Server add-in that you no longer use or that is causing problems on the server, you can uninstall that add-in.

**You may also want to uninstall an add-in if you find that either the Windows Home Server Console or the Windows Home Server Settings dialog box is becoming too crowded with extra tabs created by add-ins.**

## Uninstall a Windows Home Server Add-In

1. Start the Windows Home Server Console.

*Note: For more information, see Chapter 3.*

2. Click **Settings**.

The Windows Home Server Settings dialog box appears.

3. Click the **Add-ins** tab.
4. Click the **Installed** tab.
5. Click **Uninstall** for the add-in you want to uninstall.

Windows Home Server uninstalls the add-in.

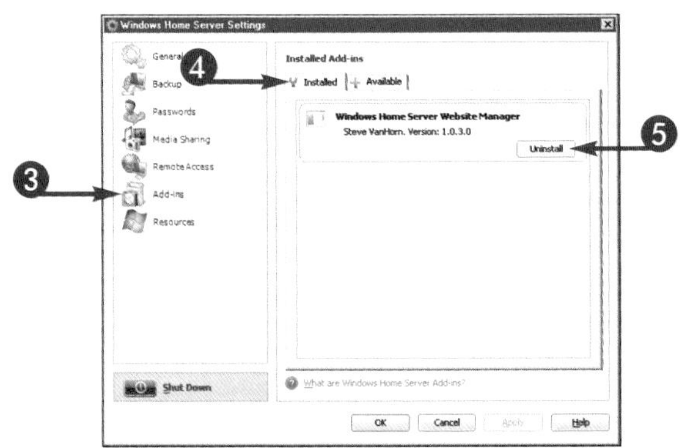

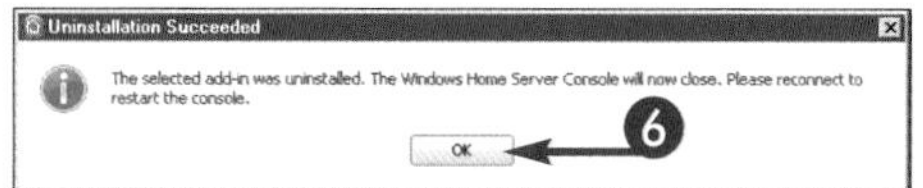


In most cases, the add-in prompts you to restart the Windows Home Server Console.

6. Click **OK**.

   The Windows Home Server Console closes.

7. Restart the Windows Home Server Console.

- Depending on the add-in, you may no longer see its tab in the Console window.
- If the add-in customized the Windows Home Server Settings dialog box, then you can click **Settings** to see the changes.

### How do I remove the add-in from the Available tab?

When you uninstall an add-in, Windows Home Server leaves the installation file in the Add-ins folder just in case you want to reinstall the add-in later. If you are sure that you do not want to reinstall the add-in, then follow these steps to remove the installation file:

1. Click **Start**.
2. Click **Computer**.

   You can also double-click the **Shared Folders** icon on the Windows desktop.

3. Navigate to the Windows Home Server shared folders, and click the **Software** folder.
4. Click the **Add-ins** folder.
5. Click the installation file you want to remove.
6. Press Delete.

   Windows asks you to confirm the deletion.

7. Click **Yes**.

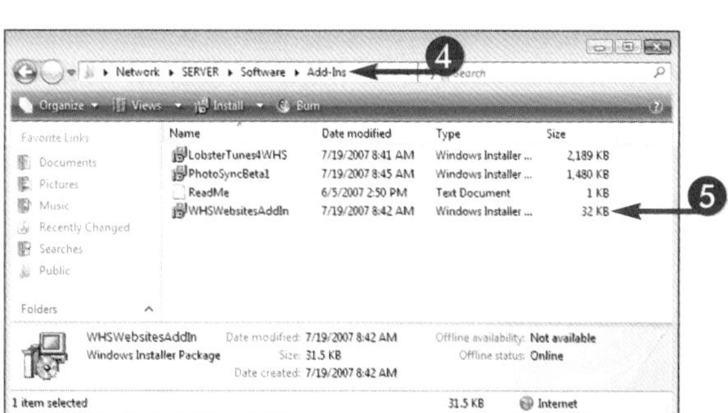

CHAPTER

# Using Windows Home Server Storage

Windows Home Server uses a single storage pool to keep your network backups and the files you copy or move to the Windows Home Server shared folders. You can view the current storage, add to the storage by attaching another hard drive, remove storage by detaching a hard drive, and even replace your main hard drive.

Understanding Windows Home Server Storage ............ 108
Learn About Hard Drive Types ............ 110
View Windows Home Server Storage ............ 112
Add Storage to Windows Home Server ............ 114
Remove Storage from Windows Home Server ............ 116
Replace Your Main Hard Drive ............ 118

# Understanding Windows Home Server Storage

Windows Home Server uses new storage technology to combine multiple hard drives into a single storage area that provides flexibility, simplicity, and features such as folder duplication and load balancing.

### Hard Drives

Windows Home Server's storage is a collection of one or more hard drives that are attached to the home server computer. If the server includes other types of storage drives – such as a USB Flash drive or a memory card reader – those drives are not used for Windows Home Server's main storage.

### Storage Pool

If your home server computer has multiple hard drives, Windows Home Server combines the drives into a single area called a *storage pool*. Part of the storage pool is set aside for the Windows Home Server system files, while the rest of the storage pool is used for backups and the shared folders.

### Flexible Storage

The Windows Home Server storage pool is very flexible because it enables you to easily add new hard drives to increase the storage area, or remove existing drives. Windows Home Server can work with several different types of internal and external hard drives. For more information, see the section "Learn About Hard Drive Types."

### No Drive Letters

Windows computers often have multiple drives, and the system supplies those drives with letters such as C:, D:, and so on. Windows Home Server keeps storage simple by not using drive letters for the storage pool. The Windows Home Server Console has a Server Storage tab that shows the entire storage pool as a single item without any drive letters.

### Folder Duplication

If you have at least two hard drives attached to your home server computer, Windows Home Server uses a feature called *folder duplication*. If you activate this feature for a shared folder, Windows Home Server stores a backup copy of each file on a different hard drive. If one hard drive fails, a copy of its data exists on another hard drive.

### Load Balancing

If you have at least three hard drives attached to your home server computer, Windows Home Server activates a feature called *load balancing*. This feature means that Windows Home Server attempts to improve performance by splitting the workload between all the hard drives. For example, if Windows Home Server needs to send a file and the first hard drive is currently busy, Windows Home Server will attempt to send the file using the second hard drive.

# Learn About Hard Drive Types

The flexibility of Windows Home Server storage also extends to the hard drives you can use. You can add internal or external hard drives, and you can add various drive types, including ATA, SATA, USB 2.0, FireWire, and eSATA.

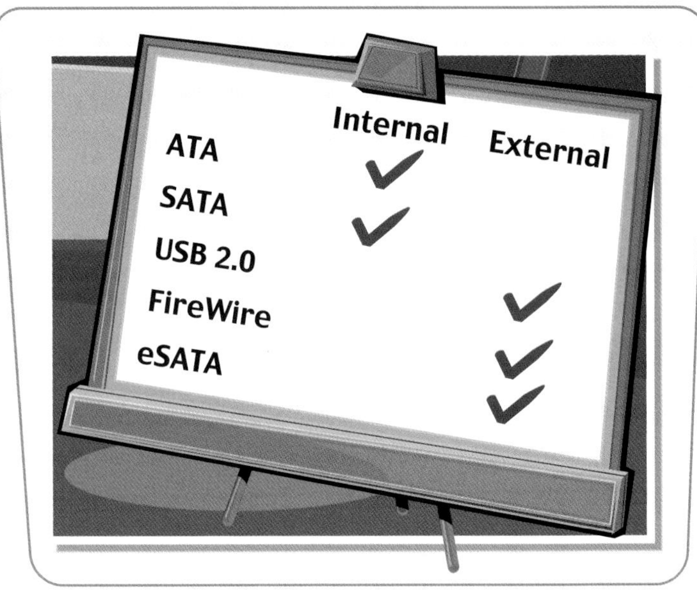


### Internal Hard Drive

The *hard drive,* also called the *hard disk drive* (HDD) or the *hard disk*, is your computer's main permanent storage area. The hard drive is a magnetic disk that holds your data even when you turn off your computer. Most current hard drives can store hundreds of gigabytes of data. An internal hard drive sits inside the computer case.

### External Hard Drive

You may want to add an additional hard drive to increase the storage space in your system. Because it can be difficult to install an internal hard drive, you may want to invest in an *external* hard drive, instead. An external hard drive remains outside of the computer case and attaches through a port, usually a USB port.

**SATA Hard Drive**

Windows Home Server accepts any type of internal hard drive that has a capacity of at least 8GB. The cheapest type of internal hard drive is ATA (Advanced Technology Attachment). However, you can greatly improve Windows Home Server's performance by using the much faster SATA (Serial ATA) hard drives.

**USB 2.0 Hard Drive**

Most computers come with several USB (Universal Serial Bus) ports, so the easiest way to add storage is to attach a USB hard drive. Note, however, that Windows Home Server does not work with older USB 1.1 hard drives, which are too slow. You must use the newer USB 2.0 hard drives, which are much faster.

**FireWire Hard Drive**

If your computer comes with at least one FireWire (also called IEEE 1394) port, you can use it to attach an external FireWire hard drive. A FireWire 800 hard drive is twice as fast as a FireWire 400 hard drive. However, your FireWire port must support FireWire 800, which most modern FireWire ports do.

**eSATA Hard Drive**

Some newer computers come with one or more eSATA (external SATA) ports, which you can use to attach an eSATA hard drive. eSATA is the fastest external drive type, with theoretical transfer rates of up to 2.4 Gbps, which compares to 480 Mbps for USB 2.0 and 800 Mbps for FireWire 800.

# View Windows Home Server Storage

You can monitor your server storage by using the Windows Home Server Console. This program offers a Server Storage tab that shows the installed hard drives, the total amount of storage, and how much storage is available.

**To view the Windows Home Server storage, you must know the password for the server's Administrator account.**

1 Start the Windows Home Server Console.

***Note:** For more information, see Chapter 3.*

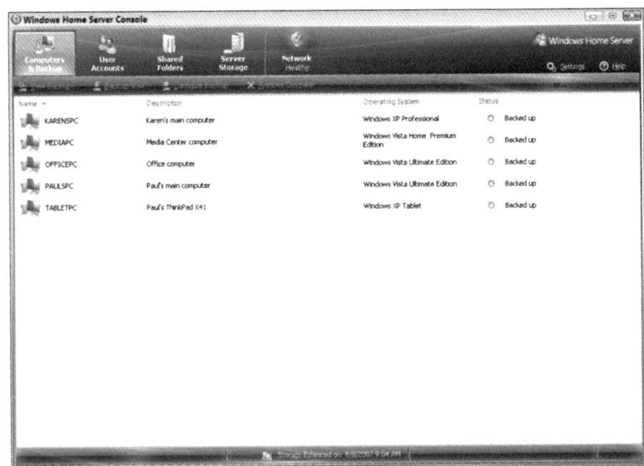


2 Click **Server Storage**.

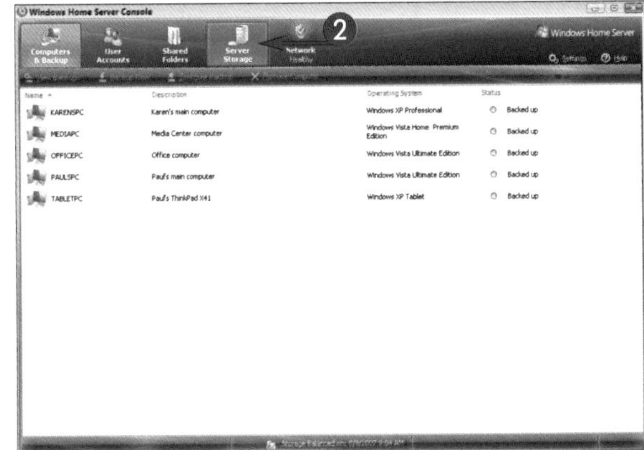

- The Server Storage tab shows the attached hard drives.
- This column shows the capacity of each drive.
- This column shows the drive type.
- This column shows the current drive status.

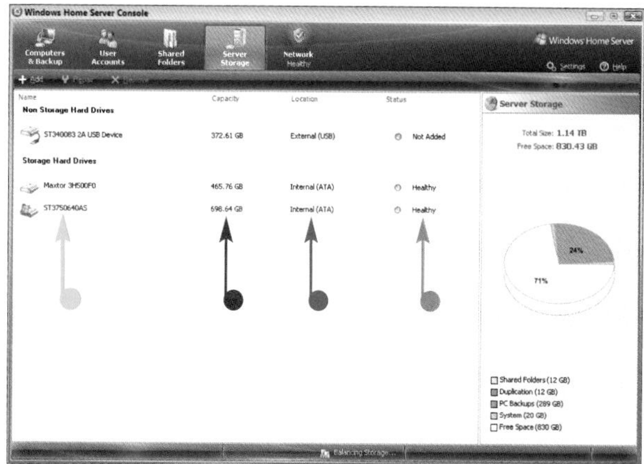


- This number tells you the size of the storage pool.
- This number tells you how much space you have left in the storage pool.
- This pie chart shows you how the storage breaks down according to the categories shown.

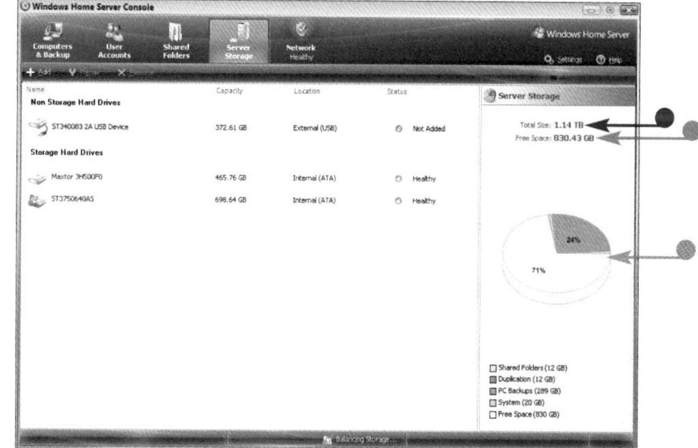

**After I attach an external hard drive, why does its status show as "Not Added" in the Server Storage tab?**

When you attach a new hard drive to the home server computer, Windows Home Server recognizes the new drive, but it does not automatically add the hard drive to the storage pool. This is just in case you have data on the drive that you want to preserve, because Windows Home Server destroys all data on a drive when you add it to the storage pool, as described in the next section.

Status

Not Added

**What is the System item that I see in the storage pie chart?**

The System category represents the files that Windows Home Server requires for its own use – the so-called *system files*. When Windows Home Server is installed, it sets aside 20GB of storage space for its own use, and you cannot change that or use that space for storing backups or shared folders.

SYSTEM

# Add Storage to Windows Home Server

After you attach a hard drive to your home server computer, you can increase the amount of storage space available to Windows Home Server by adding the new drive to the storage pool.

**Windows Home Server formats any hard drive that you add, which means that existing data on the hard drive is destroyed.**

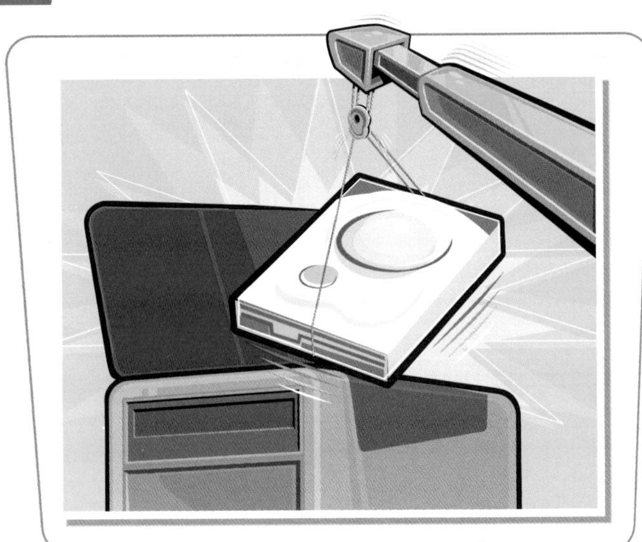

## Add Storage to Windows Home Server

1. Start the Windows Home Server Console.

*Note: For more information, see Chapter 3.*

2. Click **Server Storage**.
3. Click the hard drive you want to add.
4. Click **Add**.

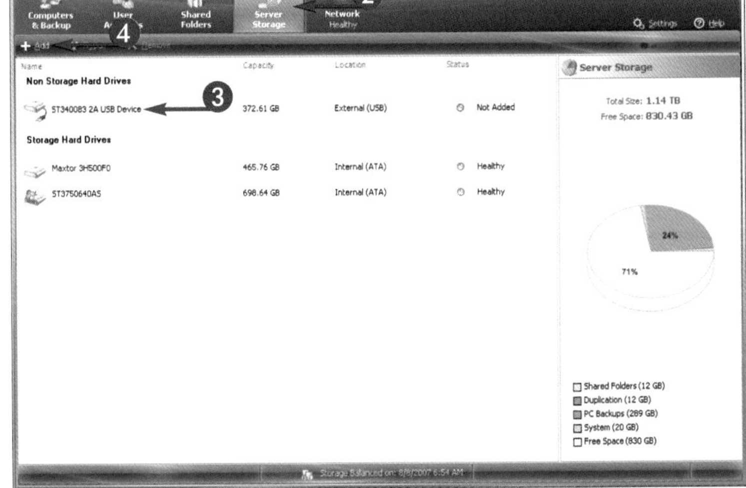


Windows Home Server launches the Add a Hard Drive Wizard.

5. Click **Next**.

- The Add a Hard Drive Wizard warns you that any files on the hard drive will be deleted.

6 Click **Finish**.

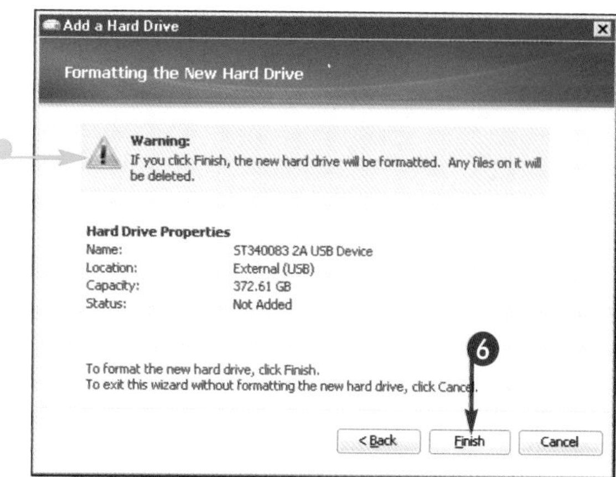


The Add a Hard Drive Wizard formats the drive and adds it to the storage pool.

7 Click **Done**.

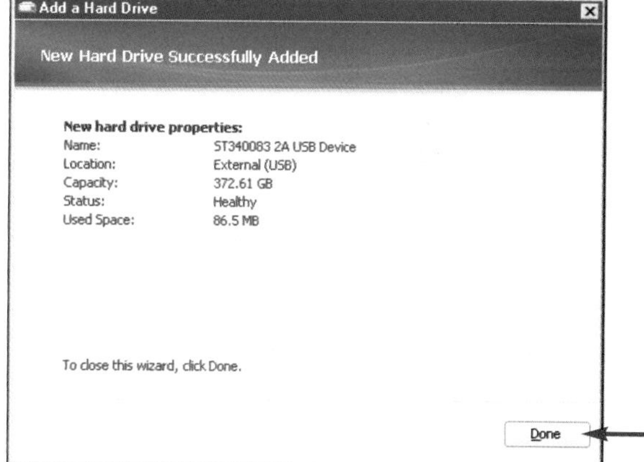

**I attached a hard drive to my home server computer, but it does not appear in the Server Storage tab. Why not?**

There are certain types of hard drives that Windows Home Server does not support. For example, Windows Home Server cannot use older USB 1.1 external hard drives because they are too slow. Similarly, Windows Home Server cannot use any hard drive that is smaller than 8GB. When you attach these drives, Windows Home Server does not display them in the Server Storage tab.

**Is there any way to prevent Windows Home Server from deleting the data that exists on a hard drive?**

No, Windows Home Server automatically formats the drive when you run the Add a Hard Drive Wizard. If you want to save the data, log on to Windows Home Server remotely (see Chapter 11), open the drive in Windows Explorer, and then copy the data to another location, such as a Windows Home Server shared folder.

# Remove Storage from Windows Home Server

You can remove a hard drive from the storage pool. This is useful if you want to use the hard drive on another system or if you want to replace the hard drive with one that is faster or has a greater capacity.

**Windows Home Server does not allow you to remove the hard drive that is currently storing the system files.**

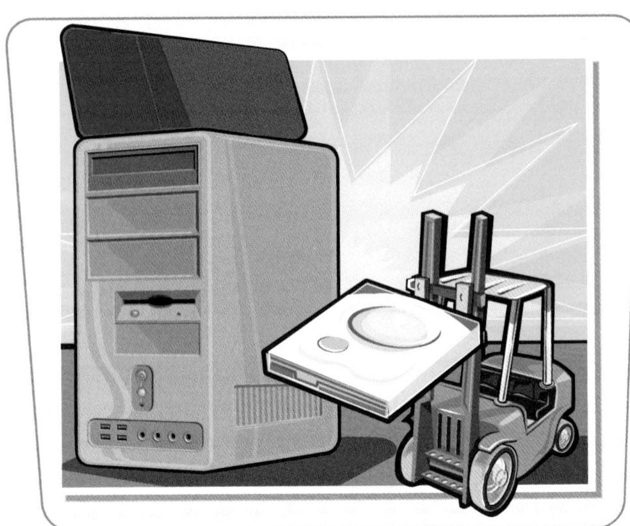

## Remove Storage from Windows Home Server

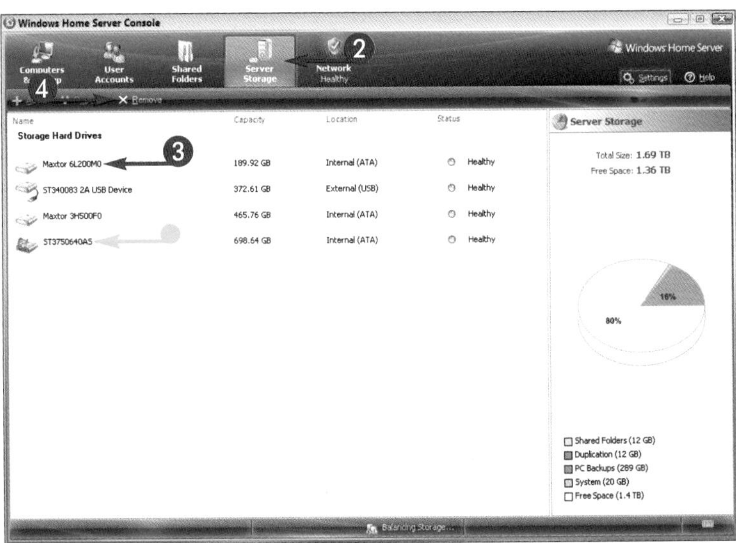

1. Start the Windows Home Server Console.

*Note: For more information, see Chapter 3.*

2. Click **Server Storage**.
3. Click the hard drive you want to remove.

- The hard drive icon that displays the Windows logo is the hard drive that stores the Windows Home Server system files. You cannot remove this drive.

4. Click **Remove**.

Windows Home Server starts the Remove a Hard Drive Wizard.

5. Click **Next**.

The Remove a Hard Drive Wizard displays the consequences of removing the drive.

6 Click **Finish**.

The Remove a Hard Drive Wizard removes the drive.

***Note:*** *Depending on the amount of data you have stored and whether folder duplication is turned on, it may take a few hours to remove the hard drive.*

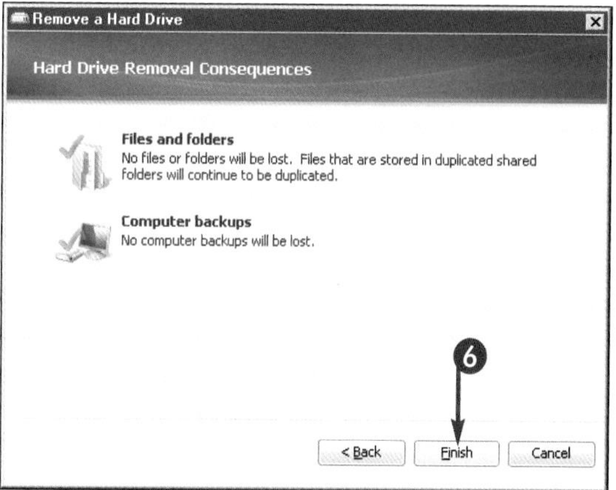


7 Click **Done**.

You can now detach the hard drive from the home server computer.

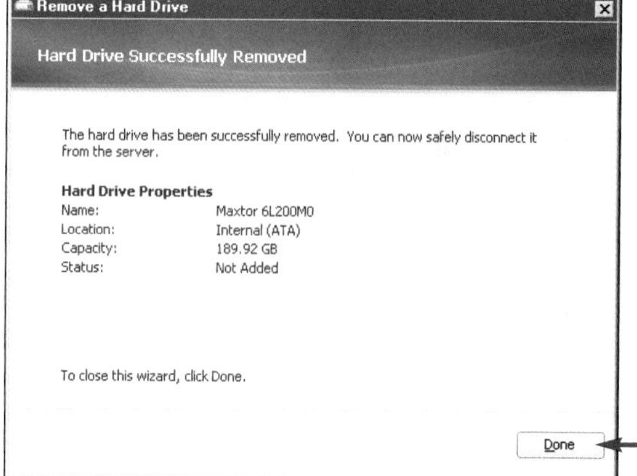

**The Server Storage tab shows a hard drive's status as Failing. Should I remove the hard drive?**

Not just yet. Instead, you should run Windows Home Server's repair feature on the hard drive. In the Server Storage tab, click the hard drive that shows the Failing status and then click **Repair**. Windows Home Server starts the Repair a Hard Drive Wizard. Click **Next** and then follow the wizard's instructions to repair the drive. (The steps you follow vary, depending on the nature of the hard drive problem.) When the wizard finishes its repairs, click **Done**. If the hard drive still does not work properly, then you should follow the steps in this section to remove it from the storage pool and replace it with a new hard drive.

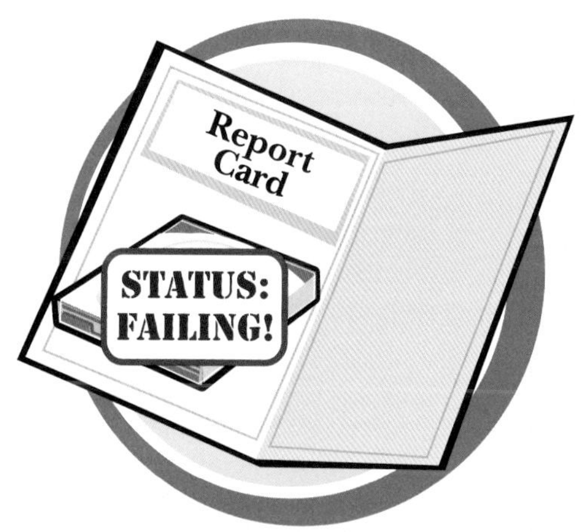

# Replace Your Main Hard Drive

If your main hard drive — the hard drive that stores the Windows Home Server system files — fails, you can get Windows Home Server up and running again by replacing the failed drive with a new hard drive.

**The main hard drive is an internal hard drive, which is more difficult to replace than an external hard drive. This task assumes that the main hard drive has already been replaced by a qualified computer technician or other knowledgeable user.**

## Replace Your Main Hard Drive

1. Attach a keyboard, mouse, and monitor to the home server computer.
2. Insert the Windows Home Server installation disc.
3. Start the home server computer.
4. Follow the instructions on the computer screen to boot from the DVD.

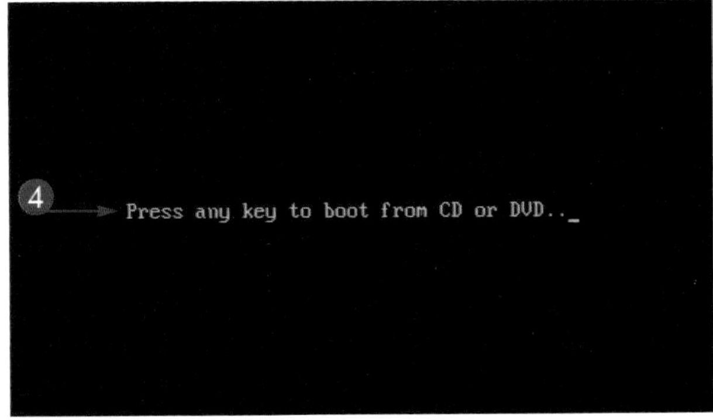


The Windows Home Server Setup Wizard appears.

5. Click **Next**.

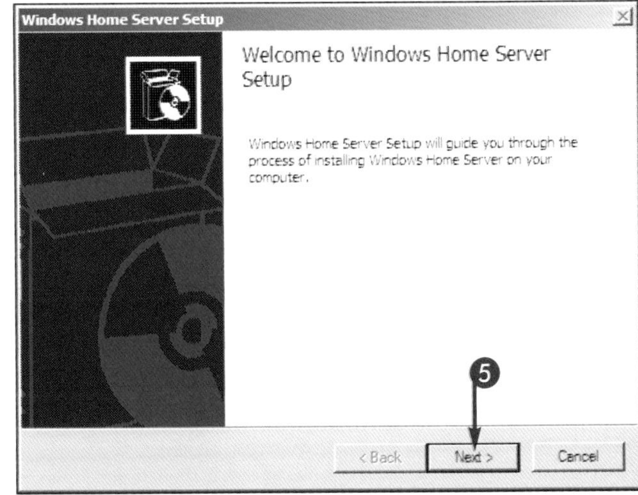

The Windows Home Server Setup Wizard displays a list of hard drives.

6. Click **Next**.

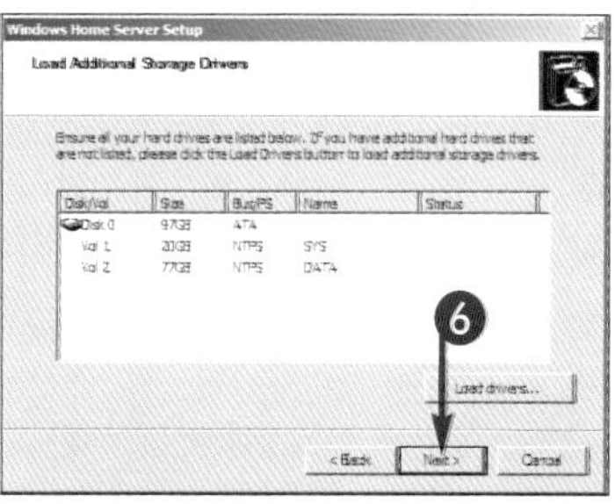

The Select an Installation Type dialog box appears.

7. From the Installation Type list, click ▾ and then click **Server Reinstallation**.
8. Click **Next**.

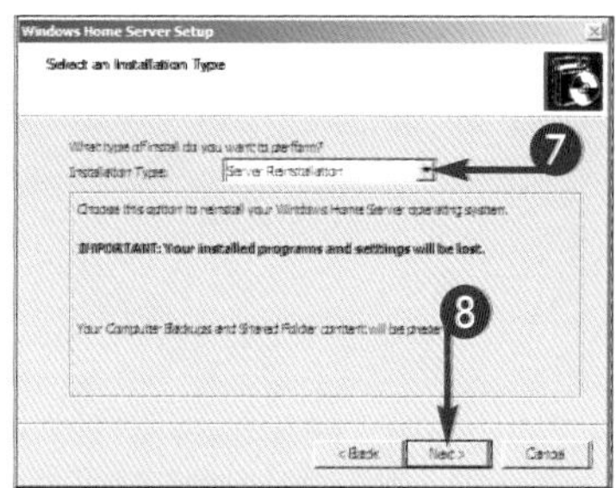

The Select Your Regional and Keyboard Settings dialog box appears.

9. Click ▾ and then click your language and country.
10. Click ▾ and then click your keyboard type.
11. Click **Next**.

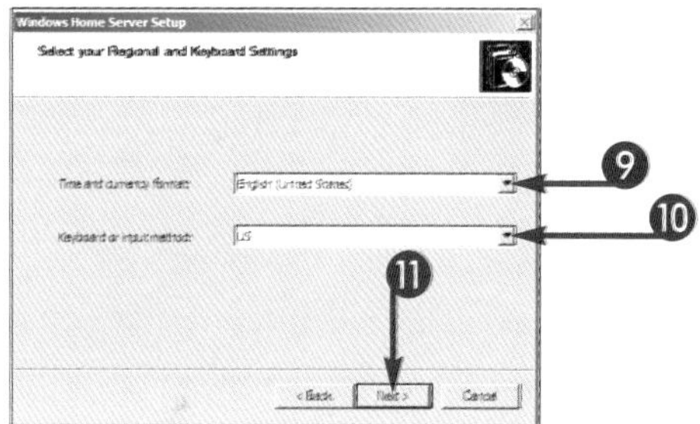

TIP

**When I replace my main hard drive, does Windows Home Server keep my user accounts and other settings?**

No, unfortunately Windows Home Server cannot recover your user accounts or any options you may have set in the Windows Home Server Settings dialog box. That data was stored on your main hard drive, so when your hard drive failed, it took that data along with it. After you finish replacing your main hard drive, you need to use the Windows Home Server Console to re-create your user accounts and reconfigure your Windows Home Server settings.

continued

# Replace Your Main Hard Drive *(continued)*

When you select Server Reinstallation as the installation type, you are telling Windows Home Server Setup not to format the other hard drives on the home server. This means that the data in the Windows Home Server shared folders will be preserved.

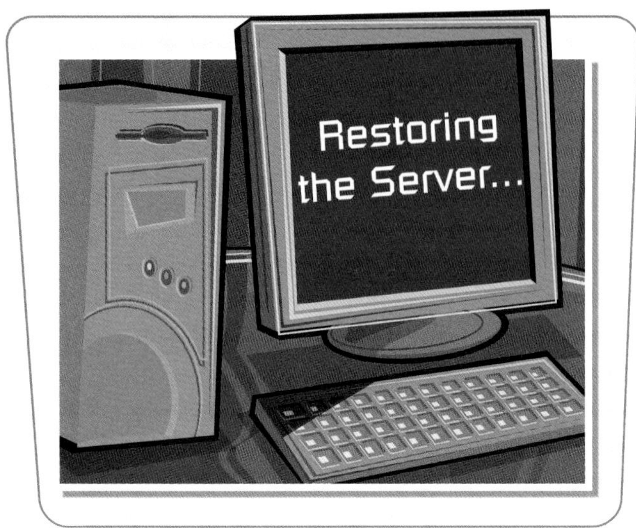


Replace Your Main Hard Drive *(continued)*

The End-User License Agreement dialog box appears.

⑫ Click **I accept this agreement** (◯ changes to ◉).

⑬ Click **Next**.

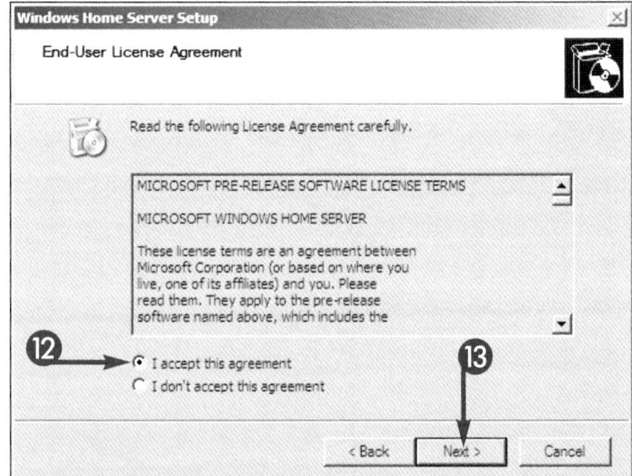


The Enter Your Windows Home Server Product Key dialog box appears.

⑭ In the Product key text boxes, type your 25-digit Windows Home Server product key.

⑮ Click **Next**.

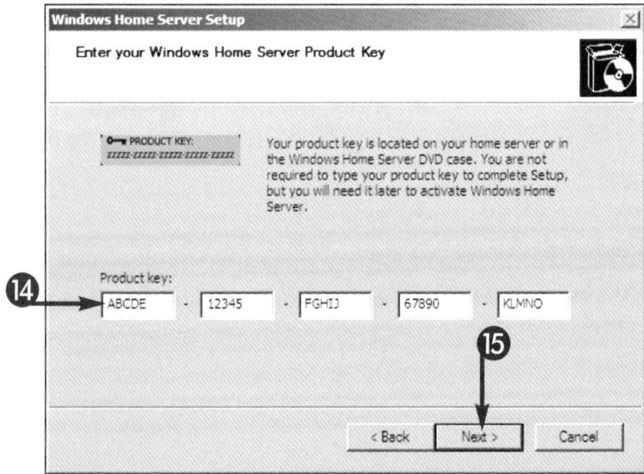

The Name Your Home Server dialog box appears.

16 Type the name you want to use for your home server.

**Note:** *To avoid problems, you should keep the home server name the same as previous Home Server installation. If you are not sure, use the default name of SERVER.*

17 Click **Next**.

The Ready to Install Windows Home Server dialog box appears.

18 Click **Start**.

The Setup Wizard begins installing Windows Home Server.

**Note:** *The installation may take an hour or more, depending on the configuration of the home server computer.*

When the installation is complete, the Windows Home Server window appears.

19 Click .

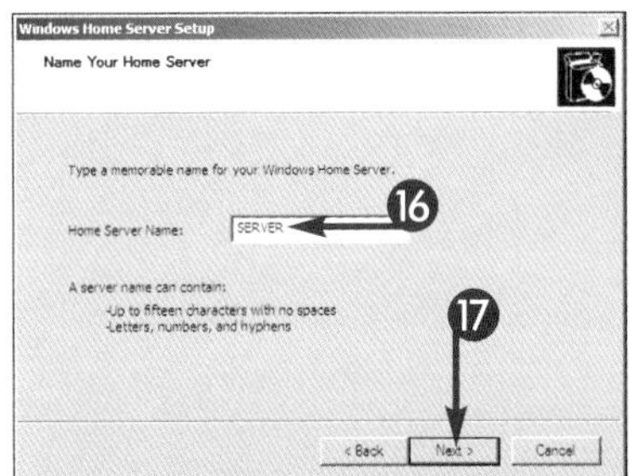


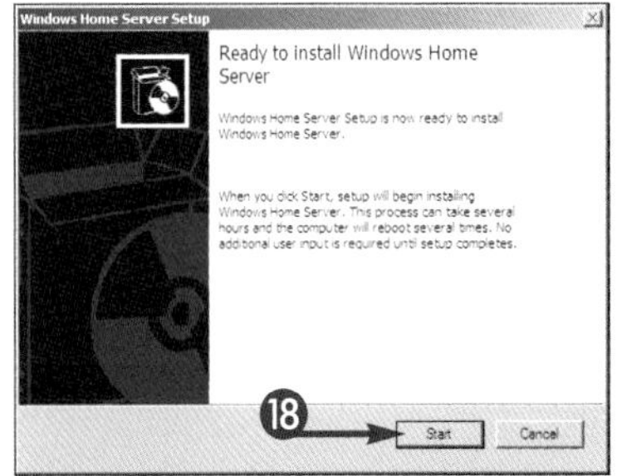


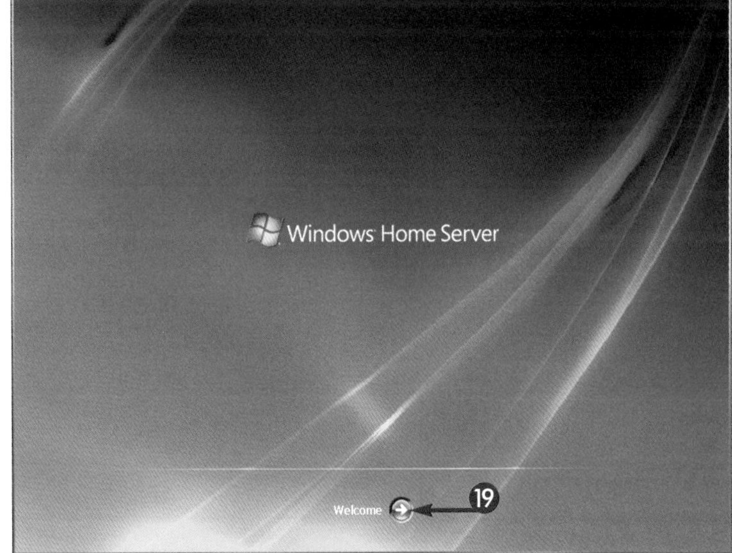


TIP

**Are my computer backups preserved when I replace the main hard drive?**

No. As with user accounts and settings, the backup database is stored on the main hard drive, so that database is lost when the hard drive fails. After you replace the main hard drive and get the server back up and running, Windows Home Server will automatically resume computer backups.

continued

# Replace Your Main Hard Drive *(continued)*

As part of the server restoration process, the Windows Home Server Setup Wizard reinstalls Windows Home Server on the new main hard drive. This means that you must run through all the initial configuration steps, such as specifying the server name and the Administrator password.

Replace Your Main Hard Drive *(continued)*

The Type a password for Windows Home Server window appears.

20. Type your Windows Home Server password.

***Note:*** *The Windows Home Server password must be at least seven characters long and it must contain at least one character from three of the following four categories: lowercase letters, uppercase letters, numbers, and symbols.*

21. Retype your Windows Home Server password.
22. Type a hint that helps you remember the password.
23. Click ➡.

The Help protect Windows Home Server automatically window appears.

24. Click **On** (◯ changes to ◉).
25. Click ➡.

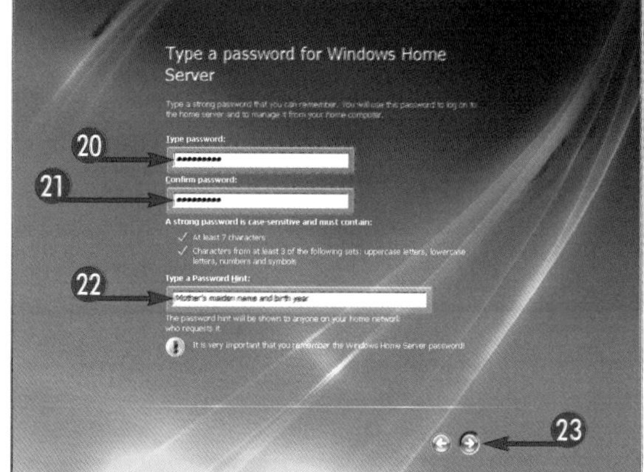


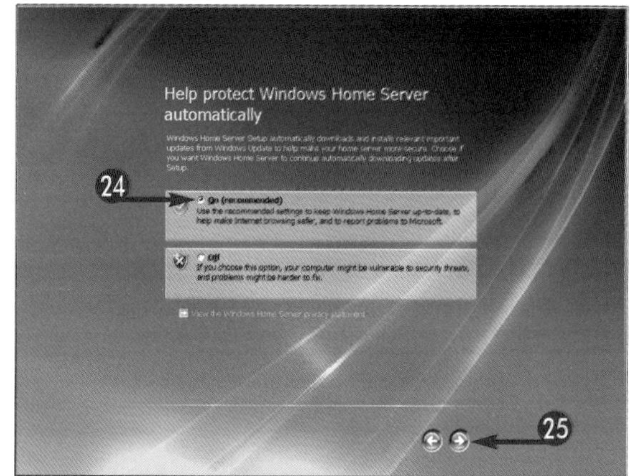

The Customer Experience Improvement Program window appears.

26 Click **Yes** (◯ changes to ◉).

27 Click ➲.

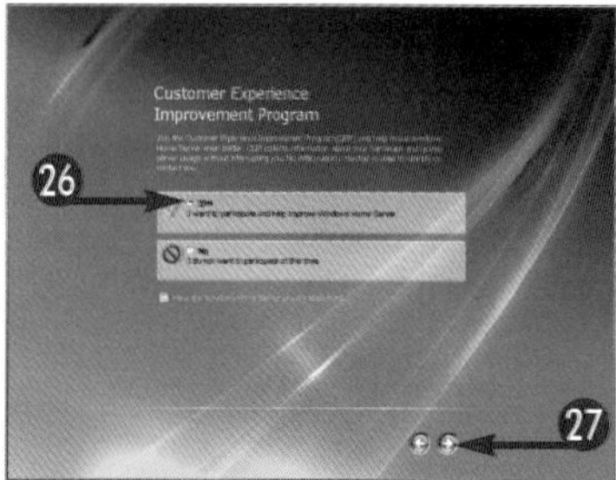

The Windows Error Reporting window appears.

28 Click **Yes** (◯ changes to ◉).

29 Click ➲.

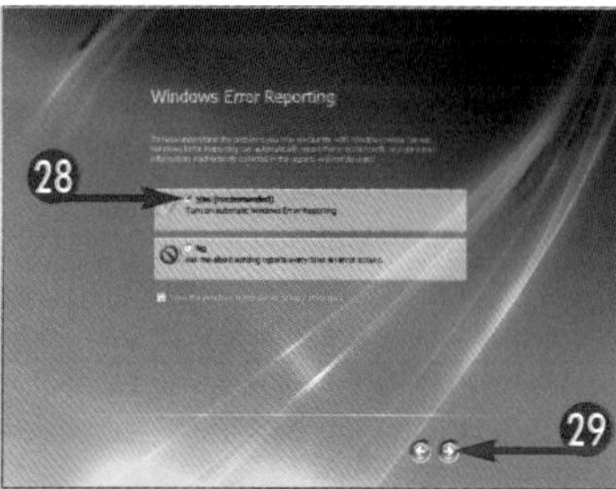

The Windows Home Server Setup is finished window appears.

30 Click ➲.

The Windows Home Server desktop appears.

You can now re-create the Windows Home Server user accounts and reconfigure the Windows Home Server system settings.

**After I have restored the home server, the Windows Home Server icon appears gray instead of green. How can I fix this?**

When the main hard drive fails, all of your home computers lose their connection to Windows Home Server. Unfortunately, when you restore the home server as described in this section, some of your home computers may not be able to reconnect to Windows Home Server, so the icon appears gray. To fix this, you need to run the Discovery program. For more information, see Chapter 3.

CHAPTER 7

# Sharing Files

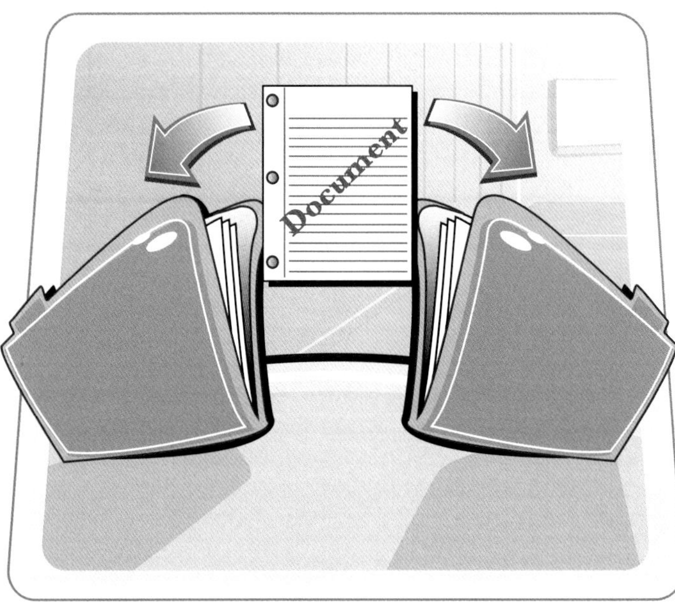


You can use Windows Home Server as a central storage area for your files. By using shared folders, you can give others on your network access to documents, music, photos, videos, and more. Windows Home Server also gives you control over who can access your shared files and what they can do with them.

Understanding Windows Home Server File Sharing....126
Access the Windows Home Server Shared Folders....128
Map a Shared Folder to a Drive Letter ....130
View the Shared Folders in the Console ....132
Rename a Shared Folder ....134
Turn Folder Duplication On and Off ....136
Apply User Permissions on a Shared Folder ....138
Apply User Permissions on All Shared Folders ....140
View Shared Folder History ....142
Create a New Shared Folder....144
Delete a Shared Folder ....146
Work with a Shared Folder Offline....148

# Understanding Windows Home Server File Sharing

To get the most out of Windows Home Server's file-sharing features, you need to understand a few key concepts such as shared folders, user permissions, and shared folder duplication.

### Shared Folder

A *shared folder* is a folder that has been configured to allow people on the network to see the folder and access its contents. A shared folder is useful because it enables network users to work with files on another computer without having to create copies of those files.

### Windows Home Server Shared Folders

Windows Home Server comes with six shared folders. You can use the Music, Photos, and Videos folders to store specific files. The Software shared folder can store installation files for Windows Home Server add-ins and other programs, and you can use the Public shared folder for other types of files. You learn about the Users folder on the next page.

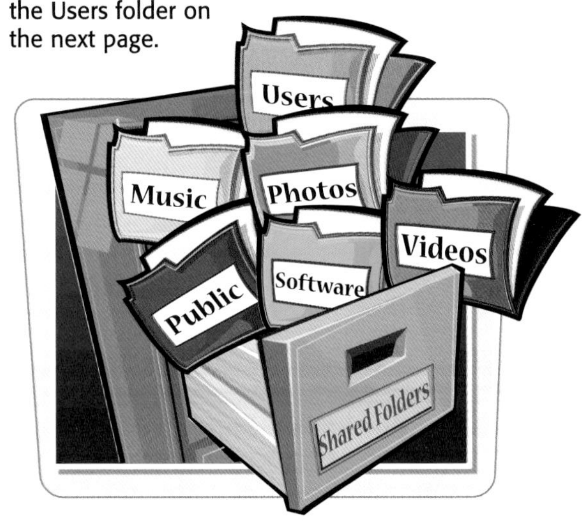

### User Folders

Windows Home Server's predefined Users shared folder contains subfolders for each user account that you set up. Each time you create an account, Windows Home Server automatically adds a subfolder to Users for that account. The subfolder name is the same as the person's logon name.

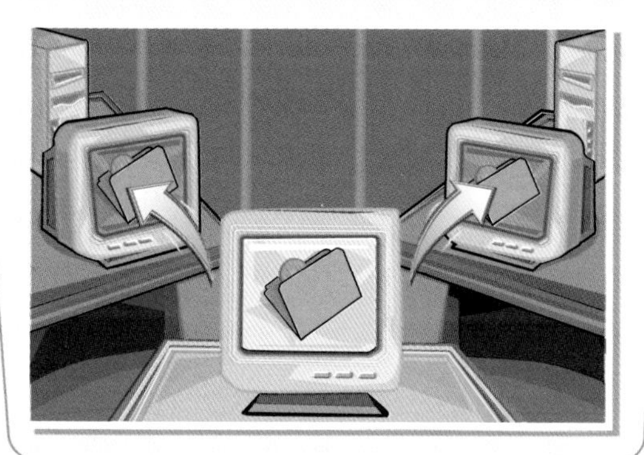

### Shared Folder Duplication

If you have at least two hard drives in your Windows Home Server system, you can activate folder duplication for some or all of the shared folders. This creates a second copy of each file, which means that if one of your hard drives fails, your data remains safe because a copy exists on another hard drive.

## User Permissions

### Full

*User permissions* specify the level of access that each user is given for a particular folder. If a user has Full access, the user can do almost anything with the shared folder, including viewing the folder, opening files, editing files, creating new files and subfolders, and deleting files. However, the user cannot delete the shared folder.

### Read

If a user has Read access to a shared folder, the user can open the shared folder to view its contents, as well as open any files in the folder. However, the user cannot save changes to those files, create new files, or delete existing files.

### None

If a user has None access to a shared folder, the user cannot open the shared folder to view its contents. For example, on the shared folder associated with your Windows Home Server user account, you are given Full access to the folder, but all other users are given None access.

# Access the Windows Home Server Shared Folders

To work with the Windows Home Server shared folders, you must first access the folders by using your local computer.

## Access the Windows Home Server Shared Folders

1. Click **Start**.
2. Click **Network**.

The Network window appears.

3. Double-click the icon for Windows Home Server.

***Note:*** *The default name of the Windows Home Server computer is SERVER.*

***Note:*** *If you see more than one icon for the Windows Home Server computer, be sure to double-click the icon that displays the monitor and computer, as shown here.*

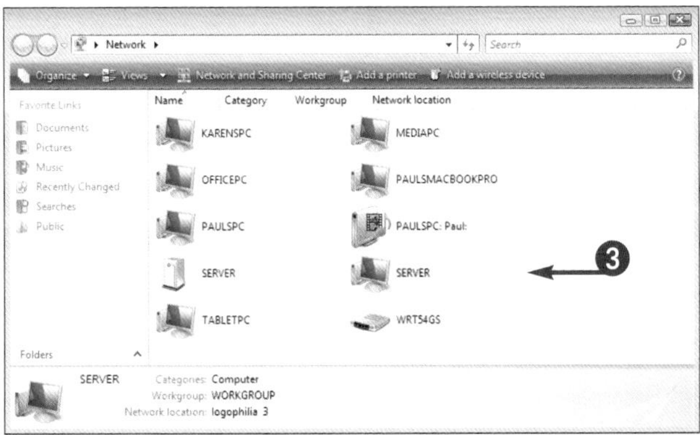

- The Windows Home Server shared folders appear.

4. Double-click the folder you want to access.

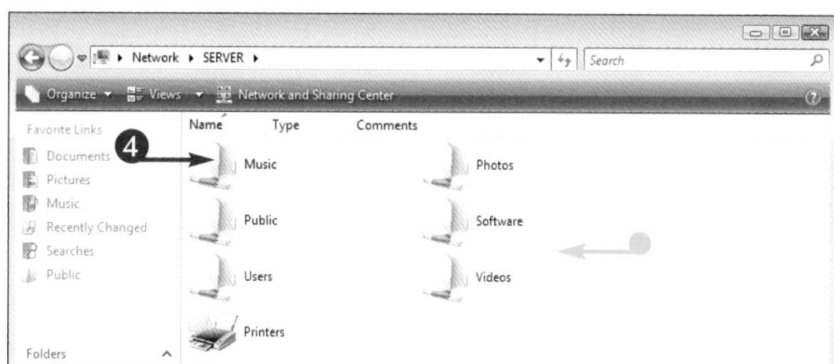

The folder contents appear.

***Note:** If your user account has None access to the shared folder, an Access Denied message appears, instead.*

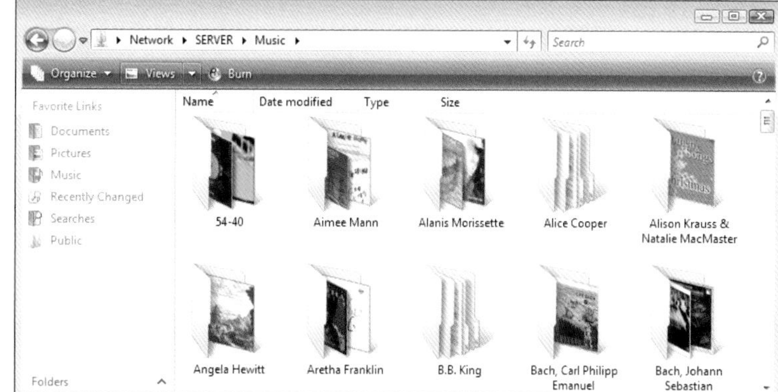

**Is there a faster way to access the Windows Home Server shared folders?**

Yes. When you install the Windows Home Server Connector software (see Chapter 3), the setup program automatically adds a desktop shortcut named "Shared Folders on *Server*" (where *Server* is the name of your Windows Home Server computer). Double-click that shortcut to access the shared folders.

**How do I access the Windows Home Server shared folders in Windows XP?**

Either double-click the **Shared Folders on *Server*** desktop shortcut, or follow these steps:

1. Click **Start**.
2. Click **My Network Places**.

   You may see the Windows Home Server shared folder in the My Network Places window. If not, continue to step **3**.
3. Click **View workgroup computers**.
4. Double-click the Windows Home Server icon.

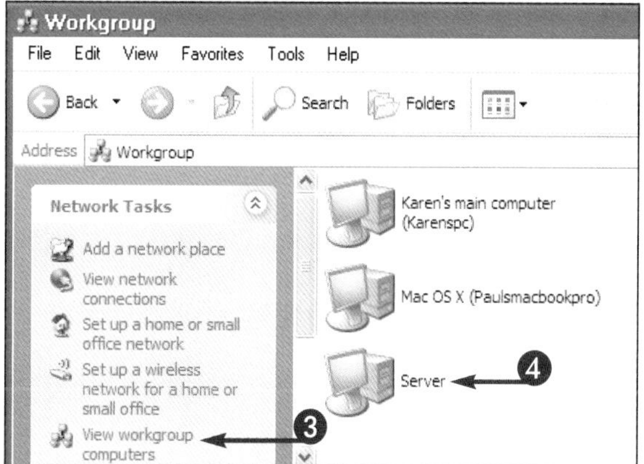

# Map a Shared Folder to a Drive Letter

You can set up a connection to a Windows Home Server shared folder that makes the folder appear as though it is a disk drive on your computer. This gives you even easier access to the shared folder through the Computer window.

## Map a Shared Folder to a Drive Letter

1. Click **Start**.
2. Right-click **Network**.
3. Click **Map Network Drive**.

   The Map Network Drive dialog box appears.

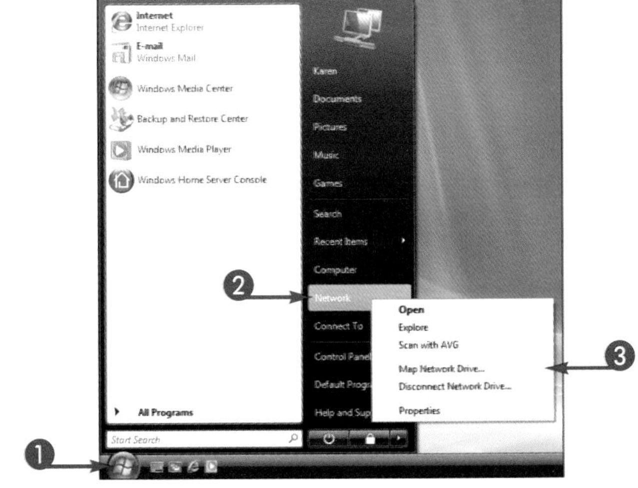


4. Click ▾ in the Drive list and then click the drive letter you want to use for the shared folder.
5. In the Folder text box, type the address of the shared folder you want to work with, or click **Browse** to select the folder.

***Note:*** *A shared folder address takes the form* \\server\share, *where* server *is the name of the Windows Home Server computer and* share *is the name of the shared folder.*

6. Click **Finish**.

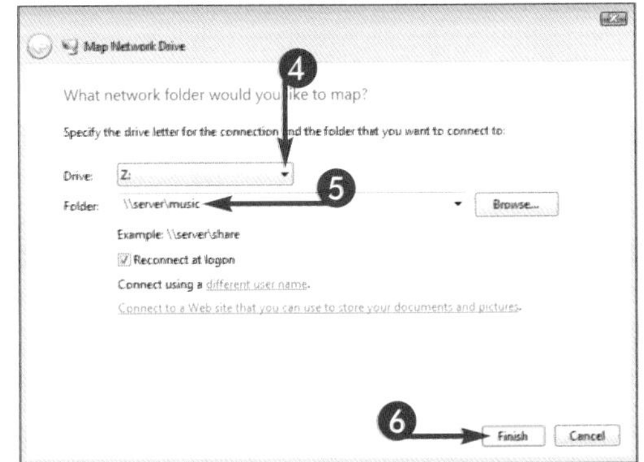

Windows sets up the drive letter and displays a window showing the contents of the shared folder.

7 Click **Computer**.

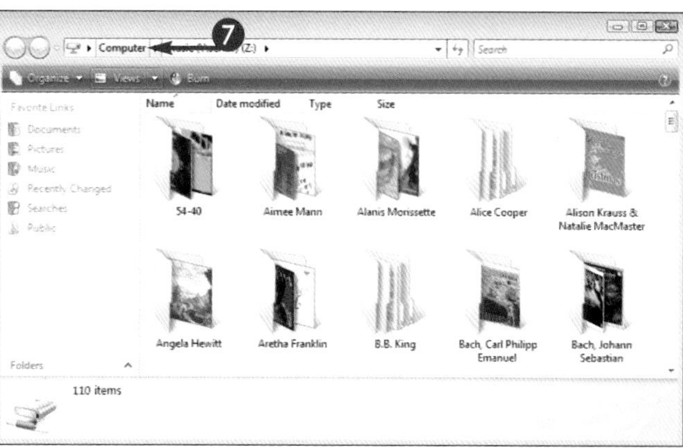

The Computer window appears.

- The shared folder appears as a disk drive in the Computer window.

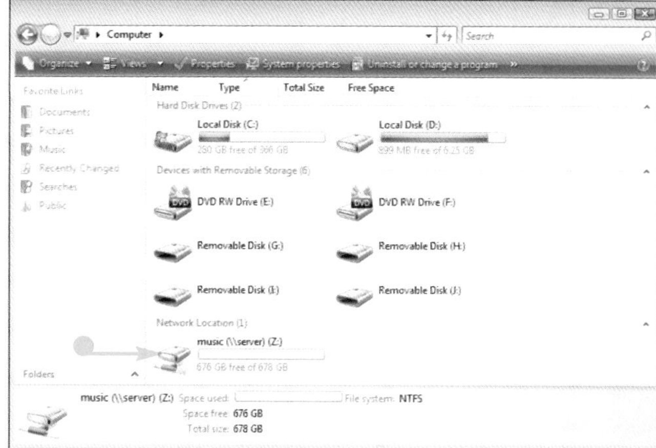

TIPS

**Does the network folder become an actual disk drive on my computer?**

No. The folder remains on the network, but Windows maps the folder to appear as though it is a disk drive on your computer.

**How do I disconnect a drive letter assigned to a shared folder?**

1. Click **Start**.
2. Right-click **Network**.
3. Click **Disconnect Network Drive**.

   The Disconnect Network Drives dialog box appears.
4. Click the drive you want to disconnect.
5. Click **OK**.

   Windows disconnects the drive letter.

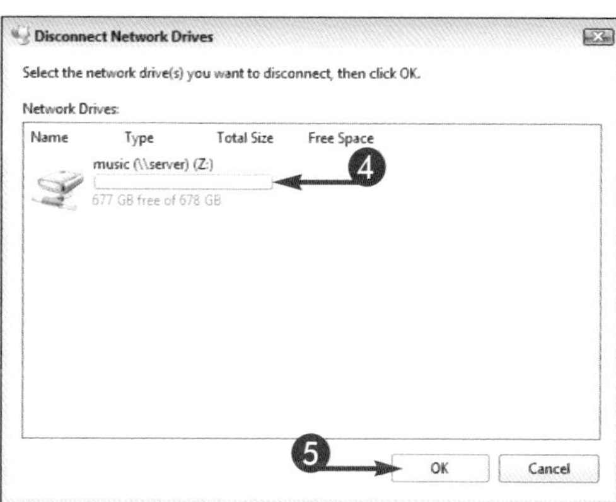

# View the Shared Folders in the Console

You can monitor and work with a shared folder by using the Windows Home Server Console. This program offers a Shared Folders tab that shows the shared folders. It also shows the description, used space, duplication setting, and current status for each folder.

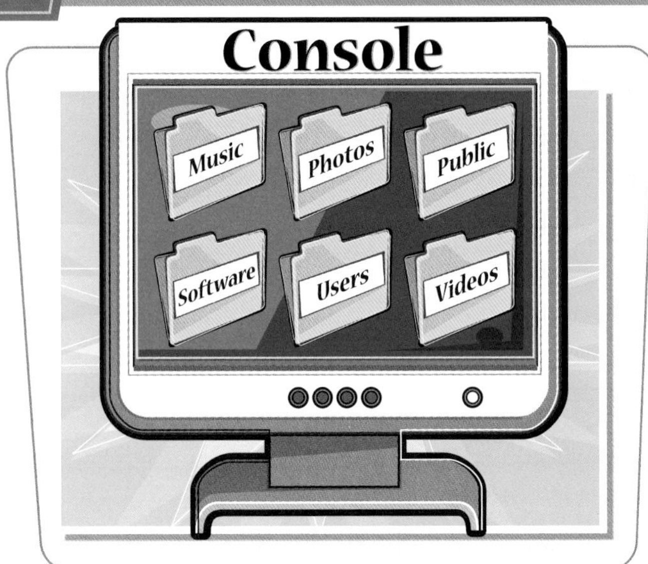


**To view the Windows Home Server storage, you must know the password for the server's Administrator account.**

## View the Shared Folders in the Console

1. Start the Windows Home Server Console.

***Note:*** *For more information, see Chapter 3.*

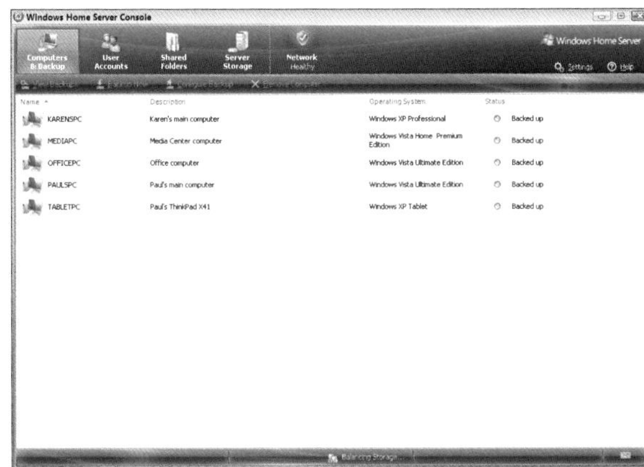


2. Click **Shared Folders**.

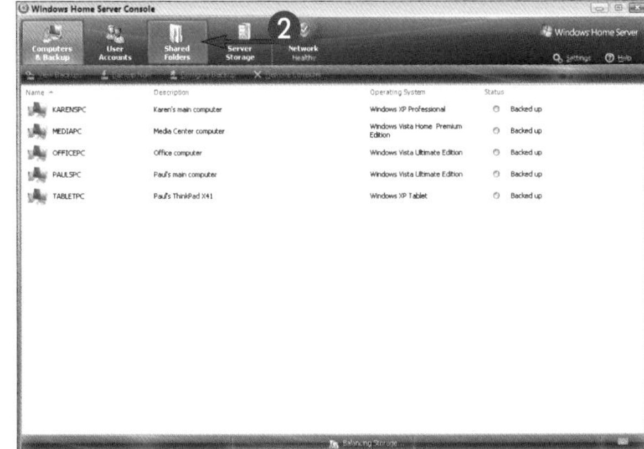

- The Shared Folders tab shows the predefined shared folders and the user folders.
- This column shows a description for each folder.
- This column shows the amount of space each folder is using.

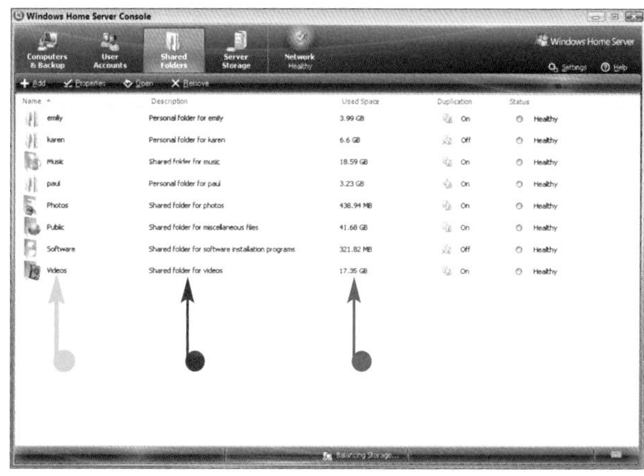


- This column tells you whether duplication is turned on for each folder.
- This column tells you the current health status for each folder.

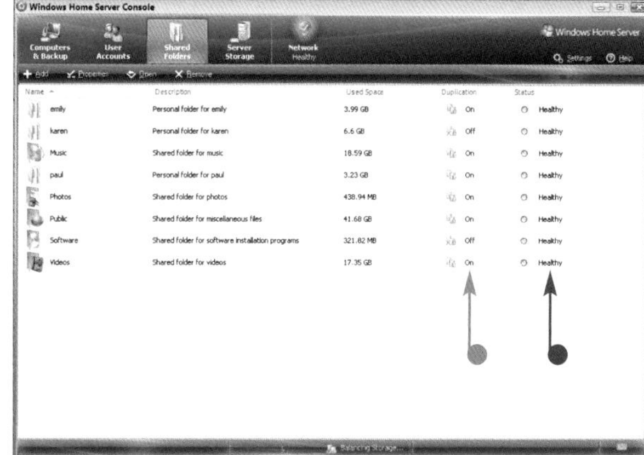


## TIP

### Can I change the description associated with a shared folder?

Yes. Follow these steps:

1. In the Shared Folders tab, click the shared folder you want to work with.
2. Click **Properties**.

   The folder's Properties dialog box appears.
3. In the Description text box, type the new description for the folder.
4. Click **OK**.

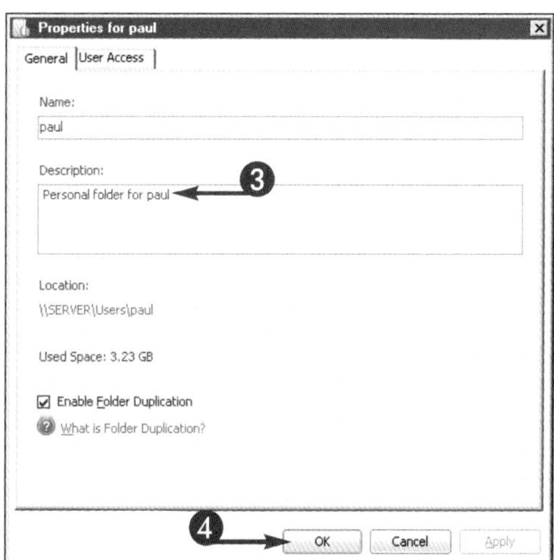

# Rename a Shared Folder

You can customize how a shared folder appears within the home server's folder window and the Windows Home Server Console's Shared Folders tab by renaming the shared folder.

**To rename a shared folder in Windows Home Server, you must know the password for the server's Administrator account. Keep in mind that you can only rename user folders and any shared folders that you have created.**

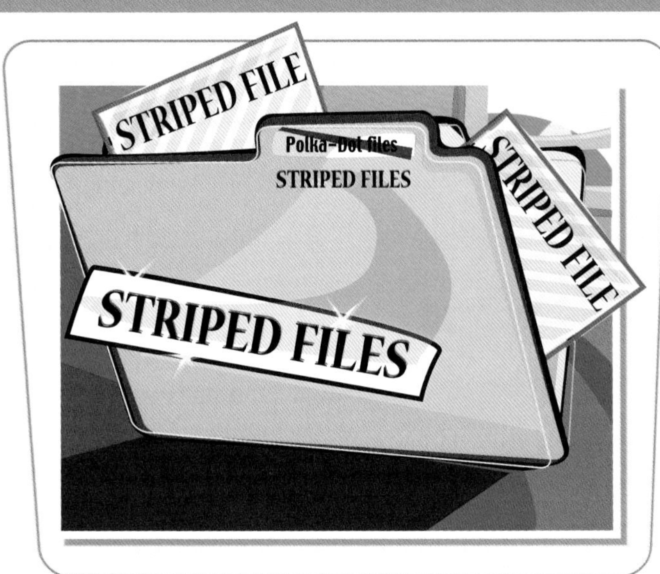


## Rename a Shared Folder

1. Start the Windows Home Server Console.

*Note:* *For more information, see Chapter 3.*

2. Click **Shared Folders**.

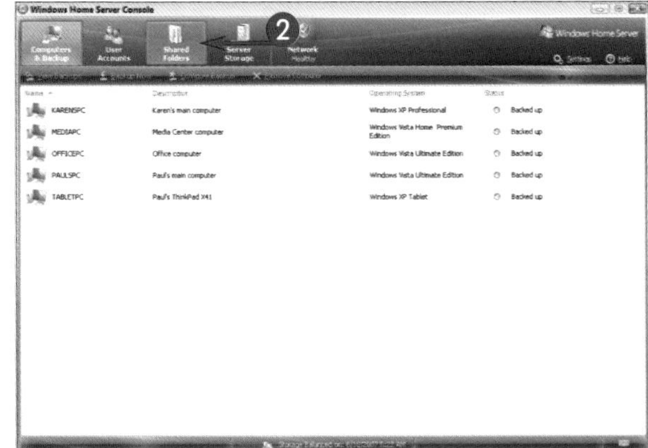

- This column shows the name for each shared folder.

3. Click the shared folder you want to rename.
4. Click **Properties**.

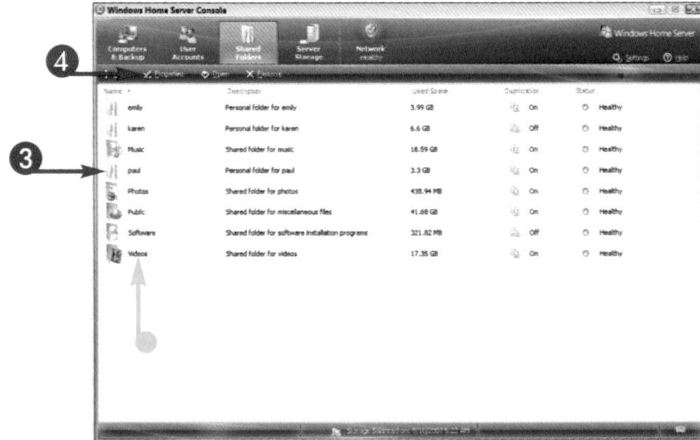

The shared folder's Properties dialog box appears.

5 Click the **General** tab.

6 In the Name text box, edit the shared folder's name.

7 Click **OK**.

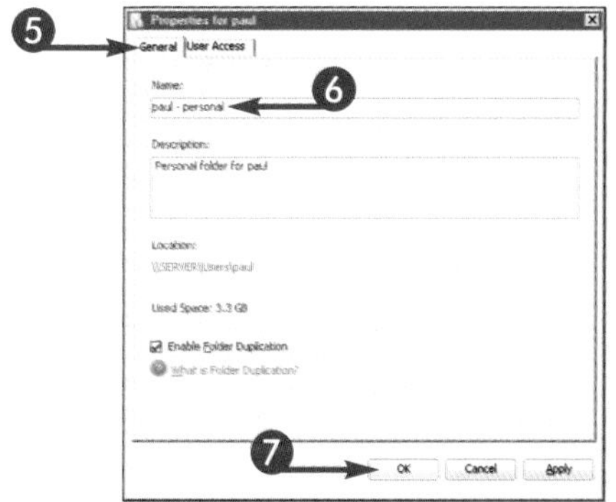

- Windows Home Server displays the shared folder's new name.

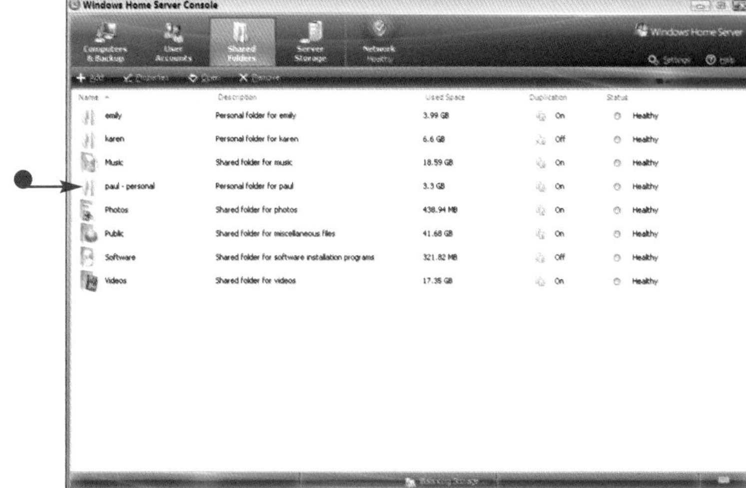

### Are there any restrictions on the shared folders' names?

Yes, there are several restrictions that you need to be aware of. The maximum length of a shared folder name is 64 characters, and the name must contain only letters, numbers, spaces, or any of the following characters: dot (.), dash (-), or underscore (_). In addition, the shared folder name must end with either a letter or a number.

### Are there faster methods I can use to open a shared folder's Properties dialog box?

Yes. Probably the fastest method is to double-click the folder in the Shared Folders tab. You can also right-click the shared folder and then click **Properties**.

# Turn Folder Duplication On and Off

You can toggle a folder's duplication setting on and off. When duplication is on and your home server computer has multiple hard drives, Windows Home Server keeps a copy of each file on a second drive just in case one drive fails.

**To turn duplication on and off in Windows Home Server, you must know the password for the server's Administrator account.**

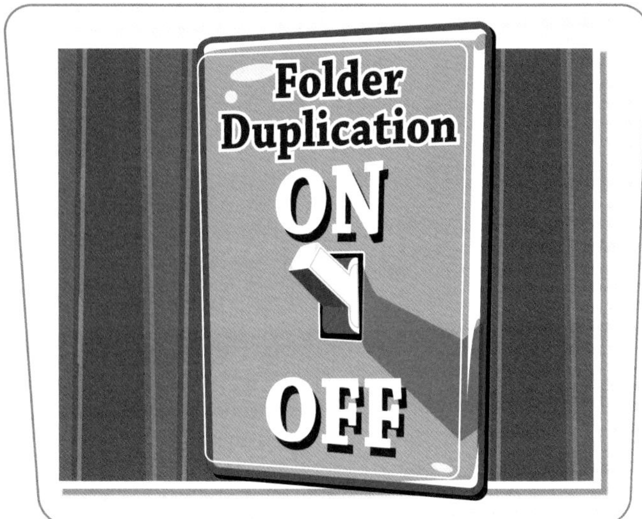


## Turn Folder Duplication On and Off

1. Start the Windows Home Server Console.

*Note:* *For more information, see Chapter 3.*

2. Click **Shared Folders**.

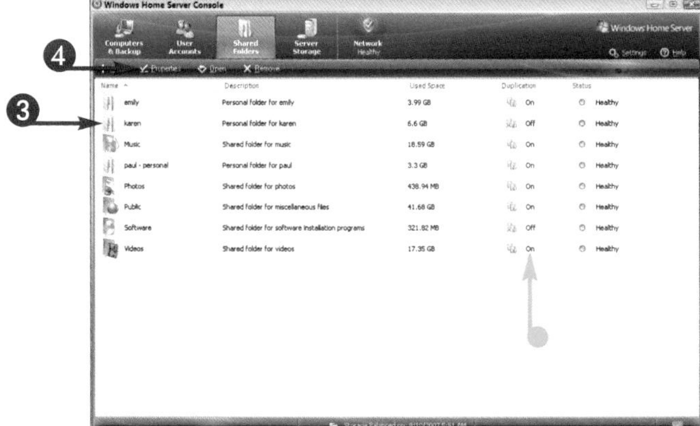


- This column shows the duplication setting for each shared folder.

3. Click the shared folder you want to work with.
4. Click **Properties**.

The shared folder's Properties dialog box appears.

5. Click the **General** tab.

6. Click the **Enable Folder Duplication** check box to turn duplication on (☐ changes to ☑) or off (☑ changes to ☐).

7. Click **OK**.

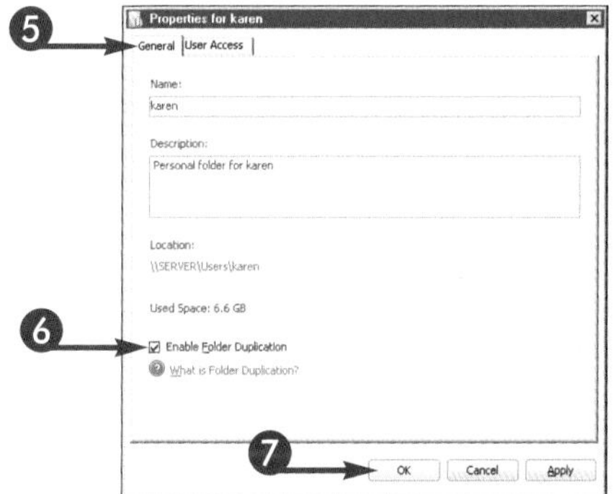


- Windows Home Server displays the new duplication status for the shared folder.

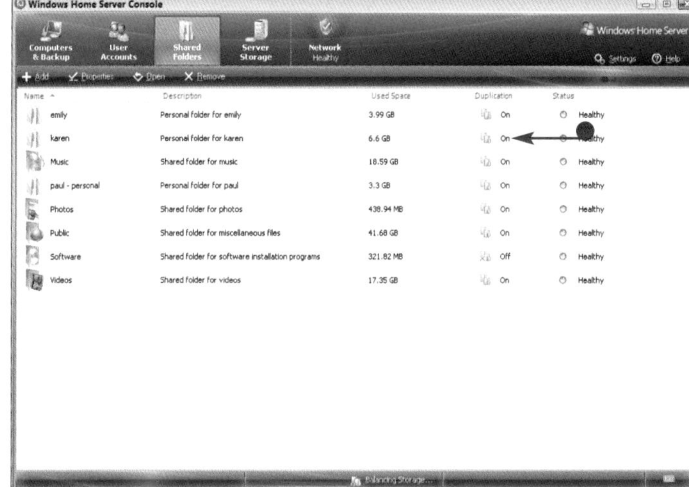

### Why would I want to turn duplication off for a shared folder?

The most common reason is to improve performance when you are transferring a large amount of data to a shared folder. If duplication is turned on for that folder, Windows Home Server immediately starts making copies of the incoming files, which slows down the transfer. It is faster to first turn off duplication for the shared folder, complete the file transfer, and then turn duplication back on. You may also want to turn off duplication for one or more folders if you are running low on disk space in Windows Home Server.

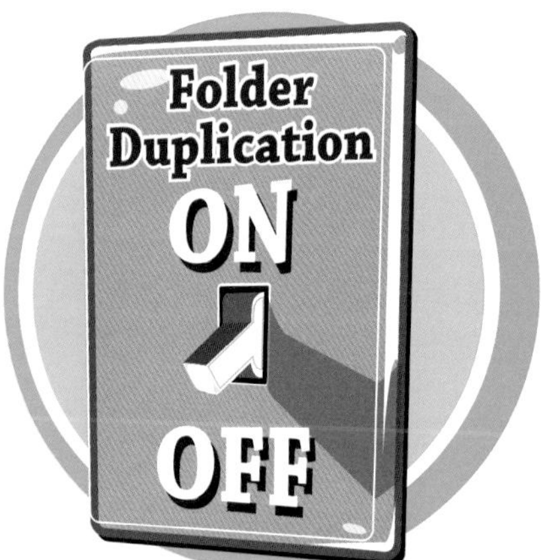

# Apply User Permissions on a Shared Folder

*User access permissions* determine what each Windows Home Server user can and cannot do with a shared folder. For example, giving users Read permission enables them only to open files for viewing. Giving users Full permission enables them to also make changes to a file and create new files.

**To modify permissions on a shared folder in Windows Home Server, you must know the password for the server's Administrator account.**

## Apply User Permissions on a Shared Folder

1. Start the Windows Home Server Console.

**Note:** *For more information, see Chapter 3.*

2. Click **Shared Folders**.

3. Click the shared folder you want to work with.
4. Click **Properties**.

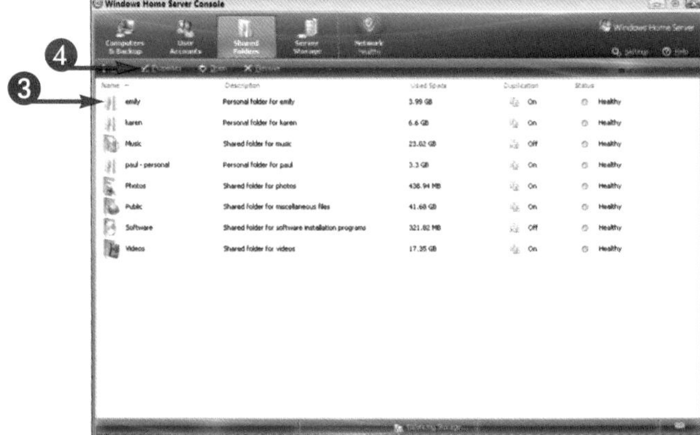

The shared folder's Properties dialog box appears.

5 Click the **User Access** tab.

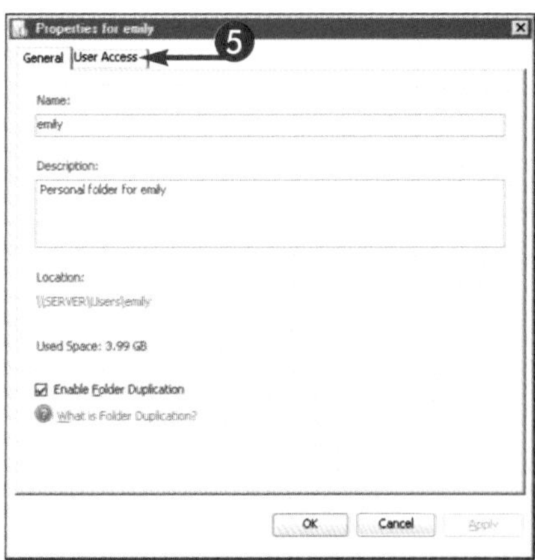

6 For each user, click **Full**, **Read**, or **None** (◯ changes to ◉).

7 Click **OK**.

Windows Home Server puts the new permissions into effect.

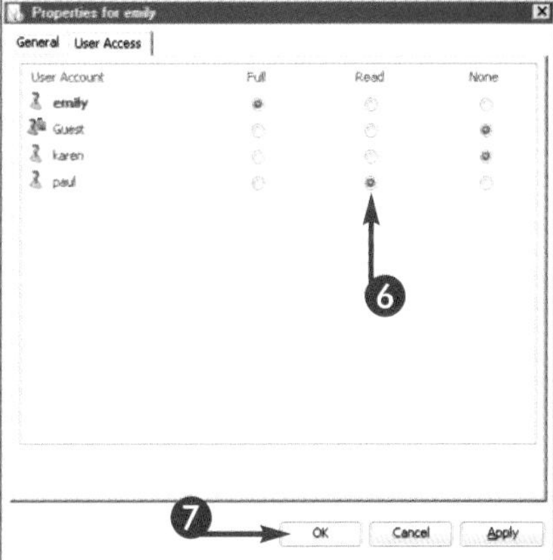

**I have private files in my user folder. How can I prevent others from even seeing those files?**

To secure a shared folder, follow steps **1** to **5** in this section, and then for step **6**, apply the **None** access to every user (◯ changes to ◉). Click **OK** to put the settings into effect. Now, when users try to open your shared folder, they see an Access is denied error message, as shown here. Note, however, that the Windows Home Server Administrator account always has Full user access permission on every shared folder.

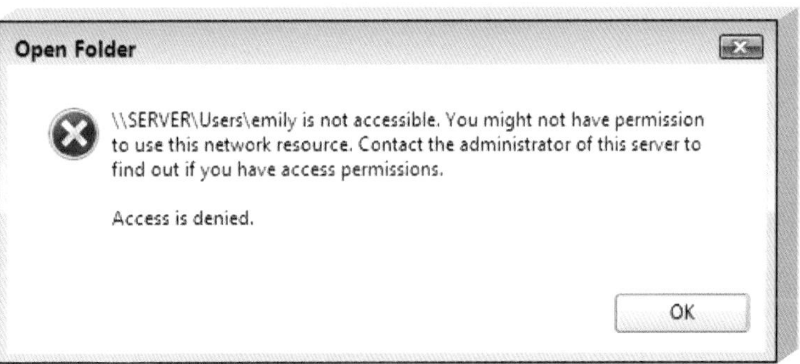

# Apply User Permissions on All Shared Folders

If you are interested in applying shared folder permissions for a specific user, Windows Home Server offers a quick method for applying a user's permissions to all of the shared folders. This method is much faster than applying permissions one folder at a time, as described in the previous section.

**To modify a user's permissions in Windows Home Server, you must know the password for the server's Administrator account.**

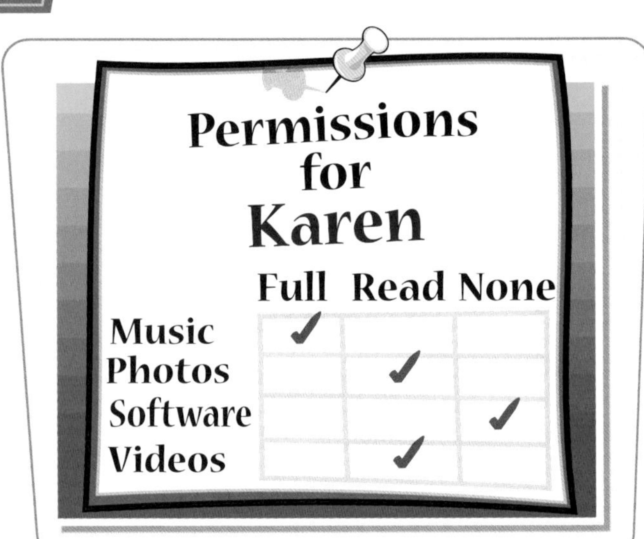


## Apply User Permissions on All Shared Folders

1. Start the Windows Home Server Console.

*Note: For more information, see Chapter 3.*

2. Click **User Accounts**.

3. Click the user account you want to work with.
4. Click **Properties**.

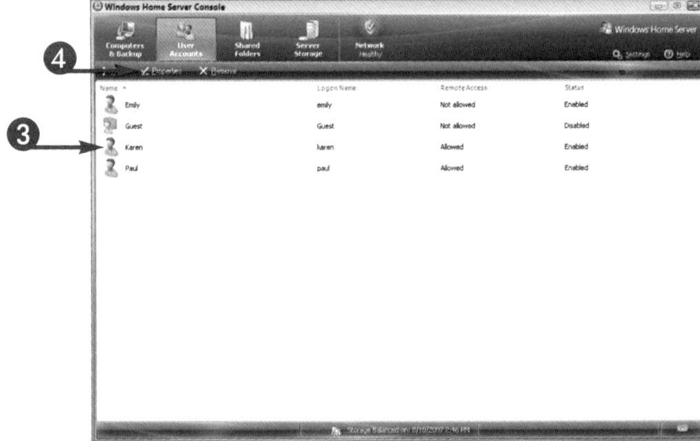

The user account's Properties dialog box appears.

5 Click the **Shared Folder Access** tab.

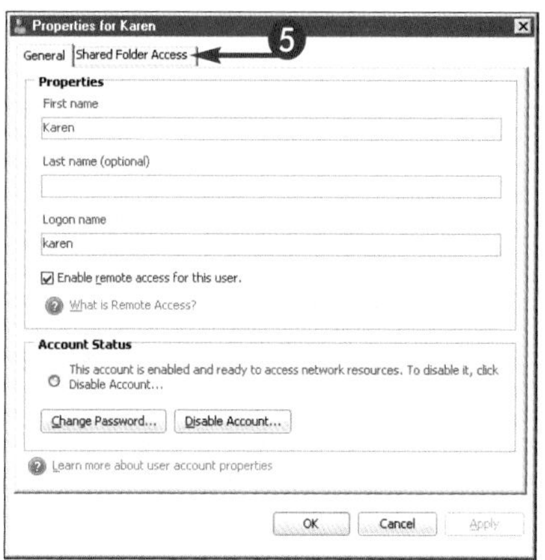

6 For each shared folder, click **Full**, **Read**, or **None** (◯ changes to ◉).

7 Click **OK**.

Windows Home Server puts the new permissions into effect.

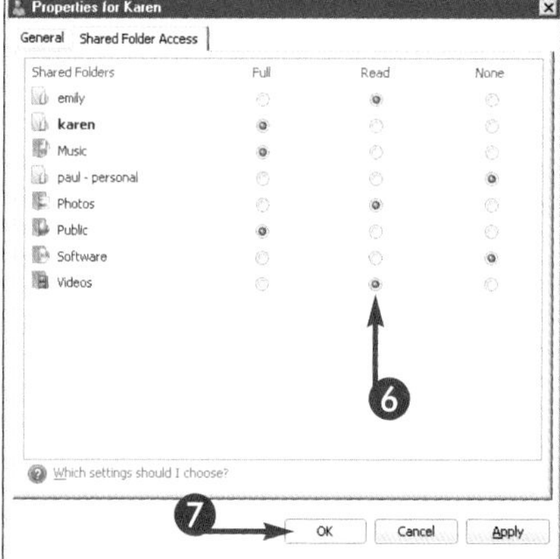

**I set up a user to have Read access on all the shared folders, but that person can still make changes to the files. Why?**

Giving a user Read access does not prevent that user from making changes to a file, but it does prevent them from saving those changes. If the user edits a file and then clicks the program's **Save** command, the program will generate an error message, such as the WordPad message shown here. Note that similar messages appear if the user tries to create a new file, rename a file, or delete a file.

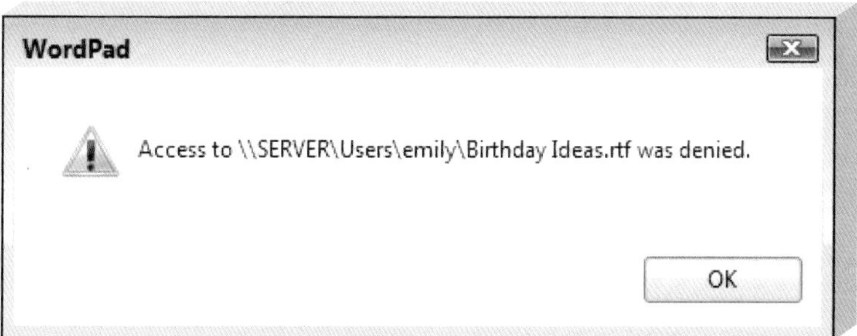

# View Shared Folder History

You can monitor the growth of the space used by a shared folder by examining the shared folder history. This feature displays a graph that shows how a folder's used space has changed over time.

**To view a shared folder's history in Windows Home Server, you must know the password for the server's Administrator account.**

## View Shared Folder History

1. Start the Windows Home Server Console.

*Note: For more information, see Chapter 3.*

2. Click **Shared Folders**.

3. Right-click the shared folder you want to work with.
4. Click **View History**.

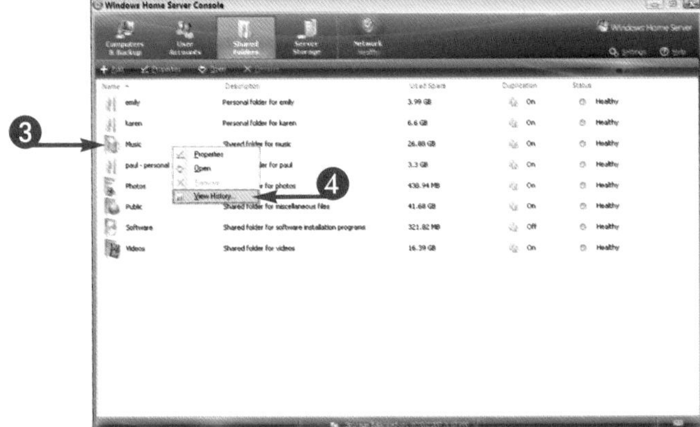

The Shared Folder History dialog box appears.

5. Click the **History range** option you want to use (◯ changes to ◉).

- The graph shows the changes in the folder's used space over the history range you selected.

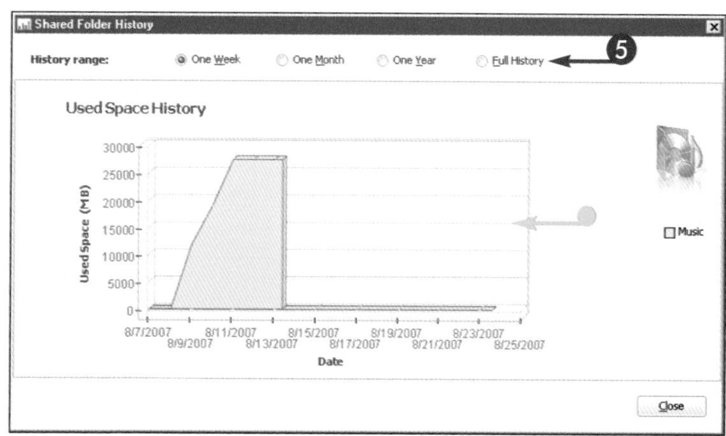

6. Click **Close**.

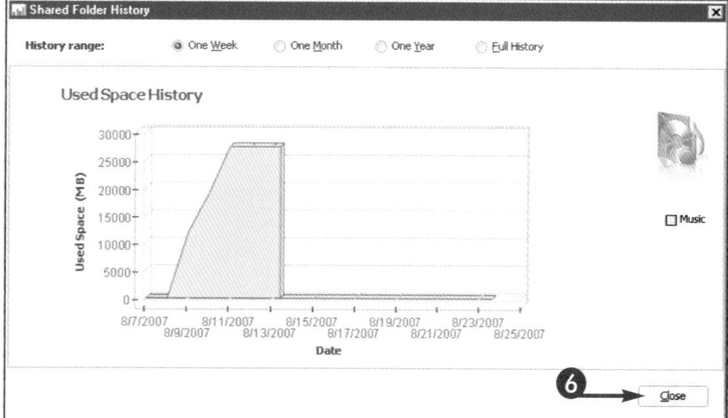


TIP

**Is there a way to see the history of more than one shared folder at a time?**

Unfortunately, Windows Home Server does not allow you to select multiple shared folders, so you cannot run the View History command on two or more folders. However, Windows Home Server does offer a method whereby you can see the history for all of the shared folders:

1. Follow steps **1** and **2** in this section.
2. Right-click an empty section of the Shared Folder tab.
3. Click **View History**.
4. Click the **History range** option you want to use (◯ changes to ◉).
   - The graph shows the changes in the folder's used space over the history range you selected.
5. Click **Close**.

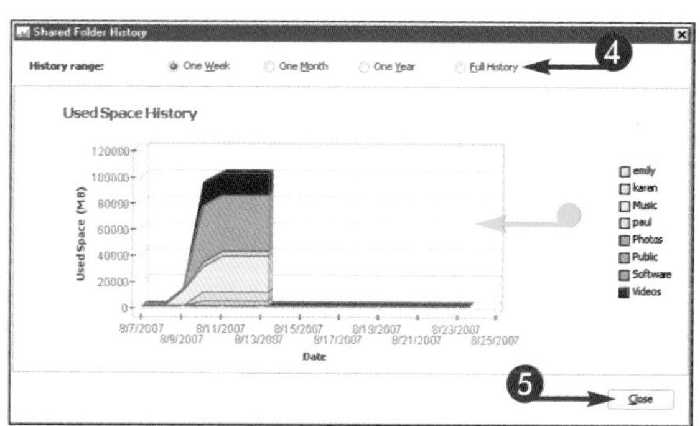

# Create a New Shared Folder

You can customize the collection of shared folders on Windows Home Server by creating your own shared folders. For example, you can create shared folders to store recorded TV shows, Internet downloads, or work-related documents.

**To create a new shared folder in Windows Home Server, you must know the password for the server's Administrator account.**

## Create a New Shared Folder

1. Start the Windows Home Server Console.

*Note: For more information, see Chapter 3.*

2. Click **Shared Folders**.
3. Click **Add**.

The Add a Shared Folder Wizard appears.

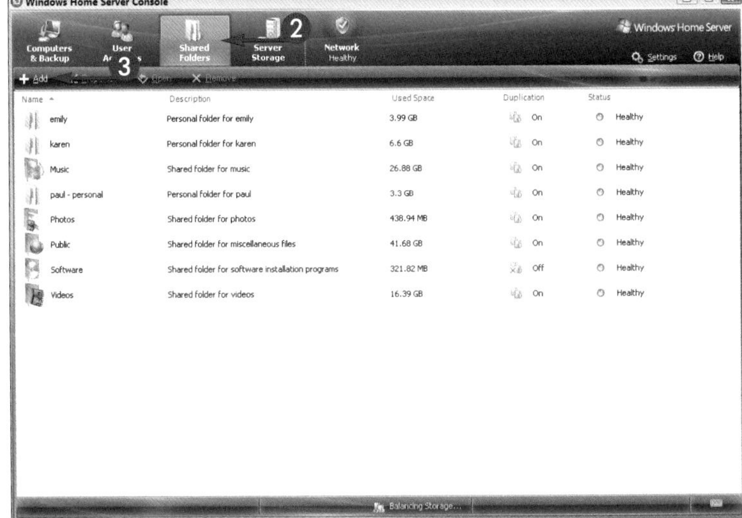


4. In the Name text box, type the name you want to use for the new folder.
5. In the Description text box, type an optional description of the folder.

- If you do not want Windows Home Server to duplicate the folder, click **Enable Folder Duplication** (☑ changes to ☐).

6. Click **Next**.

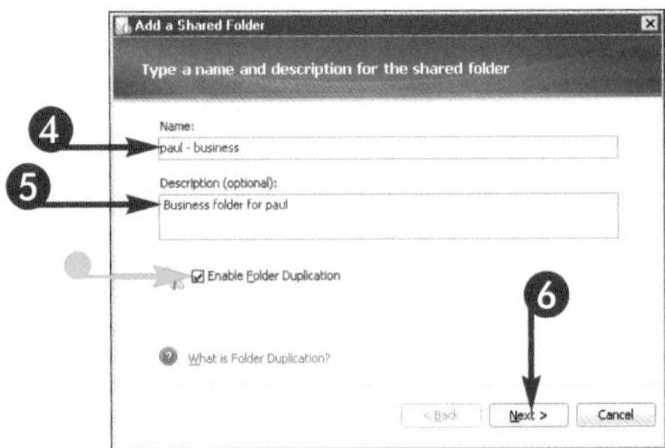

The Choose the level of access dialog box appears.

7. For each user account, click **Full**, **Read**, or **None** (◯ changes to ◉).
8. Click **Finish**.

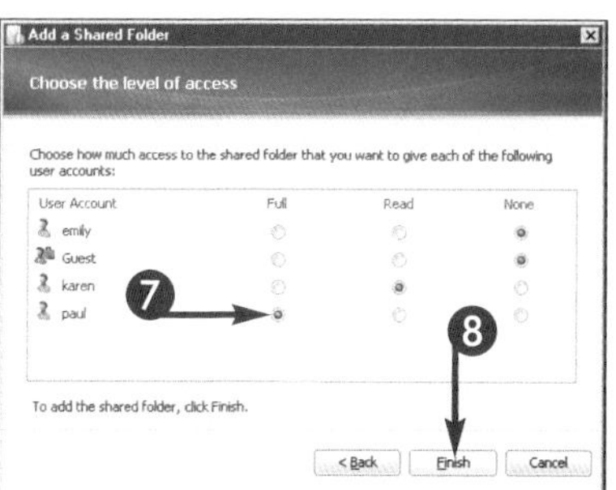

Windows Home Server creates and configures the new shared folder.

9. Click **Done**.

- The new folder appears in the Shared Folders tab.

You can now use the new shared folder to store files.

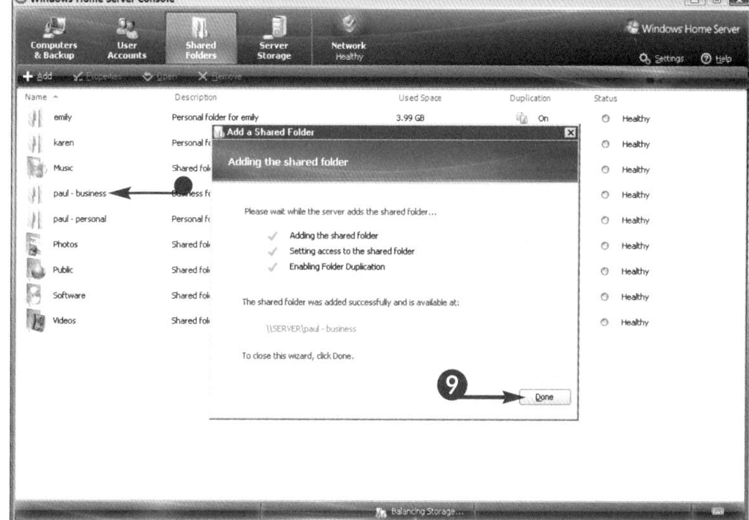

**Are there any restrictions on new shared folder names?**

Yes, the restrictions are the same as when you rename a shared folder. That is, the maximum length of a new shared folder name is 64 characters, and the name of the new folder must contain only letters, numbers, spaces, or any of the following characters: dot (.), dash (-), or underscore (_). In addition, the new shared folder name must end with either a letter or a number.

# Delete a Shared Folder

When you have a Windows Home Server shared folder that you no longer need, you should delete it. This frees up disk space and reduces the clutter in the Console's Shared Folders tab.

**To delete a shared folder in Windows Home Server, you must know the password for the server's Administrator account.**

## Delete a Shared Folder

1. Start the Windows Home Server Console.

*Note:* *For more information, see Chapter 3.*

2. Click **Shared Folders**.

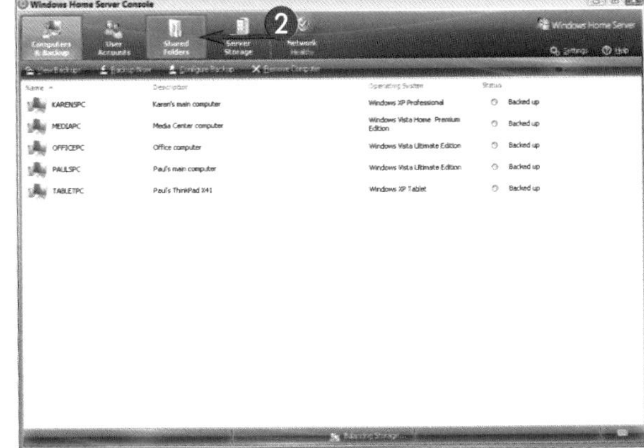

3. Click the shared folder you want to delete.
4. Click **Remove**.

The Remove a Shared Folder Wizard appears.

5 Click **Finish**.

Windows Home Server deletes the folder and its contents.

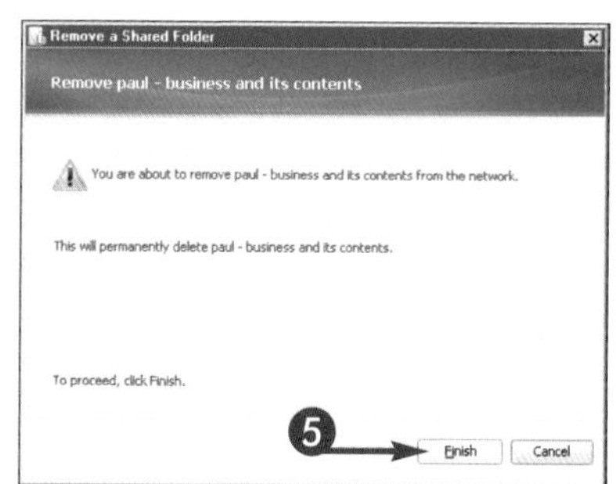

- The folder no longer appears in the Shared Folders tab.

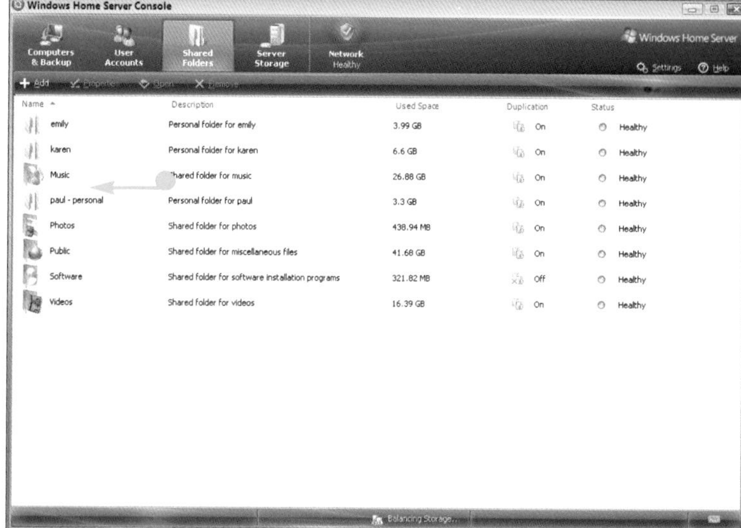

### Why is the Remove button disabled when I click certain shared folders?

Windows Home Server does not allow you to delete any of the following five predefined shared folders: Music, Photos, Public, Software, and Videos. When you click any of these folders, Windows Home Server disables the Remove button. The only shared folders that you are allowed to delete are the folders associated with each user account and any folders that you have created.

### Is there any way to recover a shared folder that I deleted accidentally?

No, this is not possible. When you delete a shared folder through the Windows Home Server Console, the deletion is permanent and irreversible. If the shared folder that you want to delete has one or more files that you would like to preserve, you should first open the shared folder and then copy those files to another location.

# Work with a Shared Folder Offline

You can work with the contents of a Windows Home Server shared folder even when you are not connected to the network. By making the folder available offline, you get copies of the folder's files on your own computer, and you can then work with those files wherever and whenever you want.

**If you make changes to the files while offline, or if the original files change while you are offline, Windows automatically synchronizes the folder contents the next time you connect to the network.**

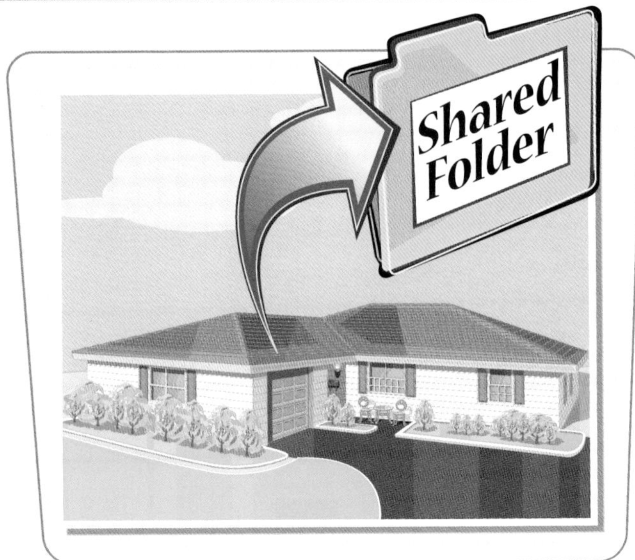


## Work with a Shared Folder Offline

1. Click **Start**.
2. Click **Network**.

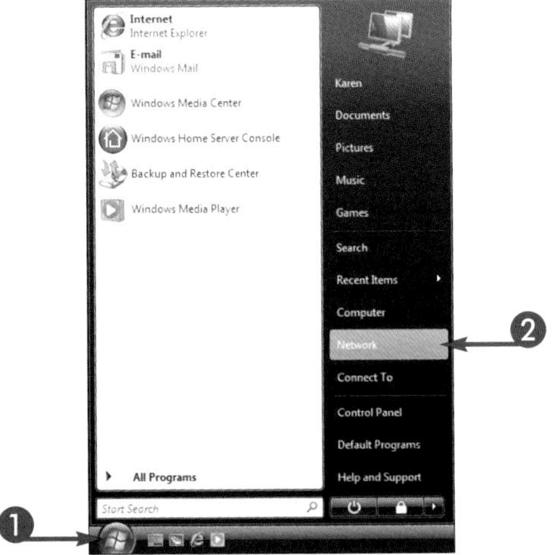

The Network window appears.

3. Double-click the icon for Windows Home Server.

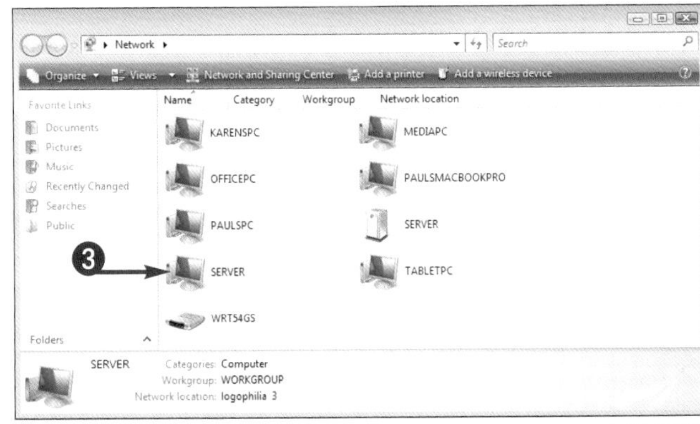

The Windows Home Server shared folders appear.

4. Right-click the folder you want to use offline.

5. Click **Always Available Offline**.

Windows Vista makes local copies of the folder's files.

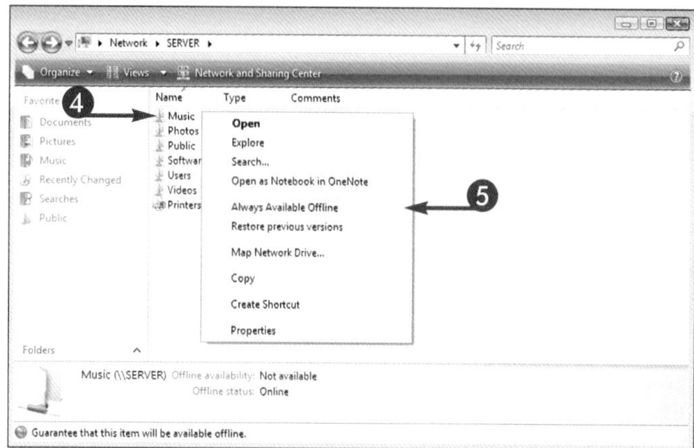

- The Always Available Offline dialog box appears.

6. Click **Close**.

***Note:*** *The Always Available Offline dialog box closes automatically after a few seconds.*

- Windows Vista adds the Sync icon to the folder's regular icon.

You can now use the folder's files even when you are disconnected from the network.

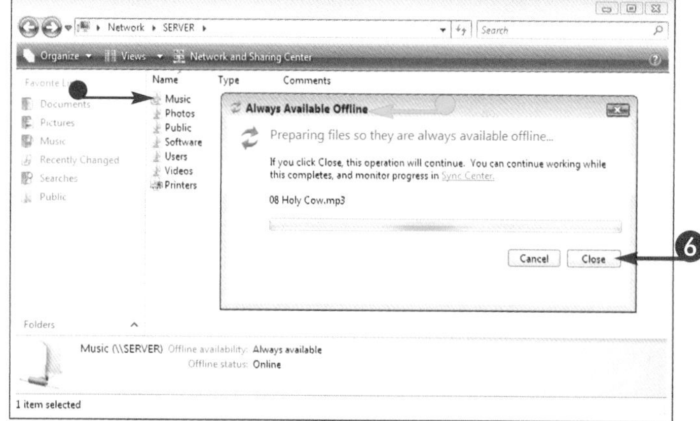

### When I right-click a shared folder, why do I not see the Always Available Offline command?

Always Available Offline
Ultimate ✓
Enterprise ✓
Business ✓
Home N/A
Home Premium N/A


The Always Available Offline feature is not found in all versions of Windows Vista. You only see this command if you are using Windows Vista Ultimate, Windows Vista Business, or Windows Vista Enterprise. If you are using Windows Vista Home or Windows Vista Home Premium, you cannot use network files offline as described in this section.

### If I know that the shared folder's files have changed, is there a way that I can synchronize them before logging off the network?

Yes, you can also synchronize the offline files manually. Follow steps **1** to **3** to display the shared network folder, double-click the folder to open it, and then click the **Sync** button in the taskbar. If you have many offline folders to synchronize, click **Start**, click **Control Panel**, click **Network and Internet**, click **Sync Center**, and then click **Sync All**.

CHAPTER

# Working with Digital Media

You can use Windows Home Server to store media such as music, photos, and videos, and then play or show that media on your home computers. Windows Home Server can also make these media files available to devices such as digital media players and personal digital assistants.

Understanding Digital Media ........................ 152

Understanding Digital Media Streaming .... 154

Turn On Media Sharing ................................ 156

Play Streamed Media in Media Player ........ 158

Play Streamed Media in Media Center ...... 160

Set Up a Photos Slide Show ......................... 162

Display Server Photos in the Vista Sidebar ............................................ 164

Add a Digital Media Folder to Media Player ............................................ 166

Rip Music to Windows Home Server .......... 168

Add a Digital Media Folder to Media Center ............................................ 170

Turn Off Media Sharing ................................ 172

# Understanding Digital Media

Digital media is the electronic version of sounds, images, and video sequences. To get the most out of the media features in Windows Home Server, you need to understand a few concepts associated with digital media.

## Understanding Digital Audio

### Digital Audio

Digital audio is an electronically formatted sequence of sounds, including music, audio CDs, sound effects, recorded sounds, and the narration or soundtrack that accompanies a digital video. You can use a program such as Windows Vista Media Player or Media Center to listen to digital audio files, and you can also incorporate digital audio into presentations, digital video projects, and Web pages.

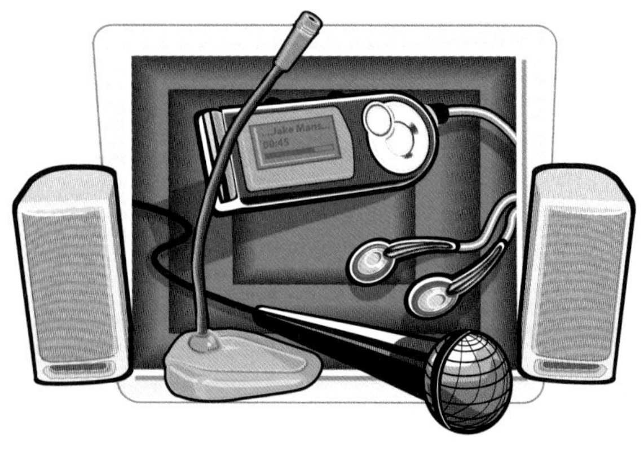

### Digital Music

Most digital audio consists of digital music files. You can obtain digital music files either by copying – also called *ripping* – tracks from an audio CD, or by downloading music files from an online service. Most music files use the MP3 audio file format, but the Windows Media Audio (WMA) format is also popular.

## Understanding Digital Images

### Digital Images

A digital image is an electronically formatted picture, such as a photo, a drawing, a scanned picture, or a piece of clip art. You can use a program such as Windows Vista Photo Gallery to view and enhance images; you can use the Paint program to create images; and you can incorporate images into presentations, reports, e-mail messages, and Web pages.

### Digital Photos

Digital images are often photos taken by a digital camera or a cellphone with a camera feature. When you are ready to work with your photos, you must first connect your digital camera to your computer (or, optionally, insert the camera's memory card into a suitable slot or port on your PC). Most digital cameras connect through a USB cable. You can then use the software that came with the camera to transfer the images to your computer.

## Understanding Digital Video

### Digital Video

A digital video is an electronically formatted series of consecutive pictures. These pictures can include files transferred from a digital video camera, live feeds from a Web cam, DVD movies, and animations. You can use a program such as Windows Vista Media Player or Media Center to view digital video, and you can use Windows Movie Maker to edit videos.

### Digital Video Files

The most common digital video file format is MPEG (Motion Picture Experts Group), which has three main standards: MPEG-1, which produces near-VHS quality; MPEG-2, which produces DVD quality; and MPEG-4, which is an enhanced version of MPEG-2 that produces smaller files. WMV (Windows Media Video) is similar to MPEG-4, but produces even smaller files. AVI (Audio Video Interleave) files are limited to a format of 320 x 240 pixels.

# Understanding Digital Media Streaming

You can configure Windows Home Server to share digital media with other computers and devices on your network. To get the most out of this useful feature, you need to understand some of the concepts behind digital media streaming.

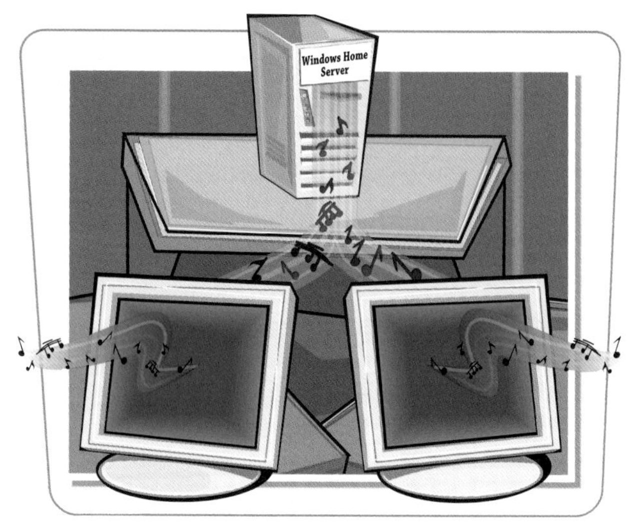


### Streaming Media

*Streaming* media refers to making the digital audio, image, or video files on a computer available to other computers or devices on a network. This enables those computers or devices to play or view the files without having to make copies of them. The files being played or viewed are called the *media stream*.

### Digital Media Receiver

A *digital media receiver* (DMR) is a device that can access a media stream and then play that stream through connected equipment such as speakers, audio receivers, a computer monitor, or a television. All Windows Vista computers can act as DMRs. Devices such as an Xbox 360, a Roku SoundBridge, and a D-Link MediaLounge are also examples of DMRs.

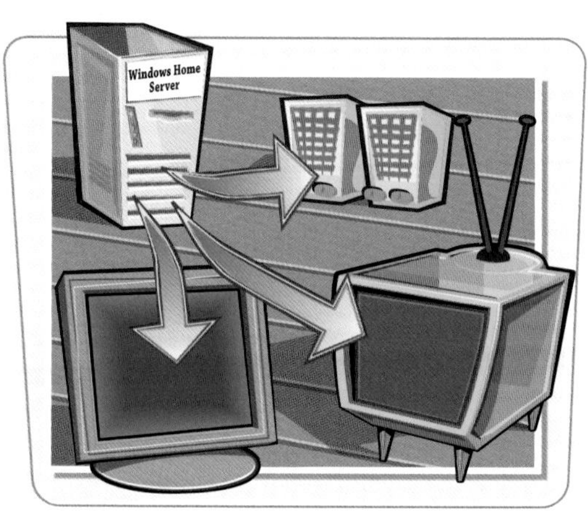

### PlaysForSure

Windows Home Server comes with software called Windows Media Connect 2.0, and this software is what gives Windows Home Server its media-streaming capability. Devices that support Windows Media Connect — and can therefore access and play the Windows Home Server media streams — come with the Microsoft PlaysForSure logo. See www.playsforsure.com for a list of compatible devices.

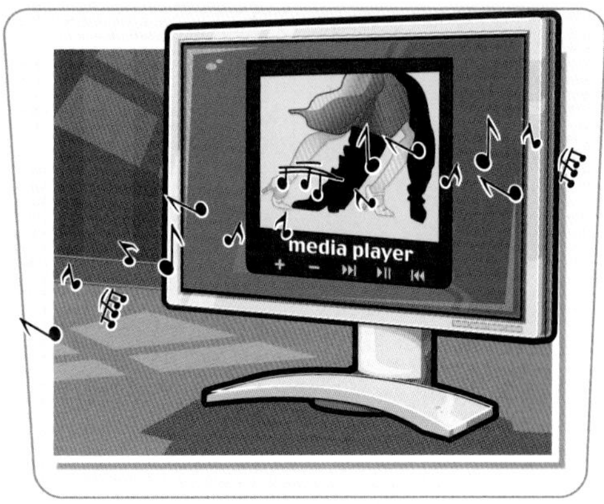


### Other Media Devices

Many devices are able to connect to a network, either with a cable or through a wireless connection, and once connected, these devices can access a media stream. A good example is a digital picture frame, which displays a series of pictures by accessing a digital image stream.

### Digital Media Shared Folders

On Windows Home Server, you store digital music files in the Music shared folder, digital photos in the Photos shared folder, and digital videos in the Videos shared folder. In each case, you can stream the contents of a folder by activating that folder's media-sharing option, as described in the section "Turn On Media Sharing."

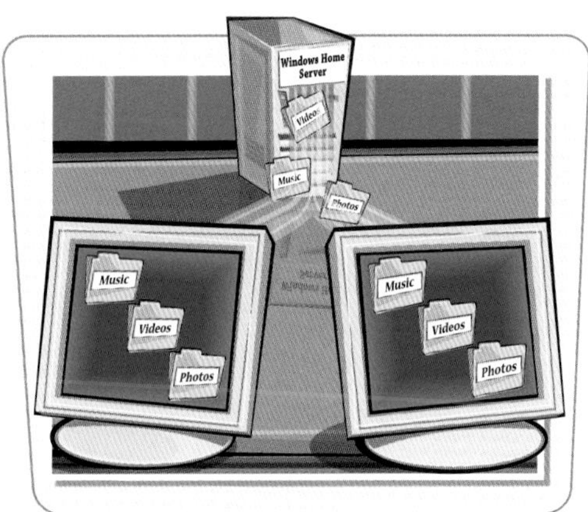

# Turn On Media Sharing

You can stream a digital media folder on Windows Home Server by turning on that folder's media-sharing feature. For example, you can turn on media sharing for the Music, Photos, or Videos folder.

**To turn on media sharing in Windows Home Server, you must know the password for the server's Administrator account.**

## Turn On Media Sharing

1. Start the Windows Home Server Console.

*Note: For more information, see Chapter 3.*

2. Click **Settings**.

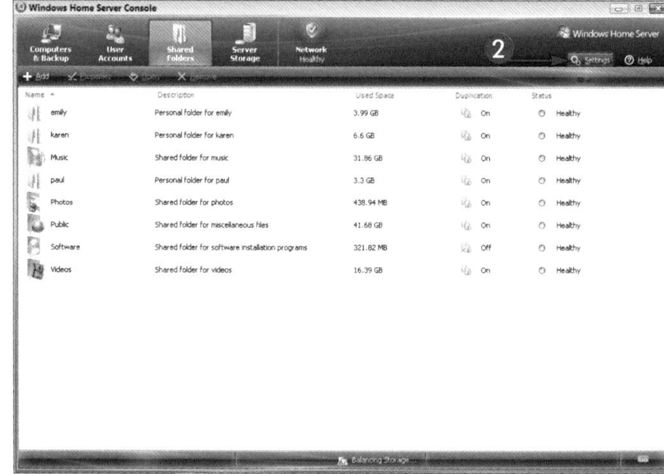

The Windows Home Server Settings dialog box appears.

3. Click the **Media Sharing** tab.

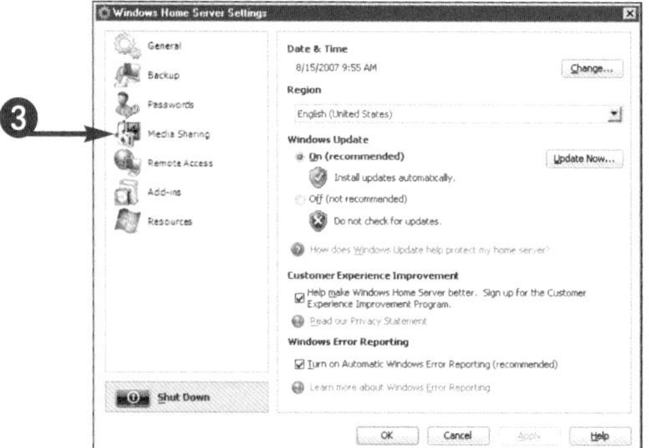

4. For each media folder that you want to stream, click **On** (○ changes to ◉).

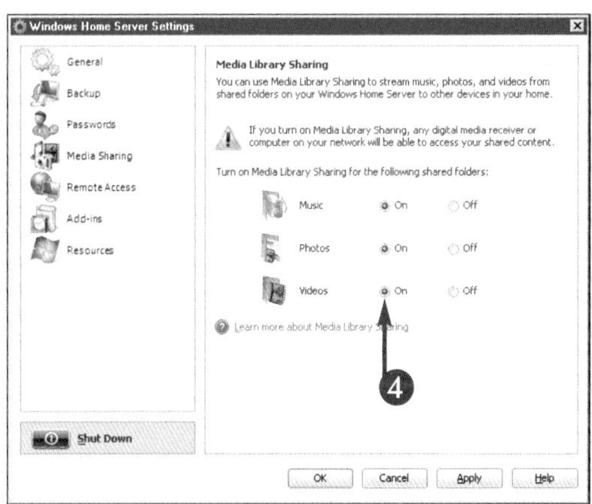


5. Click **OK**.

Windows Home Server immediately starts sharing the digital media on the network.

TIP

**After activating media sharing, I now see a third icon for Windows Home Server in the Network window. Is this normal?**

Yes, it is. After you activate media sharing, Windows Home Server creates a new network icon, usually named SERVER: 1 : Windows Media Connect. This is the network item that sends the media stream. You do not need to work with this icon directly, but its presence tells you that Windows Home Server's media-streaming feature is turned on.

- Windows Home Server's media-streaming icon.

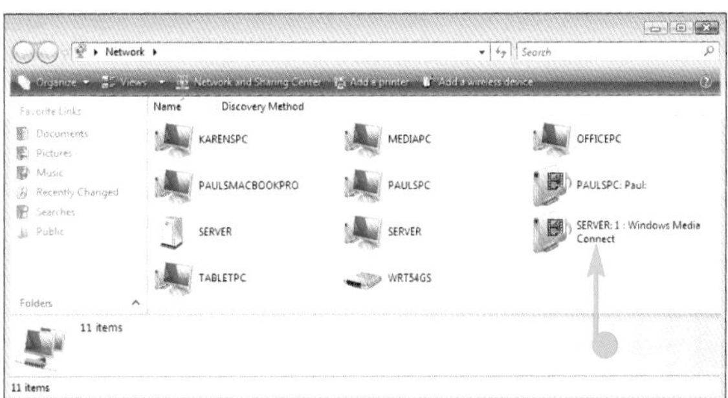

# Play Streamed Media in Media Player

After you turn on the Windows Home Server media-sharing feature for the Music, Photos, or Videos folder, you can play the contents of one of those folders on another computer using Windows Media Player.

**The streamed media from Windows Home Server appears in the Media Player Library tab as User 1 on *server*, where *server* is the name of the Windows Home Server computer.**

## Play Streamed Media in Media Player

1. Click **Start**.
2. Click **All Programs**.
   - In Windows Vista, All Programs changes to Back.
3. Click **Windows Media Player**.

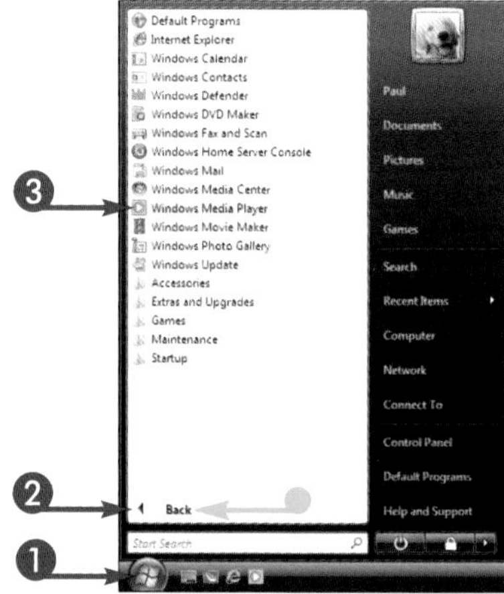

The Windows Media Player window appears.

4. Click the **Library** tab.
5. Click ▶ beside **Select a category** (▶ changes to ▼).
6. Click the media category you want to play.

7. Click **User 1 on *server***, where *server* is the name of your Windows Home Server computer.
8. Double-click the Library view you want to use.

9. Click the item you want to play.
10. Click **Play** (▶).

Windows Media Play begins playing the streamed media.

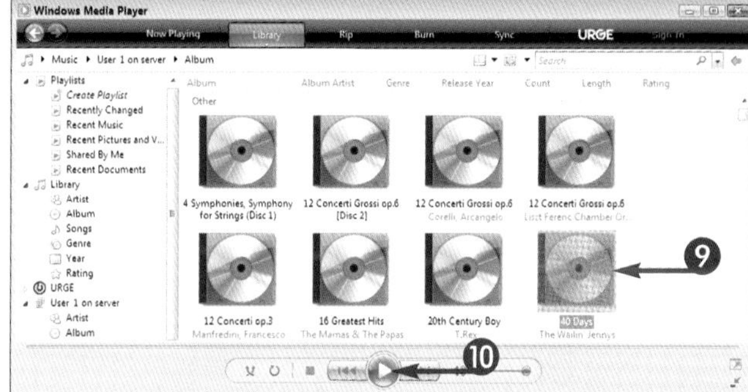

### Why do I not see any of the Windows Home Server shared media in my Media Player Library?

The feature that Windows Media Player uses to find shared media is probably turned off. To turn it back on, follow these steps:

1. Click ▾ just below the Library tab.
2. Click **Media Sharing**.
3. In the Media Sharing dialog box, click **Find media that others are sharing** (☐ changes to ☑).
4. Click **OK**.

Windows Media Player begins looking for shared media.

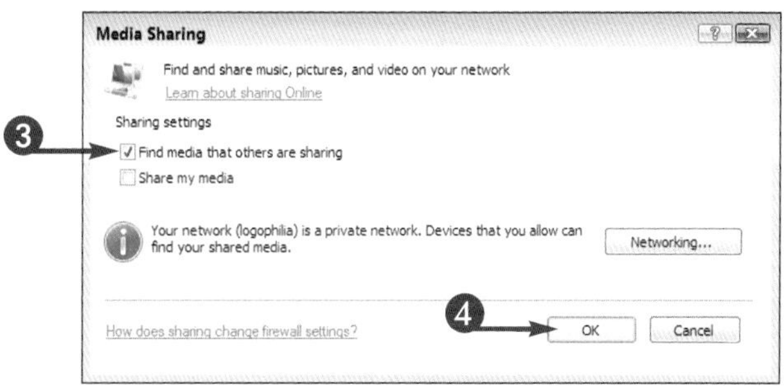

# Play Streamed Media in Media Center

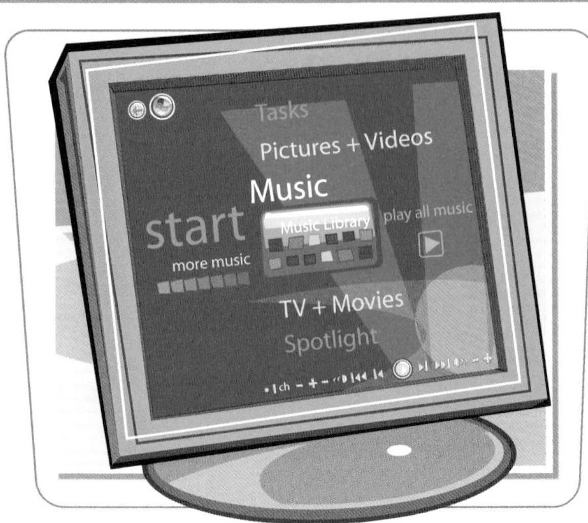


After you turn on the Windows Home Server media-sharing feature for the Music, Photos, or Videos folder, you can play the contents of one of those folders on another computer using Windows Media Center.

**The streamed media from the Windows Home Server Music folder appears in Media Center's Music Library. The streamed media from the Windows Home Server Photos and Videos folders appears in Media Center's Pictures + Videos Library.**

## Play Streamed Media in Media Center

1. Click **Start**.
2. Click **All Programs**.
   - In Windows Vista, All Programs changes to Back.
3. Click **Windows Media Center**.

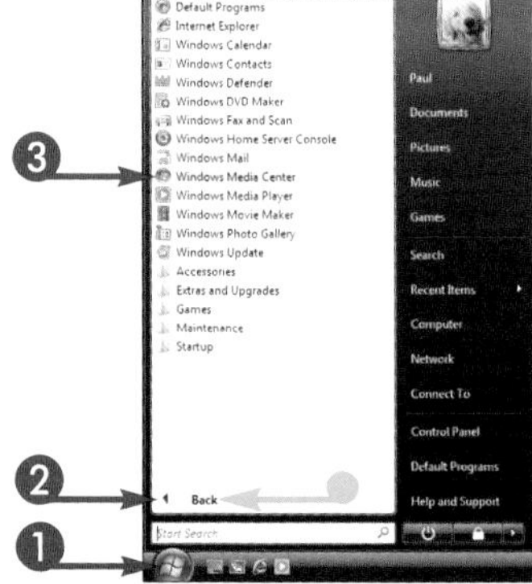

The Windows Media Center window appears.

4. Click the media category you want to work with.
5. Click the category's library icon.

   This example selects the Music Library.

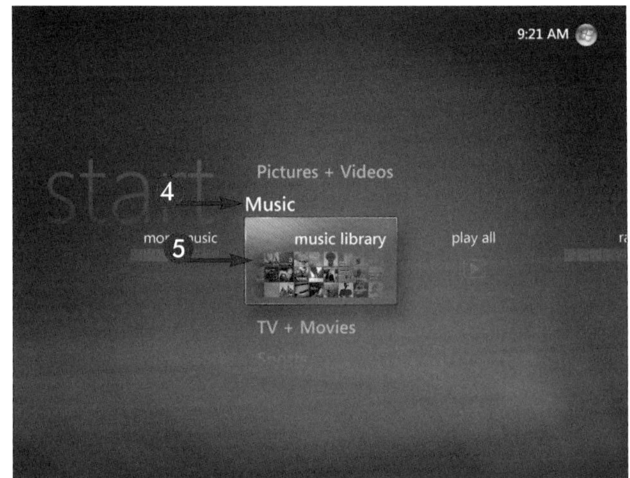

6 Click the Library view you want to use.

7 Click the item you want to play.

***Note:** If you do not see any media from Windows Home Server, you need to add the digital media folders. See the section "Add a Digital Media Folder to Media Center," later in this chapter.*

8 Click [play button].

***Note:** If you do not see the [play button] button, move the mouse to display the controls.*

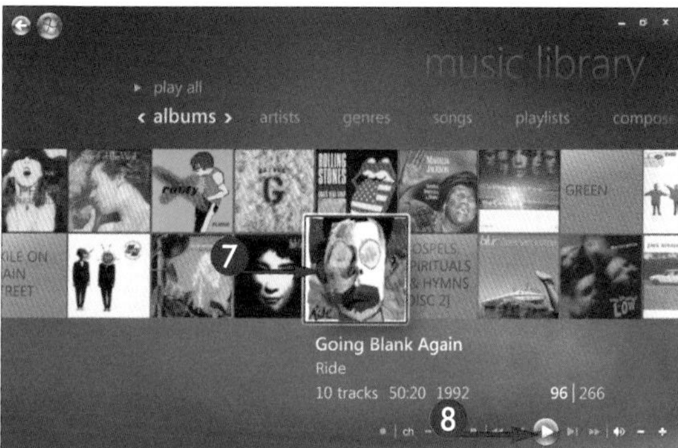


TIP

**How do I play Windows Home Server streamed media on an Xbox 360?**

Follow these steps:

1 Turn on the Xbox 360 and remove any game disc that is in the console.

2 When the Dashboard appears, display the Media blade.

3 Highlight **Music** or **Photos** and press **Select**.

4 Highlight **Computer** and press **Select**.

The Xbox 360 asks if you have installed Windows Media Connect on the computer.

5 Highlight **Yes, Continue** and press **Select**.

The Xbox 360 displays a list of Windows Media Connect computers.

6 Highlight your Windows Home Server and press **Select**.

The Xbox 360 connects to the server and displays a list of media.

7 Use the Xbox 360 interface to play the music or run a slide show.

# Set Up a Photos Slide Show

If you have copied or moved images to the Windows Home Server Photos folder, you can display the images in that folder as a slide show on another computer.

**To activate the Slide Show feature on the Photos shared folder, you need to customize that folder with the Pictures and Videos template.**

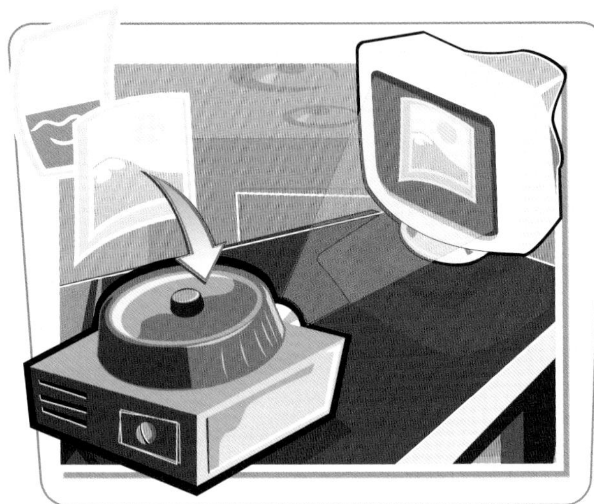

## Set Up a Photos Slide Show

### CUSTOMIZE THE PHOTOS SHARED FOLDER

1. Double-click the **Shared Folders on Server** icon.

*Note:* ***Note:*** *The icon may have a different name if your Windows Home Server computer uses a name other than Server.*

2. Right-click the **Photos** icon.
3. Click **Properties**.

   The Photos (\\SERVER) Properties dialog box appears.

4. Click the **Customize** tab.
5. Click ▾ and then click **Pictures and Videos**.
6. Click **Also apply this template to all subfolders** (☐ changes to ☑).
7. Click **OK**.

   Windows applies the template to the Photos folder.

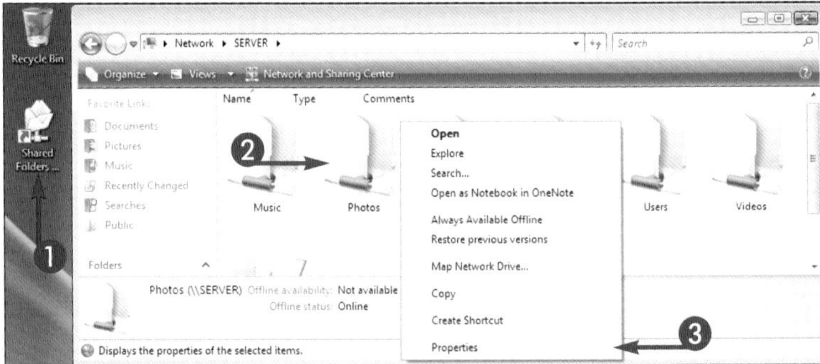


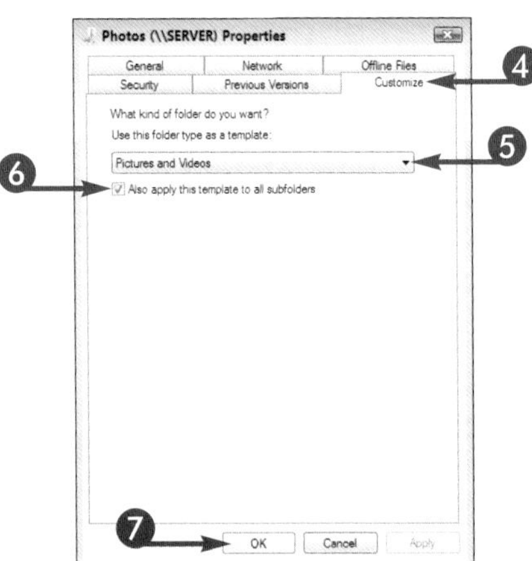

## RUN THE SLIDE SHOW

1. Double-click the **Photos** folder.

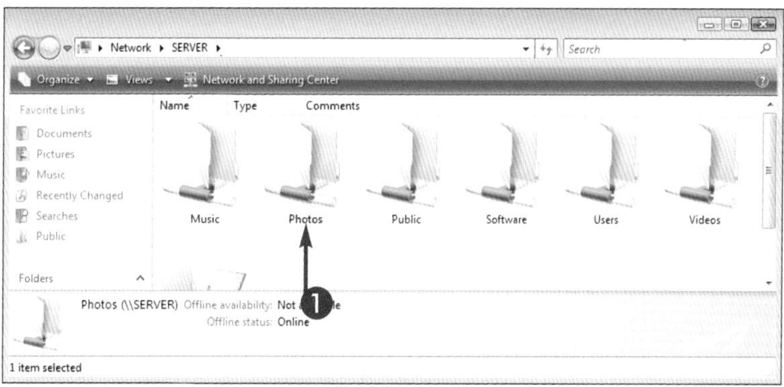

- If the photos you want to use for the slide show reside in a subfolder, double-click that subfolder.

2. Click **Slide Show**.

Windows starts the slide show.

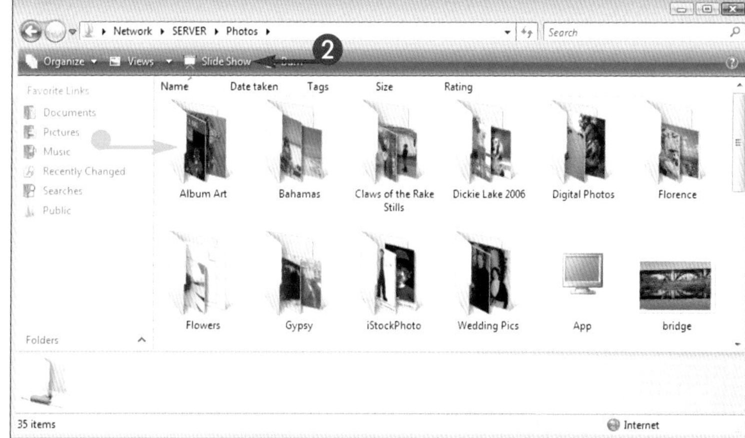

### How do I control the slide show?

When the slide show is in progress, right-click the screen to display the slide show pop-up menu. Click **Pause** to temporarily stop the slide show, and then click **Play** to restart it. Click **Back** to go back to the prior image, and click **Next** to skip to the next image. You can also use the **Slide Show Speed** commands to control the speed of the show. When you are done, click **Exit** or press Esc.

### How do I set up and run a Photos slide show in Windows XP?

Follow the steps to customize the Photos shared folder. In step **5**, click the **Pictures** template. Now, when you open the Photos folder, you see a **Picture Tasks** section in the taskbar. If the photos you want to use for the slide show reside in a subfolder, double-click that subfolder. Click the **View as a slide show** link (●) to start the show.

# Display Server Photos in the Vista Sidebar

You can customize the Windows Sidebar Slide Show gadget to display images from the Windows Home Server Photos folder.

## Display Server Photos in the Vista Sidebar

1. In the Sidebar, right-click the Slide Show gadget.

*Note:* *If you do not see the Sidebar, click* ***Start****, click* ***All Programs****, click* ***Accessories****, and then click* ***Windows Sidebar****.*

*Note:* *If you do not see the Slide Show gadget, right-click an empty section of the Sidebar, click* ***Add Gadgets****, click the* ***Slide Show*** *gadget, and then click* ***Close*** *(X).*

2. Click **Options**.

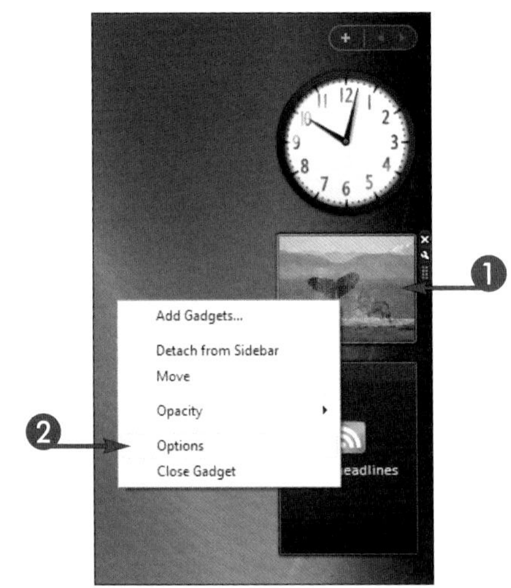


The Slide Show dialog box appears.

3. Click **Browse** (...).

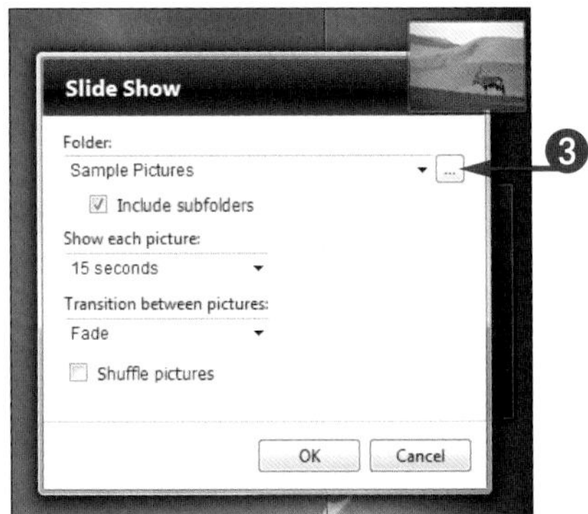

The Browse For Folder dialog box appears.

4 Click **Network**.

5 Click the icon that represents your Windows Home Server.

***Note:*** *The default name for Windows Home Server is SERVER.*

6 Click **Photos**.

7 Click **OK**.

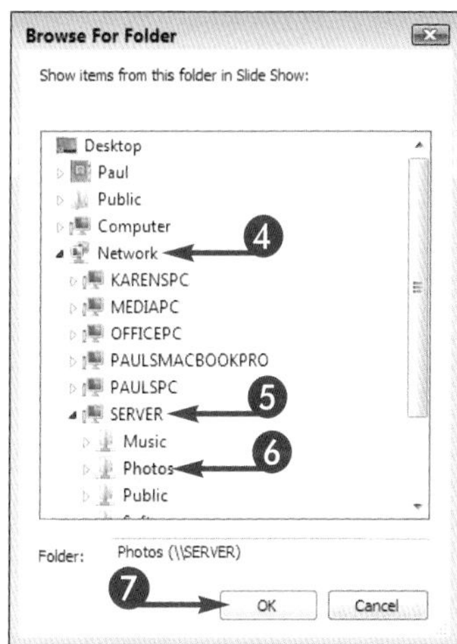


- The address of the Windows Home Server Photos folder appears in the Folder text box.

8 Click **Include subfolders** (☐ changes to ☑) if you want images in the subfolders of the Photos folder to be included in the slide show.

9 Click **OK**.

Windows Vista displays images from the Windows Home Server Photos folder in the Slide Show gadget.

### Can I customize how the Slide Show gadget displays the photos?

Yes, there are several options you can configure:

1 Follow steps **1** and **2** to open the Slide Show dialog box.

2 In the **Show each picture** drop-down list, click ▾ and then click the length of time you want each photo to appear.

3 In the **Transition between pictures** drop-down list, click ▾ and then click the effect you want the gadget to use between photos.

4 To see the photos in random order, click **Shuffle pictures** (☐ changes to ☑).

5 Click **OK**.

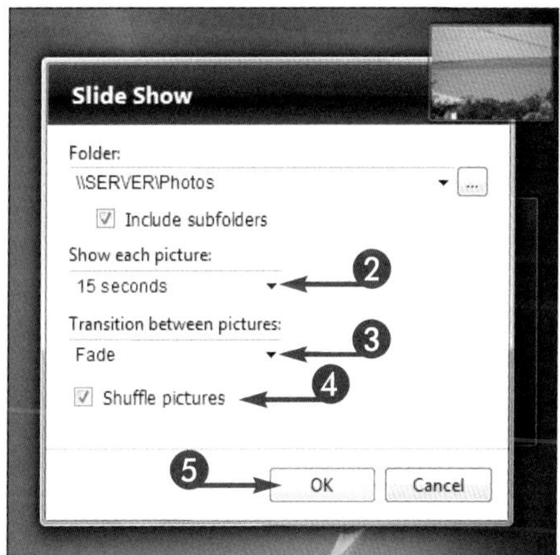

# Add a Digital Media Folder to Media Player

You can add a Windows Home Server digital media folder to the Media Player Library on your computer. This combines the Windows Home Server media with the media on your computer, which enables you to sort, shuffle, and perform other tasks on all the media at the same time.

**The Windows Home Server media files are not copied or moved to your computer. Instead, Windows Media Player simply displays the server media along with your local media.**

## Add a Digital Media Folder to Media Player

1. In Windows Media Player, click the **Library** tab.
2. Click [▶] beside the **Select a category** button ([▶] changes to [▼]).
3. Click the media category you want to work with.

4. Click [▼] under the Library tab.
5. Click **Add to Library**.

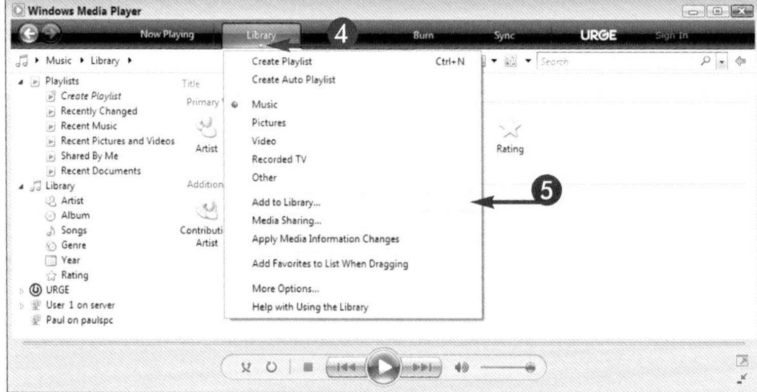

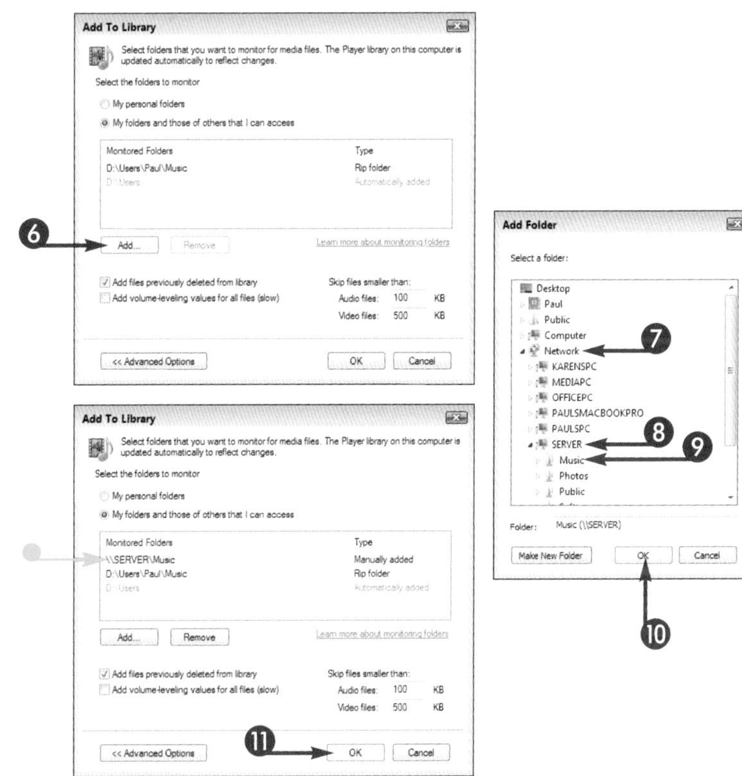

The Add To Library dialog box appears.

6 Click **Add**.

***Note:*** *If you do not see the Add button, click* ***Advanced Options****.*

The Add Folder dialog box appears.

7 Click **Network**.

8 Click the icon that represents your Windows Home Server.

***Note:*** *The default name for Windows Home Server is SERVER.*

9 Click the media folder you want to add.

This example selects the **Music** folder.

10 Click **OK**.

- The server folder appears in the list of monitored folders.

11 Click **OK**.

Windows Media Player adds the files in the folder to the Library.

### How do I remove a Windows Home Server folder from my Media Player Library?

Here are the steps to follow:

1 Follow steps **1** to **5**.

The Add To Library dialog box appears.

2 In the Monitored Folders list, click the Windows Home Server folder you want to remove from the Library.

3 Click **Remove**.

Windows Media Player removes the folder from the Monitored Folders list.

4 Click **OK**.

Windows Media Player removes the server media from the Library.

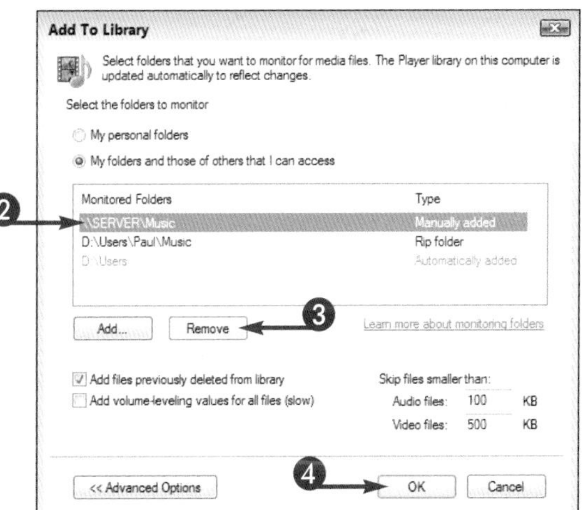

# Rip Music to Windows Home Server

You can configure Windows Media Player to use the Windows Home Server Music folder as the default location for copying, or *ripping*, tracks from an audio CD.

**Ripping music directly to the Windows Home Server Music folder saves time. Otherwise, you have to rip the music to your computer and then copy the music to Windows Home Server.**

## Rip Music to Windows Home Server

1. Click the drop-down arrow under the **Rip** tab.
2. Click **More Options**.

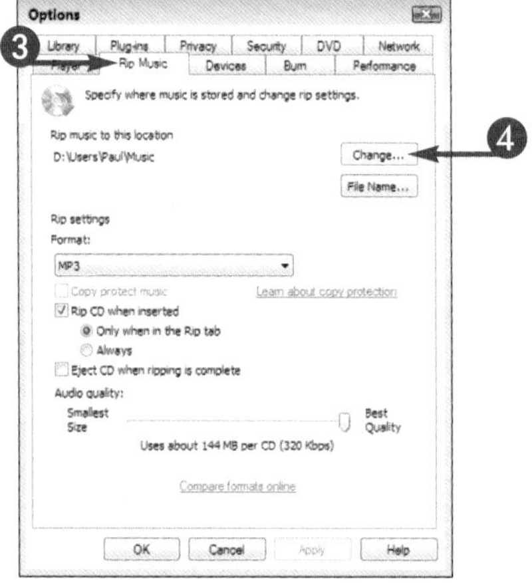

The Options dialog box appears.

3. Click the **Rip Music** tab.
4. Click **Change**.

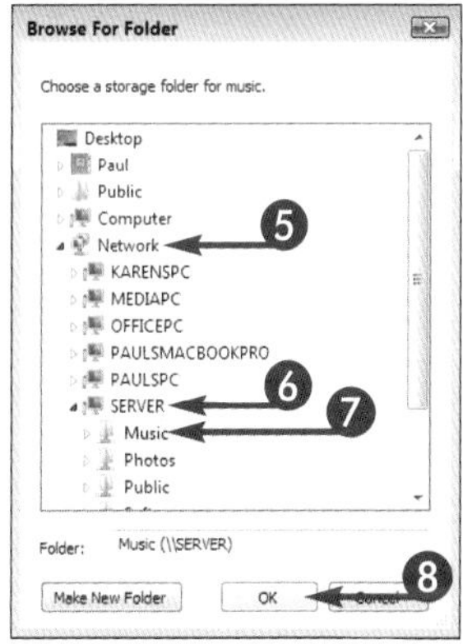


The Browse For Folder dialog box appears.

5 Click **Network**.

6 Click the icon that represents your Windows Home Server.

***Note:*** *The default name for Windows Home Server is SERVER.*

7 Click **Music**.

8 Click **OK**.

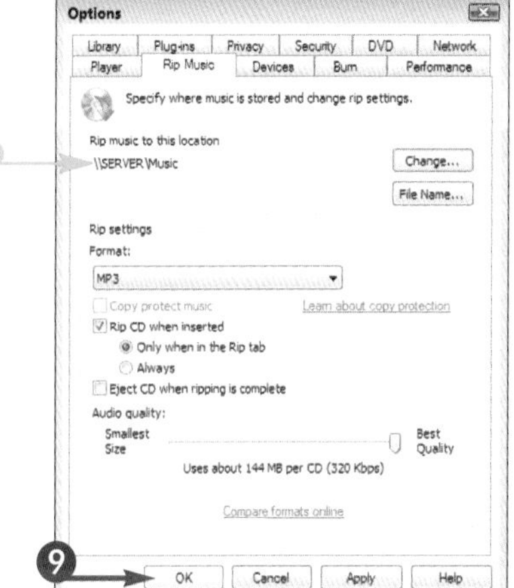


- The address of the Windows Home Server Music folder appears here.

9 Click **OK**.

Each time you rip an audio CD, Windows Media Player copies the tracks to the Windows Home Server Music folder.

### How do I perform the rip?

Insert an audio CD into your computer's CD or DVD drive. In Windows Media Player, click the **Rip** tab and then, if you have multiple disc drives, click the drive containing the music CD. Deselect the CD tracks that you do not want to copy (☑ changes to ☐) and then click **Start Rip**. Windows Media Player begins copying the track or tracks to Windows Home Server.

### Can I adjust the quality of the copies?

Yes. You do that by changing the *bit rate*, which is a measure of how much of the CD's original data is copied to your computer. The bit rate is measured in kilobits per second (Kbps): the higher the value, the higher the quality, but the more disk space each track takes up. Click ▾ under the Rip tab, click **Bit Rate**, and then click the value you want.

# Add a Digital Media Folder to Media Center

You can add a Windows Home Server digital media folder to the Windows Media Center program on your computer. This combines the Windows Home Server media with the local media managed by Windows Media Center, thus enabling you to sort, shuffle, and perform other tasks on all of the media at the same time.

**The Windows Home Server media files are not copied or moved to your computer. Instead, Windows Media Center simply displays the server media along with your local media.**

## Add a Digital Media Folder to Media Center

1. In Windows Media Center, click **Tasks**.
2. Click **settings**.

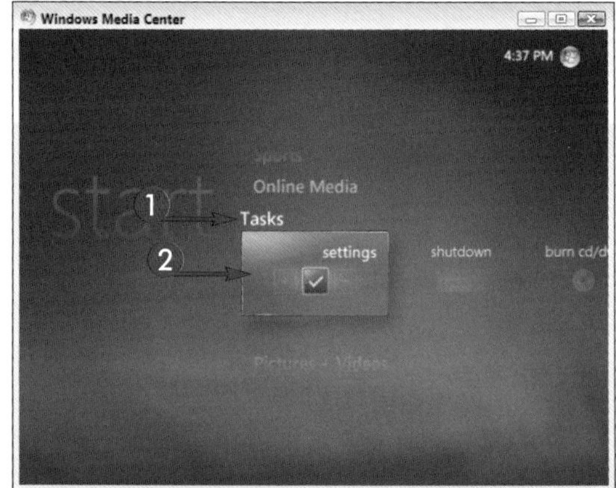


The Settings window appears.

3. Click **Library Setup**.

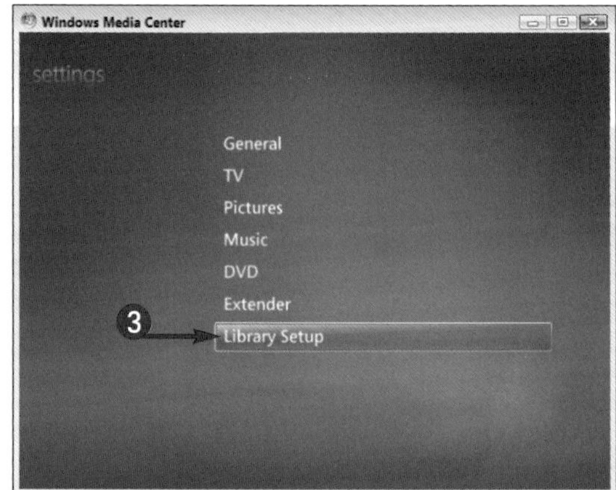

The Library Setup window appears.

4. Click **Add folder to watch** (◯ changes to ◉).
5. Click **Next**.

   The Add folders window appears.

6. Click **Add shared folders from another computer** (◯ changes to ◉).
7. Click **Next**.
8. Click **Scroll Down** (▼) and **Scroll Up** (▲) until you see the media folder you want to add.
9. Click the media folder you want (☐ changes to ☑).
10. Click **Next**.
11. Click **Finish**.

    Windows Media Center adds the folder to its library.

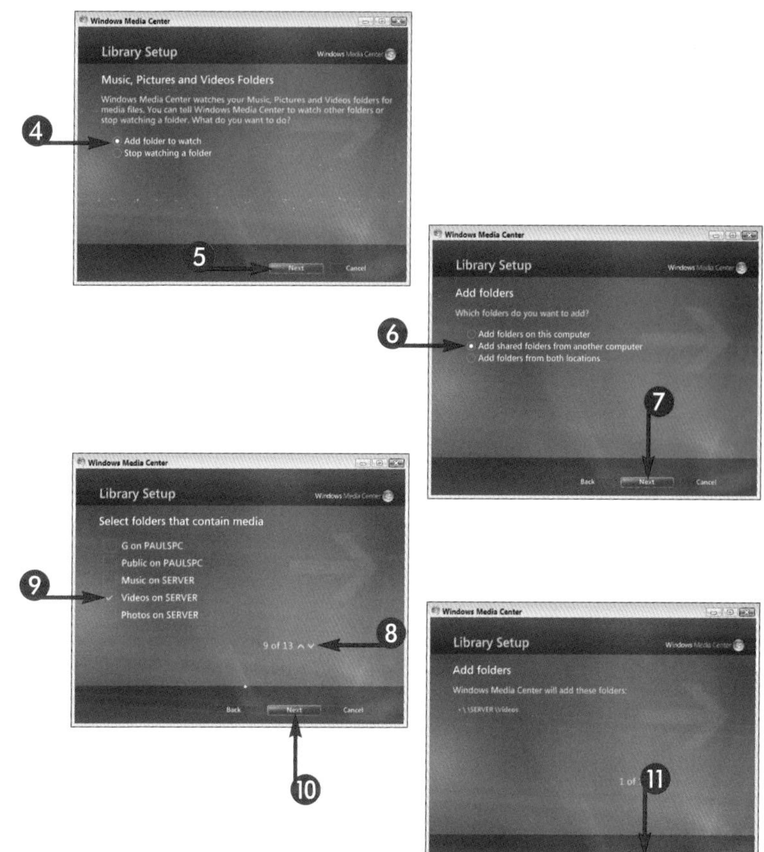

## How do I remove a digital media folder from Windows Media Center?

Follow these steps:

1. Follow steps **1** to **3** to open the Library Setup window.
2. Click **Stop watching a folder** (◯ changes to ◉).
3. Click **Next**.
4. Click the folder you want to remove (☑ changes to ☐).
5. Click **Next**.
6. Click **Finish**, and Windows Media Center removes the folder.

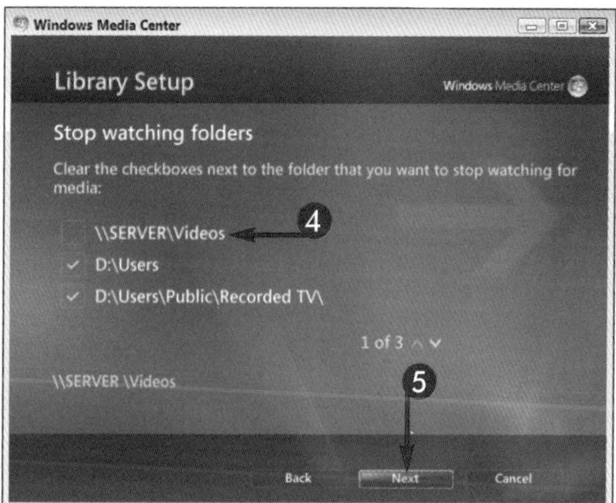

# Turn Off Media Sharing

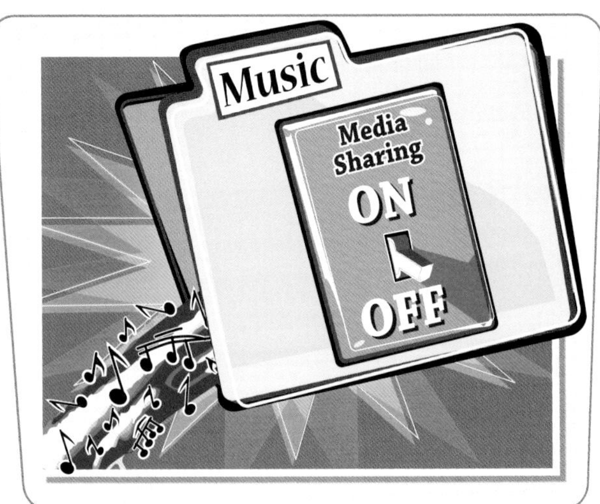


If you no longer want to stream one of the Windows Home Server digital media folders, you can turn off media sharing for that folder.

**To turn off media sharing in Windows Home Server, you must know the password for the server's Administrator account.**

## Turn Off Media Sharing

1. Start the Windows Home Server Console.

*Note: For more information, see Chapter 3.*

2. Click **Settings**.

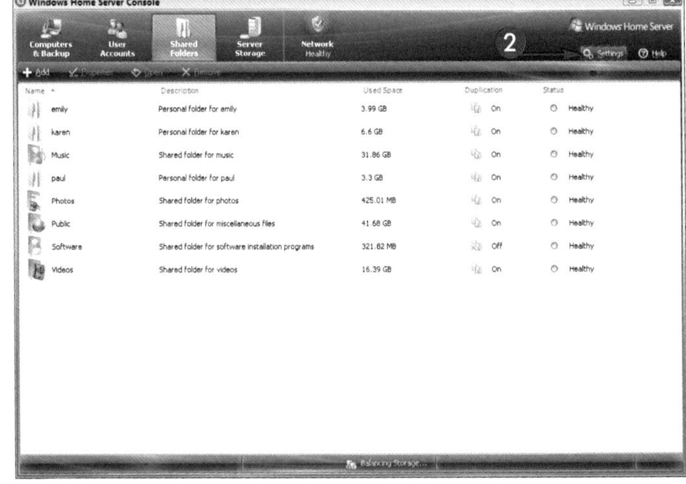

The Windows Home Server Settings dialog box appears.

3. Click the **Media Sharing** tab.

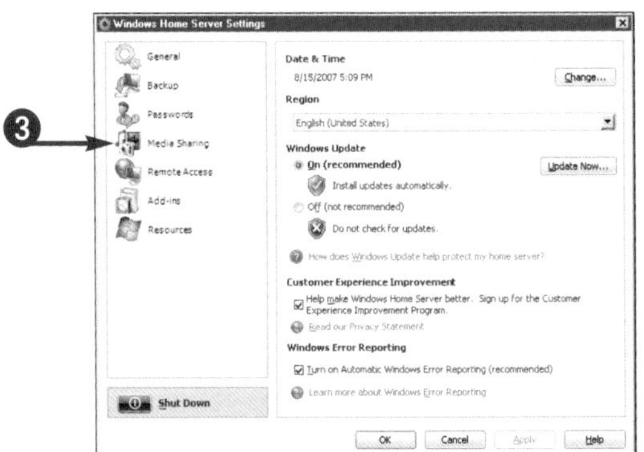

4 For each media folder that you want to turn off, click the **Off** option (◉ changes to ○).

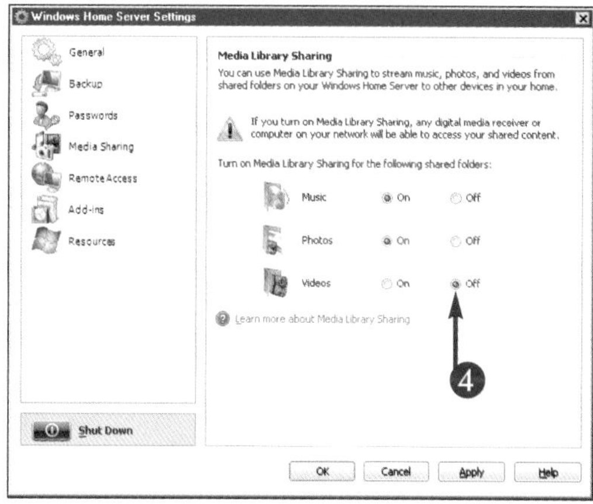

5 Click **OK**.

Windows Home Server immediately stops sharing the digital media on the network.

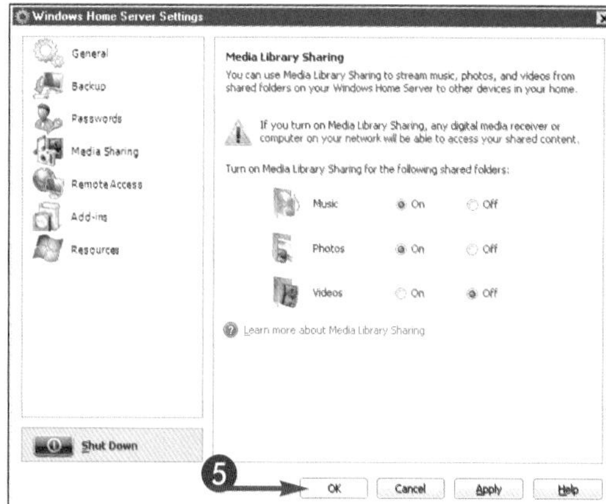


TIP

**I turned off media sharing for one of the Windows Home Server digital media folders, but that folder still shows up in Windows Media Player. Why?**

Windows Media Player does not check for changed content on the streamed media folders very often, so it may take a while before it notices that the Windows Home Server digital media folder is no longer shared. To speed up the process, exit and then restart Windows Media Player.

CHAPTER

# Backing Up Your Computers

When you connect a computer to Windows Home Server, the computer is automatically added to the list of computers that Windows Home Server backs up each night. In this chapter you learn how to configure backup options, control which drives and folders are backed up, and run a backup manually.

Understanding the Windows Home Server Backup Technology ....................176

Configure the Backup Time....................178

Configure Automatic Backup Management....................180

Add a Disk Drive to a Computer's Backup....................182

Exclude a Folder from a Computer's Backup....................184

Back Up a Computer Manually ....................188

Stop Backing Up a Computer....................190

# Understanding the Windows Home Server Backup Technology

Windows Home Server introduces a number of new technological advances that make computer backups easy, flexible, and very efficient. To get the most out of Windows Home Server backups, you need to understand a few key concepts.

### Automatic Backups

When you run the Windows Home Server Connector software on a computer, Windows Home Server adds the computer to its backup list. This means that the entire computer is backed up automatically every night at around midnight. For more information about the Windows Home Server Connector, see Chapter 3.

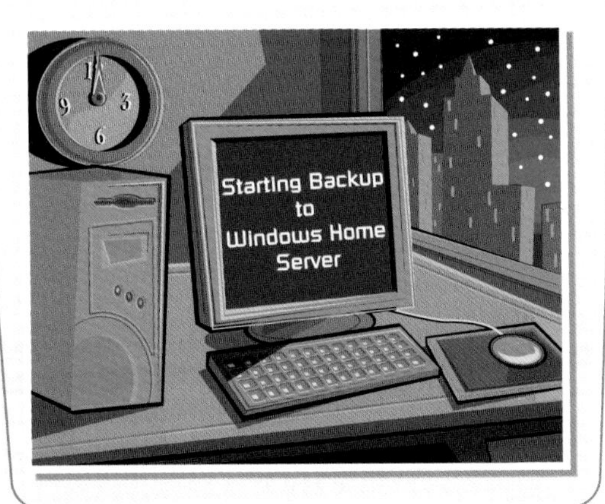


### Simplified Backups

Most backup programs offer complex backup options such as differential backups, incremental backups, and daily backups. Windows Home Server simplifies the process of backing up by doing away with these distinctions. As a result, every Windows Home Server backup is a full backup of the computer.

## Efficient Backups

Windows Home Server backups take up less room than most backups because they do not back up the same file twice. For example, if two computers have the same music file, Windows Home Server only backs up the file once for both computers. Windows Home Server also avoids backing up useless files such as temporary files used by Windows and the contents of the Recycle Bin.

## Backup Process

Windows Home Server begins the backup process at midnight, but it only backs up one computer at a time. It begins with one computer and puts the other computers in a queue. When one computer's backup is complete, Windows Home Server moves on to the next computer. If that computer happens to be in sleep mode, the computer wakes itself up for the backup, and then returns to sleep mode.

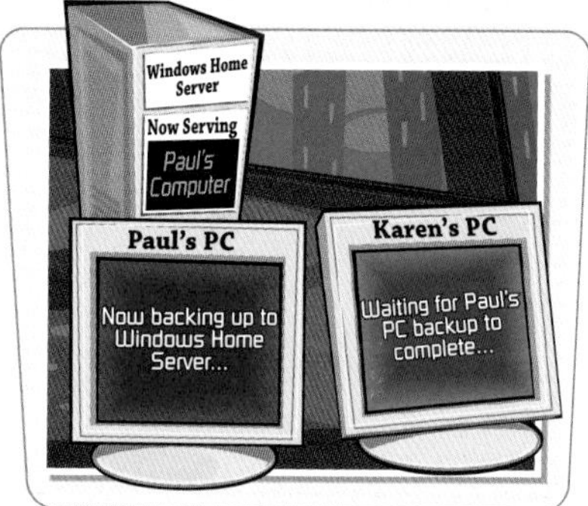


## Manual Backups

If you have added or created important files on your computer, you might not want to wait until midnight for that data to be backed up. In that case, you can initiate a manual backup to preserve the data on Windows Home Server right away. For more information, see the section "Back Up a Computer Manually."

## Backup Management

With backups occurring daily, you could quickly run out of disk space on Windows Home Server. To avoid this, Windows Home Server automatically deletes old backups once a week. To learn more about this feature and to customize it to suit your needs, see the section "Configure Automatic Backup Management."

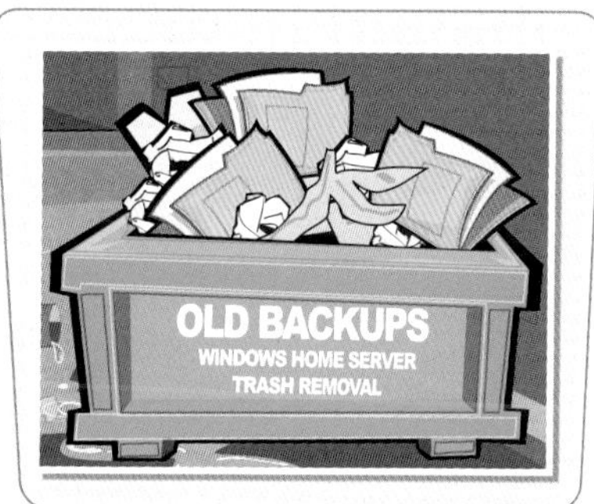

# Configure the Backup Time

You can customize the Windows Home Server backup start time to one that is more suitable for you. Windows Home Server also stops all pending backups at 6:00 AM, and you can configure that time, as well.

**To configure the backup time in Windows Home Server, you must know the password for the server's Administrator account.**

## Configure the Backup Time

1. Start the Windows Home Server Console.

*Note: For more information, see Chapter 3.*

2. Click **Settings**.

The Windows Home Server Settings dialog box appears.

3. Click the **Backup** tab.

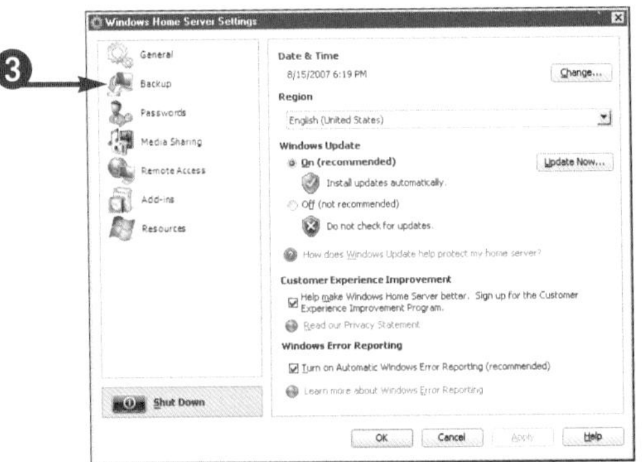

4. In the Start time text box, type the time you want Windows Home Server to begin backing up the computers.

5. In the End time text box, type the time you want Windows Home Server to stop backing up the computers.

***Note:** If Windows Home Server is currently backing up a computer when the end time occurs, it finishes backing up that computer.*

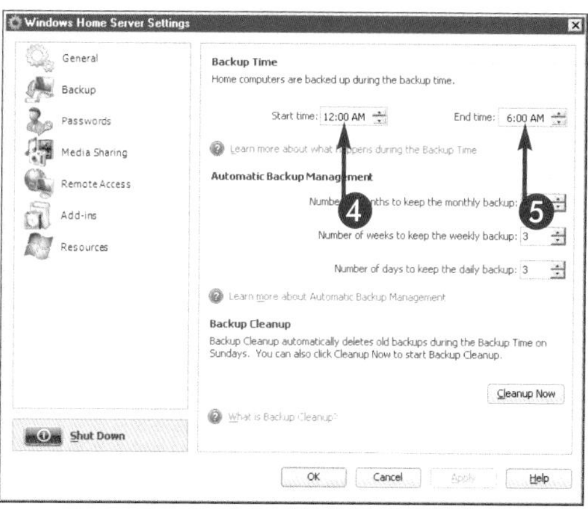

6. Click **OK**.

Windows Home Server activates the new backup times.

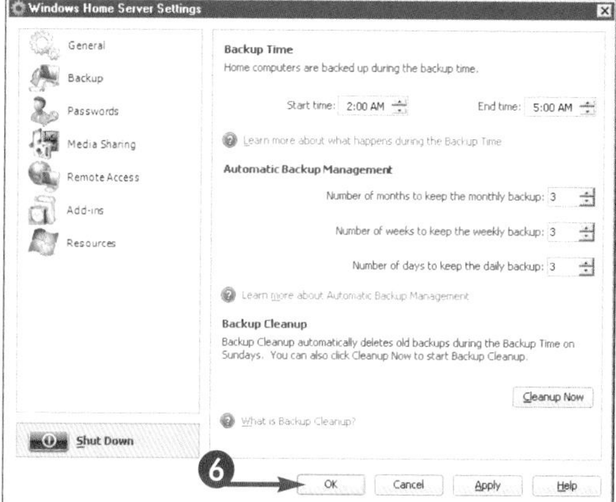


## TIPS

### Can I choose any time for the backup to start and end?

Yes, with one exception. You have to make sure that the value you specify for the end time is at least one hour later or at least one hour earlier than the value for the start time. For example, if you leave the start time at 12:00 AM, the end time cannot be earlier than 1:00 AM or later than 11:00 PM.

Backup Time

### Does Windows Home Server perform any other chores during the backup time?

Yes. Besides backing up the computers, Windows Home Server also uses the backup time to check for and install system updates. This is assuming you have automatic updates turned on. For more information, see Chapter 5. Windows Home Server also uses the backup time to remove old backups from the system.

Backup Time Chores
✓ Back Up Computers
✓ Install Updates
✓ Delete Old Backups

# Configure Automatic Backup Management

You can control the number of old backups kept by Windows Home Server. You can increase the number of kept backups to improve file safety, or you can decrease the number of kept backups to save disk space.

**To configure automatic backup management in Windows Home Server, you must know the password for the server's Administrator account.**

## Configure Automatic Backup Management

1. Start the Windows Home Server Console.

*Note: For more information, see Chapter 3.*

2. Click **Settings**.

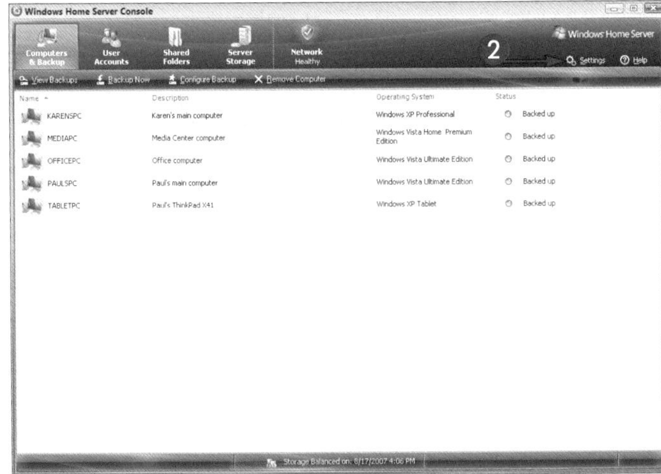


The Windows Home Server Settings dialog box appears.

3. Click the **Backup** tab.

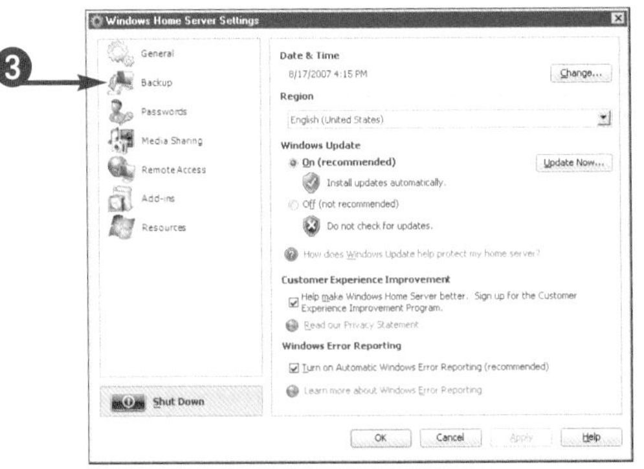

4 In this text box, type the number of months that Windows Home Server should keep the first backup of each month.

5 In this text box, type the number of weeks that Windows Home Server should keep the first backup of each week.

6 In this text box, type the number of days that Windows Home Server should keep the first backup of each day.

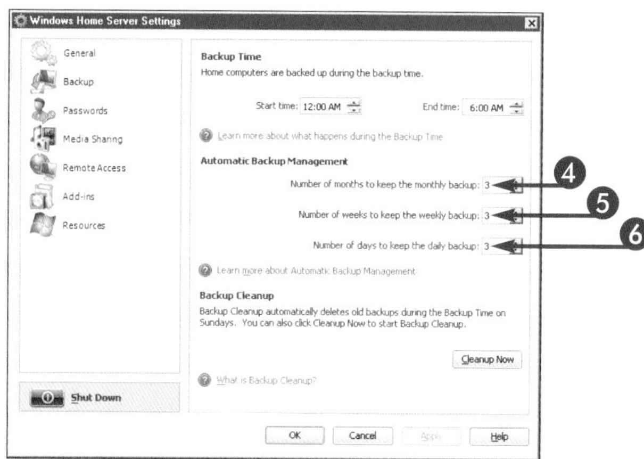

7 Click **OK**.

Windows Home Server activates the new automatic backup management settings.

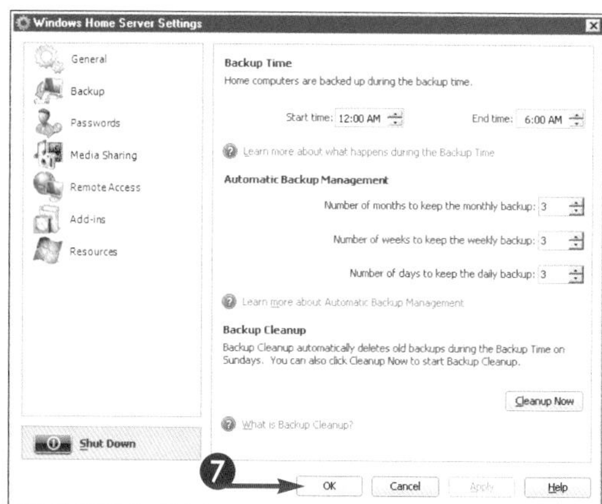

TIPS

### Why does Windows Home Server keep old backups if every backup is a complete backup of my computer?

Old backups help you recover data that no longer exists in newer backups or that has changed in newer backups. For example, if you delete a file on Monday and then decide you want to restore that file on Wednesday, you would be unable to retrieve the file if you only had Tuesday's backup, which does not include the file. By keeping old backups, you can restore the file using Monday's backup, which does include the file.

### If I use the maximum values for each setting, would that give me maximum file protection?

Yes, it probably would. However, keeping so many backups would use up a great deal of disk space on Windows Home Server. If the backups use too much disk space, this would actually *reduce* file protection because Windows Home Server would be forced to turn off folder duplication.

# Add a Disk Drive to a Computer's Backup

If you have attached a new hard drive to a computer, you can protect that drive by configuring Windows Home Server to include the new drive in the computer's backups.

**To add a disk drive to a computer's backup in Windows Home Server, you must know the password for the server's Administrator account.**

## Add a Disk Drive to a Computer's Backup

1. Start the Windows Home Server Console.

***Note:*** *For more information, see Chapter 3.*

2. Click **Computers & Backup**.
3. Click the computer you want to work with.
4. Click **Configure Backup.**

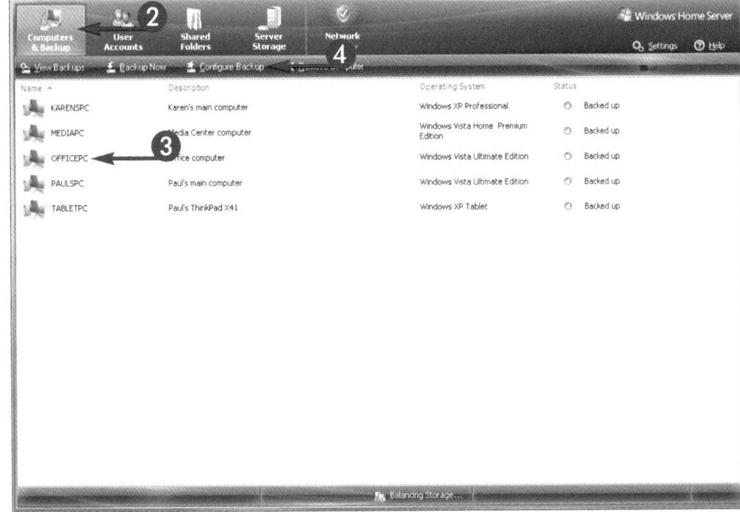


The Backup Configuration Wizard appears.

5. Click **Next**.

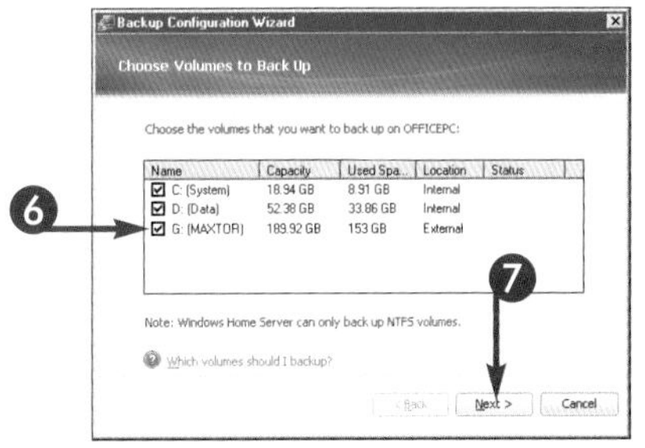

The wizard displays the Choose Volumes to Back Up dialog box, which includes a list of hard drives attached to the computer.

6. Click the hard drive you want to add to the backup (☐ changes to ☑).
7. Click **Next**.

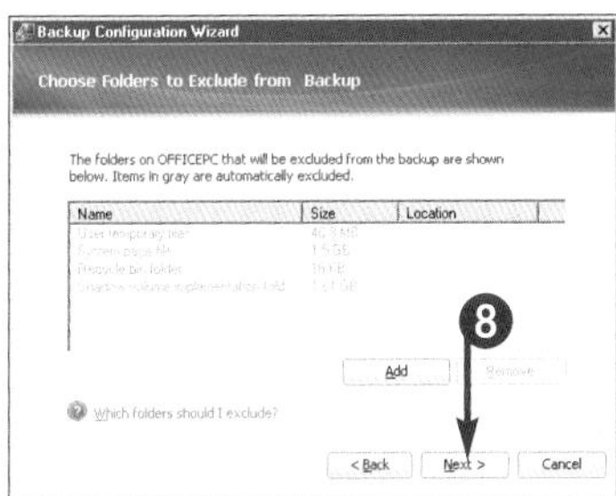

The Choose Folders to Exclude from Backup dialog box appears.

8. Click **Next**.

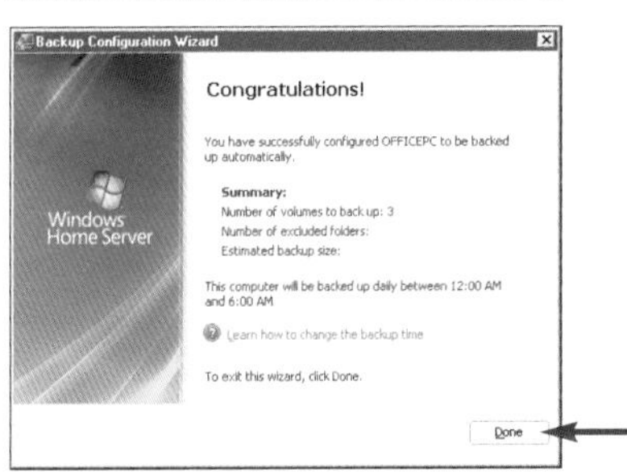

The final wizard dialog box displays a summary of your changes.

9. Click **Done**.

Windows Home Server includes the hard drive the next time it backs up the computer.

### How do I remove a drive from a backup?

Here are the steps to follow:

1. Follow steps **1** to **5**.
2. Click the hard drive to remove (☑ changes to ☐).
3. Click **Next**.
4. In the Choose Folders to Exclude from Backup dialog box, click **Next**.

   The Confirm Configuration of Backup dialog box asks whether you want to keep the drive's existing backups.
5. Click **Delete them from the server** (○ changes to ●).
6. Click **Next**.
7. Click **Done**.

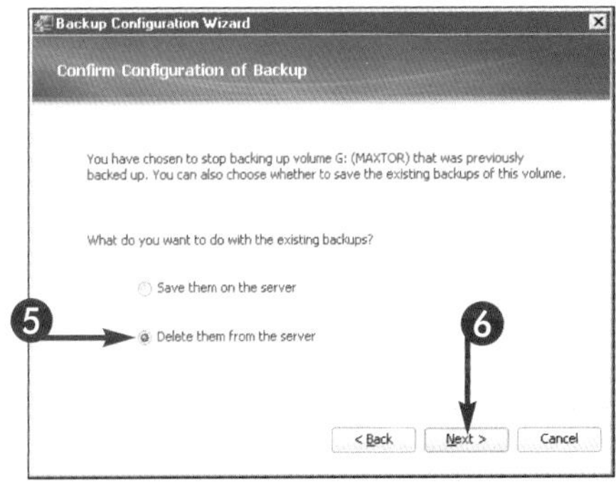

# Exclude a Folder from a Computer's Backup

You can customize a computer's backup to exclude a particular folder. This can reduce the amount of time it takes to back up the computer, and it saves disk space on Windows Home Server.

**To exclude a folder from a computer's backup in Windows Home Server, you must know the password for the server's Administrator account.**

## Exclude a Folder from a Computer's Backup

1. Start the Windows Home Server Console.

*Note: For more information, see Chapter 3.*

2. Click **Computers & Backup**.
3. Click the computer you want to work with.
4. Click **Configure Backup.**

The Backup Configuration Wizard appears.

5. Click **Next**.

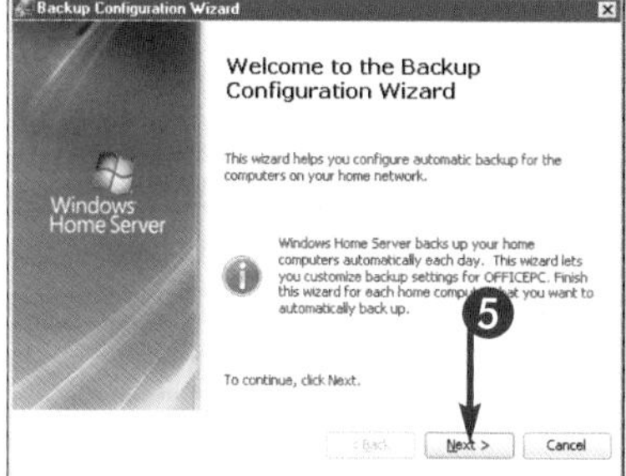

The wizard displays the Choose Volumes to Back Up dialog box, which includes a list of volumes that will be backed up.

6 Click **Next**.

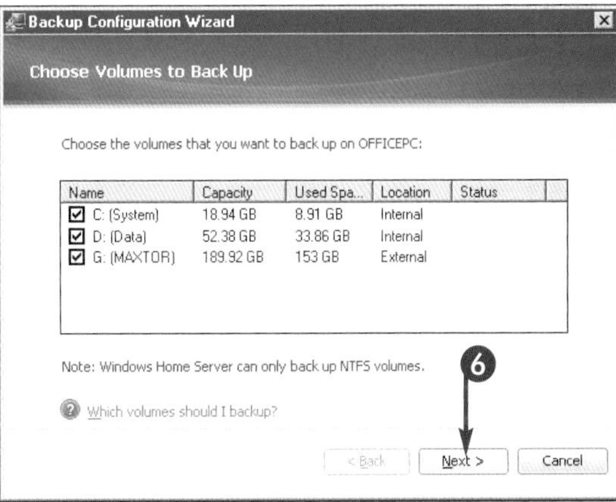


The Choose Folders to Exclude from Backup dialog box appears.

7 Click **Add**.

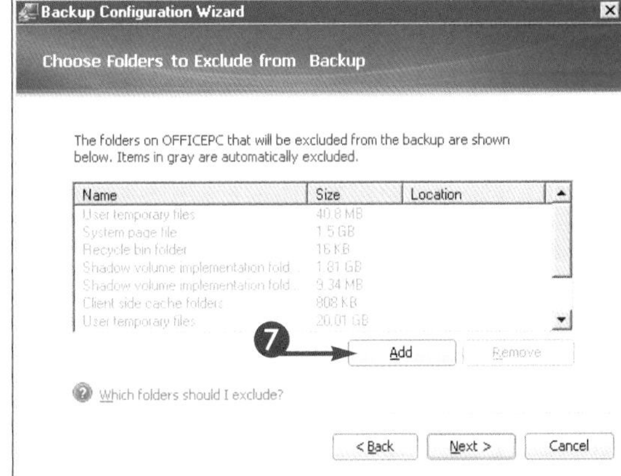

**Why would I want to exclude a folder from a computer's backup?**

The most common reason is that you have a folder that contains files you are going to delete soon. For example, if you have a folder that holds files for recorded TV shows, you probably delete each file after you watch the show. Similarly, you might have a folder that contains extremely large files, such as movie files, and you might not have enough room on Windows Home Server to back up these large files.

continued

# Exclude a Folder from a Computer's Backup *(continued)*

Windows Home Server keeps backup sizes to a minimum by automatically excluding certain system folders from the backup.

**These automatically excluded folders include your system's temporary files and the contents of the Recycle Bin. You can see a list of them in the Choose Folders to Exclude from Backup dialog box.**

## Exclude a Folder from a Computer's Backup *(continued)*

The Exclude a folder dialog box appears.

8. Click [−] to open the hard drive that contains the folder you want to exclude ([−] changes to [+]).

*Note: If the folder you want to exclude is a subfolder, click [−] to open the folder that contains the subfolder.*

9. Click the folder you want to exclude.

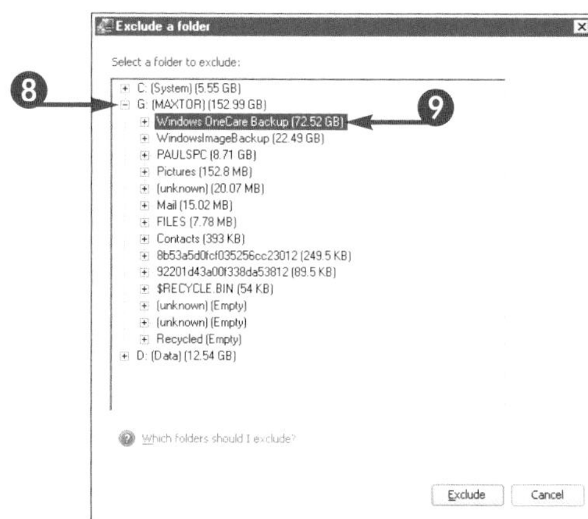


10. Click **Exclude**.

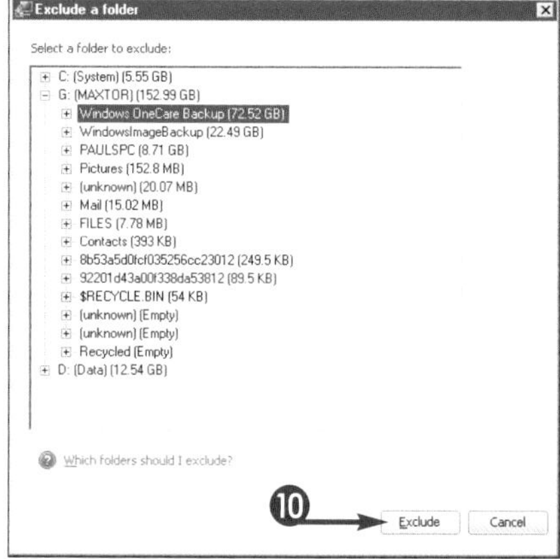

- The wizard adds the folder to the list of excluded folders.

11. Repeat steps **7** to **10** for any other folders you want to exclude.
12. Click **Next**.

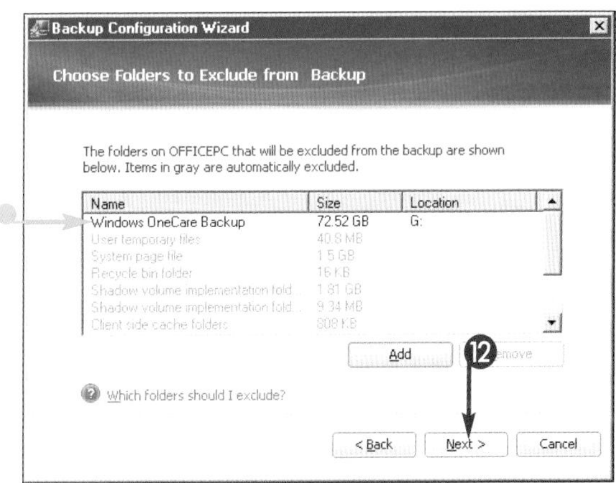


The final wizard dialog box displays a summary of your changes.

13. Click **Done**.

Windows Home Server excludes the folder or folders the next time it backs up the computer.

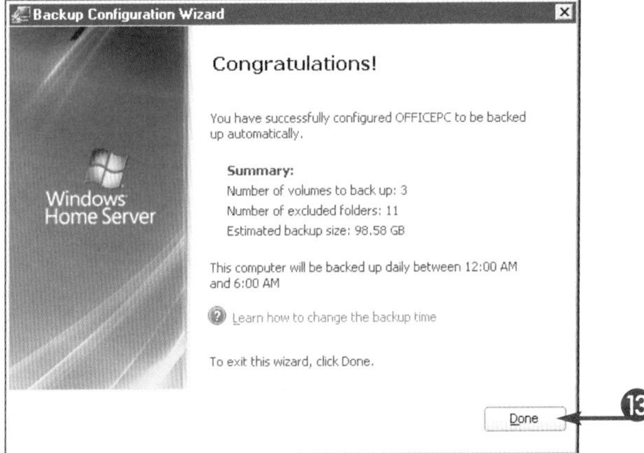

### How do I return an excluded folder to a computer's backup?

Here are the steps to follow:

1. Follow steps **1** to **6** on the previous page.
2. Click the excluded folder that you want to return.
3. Click **Remove**.

   The wizard removes the folder from the list of excluded folders.
4. Click **Next**.
5. In the final wizard dialog box, click **Done**.

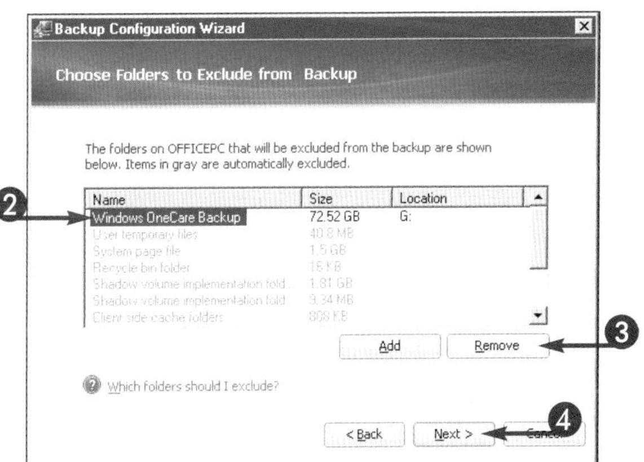

# Back Up a Computer Manually

If you have important documents on your computer that you want to back up right away, you can run a manual backup on your computer without having to wait for the automatic backup.

**To back up a computer manually using the Windows Home Server Console, you must know the password for the server's Administrator account.**

## Back Up a Computer Manually

1. Start the Windows Home Server Console.

*Note: For more information, see Chapter 3.*

2. Click **Computers & Backup**.

3. Click the computer you want to back up.
4. Click **Backup Now**.

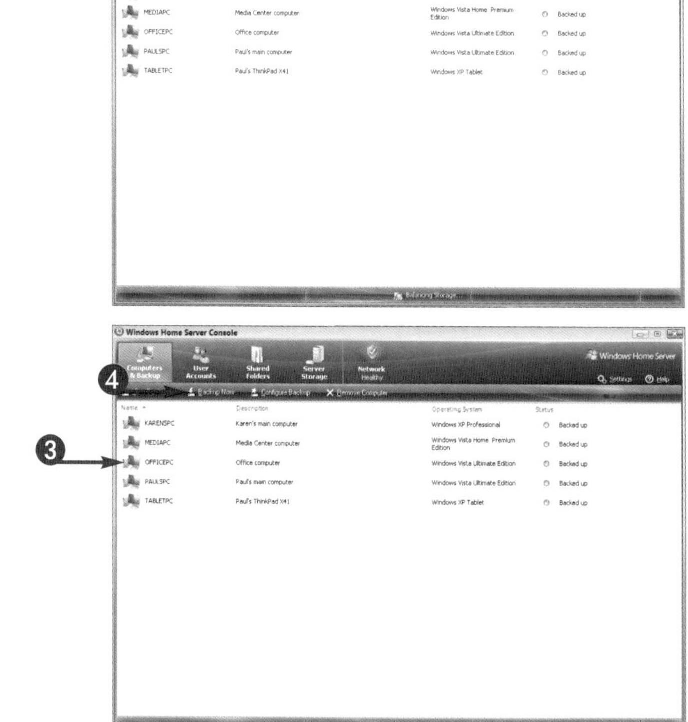

The Backup Now dialog box appears.

5. Type a description for the backup.

***Note:*** *Typing a description is optional, but it is a good idea because it will help you differentiate your manual backups.*

6. Click **Backup Now**.

Windows Home Server begins backing up the computer.

- The Status column shows you the progress of the backup.

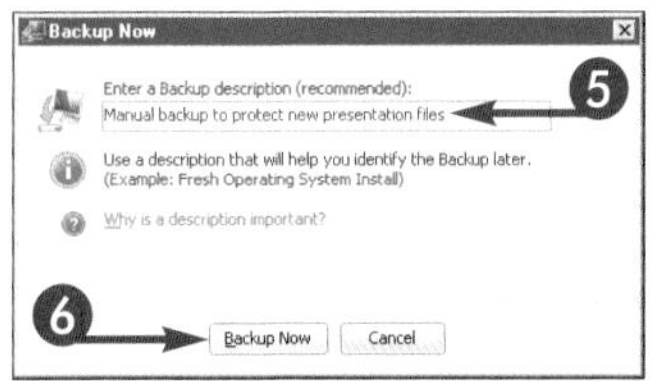


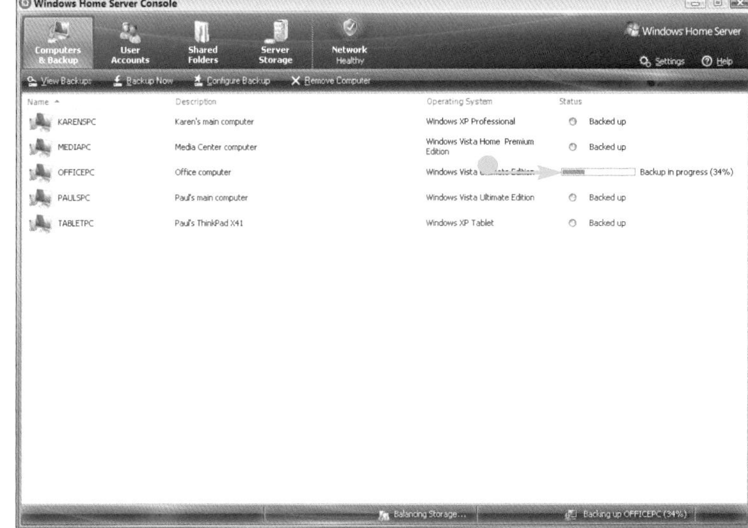

### Is there another method I can use to launch a manual backup?

Yes, by following these steps:

1. On the computer you want to back up, right-click the Windows Home Server icon (▣) in the notification area.

2. Click **Backup Now**.

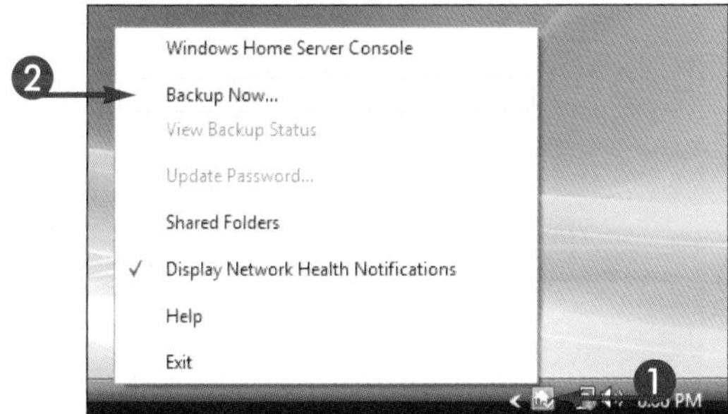


### How do I cancel a manual backup?

Follow these steps:

1. Follow steps **1** and **2**.

2. Right-click the computer that is currently being backed up.

3. Click **Cancel Backup**.

Windows Home Server cancels the manual backup.

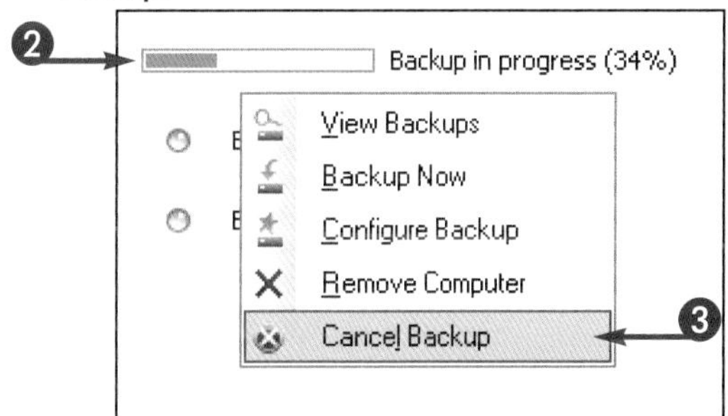

# Stop Backing Up a Computer

You can turn off a computer's backups. This is useful if you are running out of storage space on Windows Home Server or if you are going to be using the computer during the next scheduled backup time.

**To turn off a computer's backups in Windows Home Server, you must know the password for the server's Administrator account.**

## Stop Backing Up a Computer

1. Start the Windows Home Server Console.

*Note: For more information, see Chapter 3.*

2. Click **Computers & Backup**.

3. Right-click the computer you want to stop backing up.

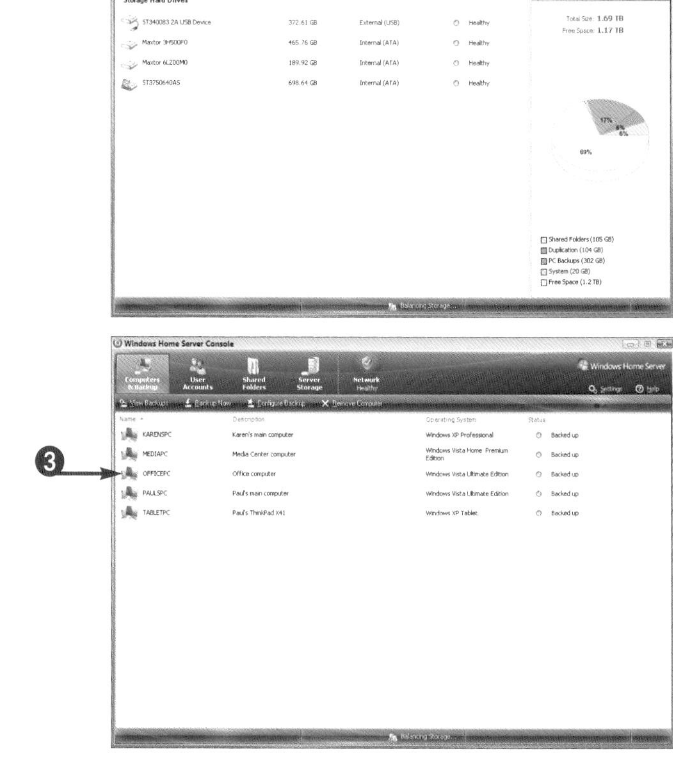

4 Click **Turn Off Backups**.

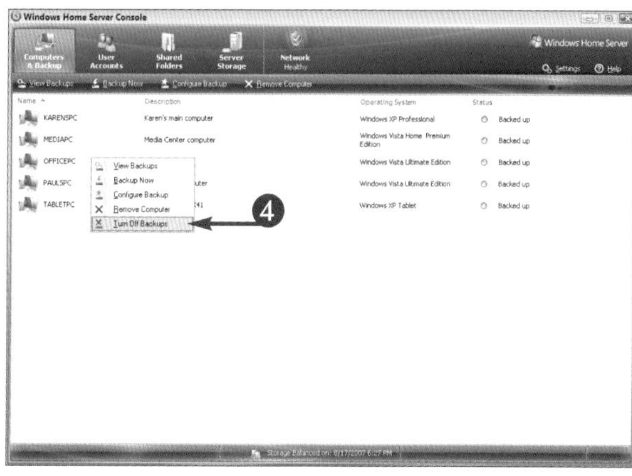

- Windows Home Server changes the computer's backup status to Off.

TIP

**How do I turn on backups for a computer?**

Follow these steps:

1 Follow steps **1** and **2**.

2 Right-click the computer you want to resume backing up.

3 Click **Turn On Backups**.

Windows Home Server includes the computer in its next backup process.

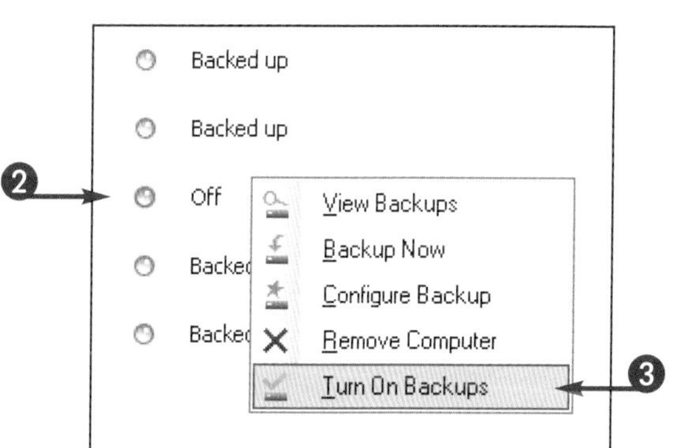

# Working with Computer Backups

To keep your data safer and to give you more data recovery choices, Windows Home Server usually keeps several backups for each computer. You can view the contents of those backups, prevent backups from being deleted, restore one or more files from a backup, and even restore an entire computer.

Understanding Computer Backups ..............194
View a Computer's Backups ..........................196
View Backup Details ........................................198
Prevent a Backup from Being Deleted........200
Schedule a Backup for Deletion ..................202
Delete Backups Manually ...............................204
View a Backup's Files......................................206
Restore a Previous Version of a File............208
Restore a Backed Up File ...............................210
Restore a Computer's Previous
Configuration ..................................................214

# Understanding Computer Backups

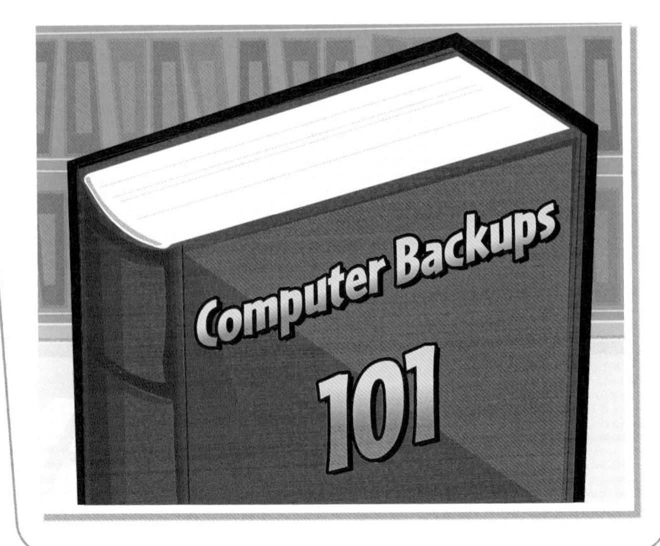


To work with computer backups in Windows Home Server, you need to know how Windows Home Server performs a backup. You also need to know about the backup cleanup process, and the various ways that Windows Home Server enables you to restore data.

### Complete Backups

When Windows Home Server backs up a computer for the first time, it backs up the entire computer. On subsequent backups, Windows Home Server includes those files that are new or that have changed, and it includes pointers to the unchanged files that are already backed up. This means that every backup is a complete backup of the computer.

### View Backups

Windows Home Server comes with a View Backups feature that displays a list of the backups that are available for each computer. This list tells you the date of the backup and the backup status. You can also open a backup to see the list of drives, folders, and files that are included in the backup.

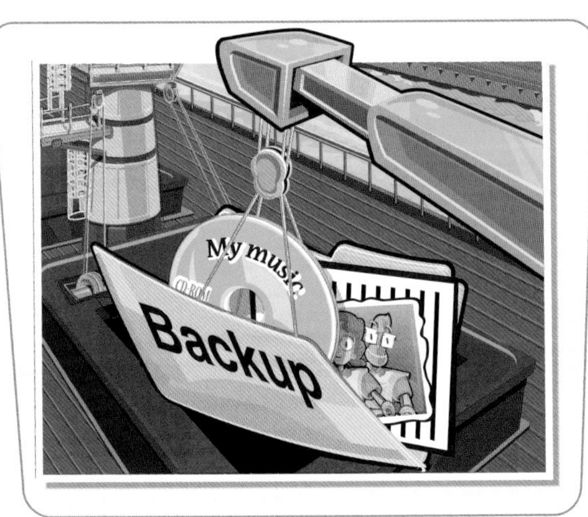

## Backup Cleanup

### Save a Backup

Backup cleanup is the weekly process that Windows Home Server uses to remove old backup files to preserve disk space. If you know that a particular backup contains a version of a file that you want to preserve in case you need to restore that version of the file later, you can tell Windows Home Server not to include the backup in the cleanup process.

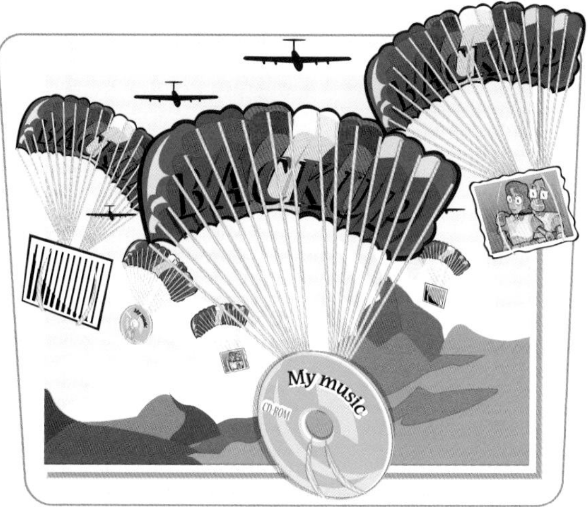


### Schedule a Deletion

If you save a backup or if you perform a manual backup of a computer, these backups are excluded from the backup cleanup process. If you find that you no longer need one of these backups, you can schedule the backup for deletion. This tells Windows Home Server to include the backup in its weekly backup cleanup process.

## Restore Data

### Restore a Previous Version

Every 12 hours – usually at 3:00 PM and 3:00 AM – Windows Home Server takes a snapshot of the contents of its shared folders. This enables Windows Home Server to preserve copies of files that change over time. You can restore a file to one of these previous versions.

### Restore a File

You can open one of the computer's backups on Windows Home Server and restore a file from the backup. This is useful if you accidentally delete a file permanently, if a file becomes corrupted, or if you make unwanted changes to a file.

### Restore a Computer

A computer may become inoperative because of a virus, hard drive crash, or some other hardware failure. Fortunately, because Windows Home Server preserves a backup of the entire computer, after fixing the underlying problem, you can then use one of the backups to restore the entire computer.

# View a Computer's Backups

You can view the dates and status of the backups that Windows Home Server is currently saving for a computer by using the Windows Home Server Console. The console displays the computer's list of backups.

**To view the backups for a computer on Windows Home Server, you must know the password for the server's Administrator account.**

## View a Computer's Backups

1. Start the Windows Home Server Console.

***Note:*** *For more information, see Chapter 3.*

2. Click **Computers & Backup**.

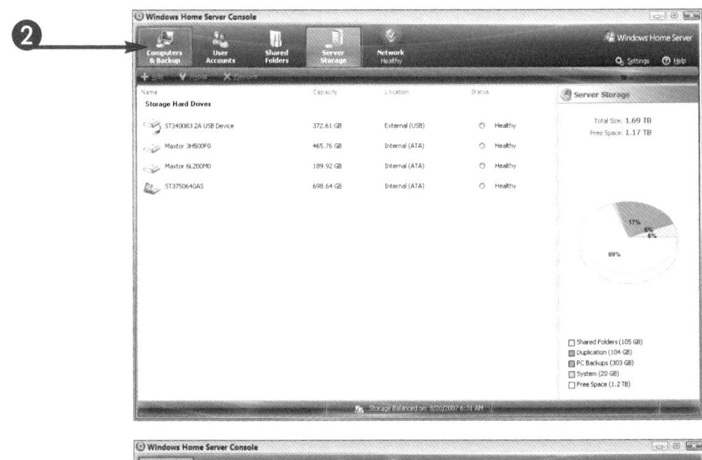

3. Click the computer you want to work with.

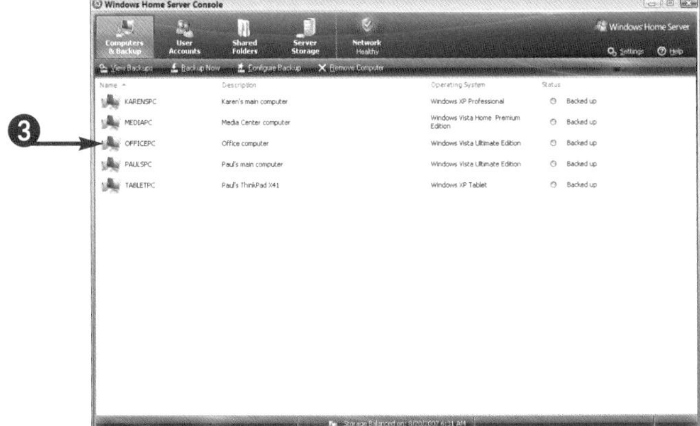

4 Click **View Backups**.

***Note:*** *You can also double-click the computer.*

The View Backups dialog box appears.

- The list of backups appears here.
- This column tells you the backup's management setting.
- This column tells you the date and time that Windows Home Server performed the backup.
- This column tells you the status of the backup.
- This column describes the backup.

5 When you have finished examining or working with the backups, click **OK**.

### What do the backup icons represent?

The icons in the first column of the backup list tell you each backup's Automatic Backup Management status. (See Chapter 9 for more information.) The icon means that Windows Home Server manages the backup according to the current Automatic Backup Management settings. The icon means that Windows Home Server will not delete the backup (see the section "Prevent a Backup from Being Deleted"); and the icon means that Windows Home Server will remove the backup during the next Automatic Backup Management session (see the section "Schedule a Backup for Deletion").

# View Backup Details

For each saved backup in Windows Home Server, you can view detailed information such as the length of time it took to perform the backup, and the hard drives included in the backup. You can also modify the backup description.

**To view backup details in Windows Home Server, you must know the password for the server's Administrator account.**

## View Backup Details

1. In the Windows Home Server Console, open the View Backups dialog box for the computer you want to work with.

***Note:*** *For more information, see the section "View a Computer's Backups."*

2. Click the backup you want to work with.
3. Click **Details**.

***Note:*** *You can also double-click the backup.*

The Backup Details dialog box appears.

- This area displays general details about the backup.
- You can edit the backup description in the Description text box.

4. Click the hard drive you want to work with.

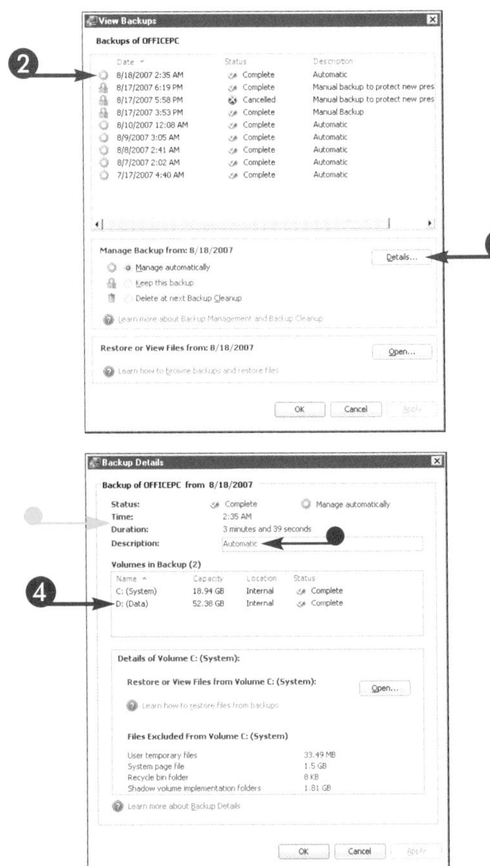

- Windows Home Server displays the backup details for the hard drive.

5 Click **OK**.

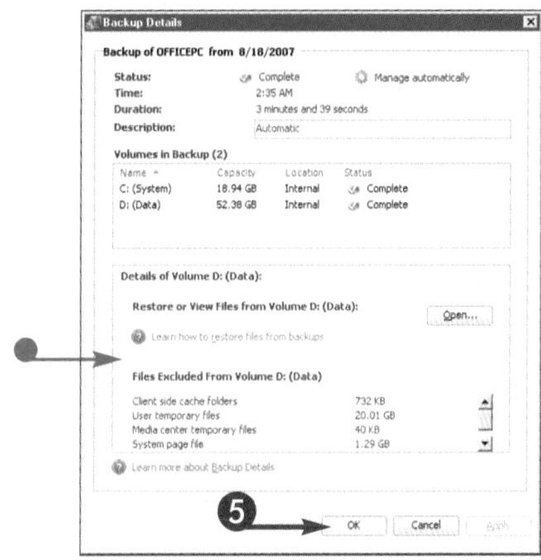

6 Click **OK**.

Windows Home Server closes the View Backups dialog box.

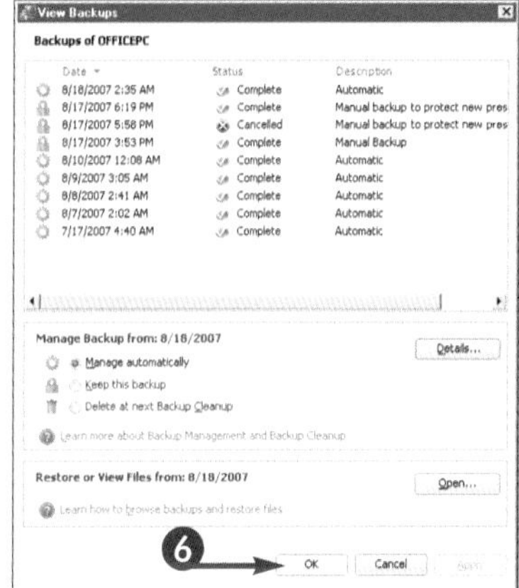

### Why do some backups take several hours while others take only minutes?

The longer backups usually occur when you first back up a computer because Windows Home Server must back up the entire system. On subsequent backups, Windows Home Server only backs up files that are new or that have changed, and these backups usually take just a few minutes. However, a backup can take much longer if you add a substantial amount of data to your computer on a particular day.

# Prevent a Backup from Being Deleted

You can stop Windows Home Server from deleting a backup when it performs its weekly cleanup of backup files. This is useful if you know that a particular backup contains important information, such as a file that you have subsequently deleted.

**To prevent a backup from being deleted in Windows Home Server, you must know the password for the server's Administrator account.**

## Prevent a Backup from Being Deleted

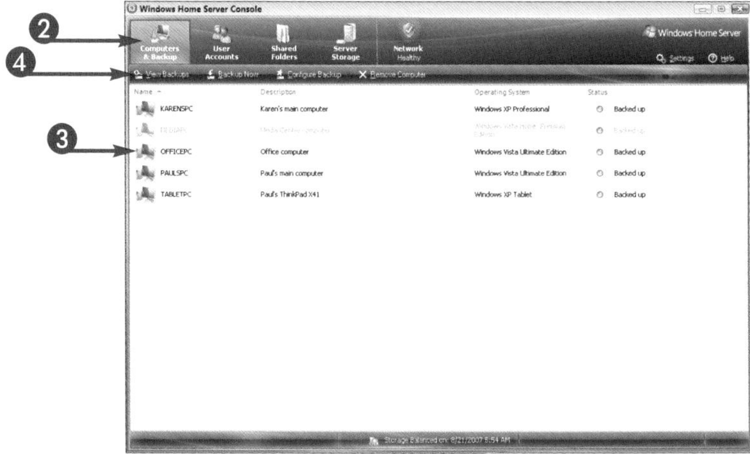


1. Start the Windows Home Server Console.

*Note:* *For more information, see Chapter 3.*

2. Click **Computers & Backup**.
3. Click the computer you want to work with.
4. Click **View Backups**.

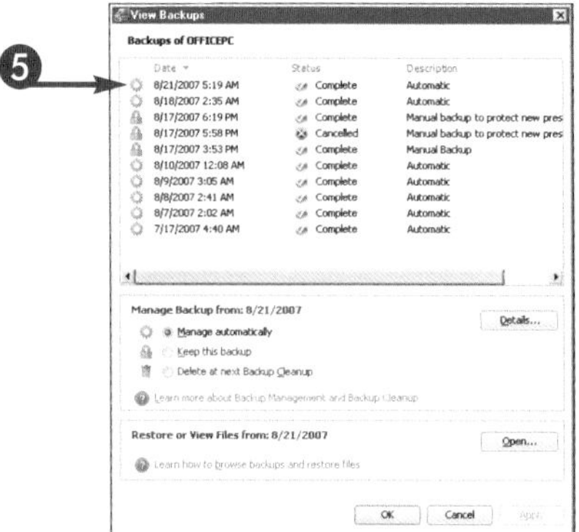


The View Backups dialog box appears.

5. Click the backup you want to save.

6 Click **Keep this backup** (◯ changes to ◉).

- Windows Home Server changes the icon for the backup to 🔒.

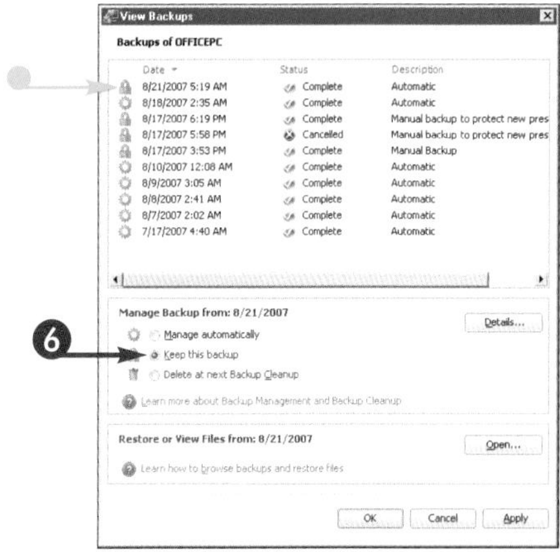

7 Click **OK**.

Windows Home Server configures the backup to prevent it from being deleted.

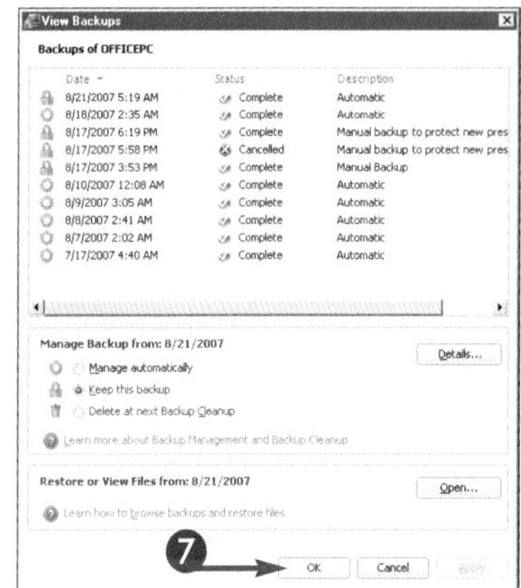

### Why does Windows Home Server automatically keep some backups?

Windows Home Server assumes that backups you perform manually are important. That is, if you cannot wait until the regularly scheduled backup time, then it must be for a good reason. Therefore, Windows Home Server automatically keeps all manual backups.

### What happens if I decide that I no longer want to keep a backup?

In most cases, it is best to let Windows Home Server manage the backup automatically. Follow steps **1** to **5**, and then click **Manage automatically** (◯ changes to ◉). Windows Home Server changes the icon for the backup to ⚙. Alternatively, you can schedule the backup for deletion, as described in the next section.

# Schedule a Backup for Deletion

If you no longer need a backup, you can schedule it to be deleted during the next backup cleanup session. This is useful if you want to reduce clutter in the list of backups, or if you want to free up some disk space on Windows Home Server.

**To schedule a backup for deletion in Windows Home Server, you must know the password for the server's Administrator account.**

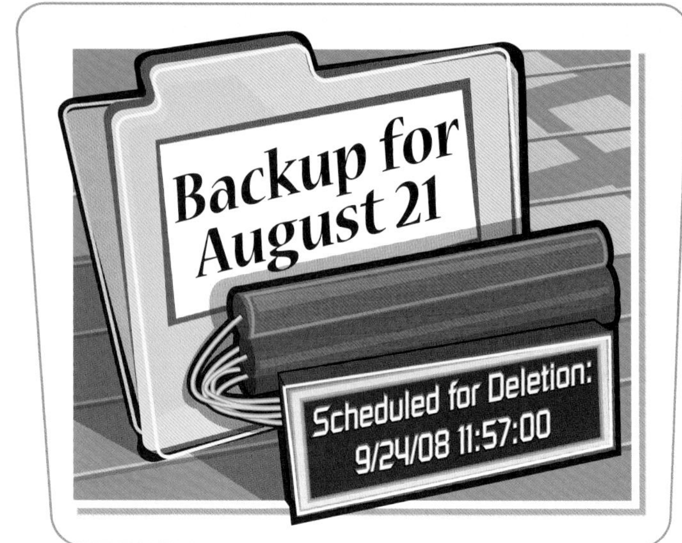


## Schedule a Backup for Deletion

1. Start the Windows Home Server Console.

*Note: For more information, see Chapter 3.*

2. Click **Computers & Backup**.
3. Click the computer you want to work with.
4. Click **View Backups.**

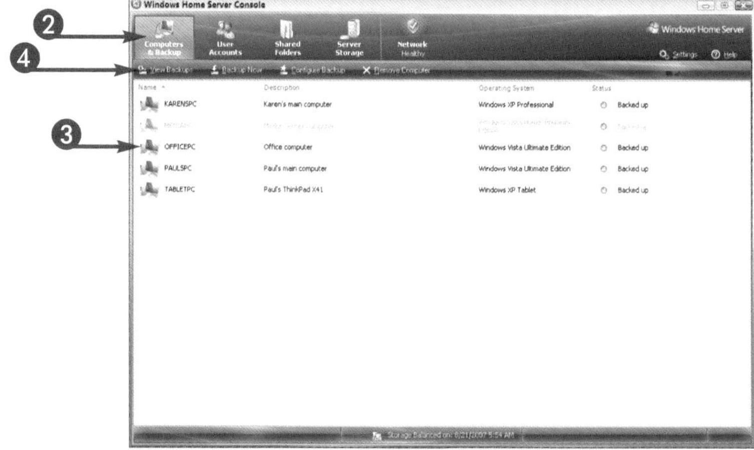


The View Backups dialog box appears.

5. Click the backup you want to schedule for deletion.

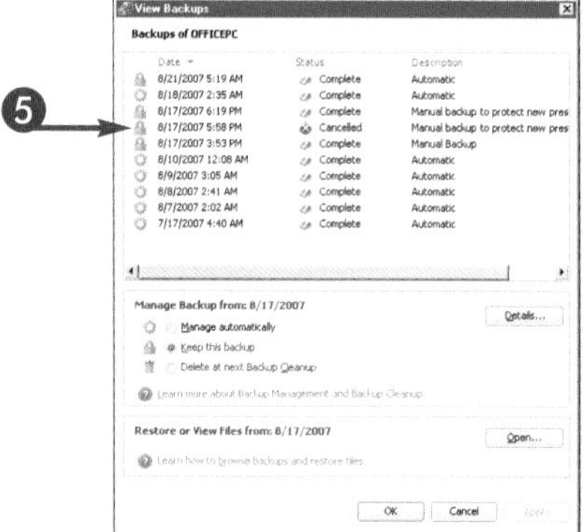

6 Click **Delete at next Backup Cleanup** (◯ changes to ◉).

- Windows Home Server changes the icon for the backup to 🗑.

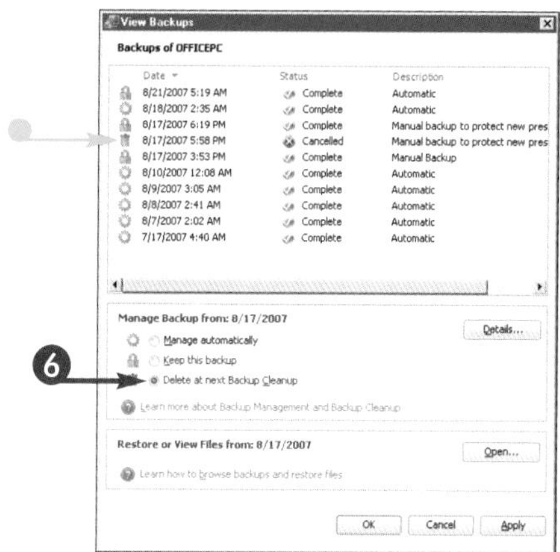

7 Click **OK**.

Windows Home Server configures the backup to be deleted during the next cleanup operation.

TIP

**What is the difference between scheduling a backup for deletion and having Windows Home Server manage the backup automatically?**

When Windows Home Server manages a backup automatically, it deletes the backup according to the Automatic Backup Management settings. (See Chapter 9 for more information.) For example, if the backup is the first backup of the month, Windows Home Server may keep the backup for as long as three months. Similarly, the first backup of the week may not be deleted for as long as three weeks. However, when you schedule a backup for deletion, Windows Home Server deletes the backup during the next backup cleanup session, which occurs every Sunday morning.

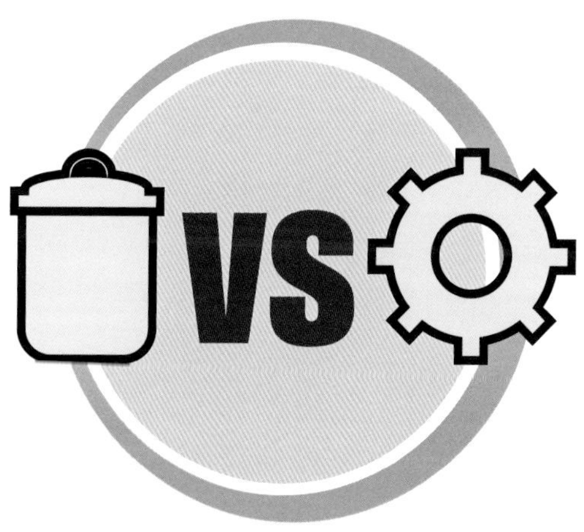

# Delete Backups Manually

You can delete backups manually by forcing Windows Home Server to run a backup cleanup session. This is useful if you want to free up disk space on Windows Home Server right away or if you have backups scheduled for deletion that you want to remove immediately.

**To delete backups manually in Windows Home Server, you must know the password for the server's Administrator account.**

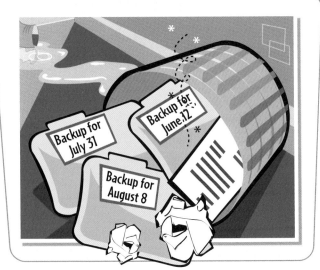

## Delete Backups Manually

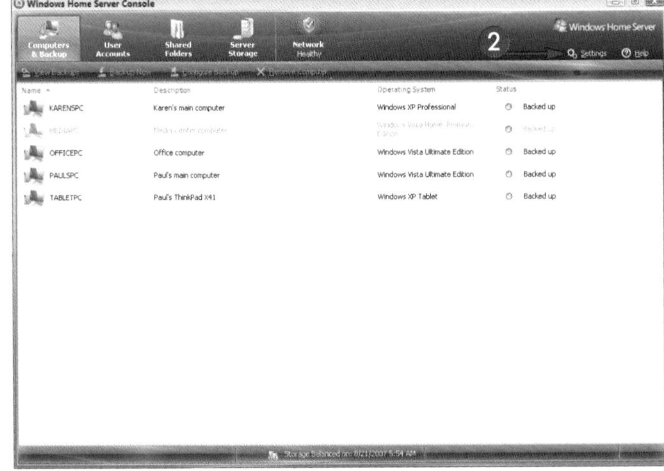


1. Start the Windows Home Server Console.

*Note: For more information, see Chapter 3.*

2. Click **Settings**.

The Windows Home Server Settings dialog box appears.

3. Click the **Backup** tab.

4 Click **Cleanup Now**.

Windows Home Server runs a backup cleanup session.

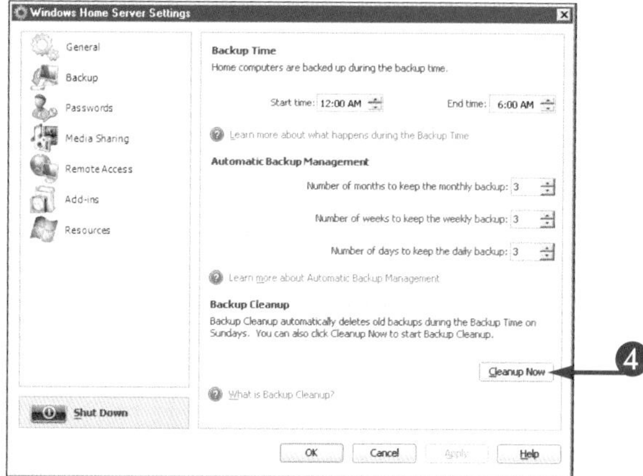

5 When the backup cleanup is complete, click **OK**.

Windows Home Server closes the Settings dialog box.

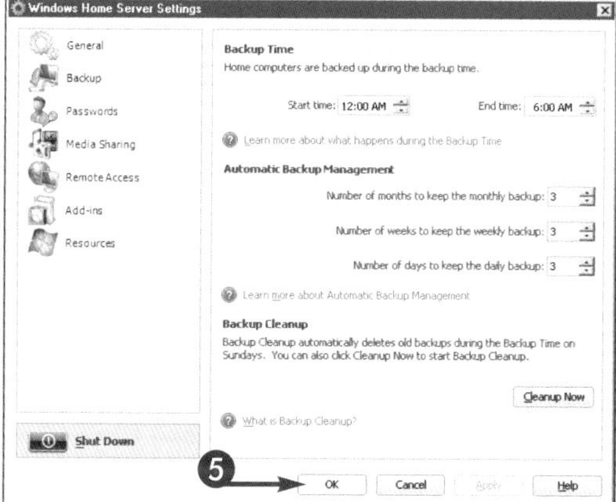

**How long does a backup cleanup session take?**

That depends on the number of backups that Windows Home Server is deleting and the size of those backups. In addition to removing the backup data, Windows Home Server must also reconfigure the remaining backups, and free up the disk space. As a result, a typical cleanup process can take at least an hour, and it is not unusual for the cleanup to take two hours or more. Therefore, you should only perform a manual backup cleanup during a time when you will not have to use the Windows Home Server Console for a while.

# View a Backup's Files

You can view the contents of a computer's backup. This is useful if you want to see whether that backup contains a particular file or a particular version of a file.

**To view a backup's files in Windows Home Server, you must know the password for both the server's Administrator account and for an Administrator account on your Windows Vista computer.**

## View a Backup's Files

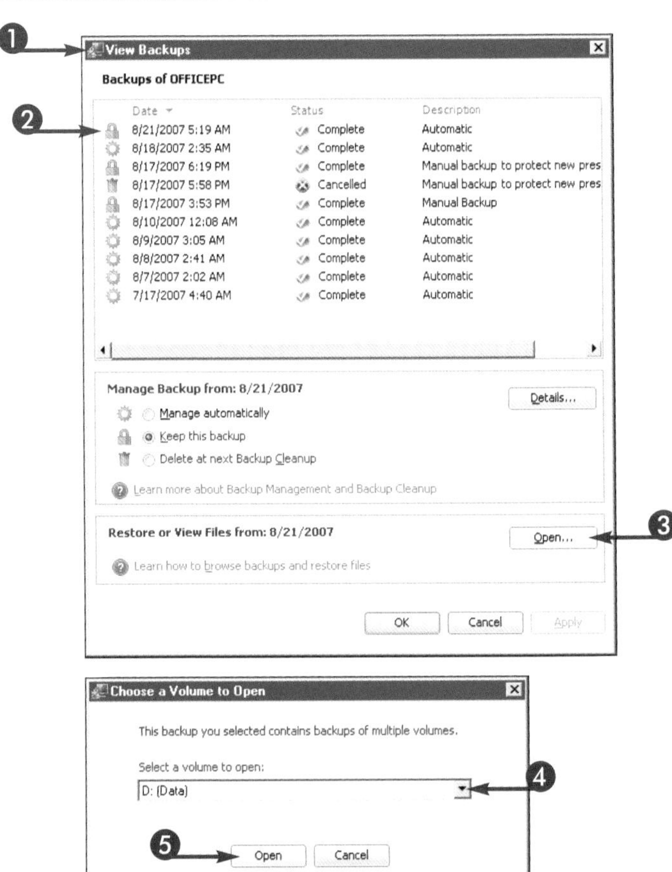


1. In the Windows Home Server Console, open the View Backups dialog box for the computer you want to work with.

***Note:*** *For more information, see the section "View a Computer's Backups."*

2. Click the backup you want to work with.
3. Click **Open**.

If you backed up multiple hard drives for this computer, the Choose a Volume to Open dialog box appears.

4. Click ▼ and then click the hard drive that contains the files you want to view.
5. Click **Open**.

***Note:*** *If you are using Windows Vista, you might see the User Account Control dialog box. Click* ***Continue*** *or type an Administrator's password and click* ***Submit****.*

Windows Home Server displays the files contained in the backup.

- Windows Home Server creates a temporary drive to display the backup files.

This example creates drive Y.

6 When you have finished examining the files, click ✕.

7 Click **OK**.

Windows Home Server closes the View Backups dialog box.

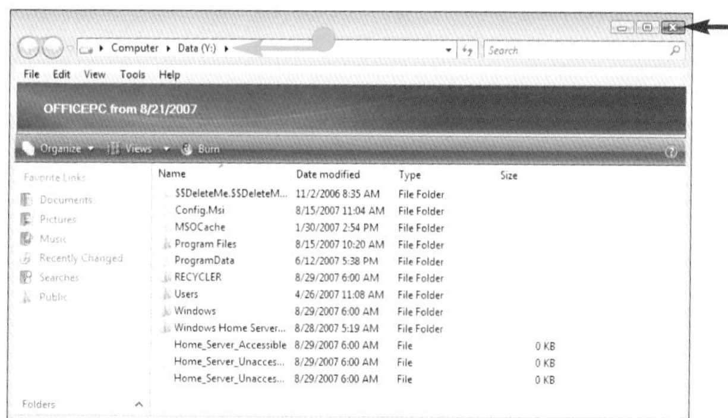


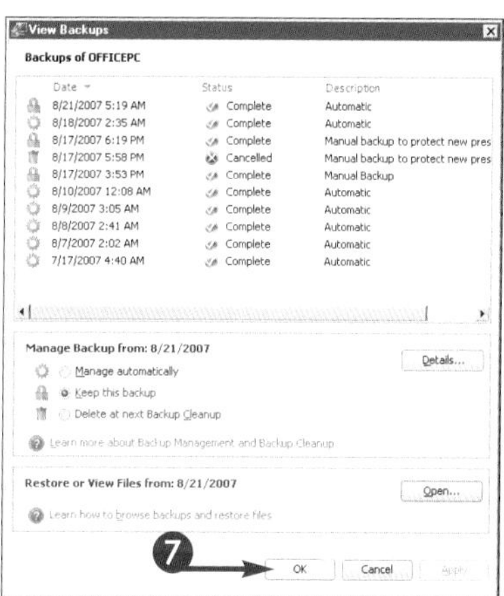

## Is there another method I can use to open backup files?

Yes, you can also open backup files as follows:

1. Open the Backup Details dialog box, as described in the section "View Backup Details."
2. Click the hard drive you want to view.
3. Click **Open**.

   Windows Home Server displays the files contained in the backup.

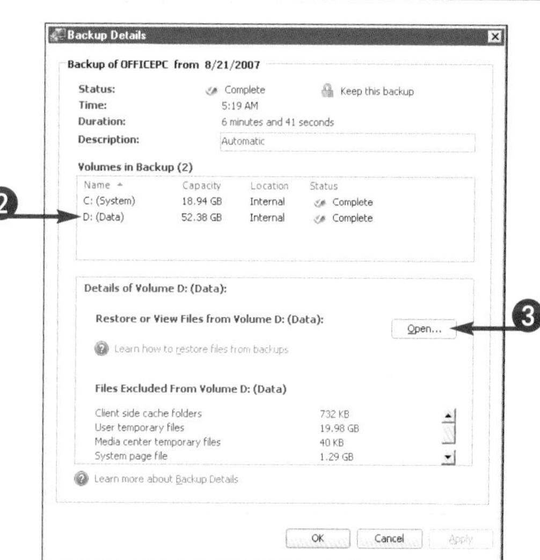

# Restore a Previous Version of a File

You can revert to a previous version of a file in a Windows Home Server shared folder. This enables you to restore a file that was accidentally overwritten, improperly edited, or lost to a program or system crash.

**Windows Home Server maintains backup copies of the files in its shared folders. This section shows you how to restore previous versions of those files, not the files in a computer's backup.**

## Restore a Previous Version of a File

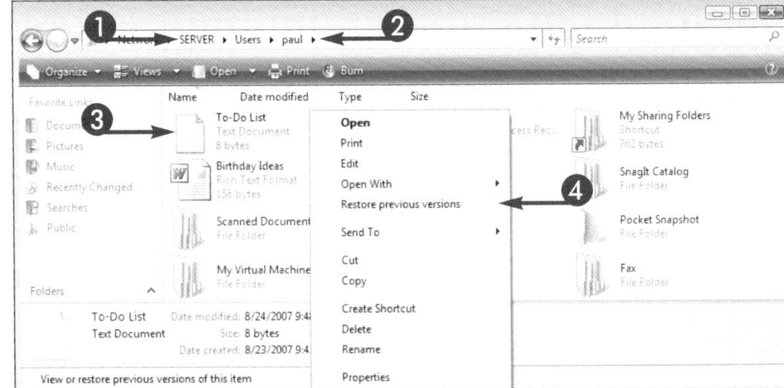


1. Display the Windows Home Server shared folders.

*Note: For more information, see Chapter 7.*

2. Navigate to the shared folder that contains the file you want to work with.
3. Right-click the file.
4. Click **Restore previous versions**.

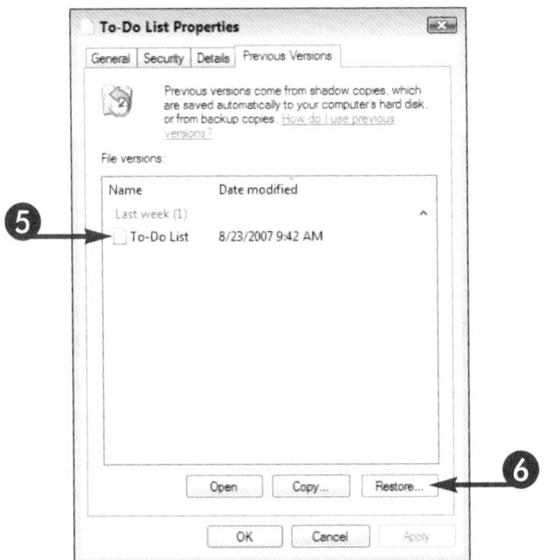


The file's Properties dialog box appears, displaying the Previous Versions tab.

5. Click the previous version you want to restore.
6. Click **Restore**.

The Previous Versions dialog box appears.

7 Click **Restore**.

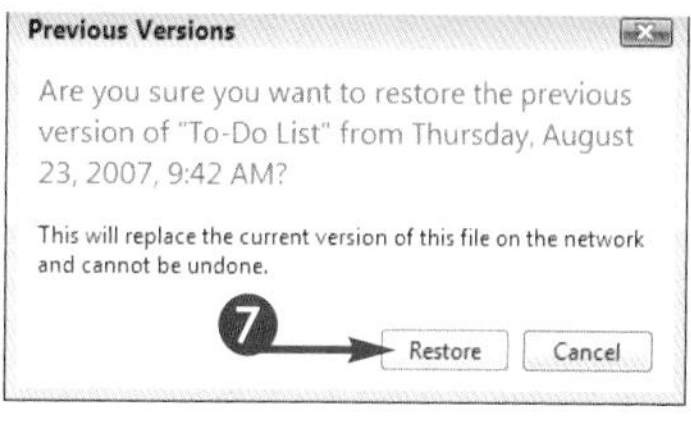


Windows tells you that the previous version was successfully restored.

8 Click **OK**.

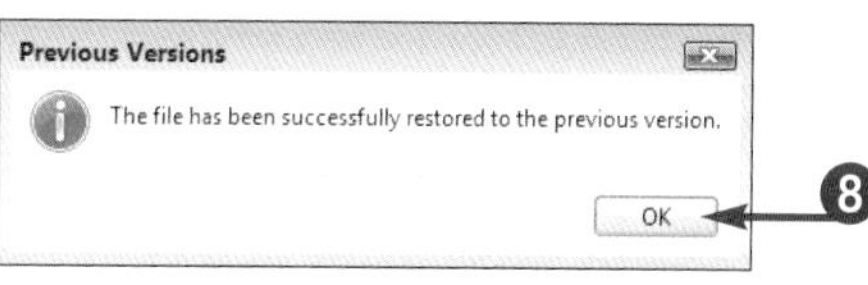


9 Click **OK**.

You can now view and work with the previous version of the file.

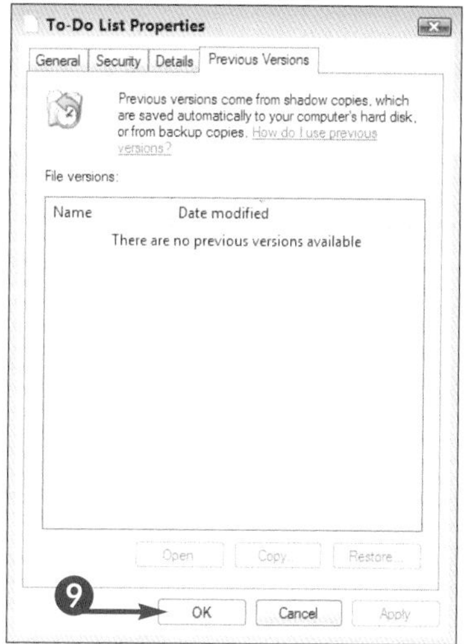

### How does Windows Home Server maintain previous versions of files?

Every 12 hours, at 3:00 AM and 3:00 PM, Windows Home Server creates a special copy — called a *shadow copy* — of the contents of the shared folders. Windows Home Server also keeps track of which files change over time, and it preserves the previous versions of each file in case you need to revert a file to an earlier version.

### Windows XP does not have the Restore Previous Versions command. How do I access the previous versions?

In Windows XP, follow steps **1** to **3**. When the shortcut menu appears, click **Properties** to open the file's Properties dialog box, and then click the **Previous Versions** tab.

# Restore a Backed Up File

You can restore a file from a computer's backup if the file is lost because of a system problem or because you accidentally deleted or overwrote the file. This way, you need not worry about losing data.

**To restore a backed up file in Windows Home Server, you must know the password for the server's Administrator account.**

❶ Display the files for the backup and hard drive that contain the file you want to restore.

***Note:*** *For more information, see the section "View a Backup's Files."*

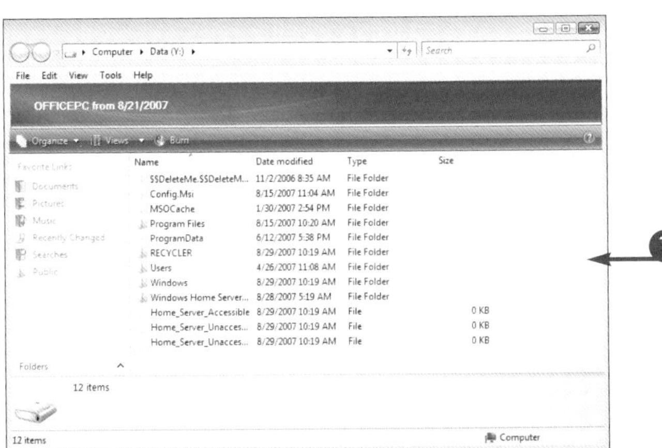


❷ Navigate to the folder that contains the file you want to restore.

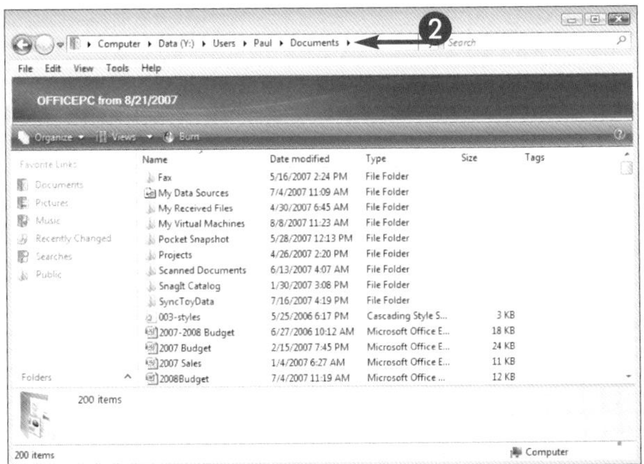

3 Click the file you want to restore.

4 Click **Organize**.

5 Click **Copy**.

Windows stores a copy of the file in memory.

6 Click **Start**.

7 Click your username.

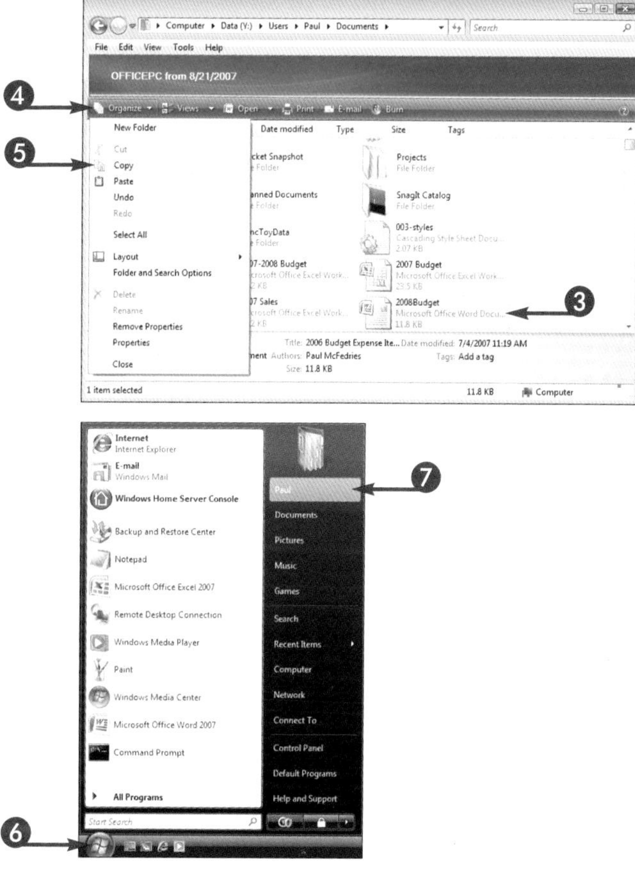

**Can I restore multiple files at once?**

Yes, you can restore as many files as you need, as long as your computer has enough disk space to handle the restored files. To restore multiple files from the same backup folder, in step **3**, press and hold Ctrl and click each backup file you want to restore. To restore an entire folder, in step **3**, click the backup folder you want to restore.

continued

# Restore a Backed Up File *(continued)*

Restoring files in Windows Home Server is a copy-and-paste operation, where you copy a file from a backup and then paste it into a folder on your computer.

## Restore a Backed Up File *(continued)*

Your user folder appears.

8. Navigate to the folder you want to use for the restored file.

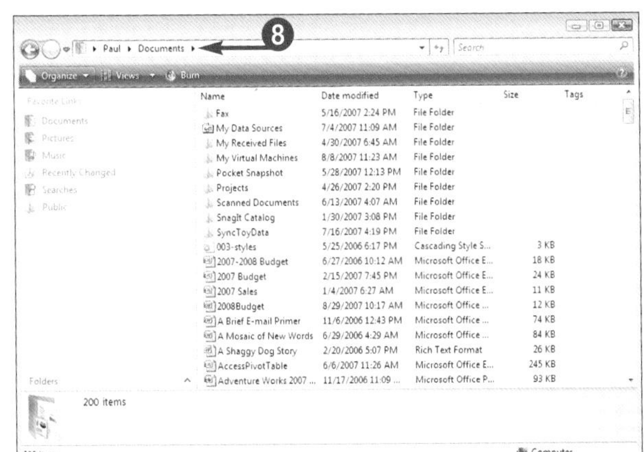


9. Click **Organize**.
10. Click **Paste**.

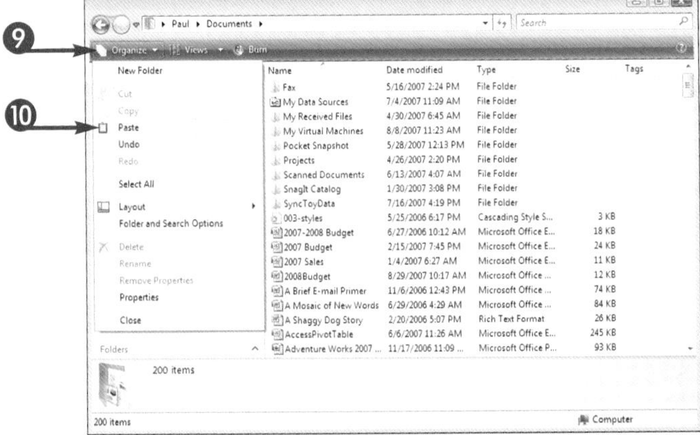

If a file with the same name already exists in the folder, the Copy File dialog box appears.

11 Click **Copy and Replace**.

- If you do not want to replace the existing file, you can click **Don't copy**, instead.
- If you want to restore the file and keep the existing file, you can click **Copy, but keep both files** to restore the file, with the text (2) added to the filename.

- Windows restores the file.

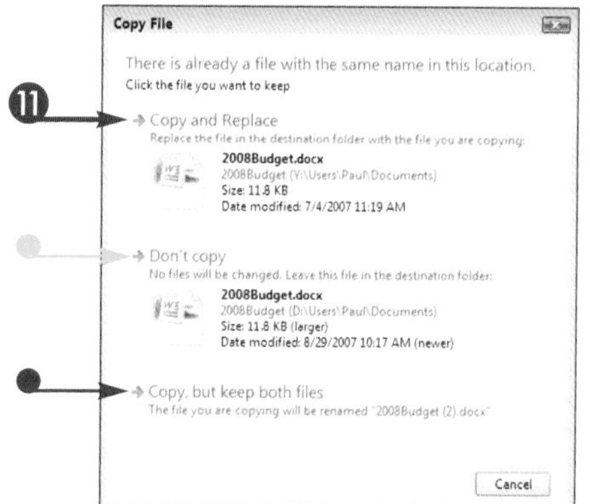


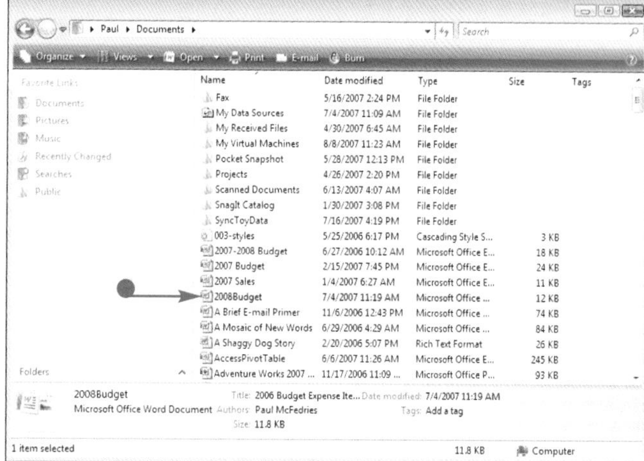

**Can I restore files from another computer?**

Yes. The restore component of most backup programs only works with files backed up from a specific computer, and it assumes that you want to restore a file to its original location on that computer. However, this is not how Windows Home Server works. Instead, it enables you to access the backups of any computer, and you can then restore a file from any backup to any folder on your computer.

# Restore a Computer's Previous Configuration

You can use the Home Computer Restore CD to restore a computer to a previous configuration. This enables you to recover a computer that no longer boots because of a hard drive crash or virus.

**To restore a computer's previous configuration in Windows Home Server, you must know the password for the server's Administrator account.**

## Restore a Computer's Previous Configuration

1. Start the computer that you want to restore.
2. Insert the Home Computer Restore CD.
3. Follow the instructions on the computer screen to boot from the CD.

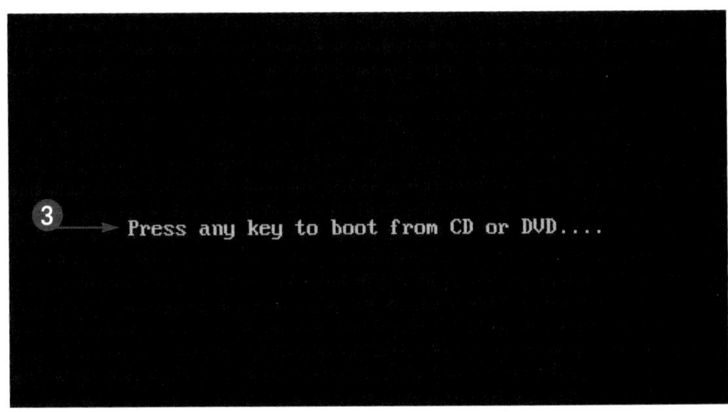


The Detect Hardware dialog box appears.

4. Click **Continue**.

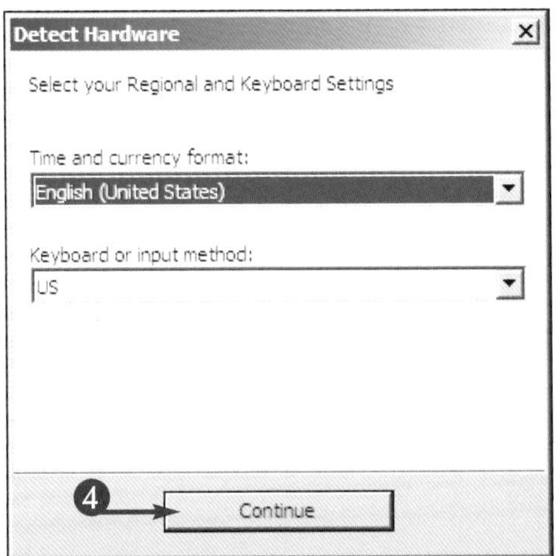

5 Click **Show Details**.

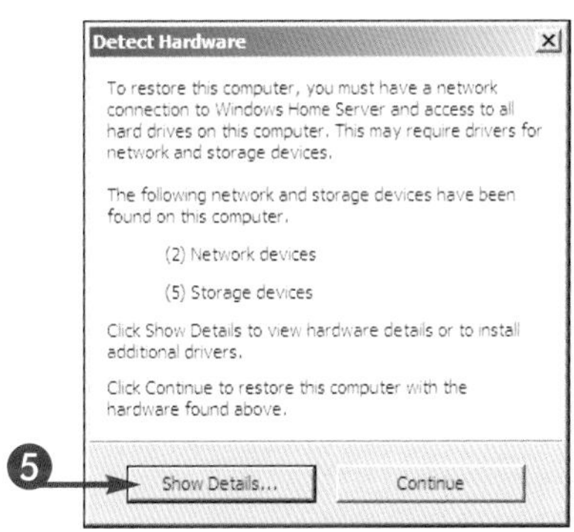


Windows Home Server displays a list of the devices that it found.

***Note:** If a device is missing — particularly a network device or a hard drive — then you must install the device.*

6 Click **Continue**.

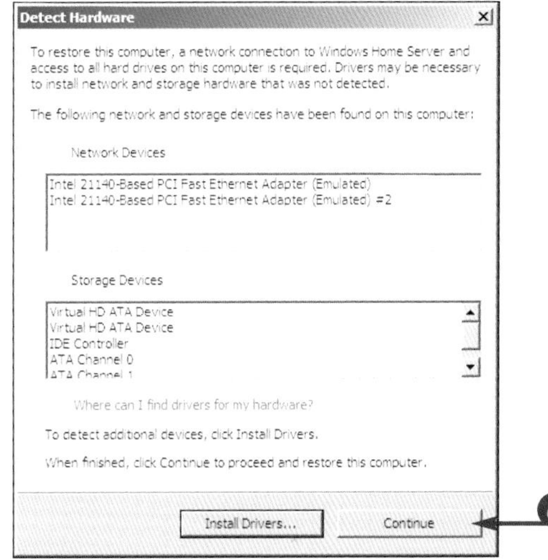

**What do I do if Windows Home Server does not recognize my network card or hard drive?**

You need to install the appropriate device drivers for the hardware and then tell Windows Home Server to install the drivers. Here are the steps to follow:

1 Use another computer to download the latest drivers from the manufacturer's Web site.

2 If the downloaded file is a ZIP file or other compressed file, decompress the file.

3 Copy all of the files onto a USB flash drive or floppy disk.

4 Insert the USB drive or floppy disk into the computer you are restoring.

5 In the dialog box showing the list of devices, click **Install Drivers**.

6 In the Install Drivers dialog box, click **Scan**.

Windows Home Server locates the drivers on the USB drive or floppy disk and then installs them.

7 Click **OK**.

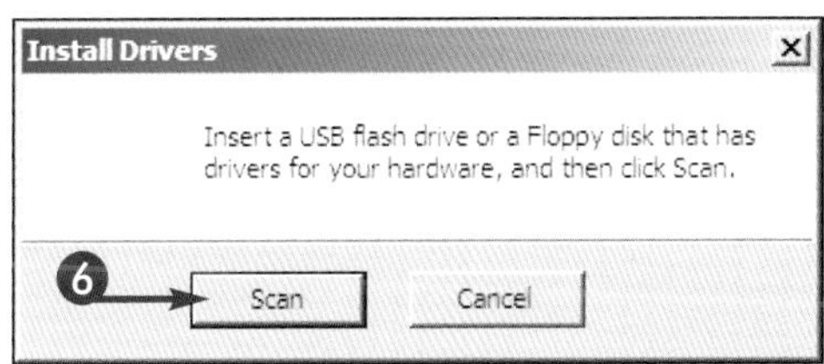

Windows Home Server makes it easy to recover your crashed computer because it has your computer backed up. Each backup is complete — containing not just your data, but also your Windows files and programs — so that you can get the computer back up and running.

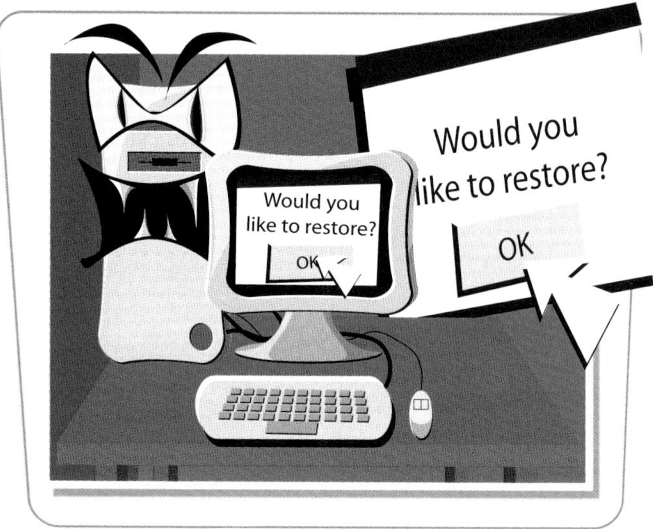


## Restore a Computer's Previous Configuration *(continued)*

The Restore Wizard appears.

7 Click **Next**.

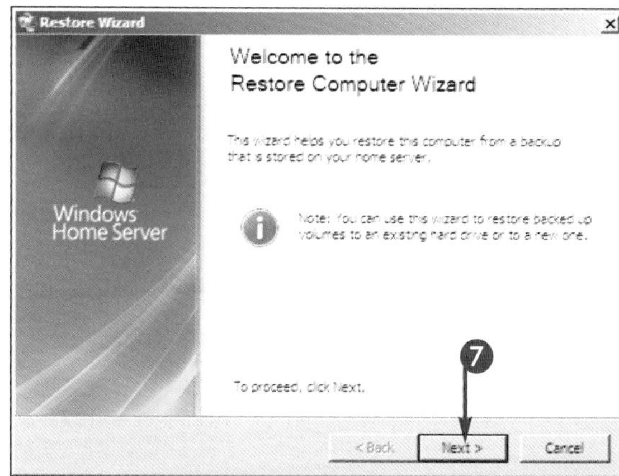


The Log On to Your Windows Home Server dialog box appears.

8 Type your Windows Home Server Administrator password.

9 Click **Next**.

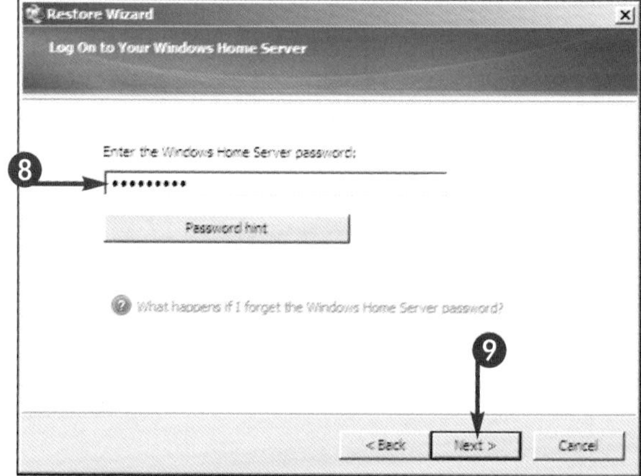

The Choose a Computer to Restore dialog box appears.

⑩ Click ▾ and then click the name of the computer you want to restore.

⑪ Click **Next**.

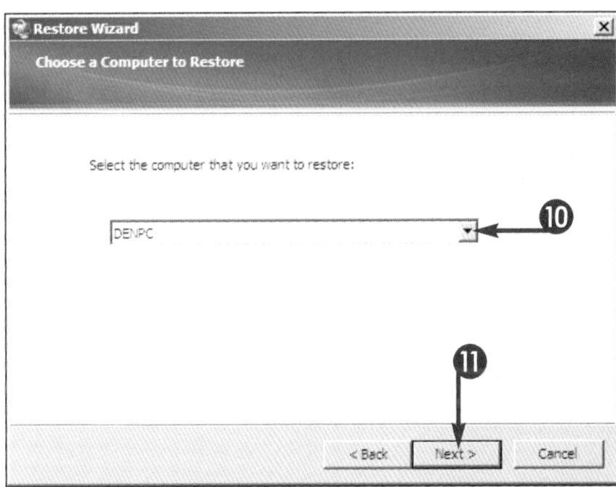


The Choose a Backup to Restore dialog box appears.

⑫ Click the backup you want to restore.

⑬ Click **Next**.

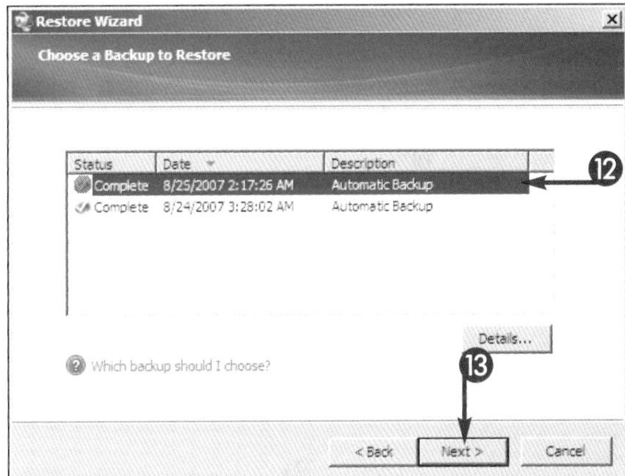

### How long does the restore take?

The time it takes Windows Home Server to restore the computer depends on how many hard drives you are restoring, and the amount of data on each hard drive. The restore might take as little as 15 minutes, but it is more likely to take as much as an hour or two. The restore is much faster if the computer has a wired connection to your network instead of a wireless connection.

continued

# Restore a Computer's Previous Configuration *(continued)*

It is possible that you may lose a small amount of data when you recover the computer. If you created any new files or modified any existing files since the last time Windows Home Server backed up the computer, this new and changed data cannot be recovered.

## Restore a Computer's Previous Configuration *(continued)*

The Choose Volumes to Restore dialog box appears.

14. Click **Next**.

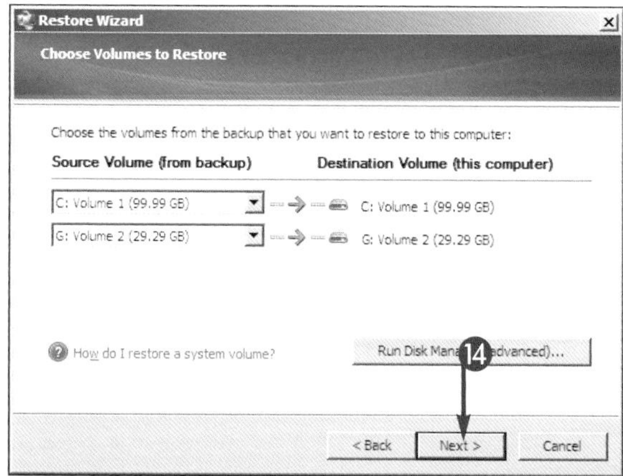


The Confirm the Restore Configuration dialog box appears.

15. Click **Next**.

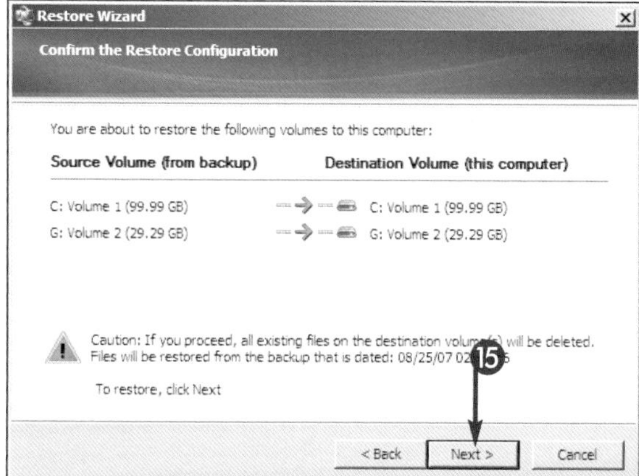

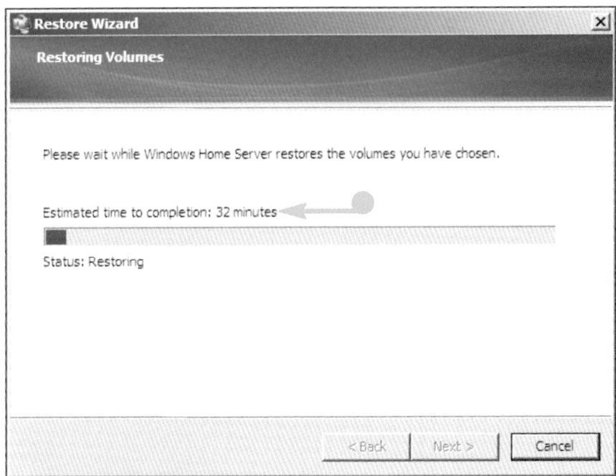


The Restoring Volumes dialog box appears.

- The Restore Wizard displays an estimate of how long the restore will take.

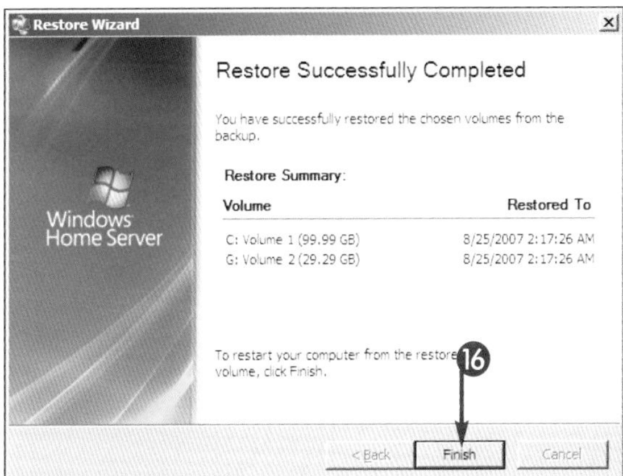


The Restore Successfully Completed dialog box appears.

16. Click **Finish**.

    The Restore Wizard restarts the computer.

17. Remove the Home Computer Restore CD.

**Do I have to restore all of the computer's hard drives?**

No, Windows Home Server does not require that you restore every hard drive. The restore goes faster if you only restore those hard drives that are no longer operative. For example, if your computer has two hard drives and only one of them crashed, you only need to restore the crashed drive. To prevent Windows Home Server from restoring a drive, when you get to the Choose Volumes to Restore dialog box, click **None** in the drive's **Source Volume** drop-down list.

- You can click ▼ and then click **None** to avoid restoring a hard drive.

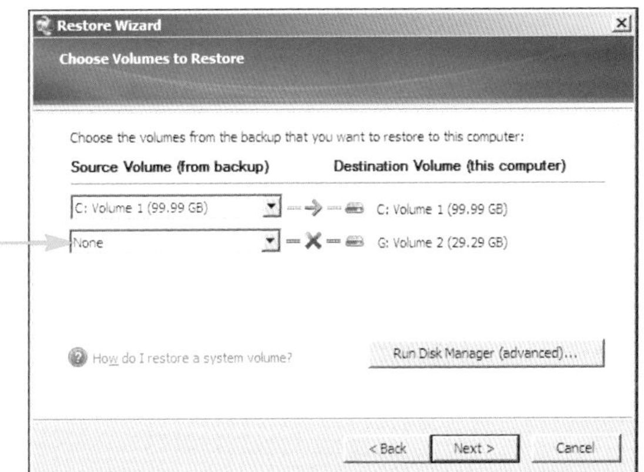

CHAPTER

11

# Making a Remote Connection to Windows Home Server

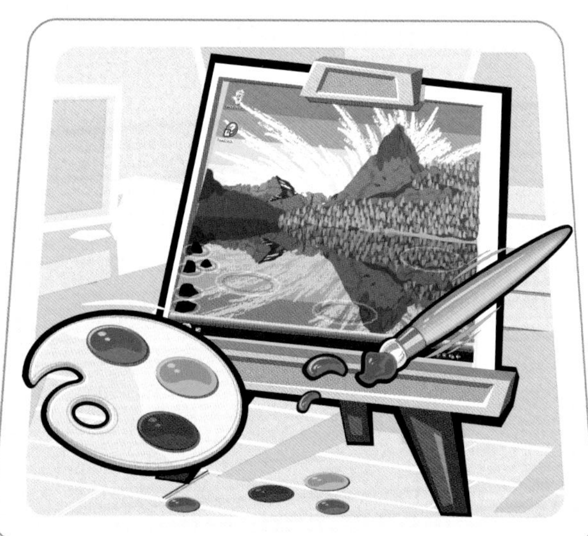

If you need to work directly with your Windows Home Server computer, you can use another computer to create a remote connection to the server's desktop. This enables you to change settings, install a program, and perform other Windows Home Server tasks.

Understanding Remote Desktop Connections ....................222
Make a Basic Connection ....................224
Work with the Connection Bar....................226
Customize the Remote Desktop Window ....................228
Customize the Remote Desktop Sounds and Keystrokes....................230
Start a Program Automatically When You Connect ....................232
Optimize the Connection Performance ......234

# Understanding Remote Desktop Connections

To get the most out of connecting remotely to Windows Home Server, you need to understand a few key concepts behind Remote Desktop connections. For example, you need to know the difference between a host and a client and what kind of performance you can expect.

### Headless Device

Most Windows Home Server computers operate as headless devices that do not have a monitor, keyboard, or mouse. If you need to work with the headless server directly to install a program or change a setting, then you must connect to the server from another computer.

### Remote Desktop Connection

Many Windows computers come with a program called Remote Desktop Connection. You use this program to connect to another computer over a network. Once you log on to the other computer, Remote Desktop Connection displays the other computer's desktop. You can then operate the remote computer as though you were sitting directly in front of it.

## Remote Desktop Host

The remote computer to which you make the connection is called a Remote Desktop host. The remote computer must be configured to act as a Remote Desktop host, or the remote connection will fail. By default, Windows Home Server is configured to act as a Remote Desktop host.

## Remote Desktop Client

The local computer that you use to connect to the Remote Desktop host is called the Remote Desktop client. All versions of Windows Vista can act as Remote Desktop clients because they come with the Remote Desktop Connection software installed. If you are using Windows XP, you must install Remote Desktop Connection from the Windows XP CD. For more information, see the section "Make a Basic Connection."

## Performance

Although Remote Desktop Connection enables you to operate Windows Home Server directly, it is not quite the same as sitting in front of the computer. This is because the network connection determines how responsive the desktop is to your mouse and keyboard inputs. A Fast Ethernet (100 Mbps) connection should provide adequate performance. For best results, use a Gigabit Ethernet (1,000 Mbps) connection.

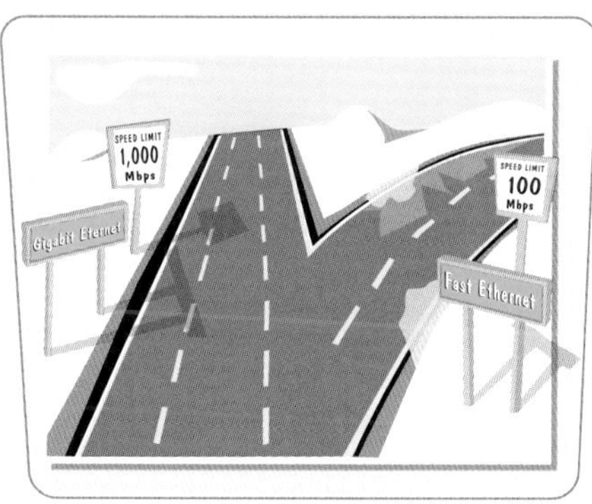


## Permissions

When you initiate a Remote Desktop session, you must log on to the remote computer to gain access to its desktop. In Windows Home Server, this means that you must log on using the server's Administrator user account.

# Make a Basic Connection

For quick access to the Windows Home Server desktop, you can establish a basic connection by using Remote Desktop Connection without options such as a custom screen size and starting a program automatically.

**The rest of this chapter shows you how to create Remote Desktop connections that are customized to suit your needs.**

## Make a Basic Connection

1. On the client computer, click **Start**.
2. Click **All Programs**.
   - In Windows Vista, All Programs changes to Back.
3. Click **Accessories**.
4. Click **Remote Desktop Connection**.

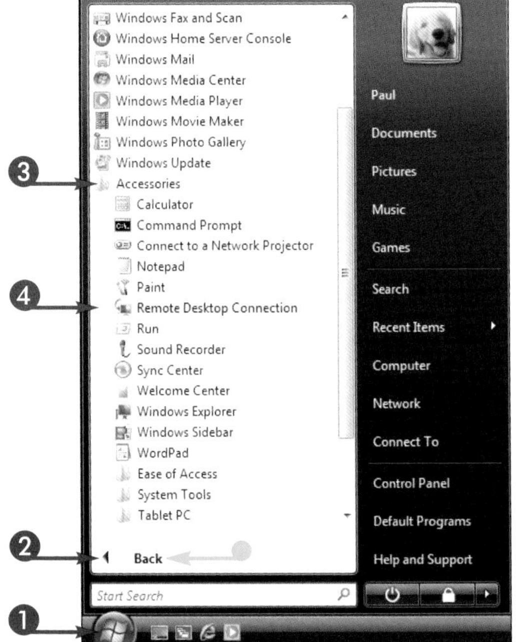


The Remote Desktop Connection window appears.

5. In the Computer text box, type the name of your Windows Home Server computer.
6. Click **Connect**.

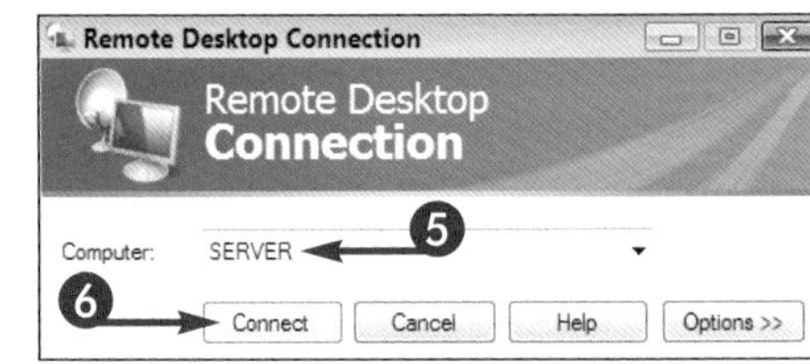

The Windows Security dialog box appears.

7. In the Username text box, type **Administrator**.
8. In the Password text box, type the password for the Windows Home Server Administrator account.
9. Click **Remember my credentials** ( changes to ) to have Windows store the username and password.
10. Click **OK**.

Windows connects to the server and then displays the Windows Home Server desktop.

***Note:*** *If you see a Web browser window with a caution message, click  to close the window.*

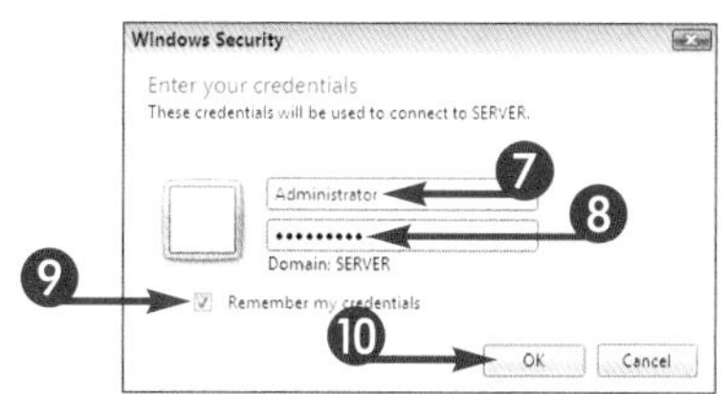

### Why can I not find Remote Desktop Connection in my version of Windows XP?

Many versions of Windows XP do not come with the Remote Desktop Connection software installed by default, so you must install the program manually. For the details, see Chapter 12.

### Is there an easier way to launch the Remote Desktop Connection program?

Yes, you can pin the program's icon to the main Start menu, as shown in these steps:

1. Follow steps **1** to **3** to display the Accessories menu.
2. Right-click **Remote Desktop Connection**.
3. Click **Pin to Start Menu**.

Windows adds an icon for Remote Desktop Connection to the main Start menu.

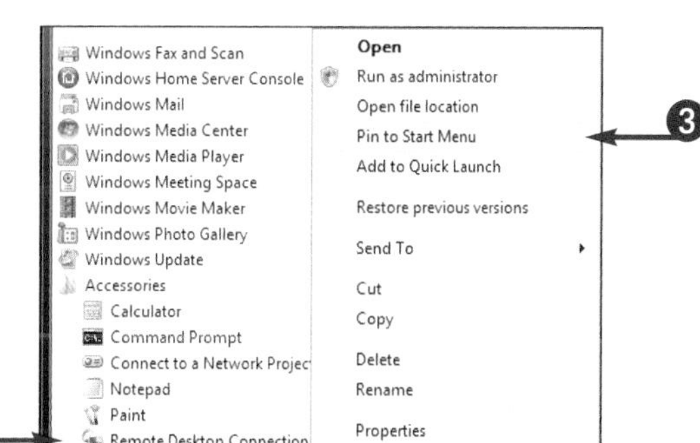

# Work with the Connection Bar

You can control the Remote Desktop connection to Windows Home Server by learning how to operate the connection bar, which enables you to minimize and restore the window and to disconnect from the server.

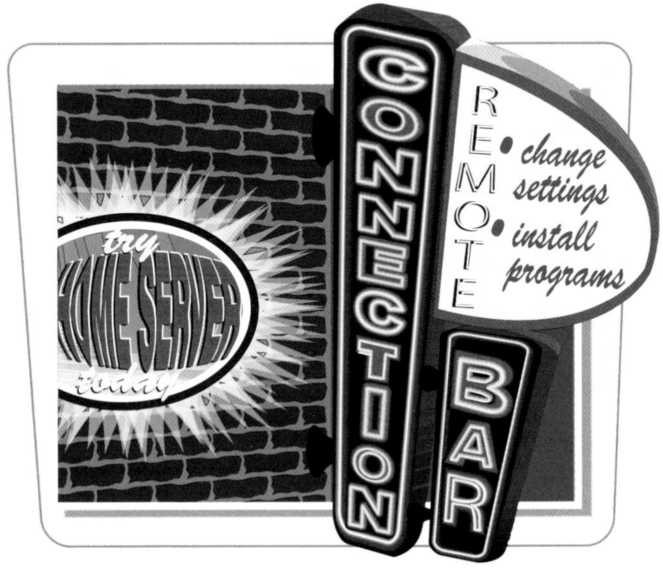


## Work with the Connection Bar

### DISPLAY THE CONNECTION BAR

1. Move the mouse to the top part of the screen, near the center.

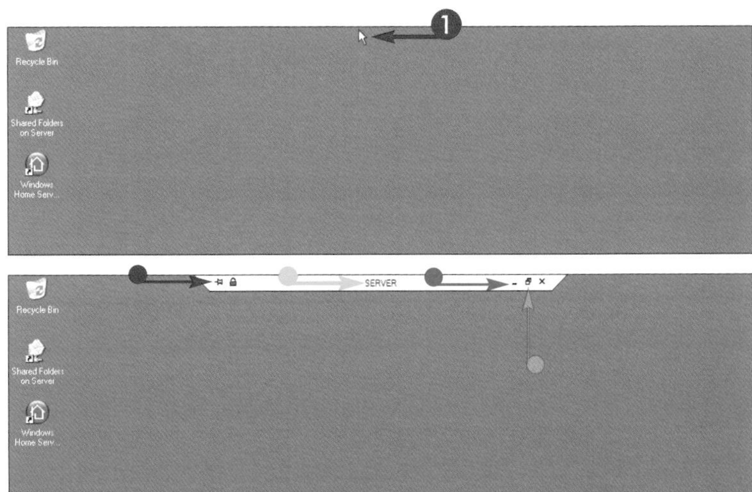


- The connection bar appears.
- Click **Pin** to keep the connection bar onscreen at all times.
- Click **Minimize** to reduce the server's desktop to a button on your computer's taskbar.
- Click **Restore** to display the server's desktop in a window.

## DISCONNECT FROM THE SERVER

1. Click **Close** (X).

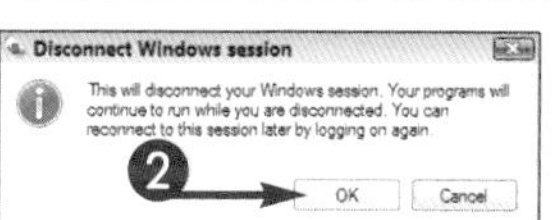


Remote Desktop Connection warns you that this will disconnect your session.

2. Click **OK**.

Remote Desktop Connection disconnects your session, but leaves your programs running.

### When I connect to Windows Home Server, the desktop appears inside a window and I cannot display the connection bar. Why?

Remote Desktop Connection only uses the connection bar when it displays the desktop in full-screen view. To switch to this view, click the Remote Desktop window's **Maximize** button (▭), or press Ctrl + Alt + Break. Windows expands the Remote Desktop window to take up the entire screen.

- Click ▭ for full-screen view.

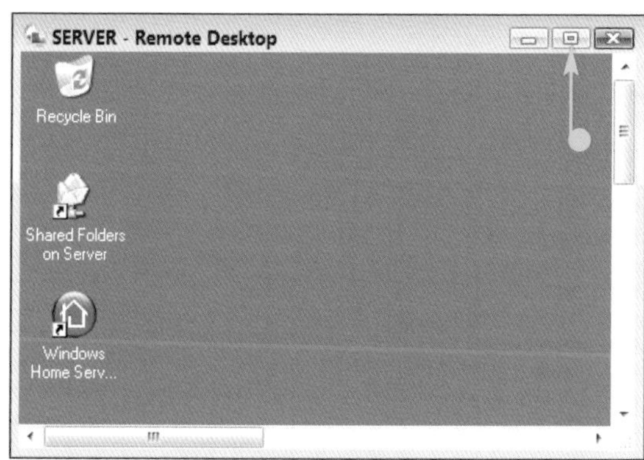


### Is there a way to disconnect from the server and also close all of the programs that I have running on the server?

Yes, by following these steps:

1. In Windows Home Server, click **Start**.
2. Click **Log Off**.

   The Log Off Windows dialog box appears.
3. Click **Log Off**.

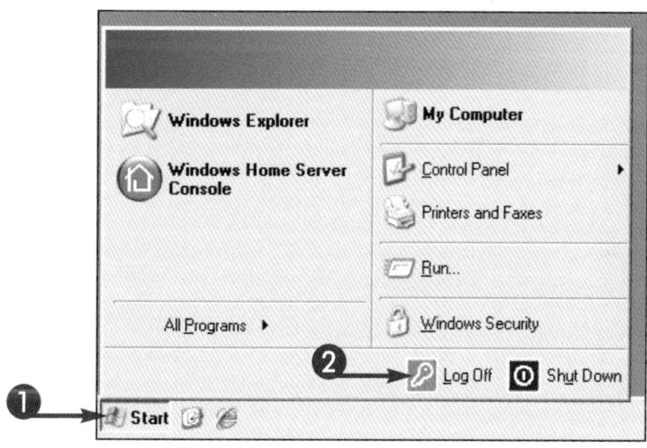

# Customize the Remote Desktop Window

You can customize the look of the Remote Desktop window to suit your needs. You can choose the size of the Remote Desktop window, the number of colors in the display, and whether the connection bar appears.

## Customize the Remote Desktop Window

1. Start Remote Desktop Connection.

*Note: For more information, see the section "Make a Basic Connection."*

2. Click **Options**.

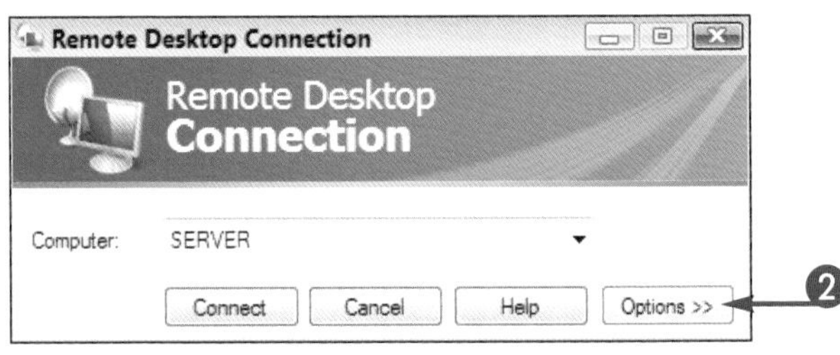


The Remote Desktop Connection dialog box expands.

3. Click the **Display** tab.
4. Click and drag the **Remote desktop size** slider (▯) to set the size of the Remote Desktop window.

- You can drag ▯ all the way to the right to display the Remote Desktop window in full-screen mode.

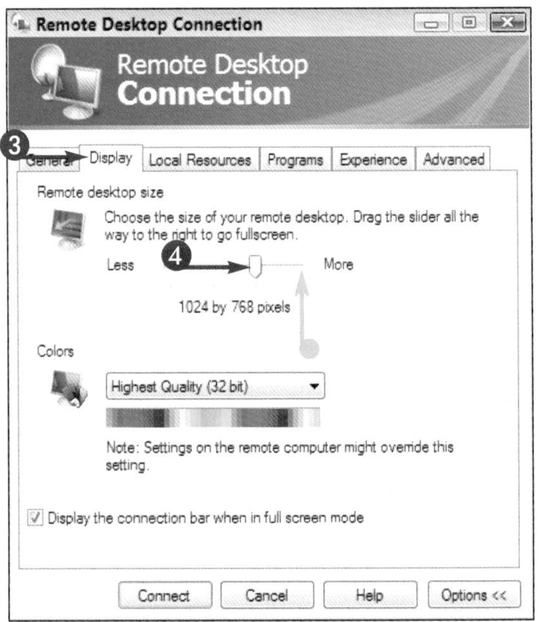

5 Click ▾ in the **Colors** drop-down list, and then click the number of colors you want to use.

***Note:*** *The greater the number of bits, the better the color quality. However, your Windows Home Server computer may not support the setting you choose, and may override your choice.*

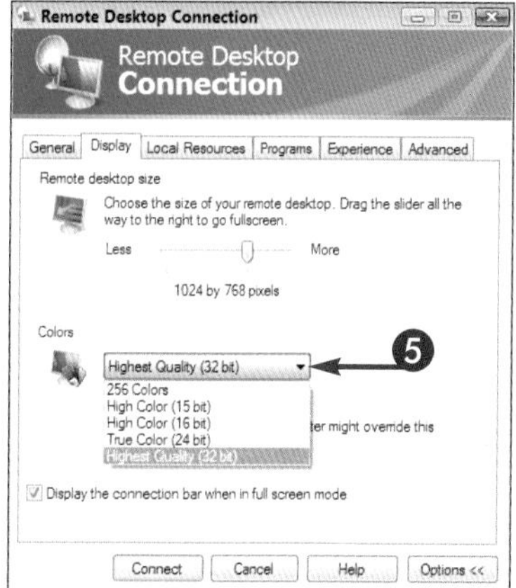

6 Click this check box to configure the Remote Desktop window to show the connection bar when you switch to full-screen view (☐ changes to ☑).

7 Click **Connect**.

***Note:*** *Alternatively, you can continue setting Remote Desktop Connection options, as described in the remaining sections of this chapter.*

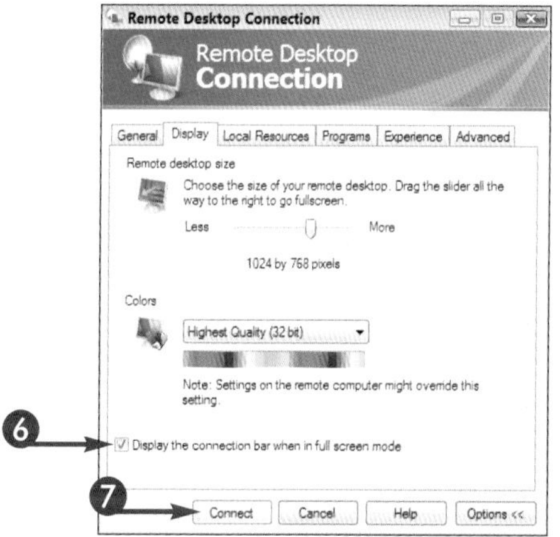

### Can I save my Remote Desktop Connection settings?

If you only use Remote Desktop Connection to connect to Windows Home Server, then Windows will retain your settings. However, if you make Remote Desktop connections to other computers, then you may want to follow these steps to save the Windows Home Server connection settings:

1. Click the **General** tab.
2. Click **Save As**.

   The Save As dialog box appears.
3. Use the File name text box to type a name for the Remote Desktop file.
4. Click **Save**.

- To reuse a Remote Desktop file, you can click **Open**.

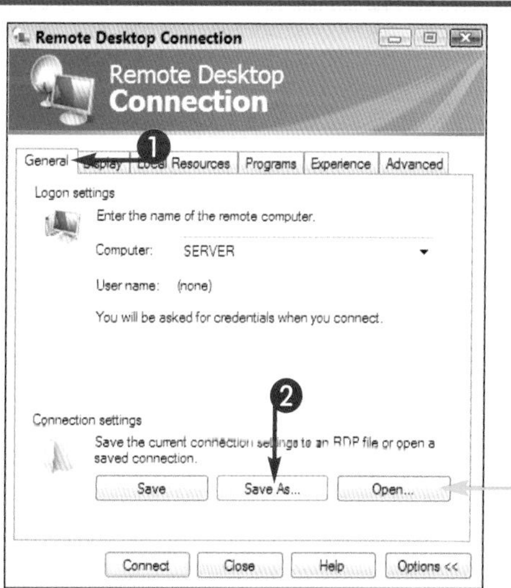

# Customize the Remote Desktop Sounds and Keystrokes

You can customize how Remote Desktop Connection processes sounds and keystrokes to suit the way you work. For example, you can have the remote computer's sounds play on your computer. You can also have keystrokes, such as Alt+Tab, either sent to the remote computer or sent to your computer.

## Customize the Remote Desktop Sounds and Keystrokes

1. Start Remote Desktop Connection.

*Note: For more information, see the section "Make a Basic Connection."*

2. Click **Options**.

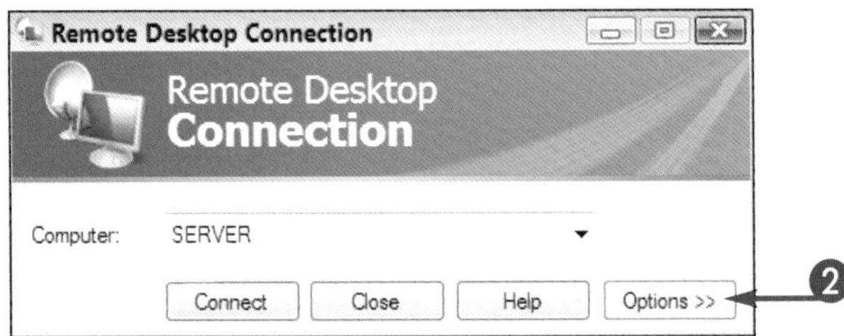


The Remote Desktop Connection dialog box expands.

3. Click the **Local Resources** tab.
4. In the **Remote computer sound** drop-down list, click ▾ and then click an option to specify where you want the remote computer's sounds to play.

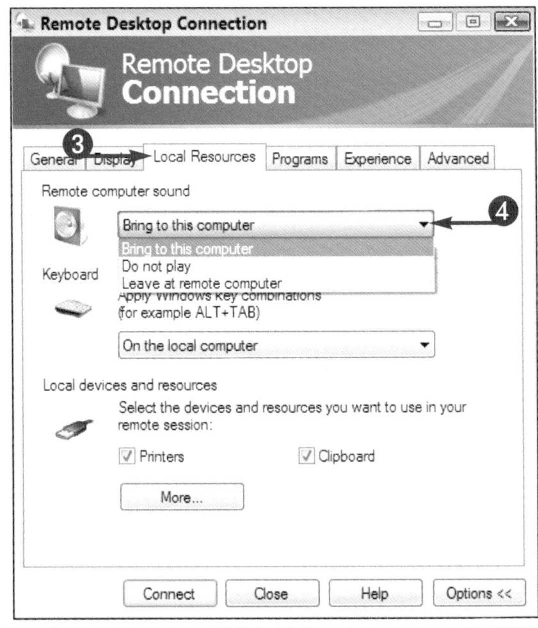

5. In the **Keyboard** drop-down list, click ▼ and then click an option to specify where you want Windows keystrokes to be sent.

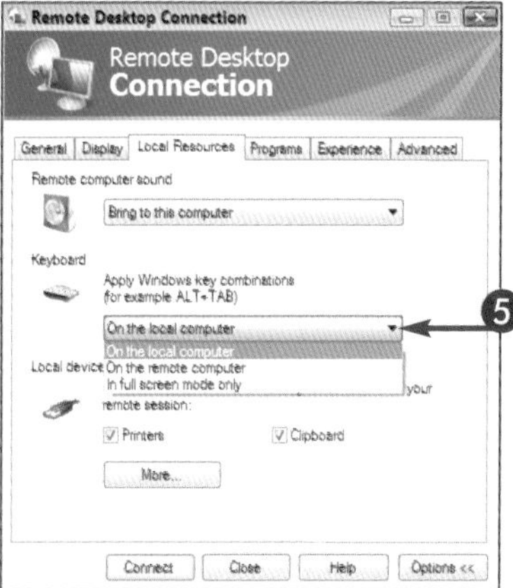


6. Click **Printers** (☐ changes to ☑) to use your computer's printers through the remote computer's desktop.

7. Click **Clipboard** (☐ changes to ☑) to cut or copy data between your computer and the Remote Desktop window.

8. Click **Connect**.

***Note:** Alternatively, you can continue setting Remote Desktop Connection options, as described in the remaining sections of this chapter.*

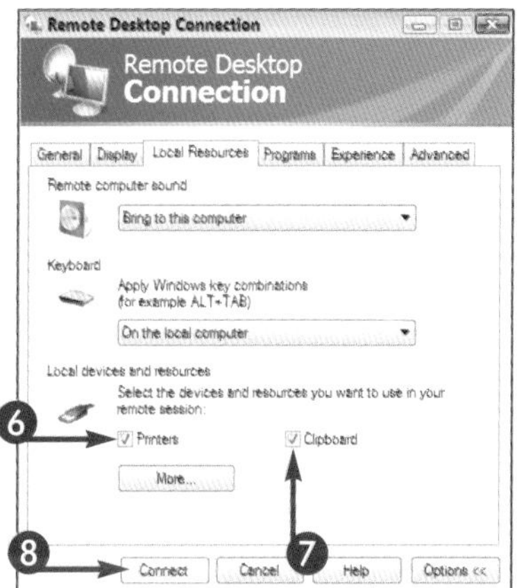

**I am sending Windows key combinations to the Remote Desktop window. What do I do if I need to use any of those keystrokes on my own computer?**

Windows comes with some alternative keystrokes you can use:

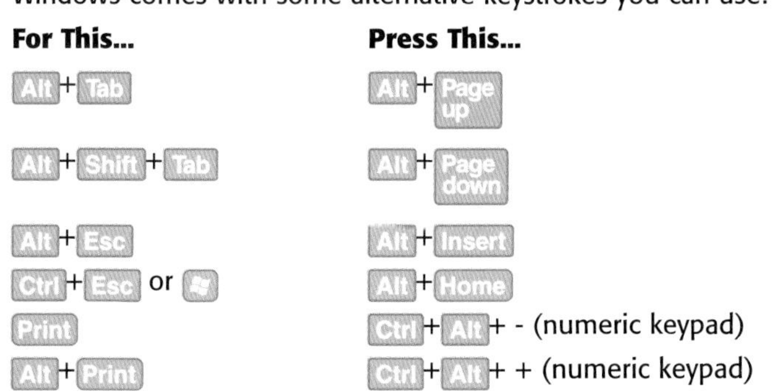

| For This... | Press This... |
|---|---|
| Alt+Tab | Alt+Page up |
| Alt+Shift+Tab | Alt+Page down |
| Alt+Esc | Alt+Insert |
| Ctrl+Esc or Windows key | Alt+Home |
| Print | Ctrl+Alt+ - (numeric keypad) |
| Alt+Print | Ctrl+Alt+ + (numeric keypad) |

# Start a Program Automatically When You Connect

If you find that you only work with a particular program when you connect to the Windows Home Server desktop, you can save a few steps by configuring Remote Desktop Connection to automatically start that program each time you connect.

## Start a Program Automatically When You Connect

1. Start Remote Desktop Connection.

*Note:* *For more information, see the section "Make a Basic Connection."*

2. Click **Options**.

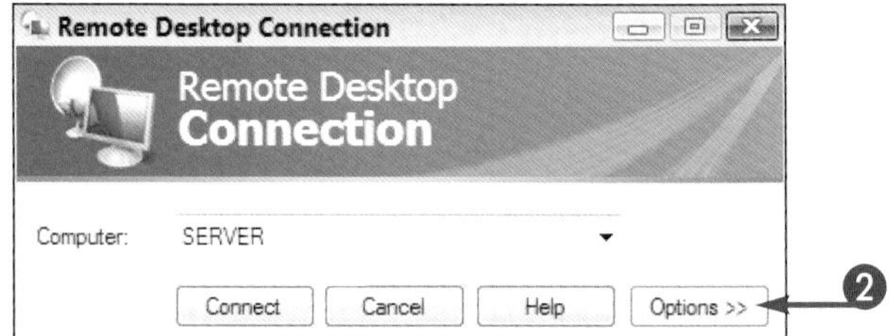


The Remote Desktop Connection dialog box expands.

3. Click the **Programs** tab.
4. Click **Start the following program on connection** (☐ changes to ☑).
5. Type the path and filename of the Windows Home Server program you want to run.
6. Click **Connect**.

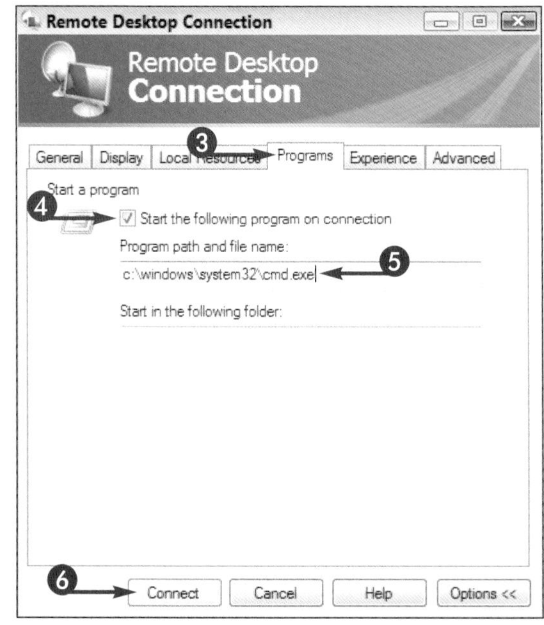

The Windows Security dialog box appears.

***Note:*** *You do not see the Windows Security dialog box if you clicked the* ***Remember my credentials*** *check box. See the section "Make a Basic Connection" for more information.*

7 Type the password for the Windows Home Server Administrator account.

8 Click **OK**.

Remote Desktop Connection connects to Windows Home Server and runs the program.

9 When you are finished working with the program, click ☒ to close the program and end your remote session.

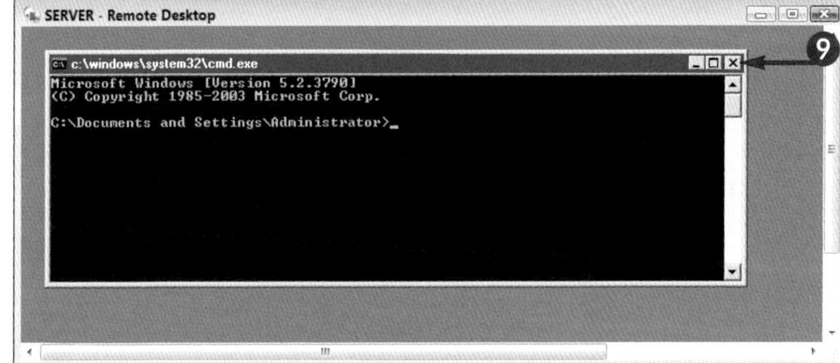

### After I specify a program, why can I no longer access the Windows Home Server desktop?

The program you specify runs instead of the Windows Home Server desktop. In a sense, that program becomes your remote Windows Home Server session. That is, when you exit the program, Remote Desktop Connection also exits your remote session. Therefore, you should only specify a program to run if you do not also want to work with the Windows Home Server desktop.

### Is there any way that I can start a program automatically *and* get access to the Windows Home Server desktop?

Yes, you can add a shortcut for the program to the Startup folder. Connect to Windows Home Server (making sure that no program is configured to run on connection). Right-click the Windows Home Server desktop, click **New**, click **Shortcut**, and then use the Create Shortcut Wizard to create a shortcut for the program. Drag the shortcut over the **Start** button, then over **All Programs**, and then drop it inside the **Startup** menu (●).

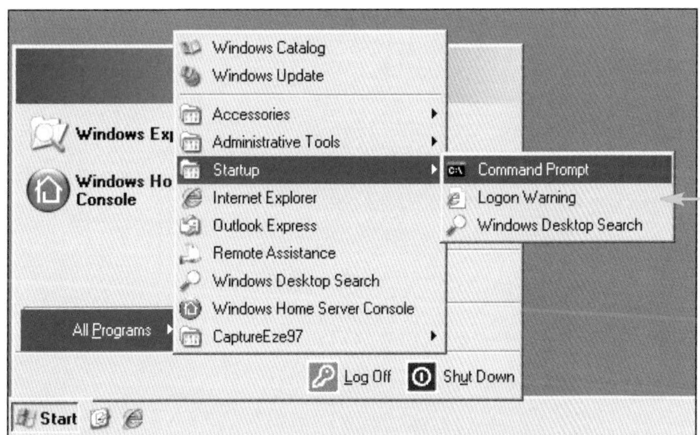

# Optimize the Connection Performance

You can make your connection perform faster and with greater stability by turning off some of the Windows Home Server graphics effects, such as themes and the animation of menus and windows.

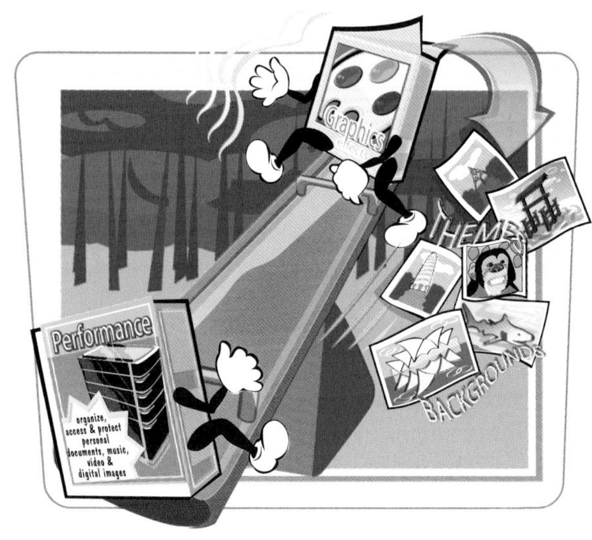


## Optimize the Connection Performance

1. Start Remote Desktop Connection.

*Note: For more information, see the section "Make a Basic Connection."*

2. Click **Options**.

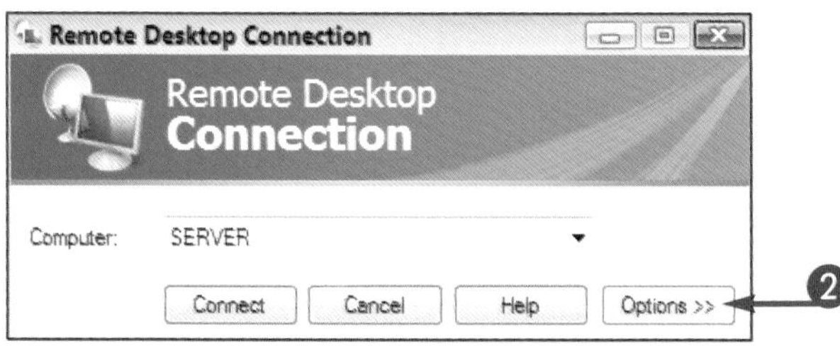


The Remote Desktop Connection dialog box expands.

3. Click the **Experience** tab.

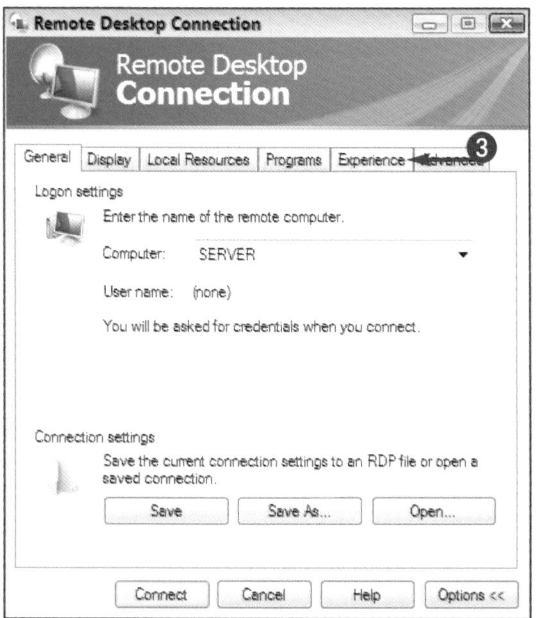

4 Click ▾ and then click **Custom**.

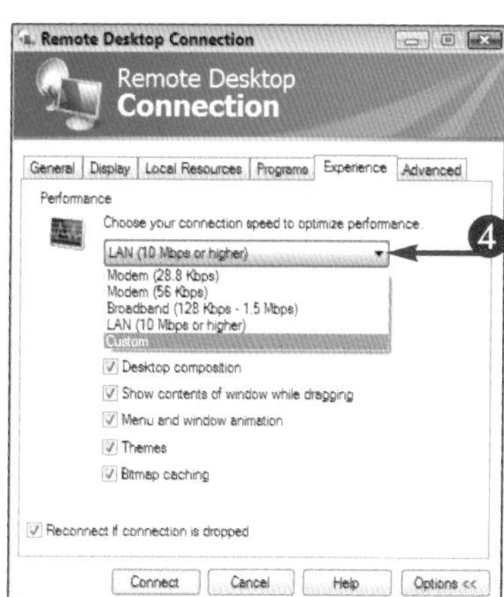


5 Click the check boxes for the graphics effects you do not want to use during the connection (☑ changes to ☐).

6 Click **Connect**.

***Note:*** *Alternatively, you can continue setting Remote Desktop Connection options, as described in the previous sections of this chapter.*

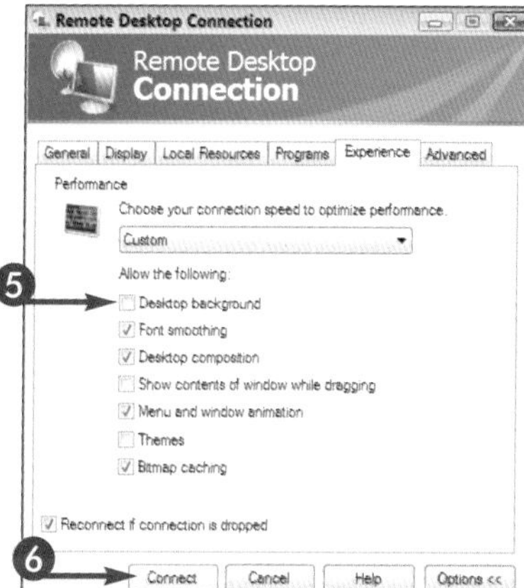

### Do I need to turn off graphics effects if I have a fast network connection to Windows Home Server?

Probably not. If you have a Fast Ethernet (100 Mbps) or Gigabit Ethernet (1,000 Mbps, or 1 Gbps) connection, then you should be able to view all of the Windows Home Server graphics effects. In step **4**, click **LAN (10 Mbps or higher)**.

If you still find that you are having performance problems, try turning off the effects one at a time until the performance is acceptable. In most cases, you should not need to turn off any of the effects unless you are connecting to Windows Home Server over a slow Internet connection. You can learn about these connections in Chapter 12.

CHAPTER

# 12

# Connecting to Other Network Computers

You can use a combination of Remote Desktop Connection and the Windows Home Server Remote Access Web page to make a remote connection to other computers on your network.

Configure Windows Vista as a Remote Desktop Host ....238
Configure Windows XP as a Remote Desktop Host ....240
Install Remote Desktop Connection on Windows XP ....242
Connect Using Remote Desktop Connection ....244
Give a User Remote Access ....246
Activate the Windows Home Server Web Site ....248
Display the Remote Access Home Page ....250
Connect Using the Remote Access Home Page ....252
Disconnect from the Remote Computer ....254
Customize the Remote Access Site Settings ....256

# Configure Windows Vista as a Remote Desktop Host

To make a remote connection to the desktop of a Windows Vista computer, you must configure that computer to act as a Remote Desktop Connection host computer.

**Unfortunately, not all versions of Windows Vista can act as Remote Desktop Connection hosts. Only computers running Windows Vista Business, Windows Vista Enterprise, and Windows Vista Ultimate can act as hosts.**

## Configure Windows Vista as a Remote Desktop Host

1. Click **Start**.
2. Right-click **Computer**.
3. Click **Properties**.

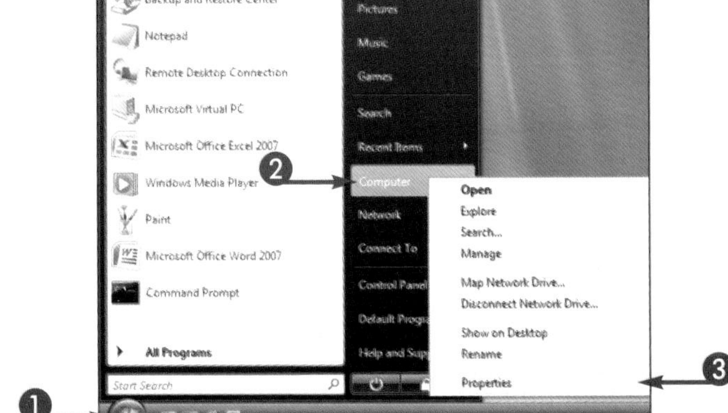

The System window appears.

4. Click **Remote settings**.

***Note:*** *If the User Account Control dialog box appears, either click* ***Continue****, or type an Administrator password and click* ***Submit****.*

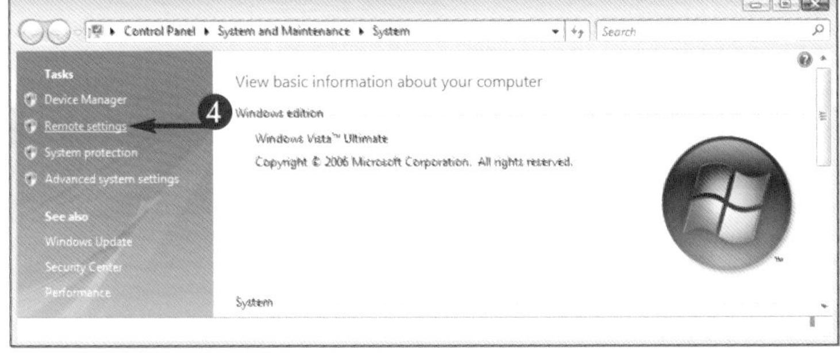

The System Properties dialog box appears with the Remote tab displayed.

5 Click **Allow connections from computers running any version of Remote Desktop** (○ changes to ◉).

6 Click **OK**.

You can now use Windows Vista as a Remote Desktop host.

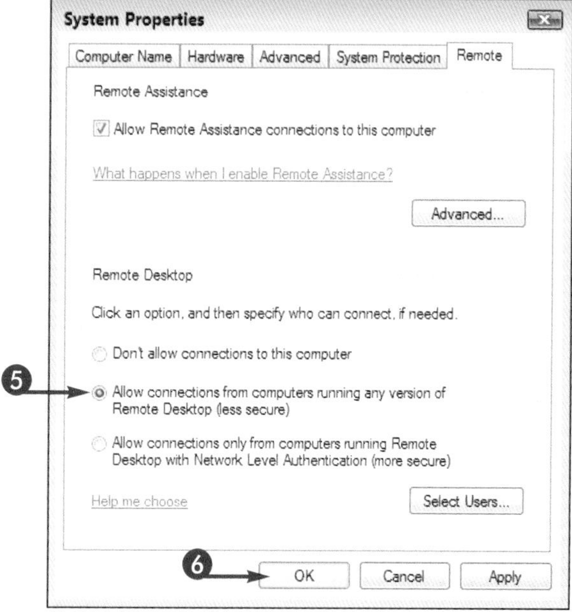

### Under what circumstances would I choose the more secure Remote Desktop option?

The Remote tab has a second Remote Desktop option called "Allow connections only from computers running Remote Desktop with Network Level Authentication." Network Level Authentication is an extra security layer built into Windows Vista that helps ensure that only authorized users can connect to the computer. Use this option if only Windows Vista computers are connected to your computer.

### How do I allow other users to connect to my Windows Vista computer?

You need to add password-protected accounts for those users to your Windows Vista computer. Click **Start**, click **Control Panel**, and then click **Add or remove user accounts**. After you have created the accounts, follow steps **1** to **5** in this section, and then click **Select Users** to open the Remote Desktop Users dialog box. For each user, click **Add**, type the user's name in the Select Users dialog box, and then click **OK**.

Remote Desktop Users

The users listed below can connect to this computer, and any members of the Administrators group can connect even if they are not listed.

Karen

Paul already has access.

Add... Remove

To create new user accounts or add users to other groups, go to Control Panel and open User Accounts.

OK Cancel

# Configure Windows XP as a Remote Desktop Host

To make a remote connection to the desktop of a Windows XP computer, you must configure that computer to act as a Remote Desktop Connection host computer.

**Most versions of Windows XP can act as Remote Desktop Connection hosts. The only version of Windows XP that cannot act as a host is Windows XP Home.**

## Configure Windows XP as a Remote Desktop Host

1. Log on to Windows XP with an Administrator-level account.
2. Click **Start**.
3. Right-click **My Computer**.
4. Click **Properties**.

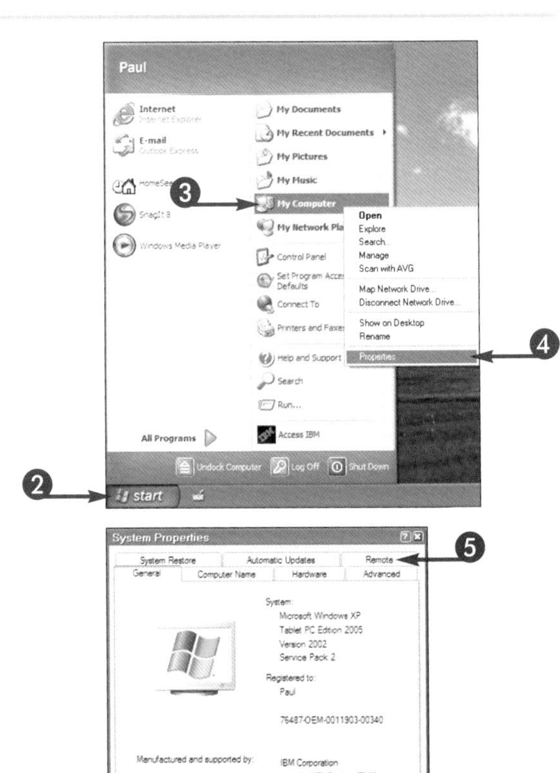

The System Properties dialog box appears.

5. Click the **Remote** tab.

6 Click **Allow users to connect remotely to this computer** (☐ changes to ☑).

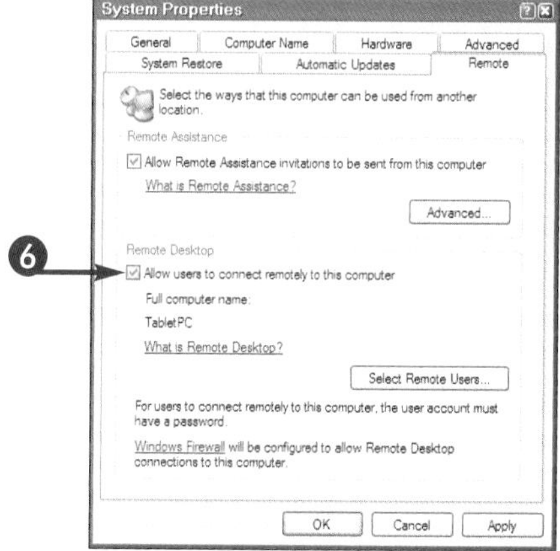


7 Click **OK**.

You can now use Windows XP as a Remote Desktop host.

### How do I allow other users to connect to my Windows XP computer?

First you need to add password-protected accounts for those users to your Windows XP computer. Click **Start**, click **Control Panel**, and then click **User Accounts**. After you have created the accounts, follow steps **1** to **6** in this section, and then click **Select Remote Users** to open the Remote Desktop Users dialog box. For each user, click **Add**, type the user's name in the Select Users dialog box, and then click **OK**.

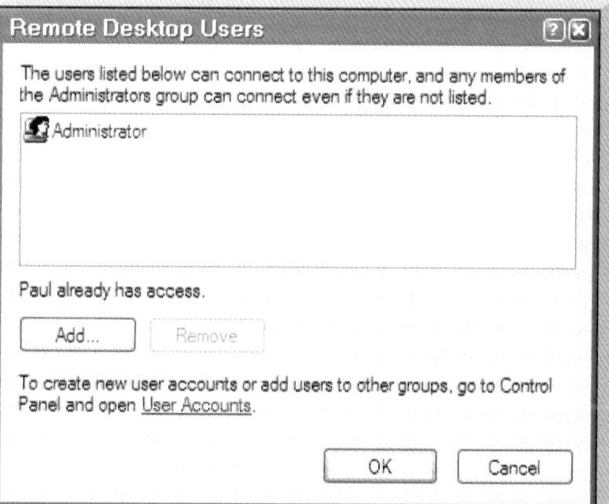

# Install Remote Desktop Connection on Windows XP

Your version of Windows XP may not include the Remote Desktop Connection software. In that case, you must install the software from the Windows XP CD.

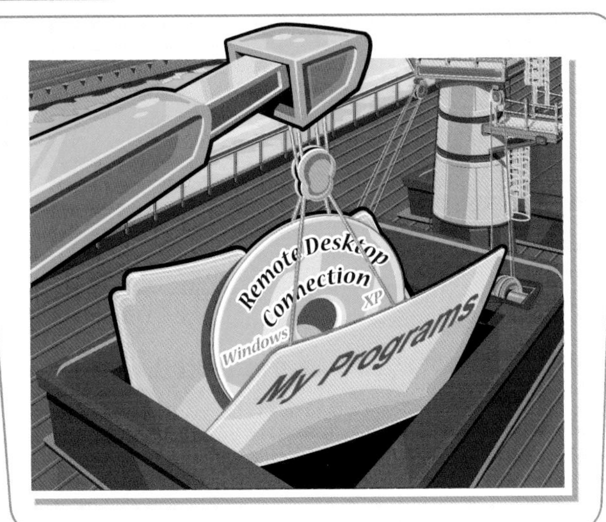


## Install Remote Desktop Connection on Windows XP

1. Insert the Windows XP CD.

   The Welcome to Microsoft Windows XP window appears.

2. Click **Perform additional tasks**.

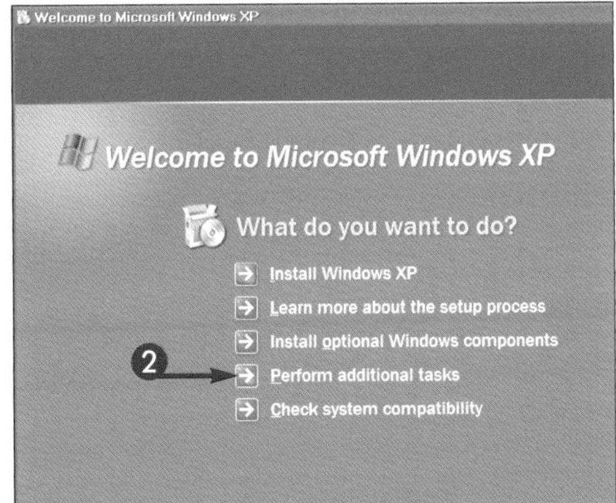


   The Welcome to Microsoft Windows XP window displays a new set of options.

3. Click **Set up Remote Desktop Connection**.

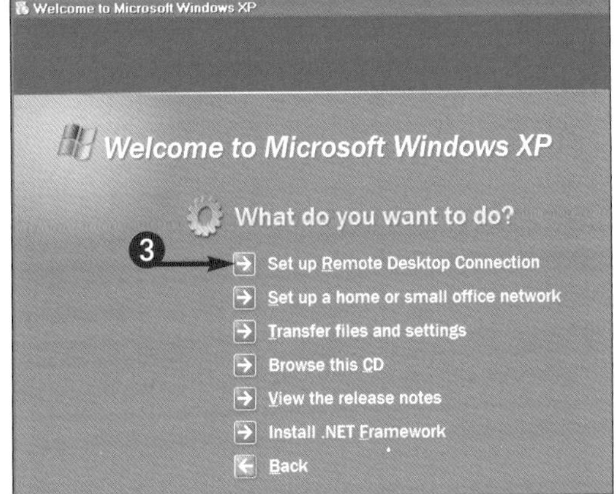

The Remote Desktop Connection - InstallShield Wizard appears.

4. Click **Next**.

The License Agreement dialog box appears.

5. Click **I accept the terms in the license agreement** (○ changes to ◉).
6. Click **Next**.

The Customer Information dialog box appears.

7. Click **Next**.

The Ready to Install the Program dialog box appears.

8. Click **Install**.

The InstallShield Wizard installs Remote Desktop Connection.

9. Click **Finish**.

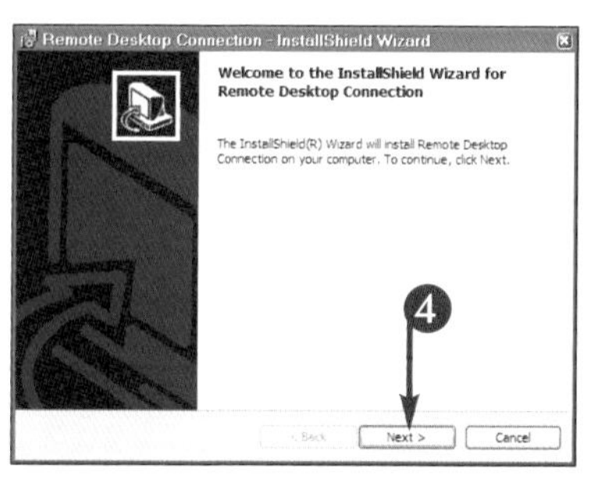
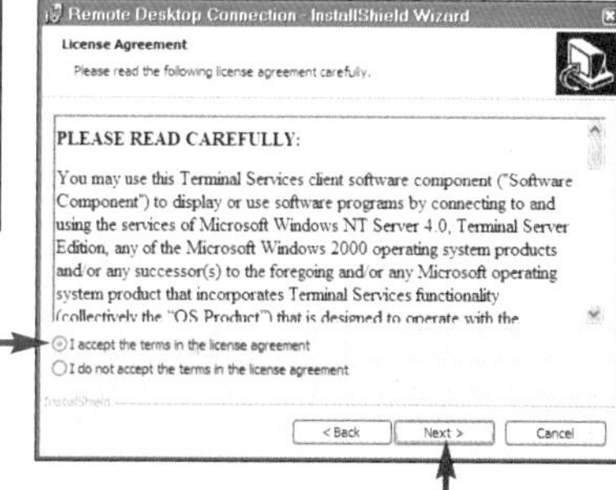
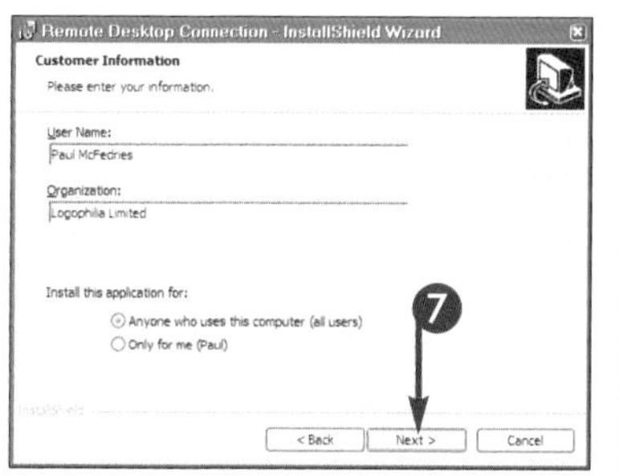
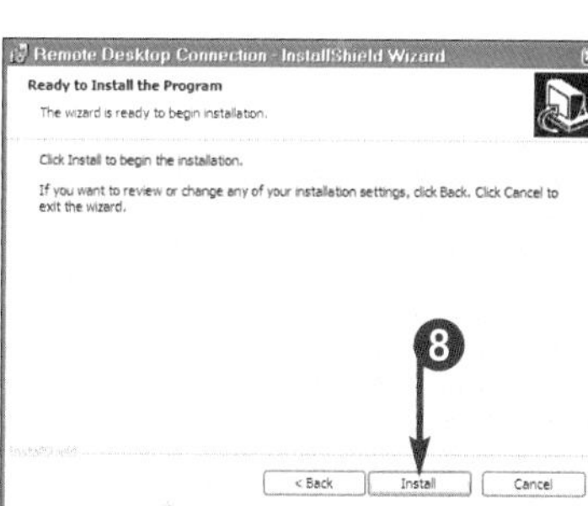

**Is there a way to check in advance whether I have Remote Desktop Connection installed on my version of Windows XP?**

Yes. The easiest way to check is to click **Start**, click **All Programs**, and then click **Accessories**. Look for the **Remote Desktop Connection** icon (●) in the Accessories menu.

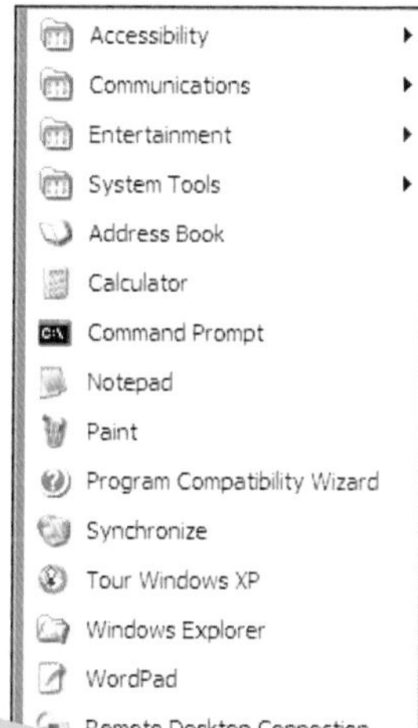


**I do not have Remote Desktop Connection installed, but I also do not have a Windows XP installation CD. How can I install Remote Desktop Connection?**

You can download Remote Desktop Connection from the Microsoft Web site. First, use a Web browser to navigate to the following address: www.microsoft.com/windowsxp/downloads/tools/rdclientdl.mspx. Click the link in the Download section(●).

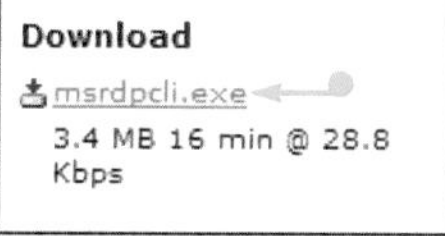

# Connect Using Remote Desktop Connection

You can use the Remote Desktop Connection software to connect to the desktop of another computer on your network.

**Remember that you can only connect to a computer that you have configured as a Remote Desktop host.**

## Connect Using Remote Desktop Connection

1. Click **Start**.
2. Click **All Programs**.
   - In Windows Vista, All Programs changes to Back.
3. Click **Accessories**.
4. Click **Remote Desktop Connection**.

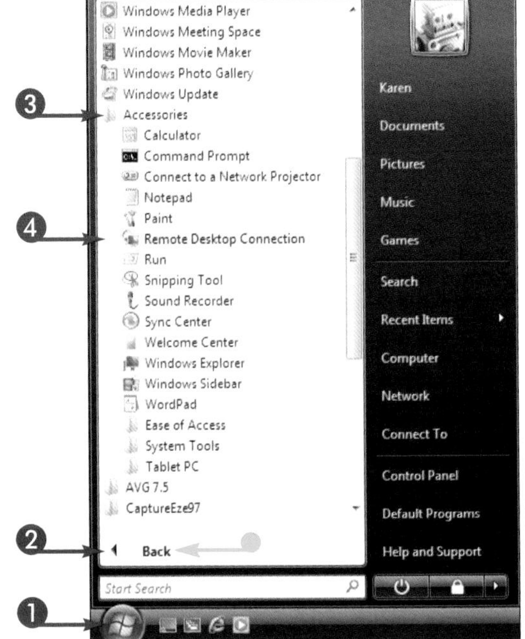

The Remote Desktop Connection window appears.

5. In the Computer text box, type the name of the Remote Desktop host computer.
6. Click **Connect**.

The Windows Security dialog box appears.

7. In the username text box, type the name of an account that has Remote Desktop access to the computer.
8. In the password text box, type the password for the account name that you typed in step **7**.
9. Click **Remember my credentials** to have Windows store the username and password (☐ changes to ☑).
10. Click **OK**.

Windows logs on to the remote computer and then displays the computer's desktop.

***Note:*** *To learn how to use the Remote Desktop window, see Chapter 11.*

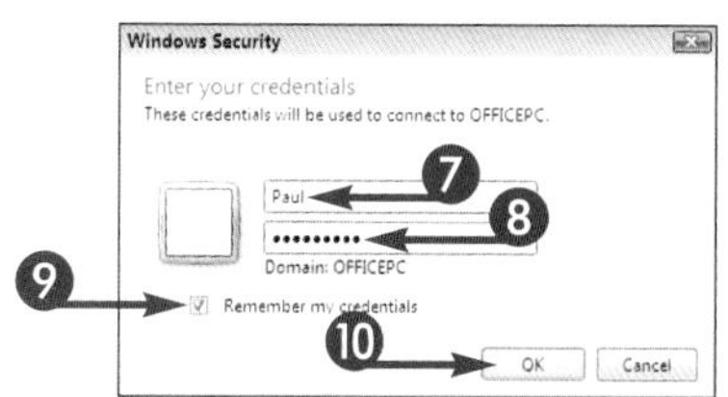

### Is there an easier way to connect to a Remote Desktop host?

Yes, Windows Home Server offers the Remote Access Web page, which enables you to connect to any Remote Desktop host on your network without using the Remote Desktop Connection software directly. The next three sections provide the details.

### Is it safe to activate the Remember my credentials check box?

Yes, in most cases, it is safe to select the **Remember my credentials** check box. However, keep in mind that this allows anyone sitting at your computer to connect to and work with the remote computer without having to enter credentials. If there is anyone who can access your computer that you do not want to give access to the remote computer, then you should not select the **Remember my credentials** check box.

Remember my credentials

# Give a User Remote Access

To give a user permission to use the Windows Home Server Remote Access Web page, you must enable remote access for that user.

**To give a user remote access in Windows Home Server, you must know the password for the server's Administrator account.**

## Give a User Remote Access

1. Start the Windows Home Server Console.

***Note:*** *See Chapter 3 for more information.*

2. Click **User Accounts**.

- This column shows the remote access setting for each user.

3. Click the user you want to work with.
4. Click **Properties**.

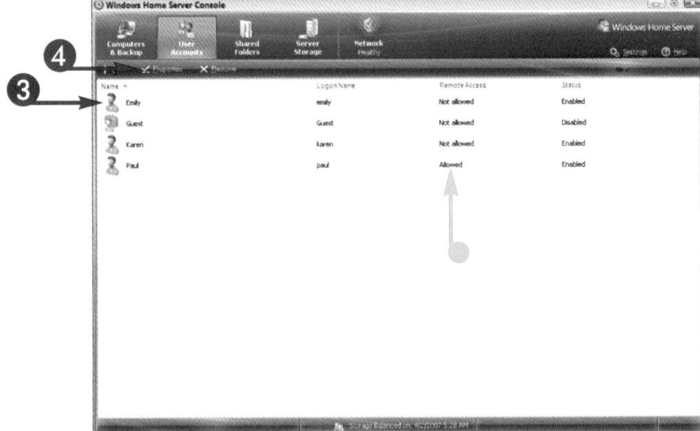

The user's Properties dialog box appears.

5. Click **Enable remote access for this user** (☐ changes to ☑).
6. Click **OK**.

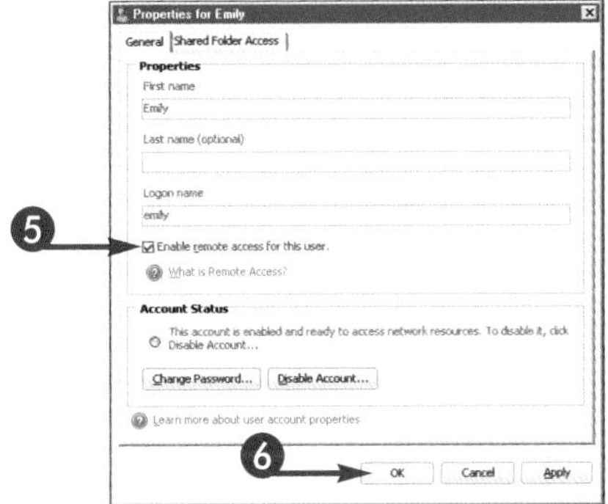

- Windows Home Server displays Allowed in the user's Remote Access column.

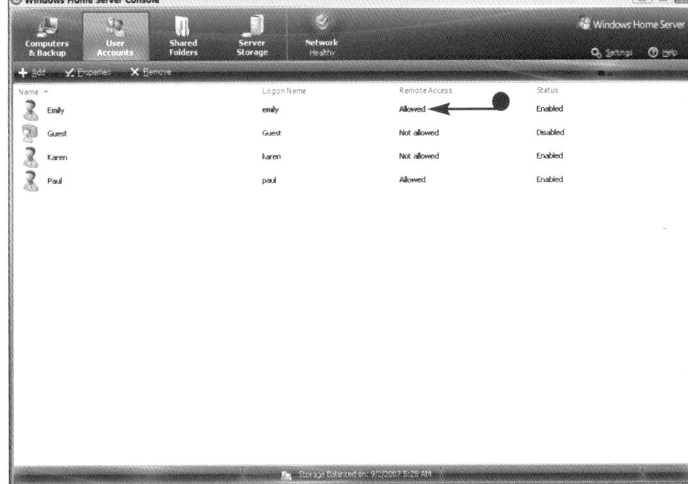

### When I enable remote access for a user, Windows Home Server tells me the account must have a strong password. Why?

The Remote Access Web page enables a user to connect to a computer's desktop either over the network, as described later in this chapter, or over the Internet, as described in Chapter 13. To prevent unauthorized access to a computer's desktop, Windows Home Server requires a strong password for each account that is given remote access. See Chapter 4 to learn more about strong passwords.

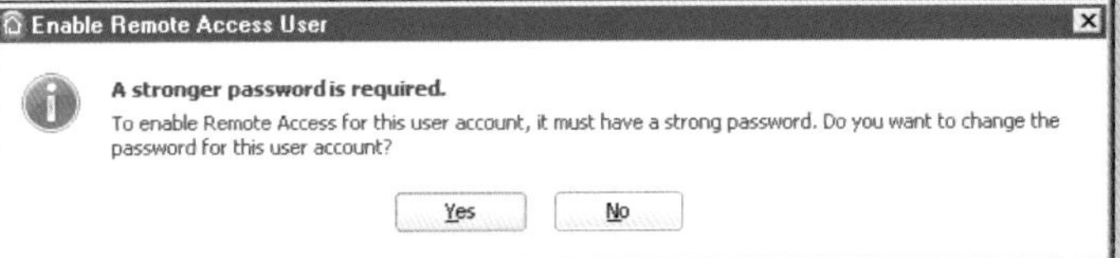

# Activate the Windows Home Server Web Site

The Windows Home Server Web site is deactivated by default, so to enable users to see the Remote Access page and other pages, you must activate the Windows Home Server Web site.

**To activate the Windows Home Server Web site, you must know the password for the server's Administrator account.**

## Activate the Windows Home Server Web Site

1. Start the Windows Home Server Console.

***Note:*** *See Chapter 3 for more information.*

2. Click **Settings**.

The Windows Home Server Settings dialog box appears.

3. Click the **Remote Access** tab.

4 Click **Turn On**.

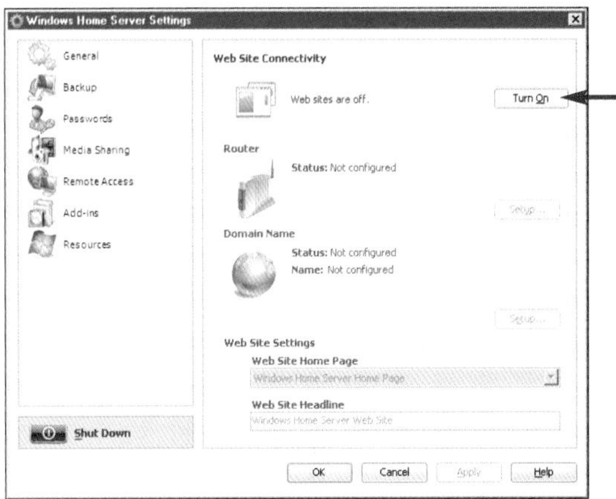


- Windows Home Server activates the Web site.

5 Click **OK**.

Windows Home Server users with remote access can now access the server's Web pages.

***Note:*** *You can learn how to configure the other settings in the Remote Access tab in Chapter 13.*

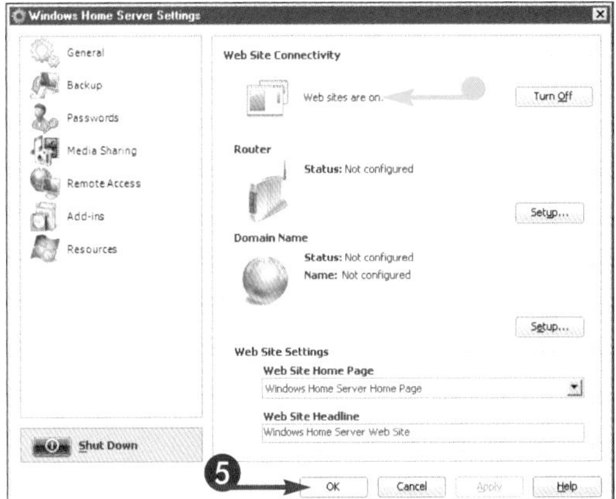

**If I find that my family never uses the Windows Home Server Web site, should I leave it turned on?**

No, it is better to turn the Windows Home Server Web site off, as a security precaution. Follow these steps:

1 Follow steps **1** to **3** in this section.

2 Click **Turn Off**.

Windows Home Server deactivates the Web site.

3 Click **OK**.

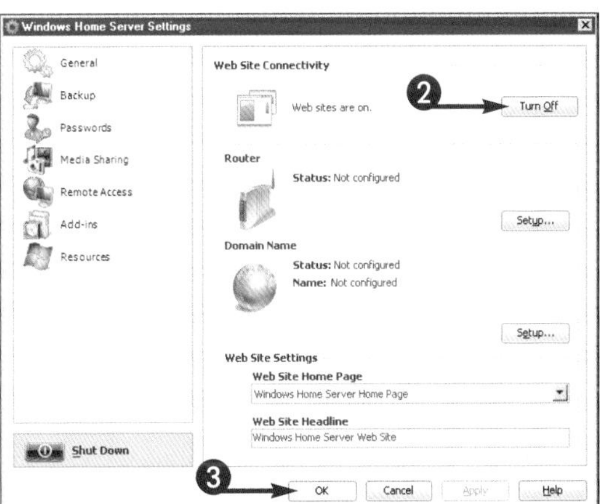

# Display the Remote Access Home Page

Windows Home Server comes with a Remote Access Web site that enables you to connect to other computers on your network. Before you can connect to any computers, you must first display the Remote Access home page.

**Remember that only users who have been given remote access permission can log on to the Remote Access home page. See the section "Give a User Remote Access," earlier in this chapter.**

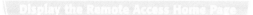

1. Click **Start**.
2. Click **Internet**.

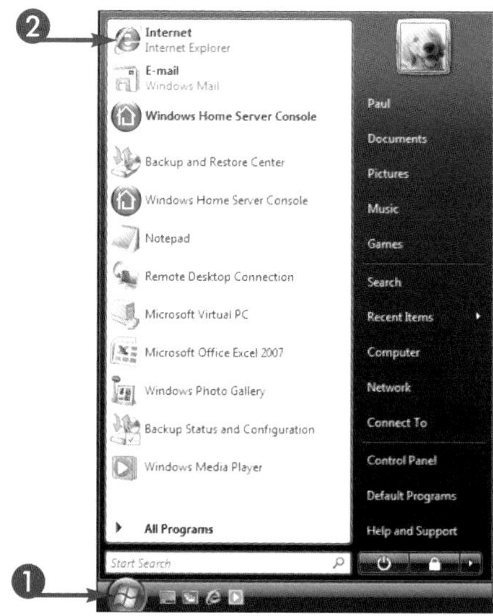


The Internet Explorer Web browser appears.

***Note:*** *Depending on your system configuration, you may see another Web browser. If you use Firefox, see the section "Connect Using the Remote Access Home Page."*

3. Type **http://*server***, where *server* is the name of your Windows Home Server computer.
4. Click **Go** (→) or press Enter.

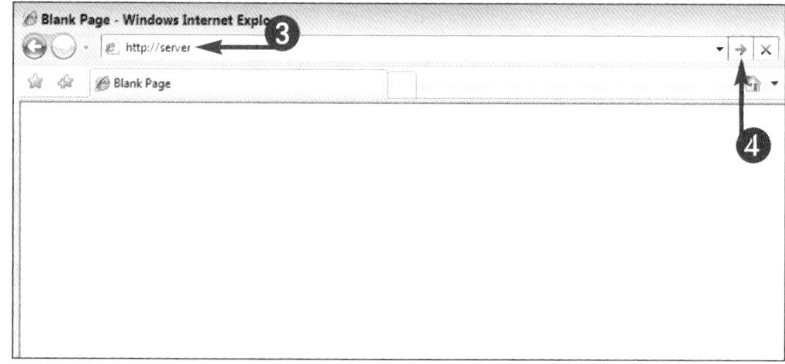

The Windows Home Server Web Site page appears.

5 Click **Log On**.

The Windows Home Server Remote Access logon page appears.

6 Type the username of a Windows Home Server account that has remote access permission.

**Note:** *For security reasons, you cannot log on to the Remote Access home page using the Administrator account.*

7 Type the password.

8 Click **Log On**.

The Windows Home Server Remote Access home page appears.

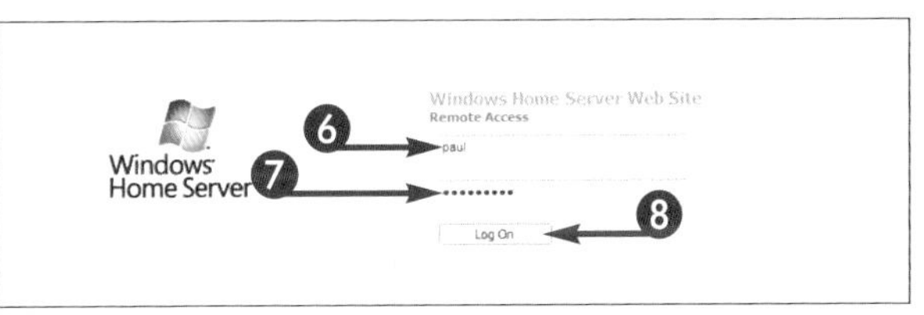


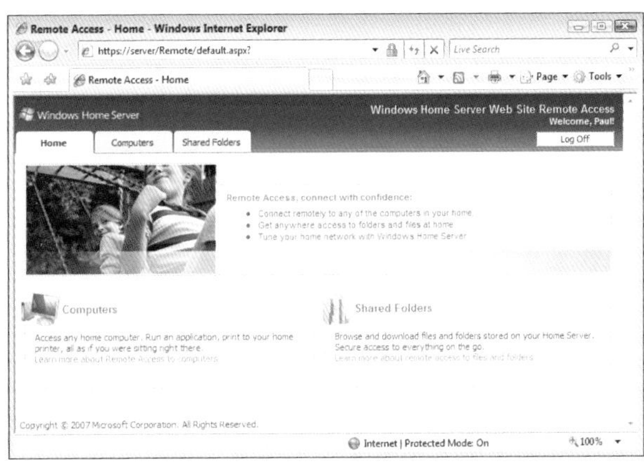

### Is there a faster way to navigate to the Windows Home Server Remote Access home page?

Yes, it is possible to skip the initial Windows Home Server Web Site page. Follow steps **1** and **2** to launch your Web browser. In the Web browser's address bar, type **https://*server*/remote** – replace *server* with the name of your Windows Home Server computer – and then click → or press Enter. This takes you directly to the Remote Access logon page. For more information, see the section "Customize the Remote Access Site Settings," later in this chapter.

### Can I display the Windows Home Server Remote Access home page by using the Firefox Web browser?

Yes, but with one problem: On the Remote Access home page, Firefox does not show the Computers tab, which prevents you from using Firefox to connect to other computers on your network. To work around this problem, install the IE Tab add-in, which is available from http://ietab.mozdev.org. With the add-in installed, right-click the Remote Access home page and then click **View page in IE Tab**.

# Connect Using the Remote Access Home Page

You can use the Windows Home Server Remote Access home page to connect to another computer on your network. This is often easier than using the Windows Remote Desktop Connection program.

**To connect to a computer, it must be configured as a Remote Desktop host. See the sections "Configure Windows Vista as a Remote Desktop Host" and "Configure Windows XP as a Remote Desktop Host" earlier in this chapter.**

## Connect Using the Remote Access Home Page

1. Use a Web browser to navigate to the Remote Access home page.

***Note:*** *See the section "Display the Remote Access Home Page," earlier in this chapter.*

2. Click the **Computers** tab.

***Note:*** *If the Information bar appears, click the bar, click* ***Run ActiveX Control****, and then click* ***Run****.*

- The Computers tab displays a list of the computers on your network.
- You can only connect to a computer with the status "Available for connection."

3. Click the computer to which you want to connect.

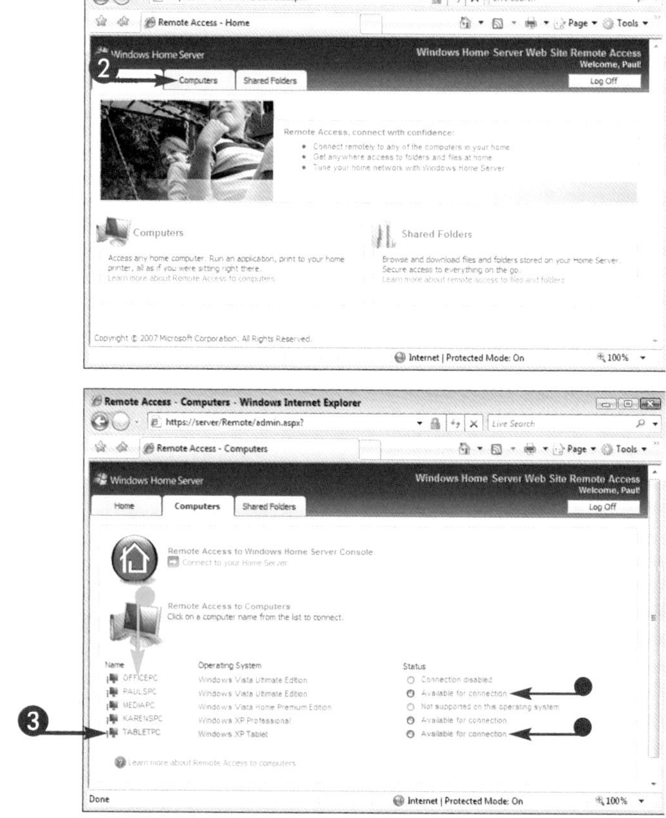

The Connection Options dialog box appears.

4. In the Connection Speed list, click ▾ and then click **Broadband**.
5. In the "Select a screen size for this connection" list, click ▾ and then click **Full Screen**.

***Note:*** *If you prefer to view the remote computer's desktop in a window, select a window size, instead.*

6. Click **OK**.

   Windows asks if you trust the computer to which you are connecting.

7. Click **Yes**.

   If you chose a screen size other than Full Screen in step **5**, press Spacebar or Enter to activate the window.

   The Log On to Windows dialog box appears.

8. In the User name text box, type the username of an account on the remote computer.
9. In the Password text box, type the account's password.
10. Click **OK**.

    Windows displays the remote computer's desktop.

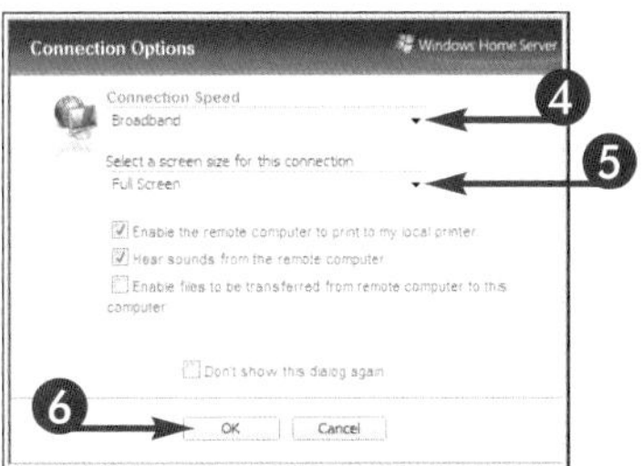

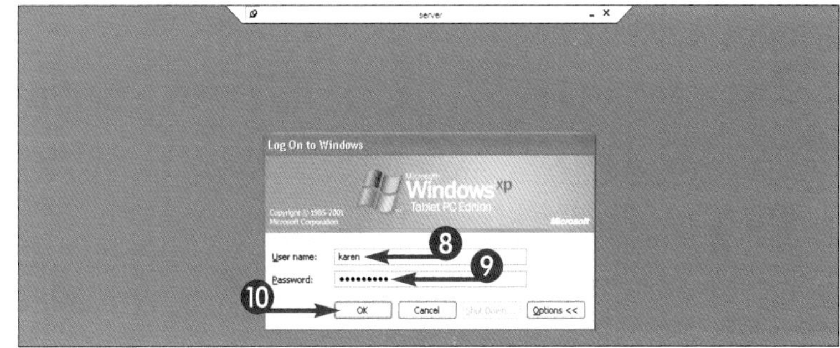

**In the Connection Options dialog box, what does the "Enable files to be transferred from remote computer to this computer" option mean?**

You would click the **Enable files to be transferred from remote computer to this computer** check box (☐ changes to ☑) to allow files to be transferred between the computers. For this to work, you must add Windows Home Server to your list of trusted sites. In Internet Explorer, click **Tools**, click **Internet Options**, click the **Security** tab, click **Trusted Sites**, and then click **Sites**. In the Trusted Sites dialog box that appears, type **https://*server***, where *server* is the name of your Windows Home Server computer. Then click **Add**, click **Close**, and click **OK**.

# Disconnect from the Remote Computer

When you have completed your work on the remote computer, you should disconnect to free up the computer for other users.

**Remember that when you log on to a remote computer, any person currently logged on to that computer is automatically logged off. Before that person logs back on, it is best to disconnect your remote desktop session.**

## Disconnect from the Remote Computer

### DISCONNECT BUT LEAVE YOUR PROGRAMS RUNNING

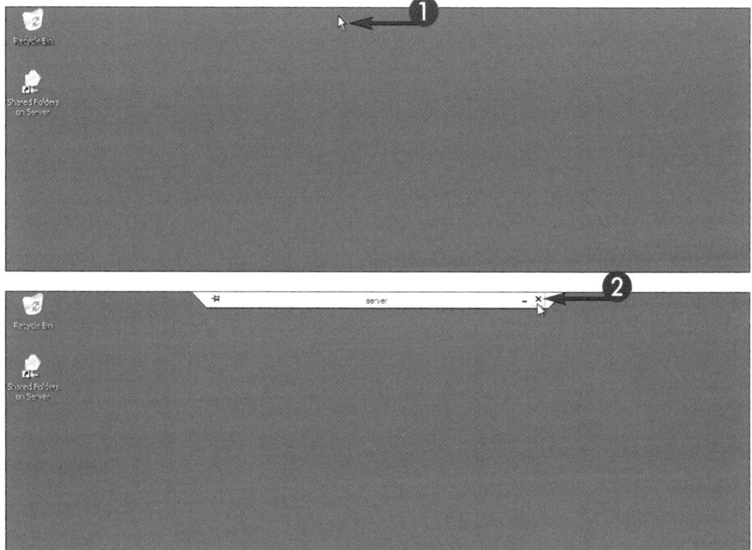

1. If you do not see the connection bar, move the mouse to the top of the screen, near the center.

   The connection bar appears.

2. Click **Close** (☒).

   Windows Home Server disconnects your session, but leaves your programs running.

### DISCONNECT AND CLOSE YOUR RUNNING PROGRAMS

1. Click **Start**.
2. Click **Log Off**.

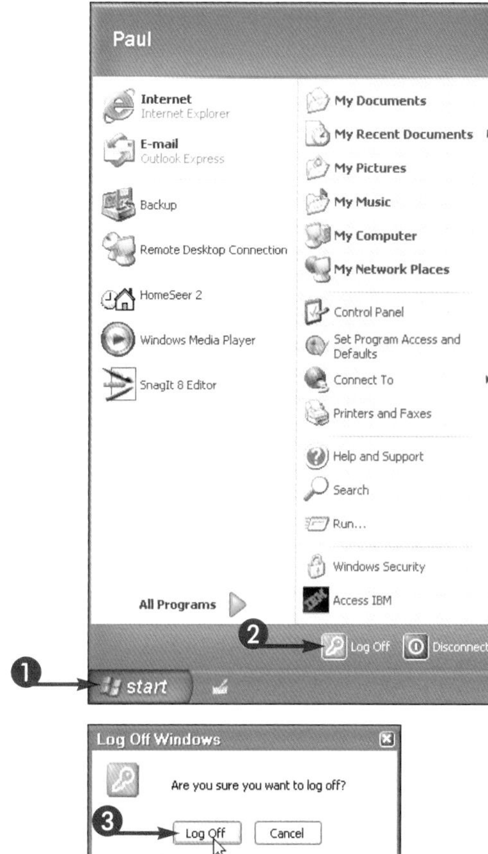


The Log Off Windows dialog box appears.

3. Click **Log Off**.

   Windows Home Server disconnects your session and closes all running programs.

**Are there any other methods I can use to disconnect from a remote computer?**

Yes, Windows Home Server offers another way to disconnect if you are running the remote computer desktop in the browser window instead of full screen. At the top of the browser window, just above the remote computer's desktop, click the **Disconnect** button (●). This closes the remote session, but leaves the session's programs running.

# Customize the Remote Access Site Settings

You can customize some aspects of the Windows Home Server Remote Access pages. For example, you can configure Windows Home Server to automatically display the Remote Access logon page. You can also change the headline that appears on the Remote Access pages.

**To customize the Remote Access site settings in Windows Home Server, you must know the password for the server's Administrator account.**

## Customize the Remote Access Site Settings

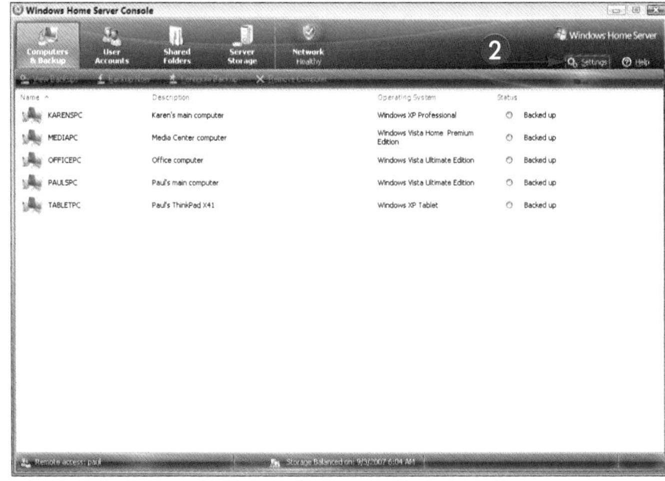


1. Start the Windows Home Server Console.

***Note:** See Chapter 3 for more information.*

2. Click **Settings**.

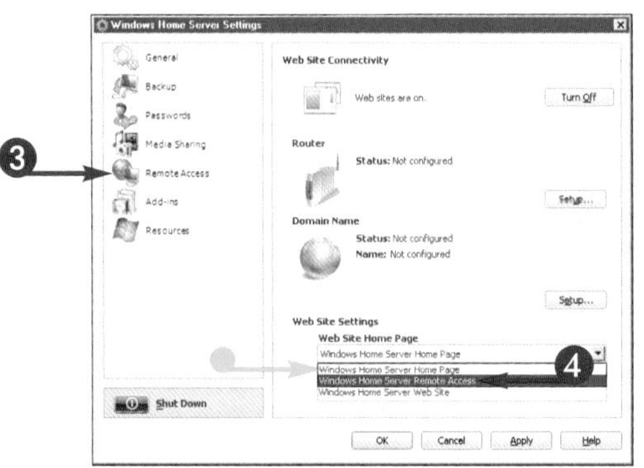


The Windows Home Server Settings dialog box appears.

3. Click the **Remote Access** tab.
4. In the Web Site Home Page list, click ▾ and then click **Windows Home Server Remote Access**.

- If you prefer to view the default home page, click **Windows Home Server Home Page**.

5 In the Web Site Headline text box, type the title you want to display on the Remote Access pages.

6 Click **OK**.

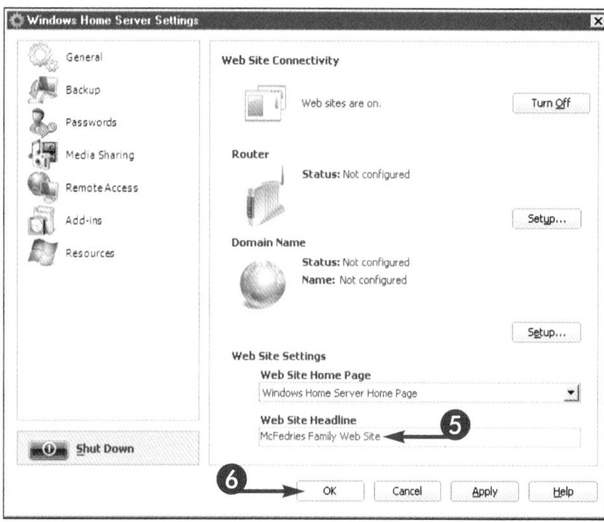


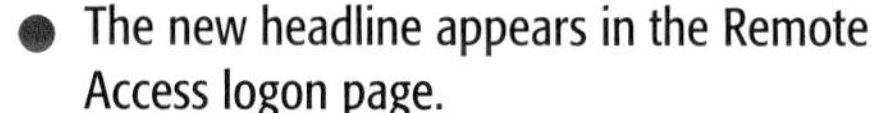

- The new headline appears in the Remote Access logon page.

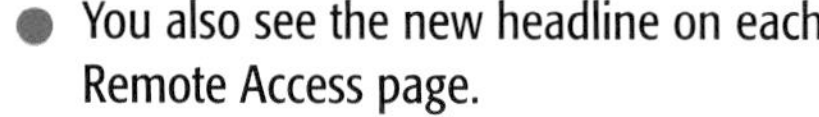

- You also see the new headline on each Remote Access page.

### What difference does it make if I choose Windows Home Server Remote Access as the home page?

This saves you a step when you want to use the Remote Access page to connect to a computer. Normally, you type the address ***http://server*** (where *server* is the name of your Windows Home Server computer) into your browser and then click **Log On** to display the Remote Access logon page. When you choose Windows Home Server Remote Access as the home page, typing ***http://server*** into the Web browser takes you directly to the Remote Access logon page.

# CHAPTER 13

# Connecting to Computers via the Internet

You can use the Windows Home Server Remote Access Web page to connect to your computer and to other computers on your home network using any Internet connection.

Understanding Remote Internet Access ....260
Configure the Router Automatically............262
Get the Windows Home Server Address....264
Configure the Router Manually ....................266
View Router Details..........................................270
Set Up a Windows Home Server Domain Name ..............................................................272
Get the Router Internet Address to Configure Your Own Domain....................274
View the Domain Name Details....................276
Display the Remote Access Home Page Over the Internet..........................................278
Connect to a Computer Over the Internet ..........................................................280
Disconnect from the Remote Computer ......................................................282
Work with Shared Folders Over the Internet ..........................................................284
Run the Windows Home Server Console Over the Internet ........................................286

# Understanding Remote Internet Access

You can use the Windows Home Server remote Internet access feature to connect to your home network. To use this feature successfully, you need to understand a few key concepts, such as routers, router addresses, and subdomains.

### Remote Internet Access

Remote Internet access means that you can connect to your home network through Windows Home Server from any location on the Internet, including your work, an Internet café, or a location with wireless Internet access, such as a coffee shop or airport. You can connect to computers that you have configured as Remote Desktop hosts. You can also use the remote Internet access feature to work with shared network folders and to use the Windows Home Server Console program.

### Connection Speed

You can connect to your home network using any Internet connection, from dial-up to broadband. However, keep in mind that a dial-up connection to a remote desktop or the Windows Home Server Console will be frustratingly slow. For these graphics-intensive operations, a broadband Internet connection is highly recommended.

### Router

A *router* is a device that enables computers on your network to request and receive Internet data. You can only use the Windows Home Server remote Internet access feature if your network has a router, and you must configure *port forwarding*, which is the feature that handles remote access. Windows Home Server can configure port forwarding for you automatically, or you can configure the router manually.

### Router Address

Every device connected directly to the Internet has a unique address, and your router is no exception. Your router's address is assigned by your Internet service provider. You connect to your home network through the Internet by typing the router address into your Web browser. Before you do this, you need to determine your router's current address.

### Domain Name

You can also access your home network with a domain name. A domain name takes the form *mydomain.domain*.com. Here, *domain*.com is the main domain name of the company providing the service, and *mydomain* is a unique name that you provide. With Windows Home Server, the domain takes the form *mydomain*.homeserver.com, and the domain is administered by Microsoft.

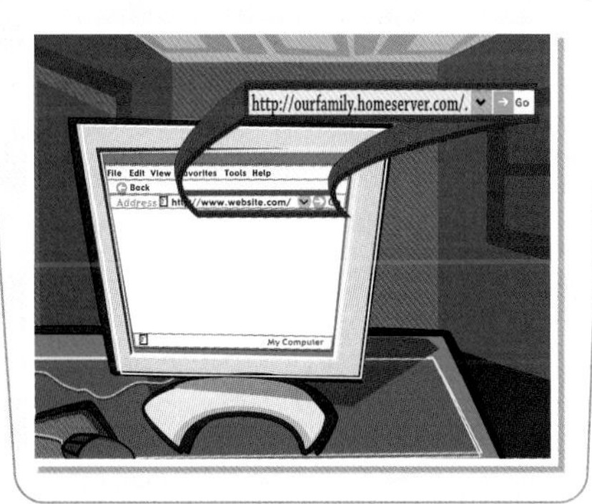


### Security

The connection to your home network over the Internet is highly secure and cannot be compromised by malicious hackers. An unauthorized user might accidentally reach your Windows Home Server Remote Access logon page, but that is not a problem because only accounts with strong passwords can access the rest of the site.

# Configure the Router Automatically

You can save time and effort by getting Windows Home Server to automatically configure your network's router port-forwarding feature to allow remote Internet access.

**To configure your router using Windows Home Server, you must know the password for the server's Administrator account.**

## Configure the Router Automatically

1. Start the Windows Home Server Console.

***Note:*** *See Chapter 3 for more information.*

2. Click **Settings**.

The Windows Home Server Settings dialog box appears.

3. Click the **Remote Access** tab.

- The router's Status value is set to "Not configured."

4. Click **Setup**.

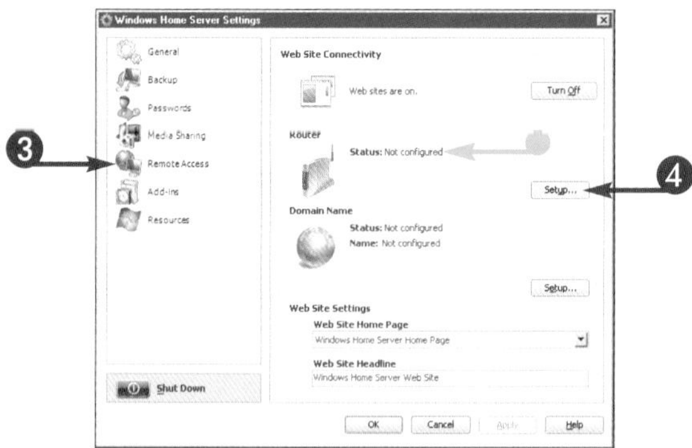

The Router Configuration dialog box appears.

5 Click **OK**.

Windows Home Server configures the router.

- If Windows Home Server is successful, the router's Status value changes to "Working."

6 Click **OK**.

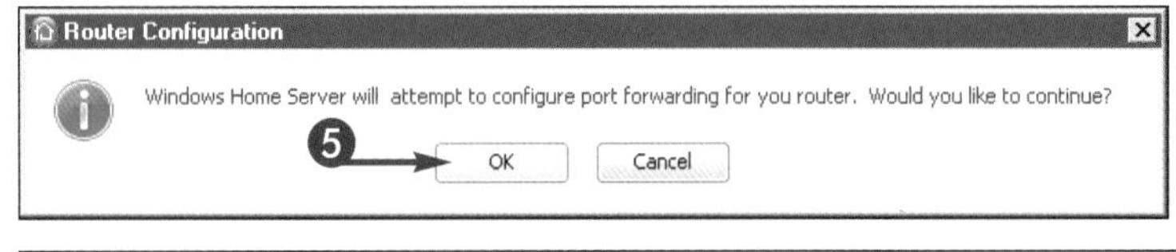


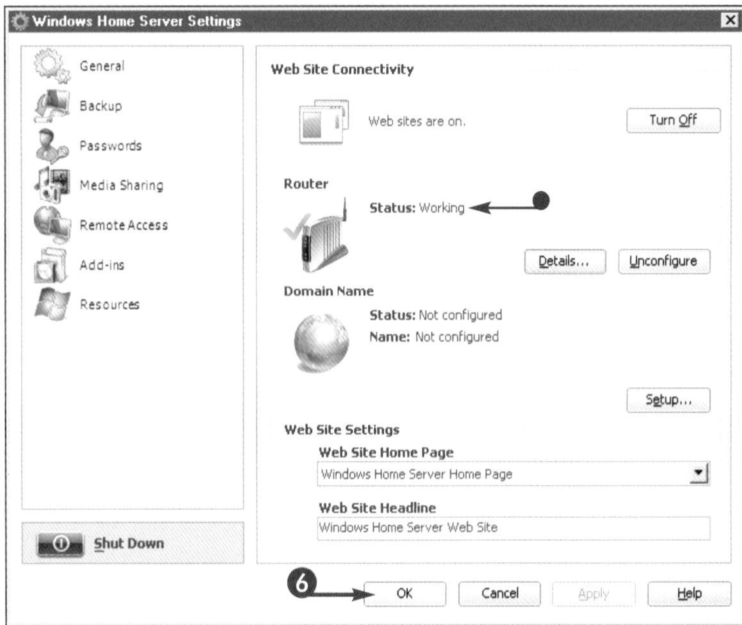

### Windows Home Server failed to configure my router. What might be wrong?

Your router must support Universal Plug and Play (UPnP), which most recent routers do. Access the router's configuration pages (see the router manual to learn how to do this) and make sure that the UPnP option is turned on (●). Also, consider upgrading the router's internal software, which is usually called *firmware*. On the router manufacturer's Web site, find the support or downloads area, and then download the latest firmware version for your router (●). Then access the configuration pages and look for the page that enables you to apply the new firmware version.

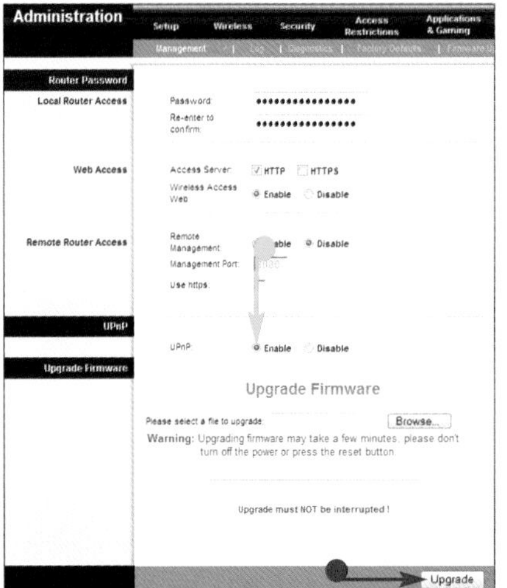

# Get the Windows Home Server Address

If you need to configure your router manually, as described in the next section, then you must know the IP address used by Windows Home Server.

**To get the Windows Home Server address, you must know the password for the server's Administrator account.**

## Get the Windows Home Server Address

1. Use Remote Desktop Connection to connect to the Windows Home Server desktop.

*Note:* *See Chapter 11 for more information about connections.*

2. Click **Start**.
3. Click **All Programs**.
4. Click **Accessories**.
5. Click **Command Prompt**.

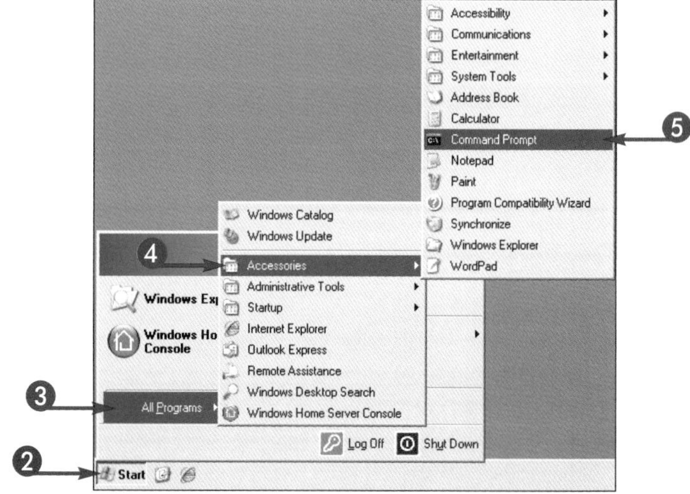


The Command Prompt window appears.

6. Type **ipconfig** and press Enter.

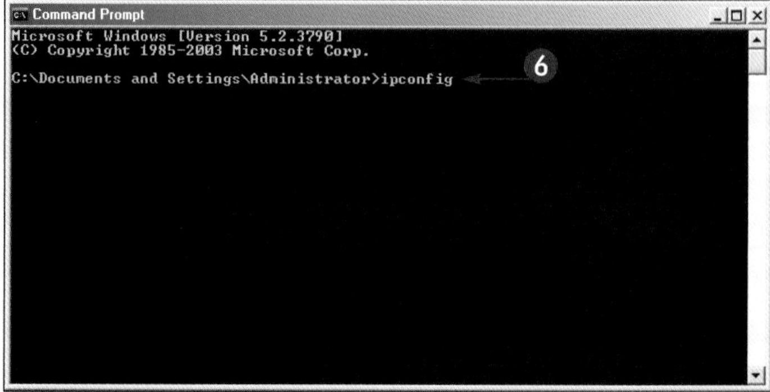

Windows Home Server displays information about its network connection.

7. Write down the IP Address value.
8. Click ☒.

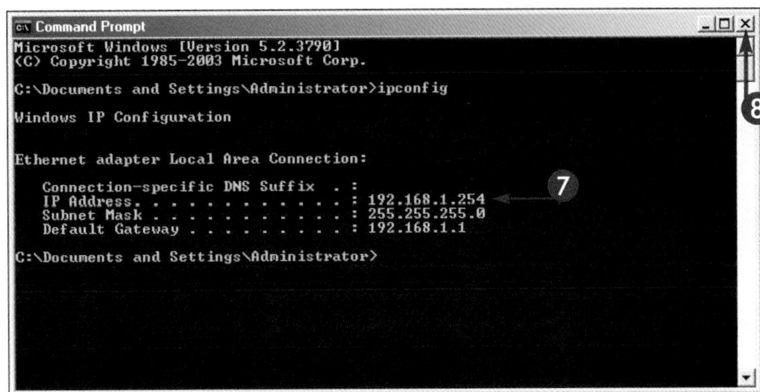


9. Click **Start**.
10. Click **Log Off**.

Windows closes the Remote Desktop session.

The Log Off Windows dialog box appears.

11. Click **Log Off**.

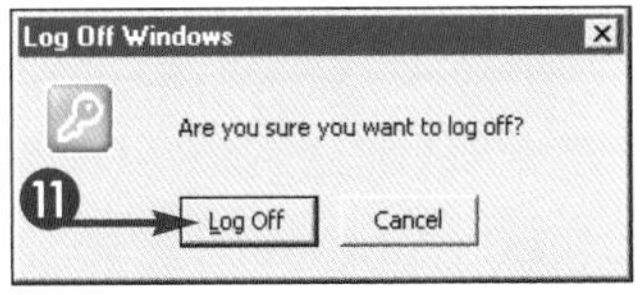

**How do I know the Windows Home Server address will not change in the future?**

In the default setup, Windows Home Server obtains its IP address from your network's router, and that address may change each time Windows Home Server reboots. However, it is possible to configure Windows Home Server to use a static IP address that will not change with each reboot. For more information, see Chapter 3.

**Is there a quicker way to open the Command Prompt window in Windows Home Server?**

Yes. Follow these steps:

1. Click **Start**.
2. Click **Run**.

   The Run dialog box appears.
3. In the Open text box, type **cmd**.
4. Click **OK**.

   The Command Prompt window appears.

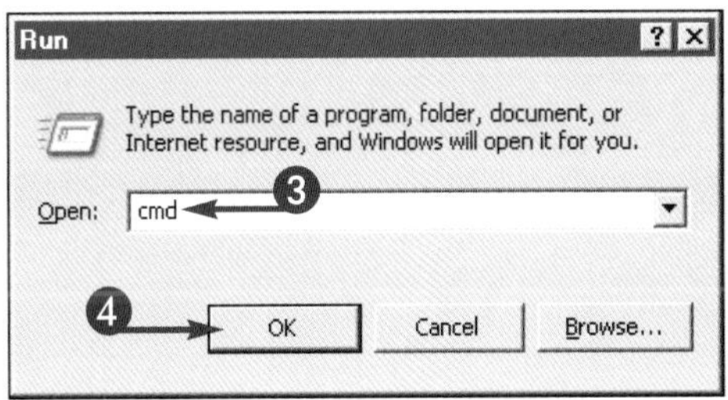

# Configure the Router Manually

If you could not get Windows Home Server to configure your router automatically, you can access the router's setup pages and configure the router manually.

**See your router's manual to learn how to access the router's setup pages. You need to know the router's IP address and the router's default username (if any) and password.**

## Configure the Router Manually

1. Click **Start**.
2. Click **Internet**.

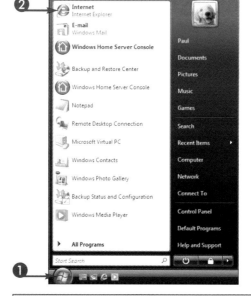

The Web browser appears.

3. Type the router's IP address.
4. Click [→].

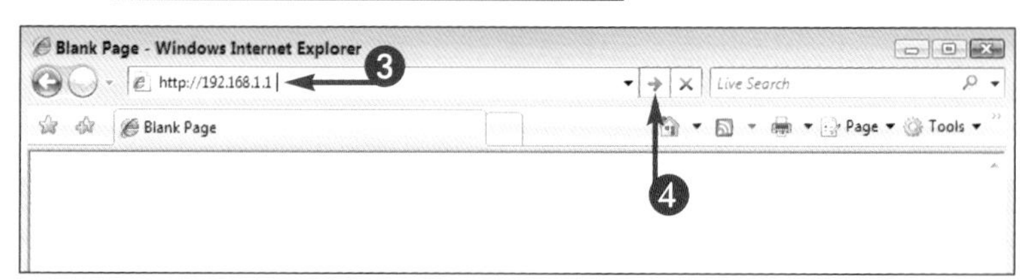

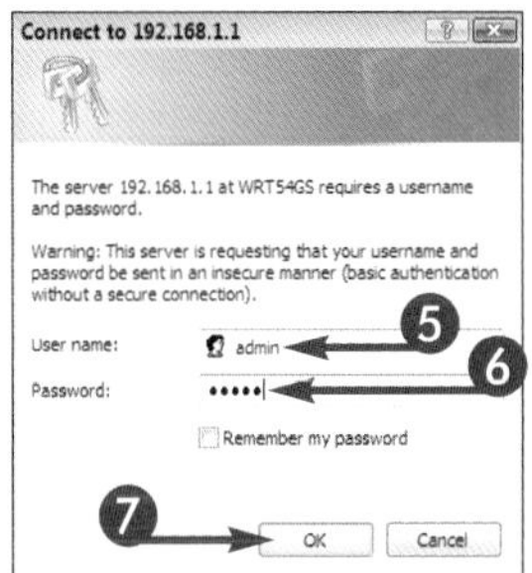


Windows prompts you to log on to the router.

5. In the User name text box, type the router's username.

***Note:*** *Many routers do not require a username to log on.*

6. In the Password text box, type the router's password.

7. Click **OK**.

   The router's setup pages appear.

***Note:*** *How you proceed from here varies from router to router. The steps that follow work for most Linksys routers. See the sections that follow for information on D-Link, Netgear, and Belkin routers.*

8. Click **Applications & Gaming**.

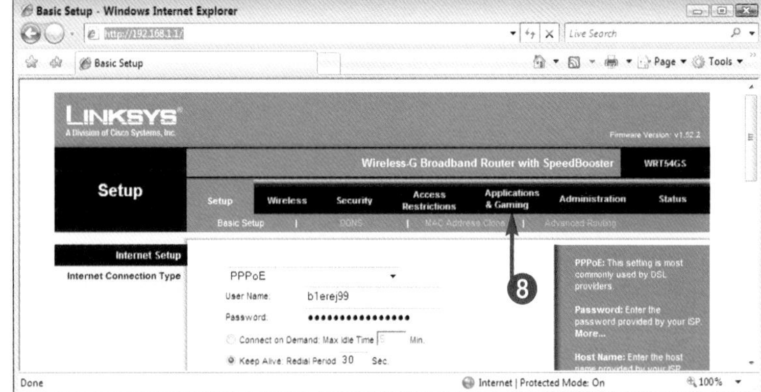

### What if I do not know my router's username and password?

On most routers, the default username is "admin" and the default password is either "admin" or "password." On some routers, you need to leave either the username or the password blank. If these default values do not work, go to the Default Password List maintained at www.phenoelit-us.org/dpl/dpl.html and see if your device is listed.

### How do I configure my D-Link router?

First, display the setup pages. The IP address is usually 192.168.0.1, the default username is usually "admin," and the default password is usually blank. Click the **Advanced** tab and then click **Port Forwarding**. Fill in the Port Forwarding Rules controls as shown here, using your own Home Server address. Click **Save Settings** (●).

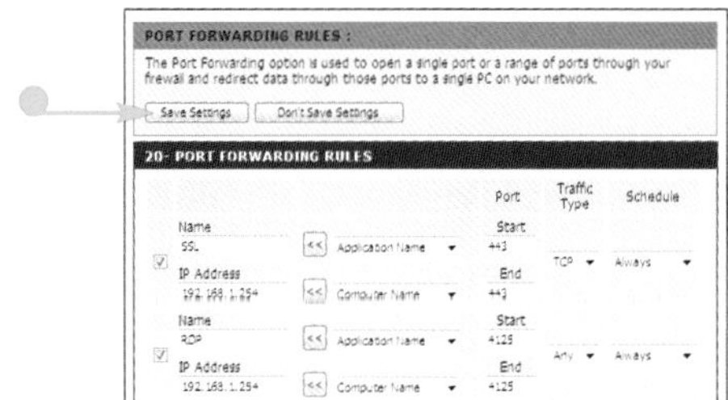

# Configure the Router Manually *(continued)*

Configuring the router means modifying its port-forwarding settings. You forward the Secure Sockets Layer (SSL) port 443 to your Windows Home Server IP address, and you forward the Remote Desktop Protocol (RDP) port 4125 to your Windows Home Server IP address.

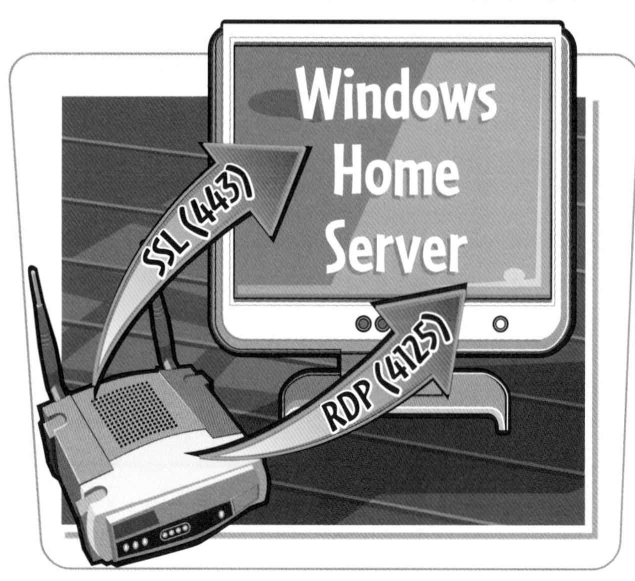


## Configure the Router Manually *(continued)*

9. For Application, type **SSL**.
10. For Start, type **443**.
11. For End, type **443**.
12. For Protocol, click ▾ and then click **TCP**.
13. For IP Address, type the address of your Windows Home Server.
14. Click **Enable** (☐ changes to ☑).

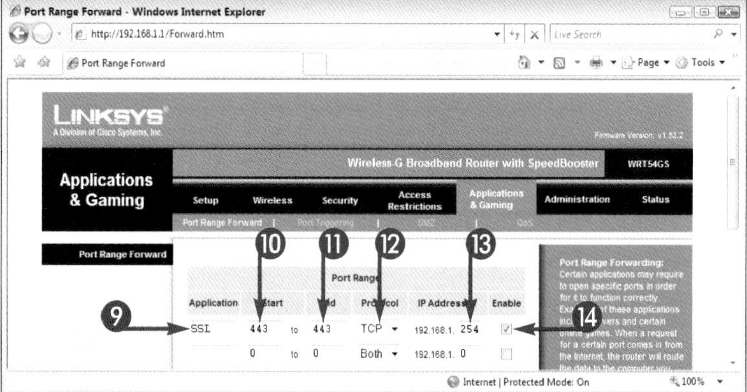

15. For Application, type **RDP**.
16. For Start, type **4125**.
17. For End, type **4125**.
18. For Protocol, click ▾ and then click **TCP**.
19. For IP Address, type the address of your Windows Home Server.
20. Click **Enable** (☐ changes to ☑).

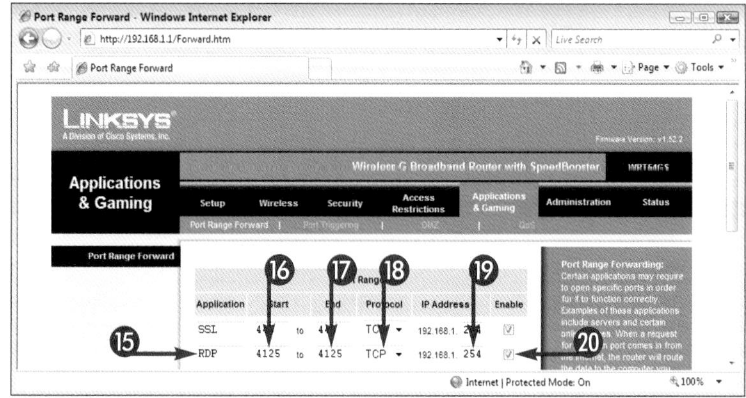

21 Click **Save Settings**.

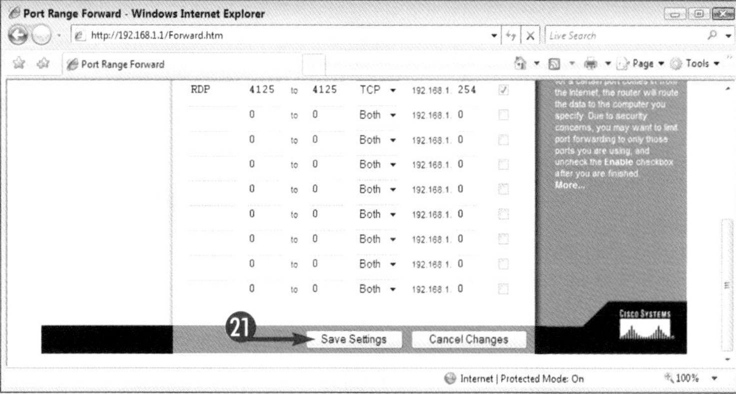


The router saves the new configuration.

22 Click **Continue**.

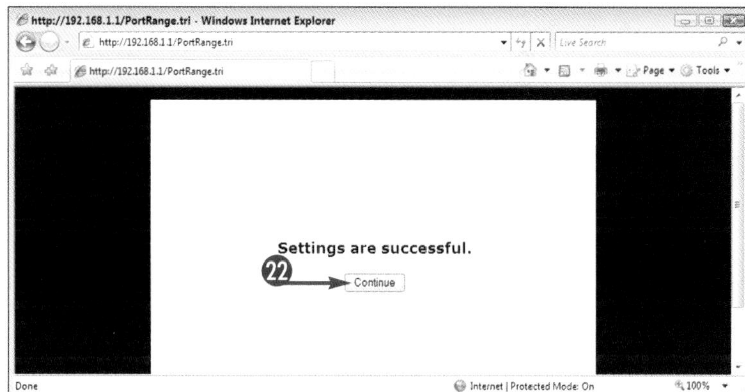

### How do I configure my Netgear router?

First, display the setup pages. The IP address is usually 192.168.1.1, the default username is usually "admin," and the default password is usually "password." In the Advanced section, click the **Port Forwarding / Port Triggering** link. Click **Add Custom Service** (●), fill in the SSL port 443 forwarding data, and then click **Apply**. Repeat for the RDP port 4125 forwarding data. You should end up with the data shown here, although with the IP address of your Home Server.

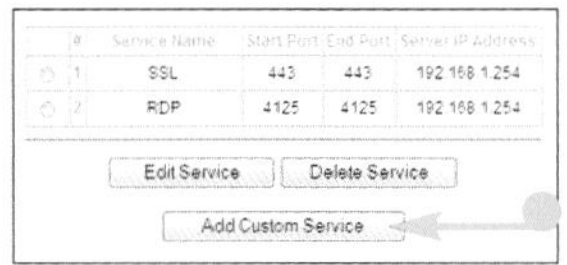


### How do I configure my Belkin router?

First, display the setup pages. Type the IP address (usually 192.168.2.1), click **Login**, type the password (the default password is usually blank), and click **Submit**. Click the **Virtual Servers** link. Then fill in the Virtual Servers Rules controls as shown here, using your own Home Server address. Click to select **Enable** (●).

Firewall > Virtual Servers

| No. | LAN IP Address | Protocol Type | LAN Port | Public Port | Enable |
|---|---|---|---|---|---|
| 1 | 192.168.2. 254 | TCP | 443 | 443 | |
| 2 | 192.168.2. 254 | TCP | 4125 | 4125 | |

# View Router Details

Before you attempt to use the Windows Home Server Remote Access pages over the Internet, you should ensure that your router is configured correctly. You do this by viewing the router details in the Windows Home Server Console.

**To view the router details in Windows Home Server, you must know the password for the server's Administrator account.**

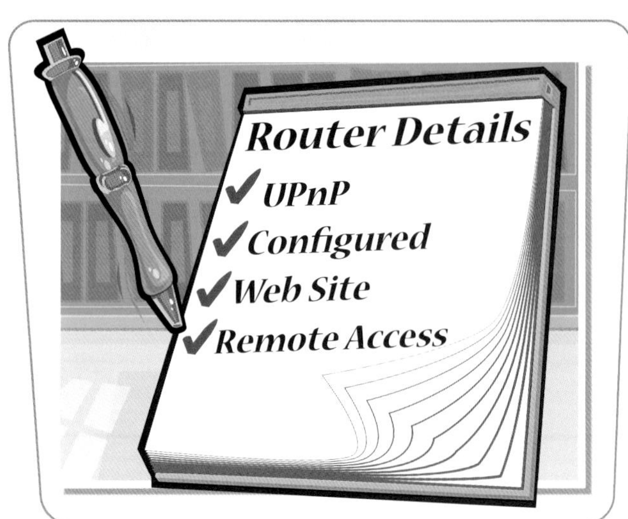


## View Router Details

1. Start the Windows Home Server Console.

*Note:* See Chapter 3 for more information.

2. Click **Settings**.

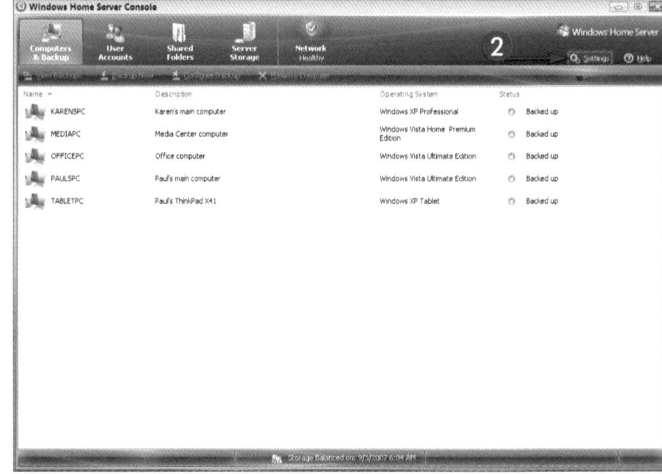

The Windows Home Server Settings dialog box appears.

3. Click the **Remote Access** tab.
4. Click **Details**.

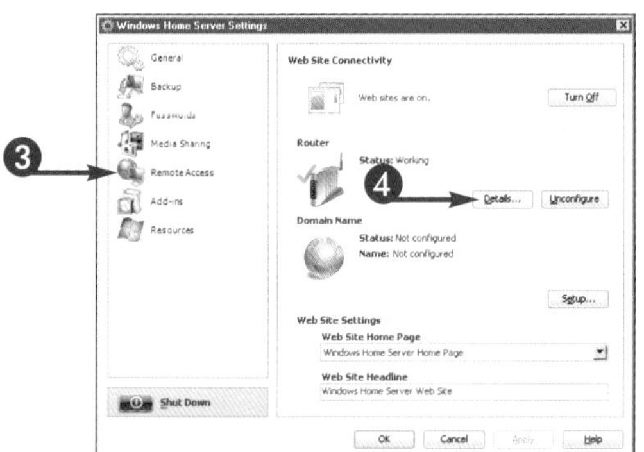

The Router Configuration Details dialog box appears.

5 Check the router details.

6 Click **Close**.

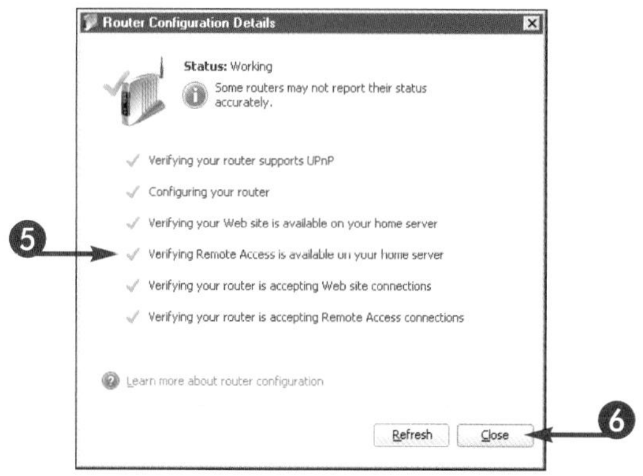

7 Click **OK**.

The Windows Home Server Settings dialog box closes.

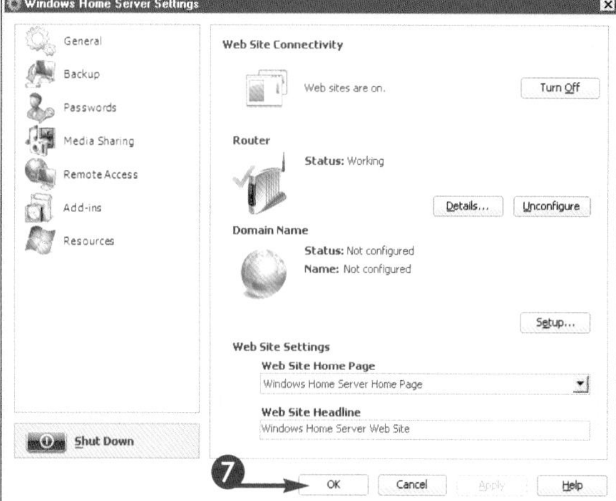

**What do I do if the Router Configuration Details dialog box tells me that my router does not support UPnP?**

First, check your router manual to see if the device supports Universal Plug and Play (UPnP). If the manual does not say, go to the manufacturer's Web site and find the router's specification data. If your router does support UPnP, it is likely turned off. See your router manual to learn how to access the device's setup pages, and then look for an option that activates UPnP.

**What do I do if the Router Configuration Details dialog box tells me that my router is not accepting Web site or Remote Access connections?**

If your router is not accepting Web site connections, then your router is not configured to forward port 443 (for Secure Sockets Layer). If your router is not accepting Remote Access connections, then your router is not configured to forward port 4125 (for Remote Desktop Protocol). Click the **Configure** button in the Remote Access tab. If that does not solve the problem, configure your router manually, as described in the previous section.

# Set Up a Windows Home Server Domain Name

You can make it easier for people to access the Windows Home Server Remote Access pages by setting up a Windows Home Server domain name.

**To set up a domain name in Windows Home Server, you must know the password for the server's Administrator account.**

## Set Up a Windows Home Server Domain Name

1. Start the Windows Home Server Console.

***Note:*** *See Chapter 3 for more information.*

2. Click **Settings**.

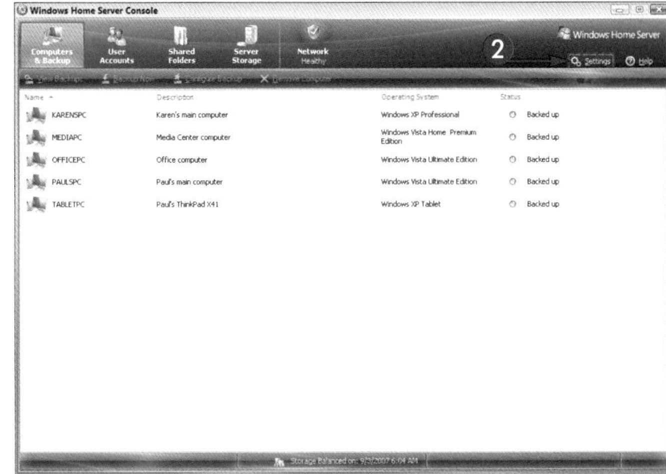


The Windows Home Server Settings dialog box appears.

3. Click the **Remote Access** tab.
4. Click **Setup**.

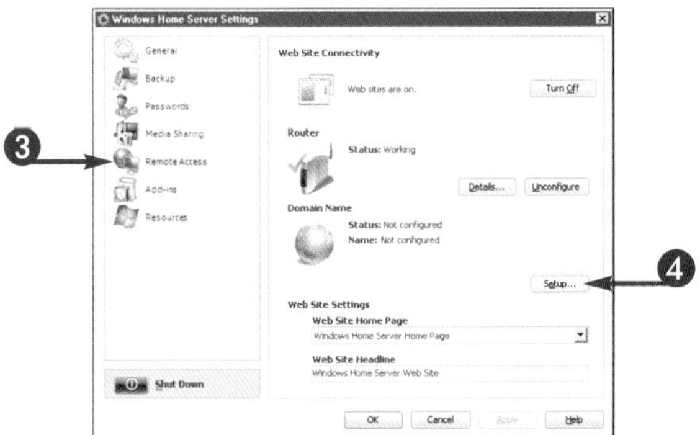

The Domain Name Setup Wizard appears.

5 Click **Next**.

The Sign In To Windows Live dialog box appears.

6 In the E-mail Address text box, type your Windows Live ID address.

7 In the Password text box, type your Windows Live ID password.

8 Click **Next**.

The Choose a Domain Name dialog box appears.

9 In the Domain Name text box, type the domain name you want to use.

- To make sure the name you want is still available, you should click **Confirm**.

10 Click ▾ and then click **homeserver.com**.

11 Click **Finish**.

Windows Home Server sets up your domain name.

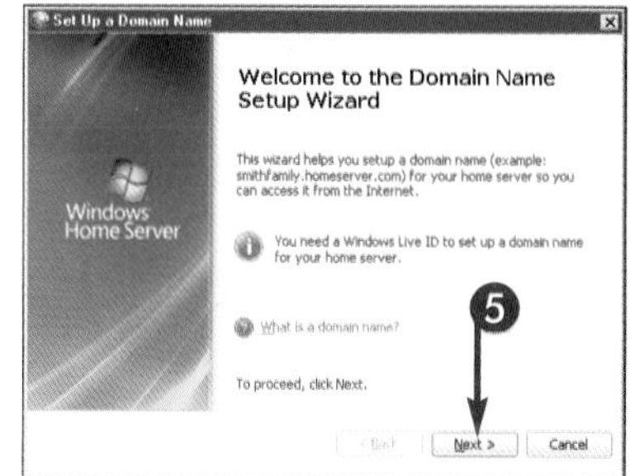


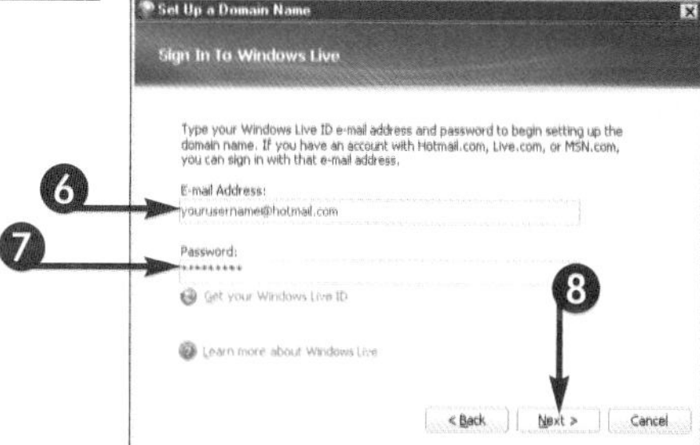


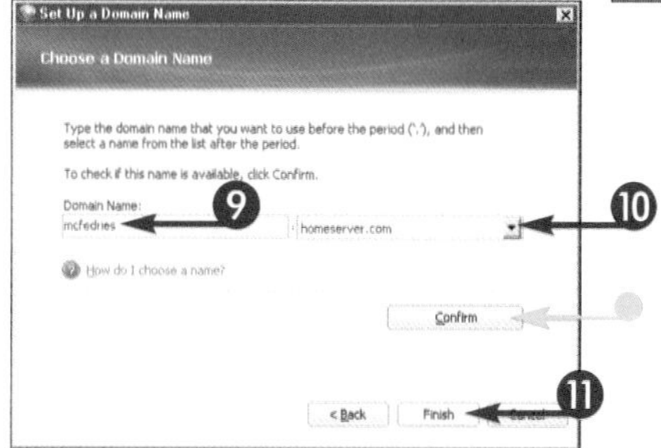

### What is the benefit of using a domain name?

Without a domain name, users would have to navigate to your Windows Home Server Web site using your router's IP address, which looks something like http://123.45.67.89/. A domain name address such as http://ourfamily.homeserver.com/ is much easier to type and to remember.

### Can I have more than one domain name?

No, you can have only one domain name associated with your Windows Live ID. If you already have a domain name and try to register a second one, Windows Home Server asks if you want to delete the existing domain name, as shown here.

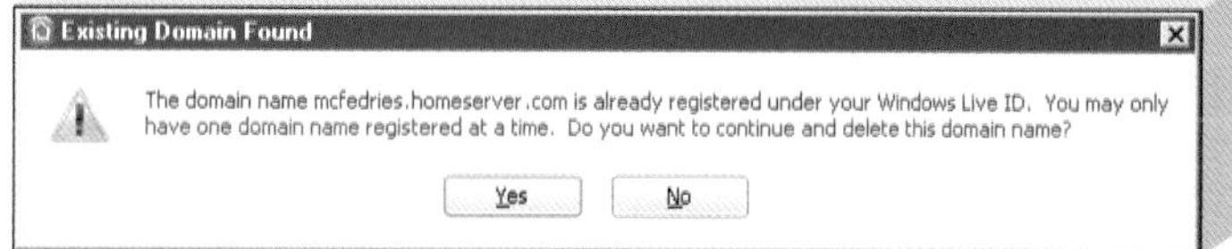

# Get the Router Internet Address to Configure Your Own Domain

If you already own a domain name, you can use a dynamic domain name system (DNS) service so that people can navigate to your Remote Access pages using the domain name. For this to work, you need to know your router's current Internet address.

**The router's Internet address is the IP address assigned to the router by your ISP. Do not confuse this with the internal IP address that you use to access the router's setup pages.**

## Get the Router Internet Address to Configure Your Own Domain

### LINKSYS ROUTER

1. Use your Web browser to log on to the Linksys router's setup pages.

*Note:* *See the section "Configure the Router Manually" to learn how to log on to a Linksys router.*

2. Click **Status**.
3. Click **Router**.

- The router address appears here.

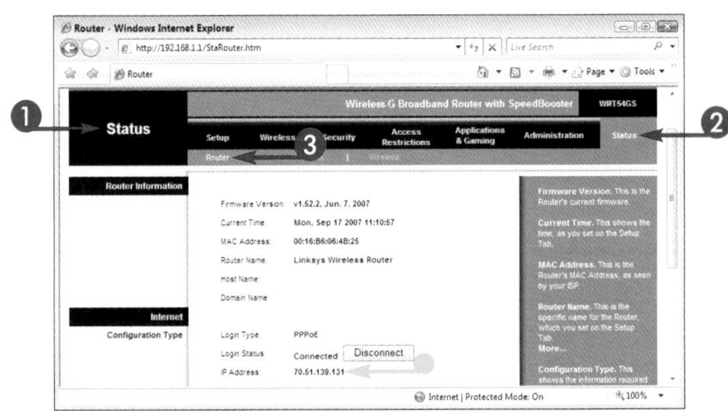


### D-LINK ROUTER

1. Use your Web browser to log on to the D-Link router's setup pages.

*Note:* *See the section "Configure the Router Manually" to learn how to log on to a D-Link router.*

2. Click **STATUS**.
3. Click **DEVICE INFO**.

- The router address appears here.

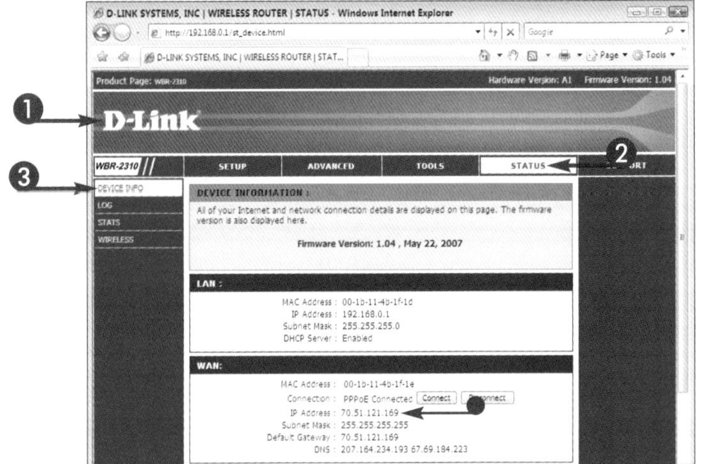

### NETGEAR ROUTER

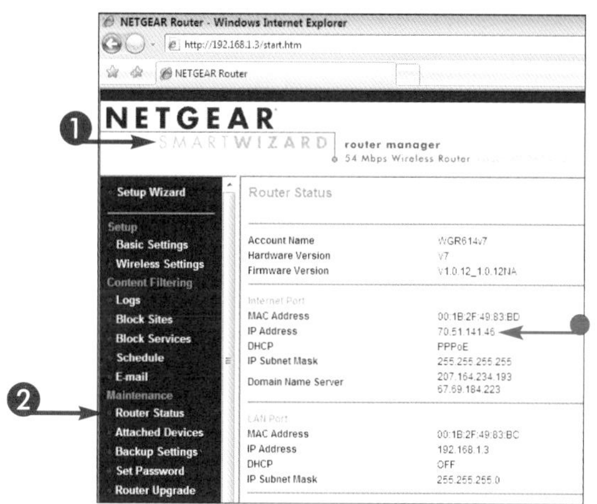

1. Use your Web browser to log on to the Netgear router's setup pages.

***Note:*** *See the section "Configure the Router Manually" to learn how to log on to a Netgear router.*

2. Click **Router Status**.

- The router address appears here.

### BELKIN ROUTER

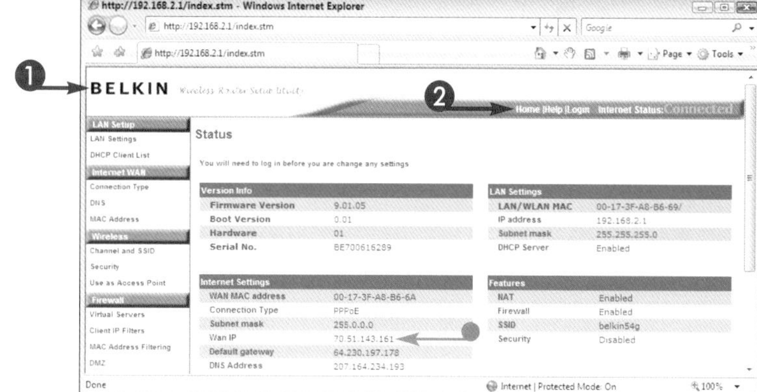

1. Use your Web browser to log on to the Belkin router's setup pages.

***Note:*** *See the section "Configure the Router Manually" to learn how to log on to a Belkin router.*

2. Click **Home**.

- The router address appears here.

## TIPS

### Is there another way that I can determine my router's Internet address?

Yes, there are several free services on the Web that can show you your router's current Internet address (●). Here are two of those services:

DynDNS (http://checkip.dyndns.org)

WhatISMyIP (www.whatismyip.com)

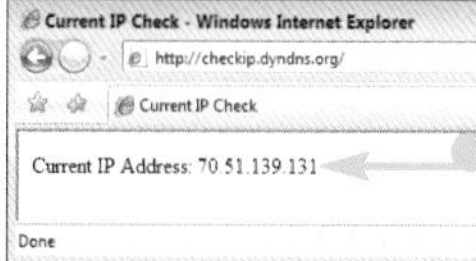

### What does a dynamic DNS service do?

A dynamic DNS service sets up a correspondence between your domain name and your router's Internet address. However, the router's Internet address usually changes each time the router makes a connection to your ISP. A dynamic DNS service monitors your router's Internet address, usually by installing a program on your computer. When the router address changes, the program updates the service's dynamic DNS servers to point your domain name to the new address.

# View the Domain Name Details

Before you attempt to navigate to the Remote Access pages using your Windows Home Server domain name, you should ensure that your domain name is working properly. You do this by viewing the domain name details in the Windows Home Server Console.

**To view the domain name details in Windows Home Server, you must know the password for the server's Administrator account.**

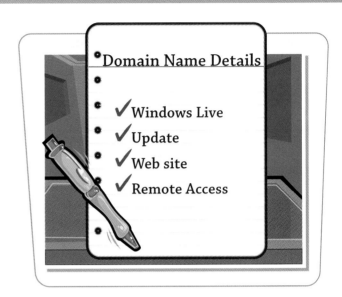

Domain Name Details
✓Windows Live
✓Update
✓Web site
✓Remote Access

## View the Domain Name Details

1. Start the Windows Home Server Console.

*Note: See Chapter 3 for more information.*

2. Click **Settings**.

The Windows Home Server Settings dialog box appears.

3. Click the **Remote Access** tab.

4. Click **Details**.

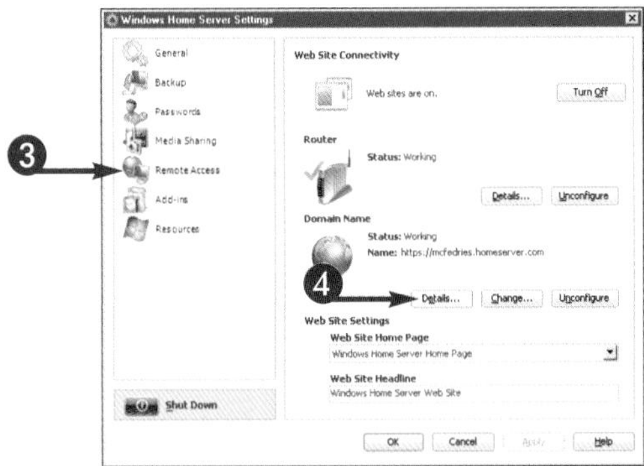

The Domain Name Details dialog box appears.

5 Check the domain name details.

6 Click **Close**.

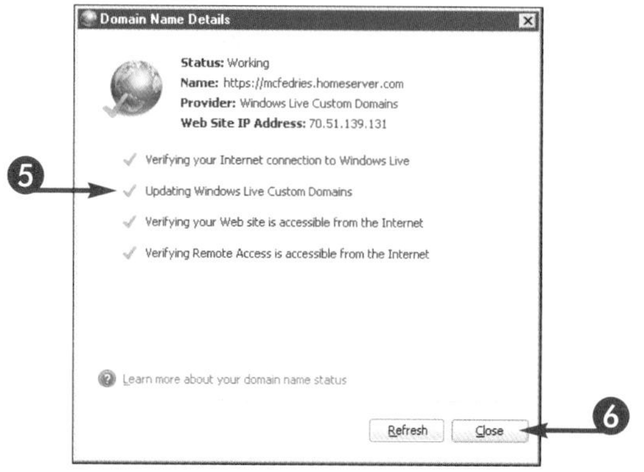

7 Click **OK**.

The Windows Home Server Settings dialog box closes.

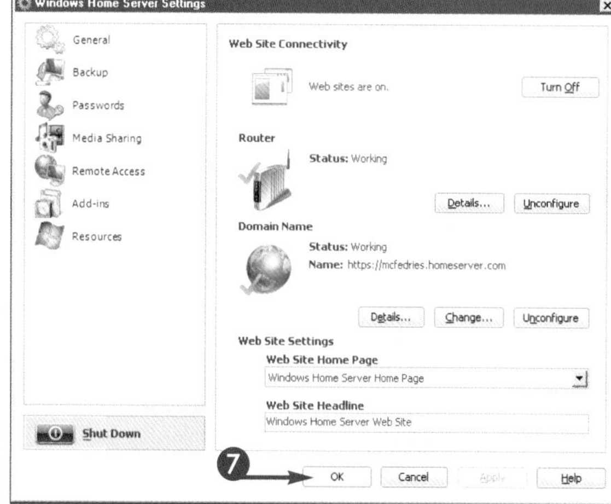

TIP

**What does the Updating Windows Live Custom Domains item mean?**

Windows Live Custom Domains is a dynamic DNS service. Windows Home Server runs a service that monitors your router's Internet address. When the address changes, Windows Home Server sends the new address to Windows Live Custom Domains. This ensures that people can always use your Windows Home Server domain name to access your Remote Access pages. When you view the domain name details, Windows Home Server also updates Windows Live Custom Domains with the current router address. See the previous section, "Get the Router Internet Address to Configure Your Own Domain," to learn about dynamic DNS.

# Display the Remote Access Home Page Over the Internet

You can use your Windows Home Server domain name or your router's Internet address to display the Remote Access home page over the Internet.

**Remember that only users who have been given remote access permission can log on to the Remote Access home page. For more information, see Chapter 12.**

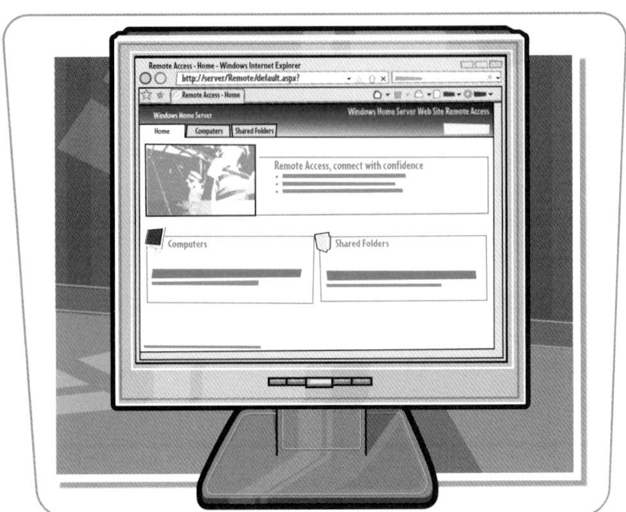

## Display the Remote Access Home Page Over the Internet

### USE A DOMAIN NAME

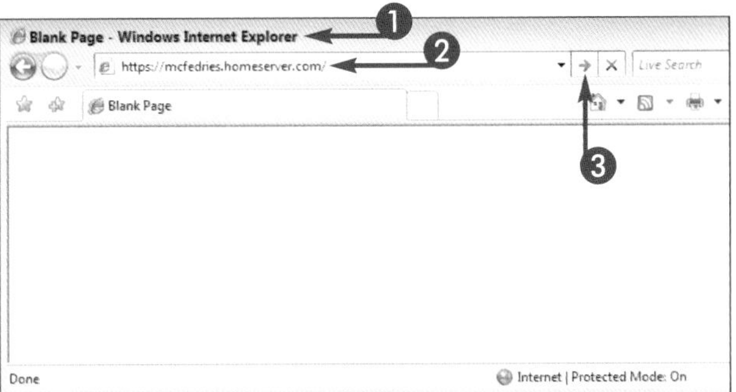


1. Launch your Web browser.
2. Type **https://*domain*.homeserver.com/**, where *domain* is your Windows Home Server domain name.

***Note:*** *If you have your own domain name and are using a dynamic DNS service, type that domain name, instead.*

3. Click **Go** (→) or press Enter.

   The Windows Home Server Web Site page appears.

***Note:*** *See the subsection "Log On to Remote Access" to learn how to proceed from here.*

### USE THE ROUTER ADDRESS

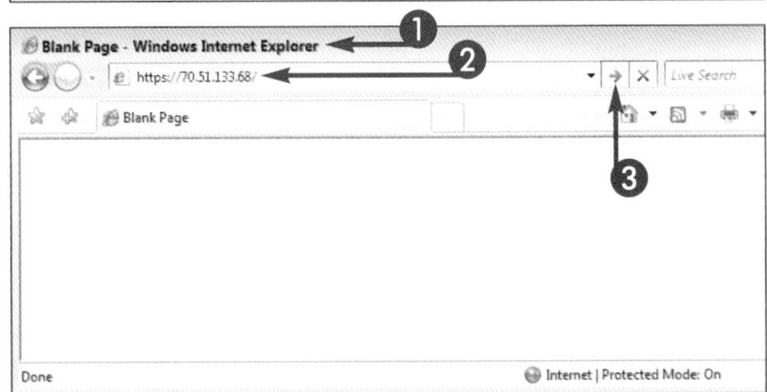


1. Launch your Web browser.
2. Type **https://*address*/**, where *address* is the Internet address of your network's router.
3. Click **Go** (→) or press Enter.

   The Windows Home Server Web Site page appears.

***Note:*** *See the subsection "Log On to Remote Access" to learn how to proceed from here.*

## LOG ON TO REMOTE ACCESS

1. Click **Log On**.

   The Windows Home Server Remote Access logon page appears.

2. Type the username of a Windows Home Server account that has remote access permission.
3. Type the account's password.
4. Click **Log On**.

The Windows Home Server Remote Access home page appears.

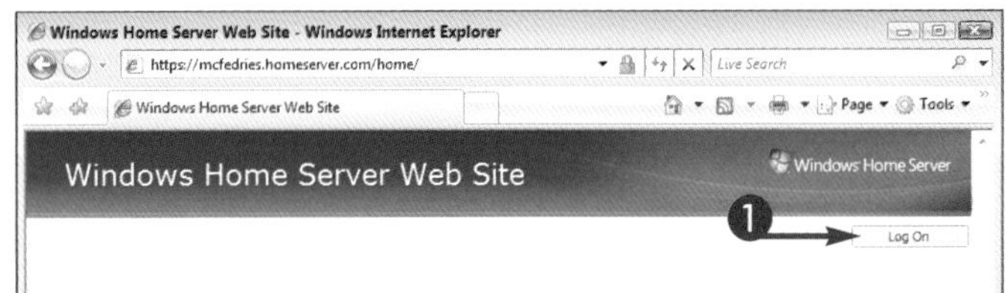


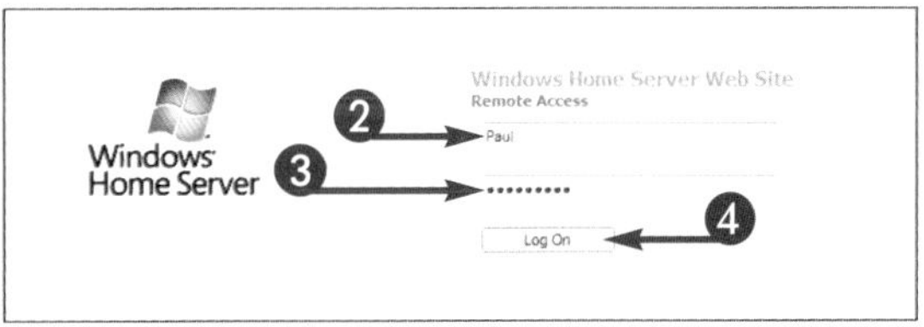


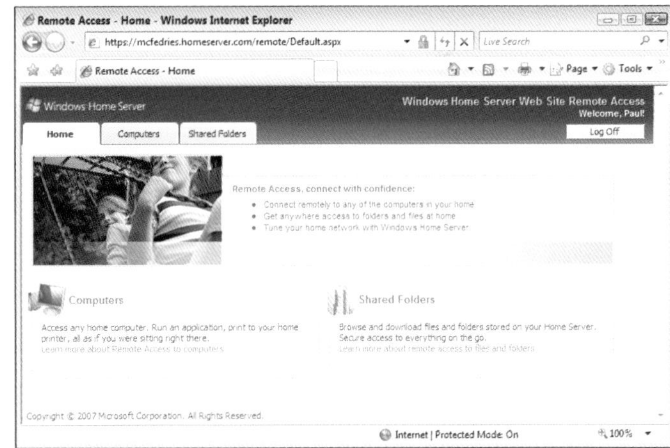

### Is there a faster way to get to the Remote Access home page over the Internet?

Yes. In your Web browser's address bar, type **https://*address*/remote** – replace *address* with either your Windows Home Server domain name or your router's Internet address – and then click [→] or press Enter. This takes you directly to the Remote Access logon page. For more information, see Chapter 12.

### Is it dangerous to use the Windows Home Server Remote Access pages over the Internet?

No. The Internet connection between your computer and Windows Home Server is encrypted, as indicated by the lock icon ([lock]) in the address bar (●). This means that no one else can read the data that is sent back and forth. If you are in a public place such as a coffee shop, ensure that no one is watching you type your password as you log on.

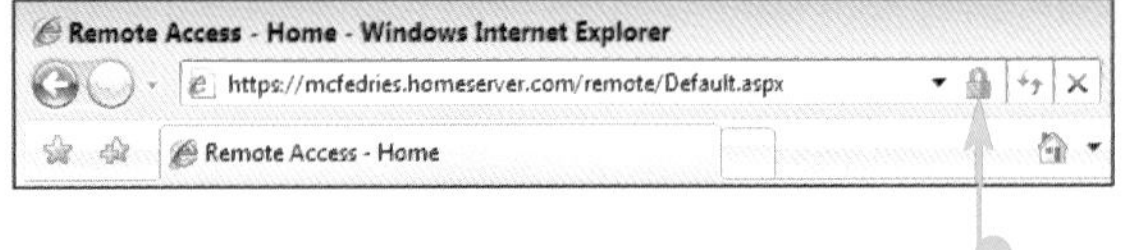

# Connect to a Computer Over the Internet

You can use the Windows Home Server Remote Access page to connect to a computer on your home network over the Internet. This is useful if you want to work on the computer remotely or if you forget a file.

**To connect to a computer, it must be configured as a Remote Desktop host. For more information, see Chapter 12.**

## Connect to a Computer Over the Internet

1. Use a Web browser to navigate to the Remote Access home page.

***Note:*** *See the section "Display the Remote Access Home Page Over the Internet" earlier in this chapter.*

2. Click the **Computers** tab.

***Note:*** *If the Information bar appears, click the bar, click **Run ActiveX Control**, and then click **Run**.*

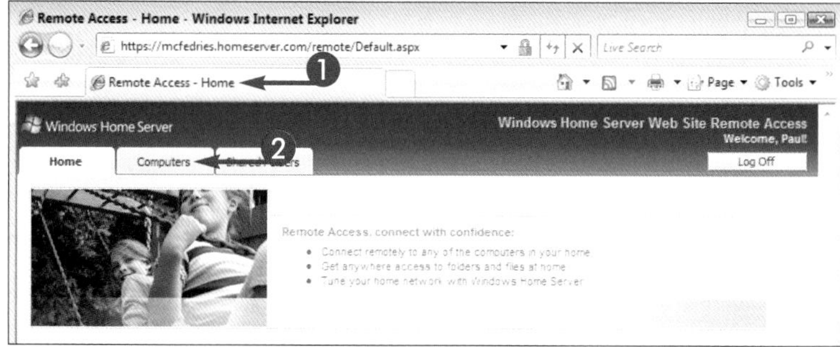


- The Computers tab displays a list of the computers on your network.
- You can only connect to a computer with the status "Available for connection."

3. Click the computer you want to connect to.

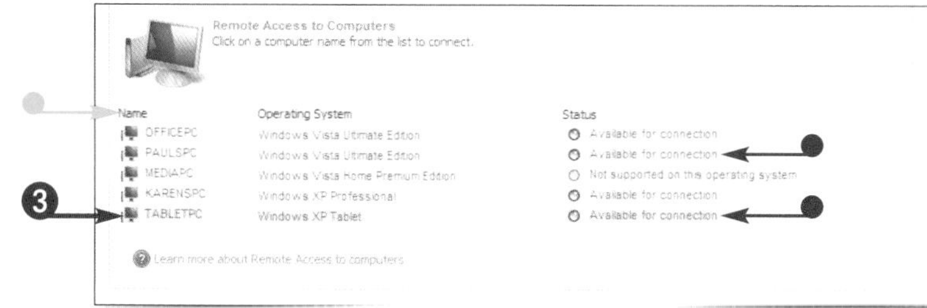

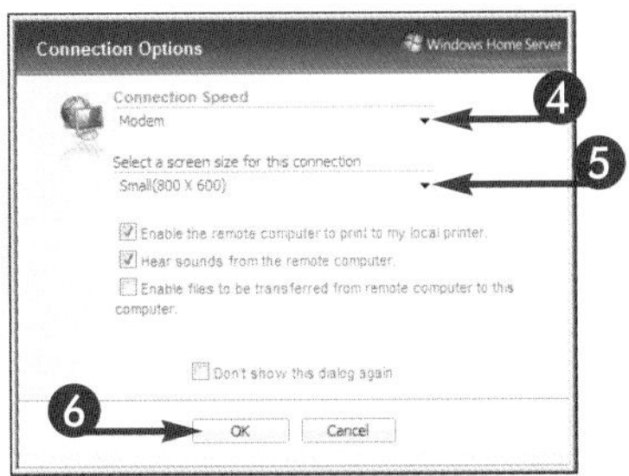


The Connection Options dialog box appears.

4. In the Connection Speed list, click ▾ and then click either **Modem** or **Broadband**.
5. In the "Select a screen size for this connection" list, click ▾ and then click a screen size.

***Note:** If you prefer that the remote computer's desktop take up the entire screen, select Full Screen, instead.*

6. Click **OK**.

   Windows asks if you trust the computer you are connecting to.

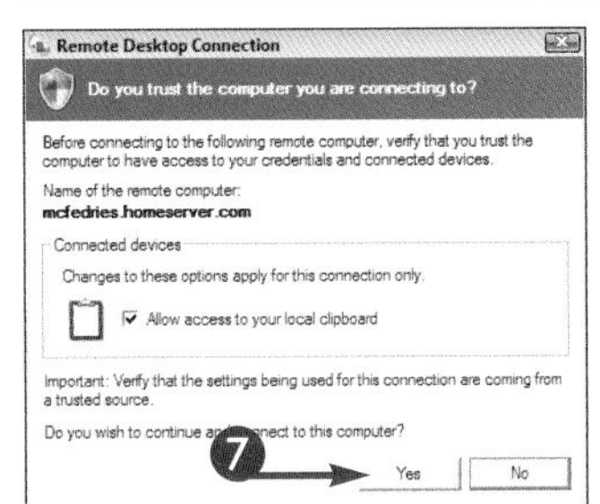

Remote Desktop Connection
Do you trust the computer you are connecting to?
Before connecting to the following remote computer, verify that you trust the computer to have access to your credentials and connected devices.
Name of the remote computer:
mcfedries.homeserver.com
Connected devices
Changes to these options apply for this connection only.
Allow access to your local clipboard
Important: Verify that the settings being used for this connection are coming from a trusted source.
Do you wish to continue and connect to this computer?
Yes
No
7


7. Click **Yes**.

   The Log On to Windows dialog box appears.

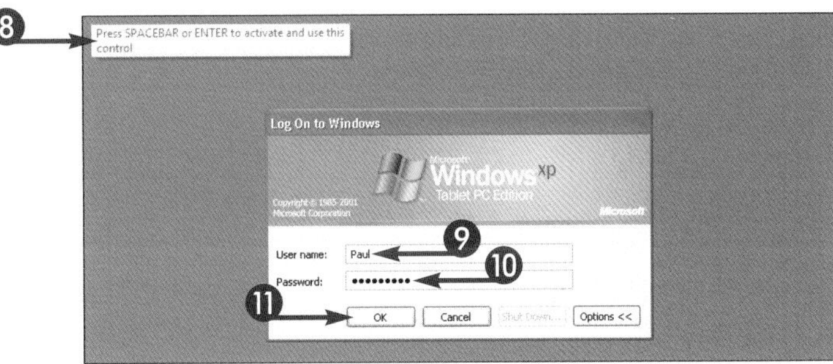


8. If you chose a screen size other than Full Screen in step **5**, press Spacebar or Enter to activate the window.
9. In the User name text box, type the username of an account on the remote computer.
10. In the Password text box, type the account's password.
11. Click **OK**.

    Windows displays the remote computer's desktop.

### How do I transfer files from the home computer to my computer?

First, add the Windows Home Server Web site to your list of trusted sites. To learn how to do this, see the section "Run the Windows Home Server Console Over the Internet." When you connect to the remote computer, click the **Enable files to be transferred from remote computer to this computer** check box (☐ changes to ☑) to allow files to be transferred between the computers. This sets up your computer's drives (●) as disk drives on the remote computer, as shown here.

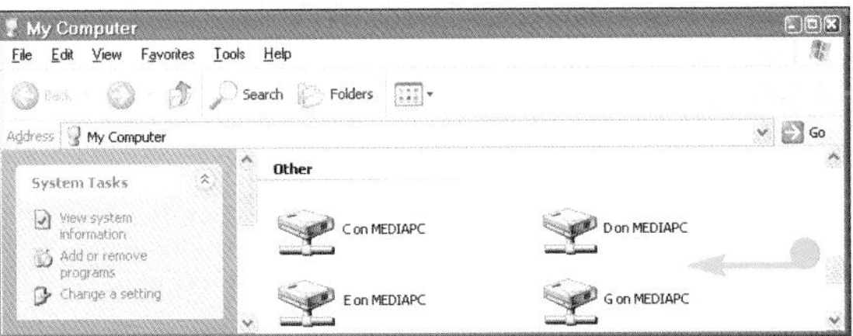

# Disconnect from the Remote Computer

When you have completed your work on the remote computer, you should disconnect. This saves connection time on a dial-up connection, and also frees up the computer for other users.

**Remember that when you log on to a remote computer, any person currently logged on to that computer is automatically logged off. Before that person logs back on, it is best to disconnect your remote desktop session.**

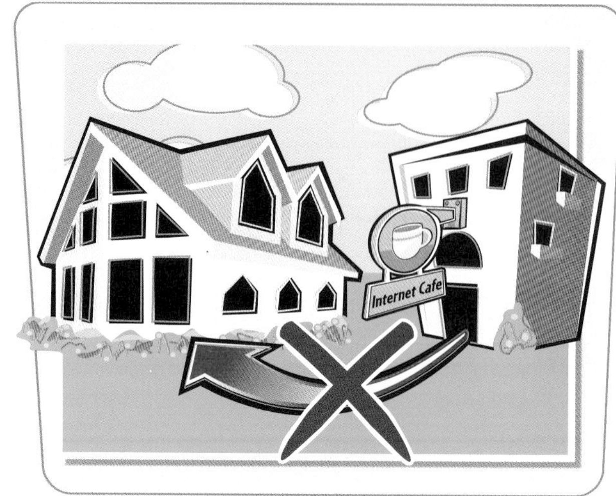


## Disconnect from the Remote Computer

### DISCONNECT BUT LEAVE YOUR PROGRAMS RUNNING

1. Click and drag the scroll bar to the top of the browser window.

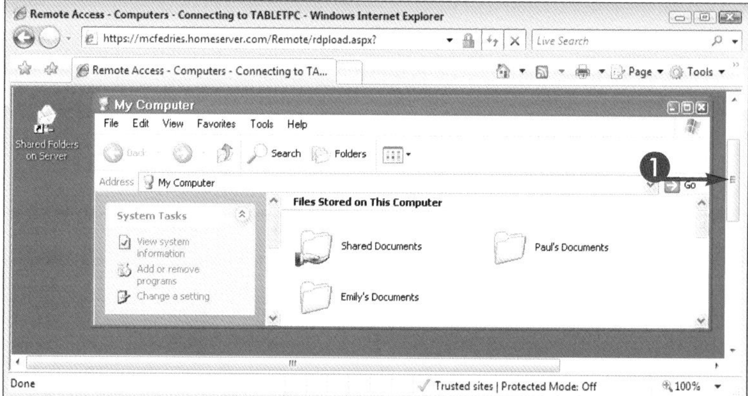


2. Click **Disconnect**.

   Windows Home Server disconnects your session, but leaves your programs running.

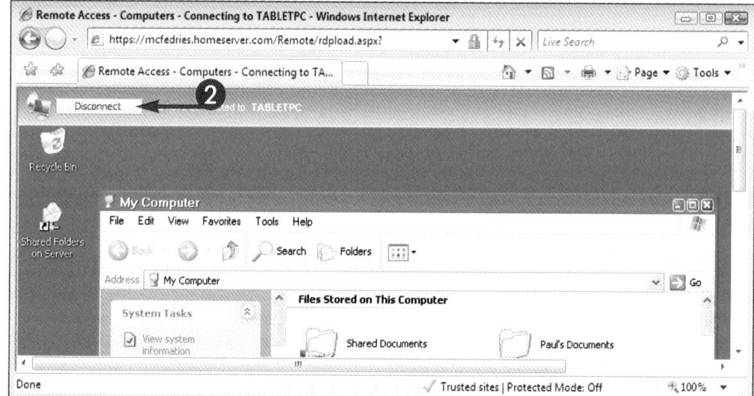

## DISCONNECT AND CLOSE YOUR RUNNING PROGRAMS

1. Click **Start**.
2. Click **Log Off**.

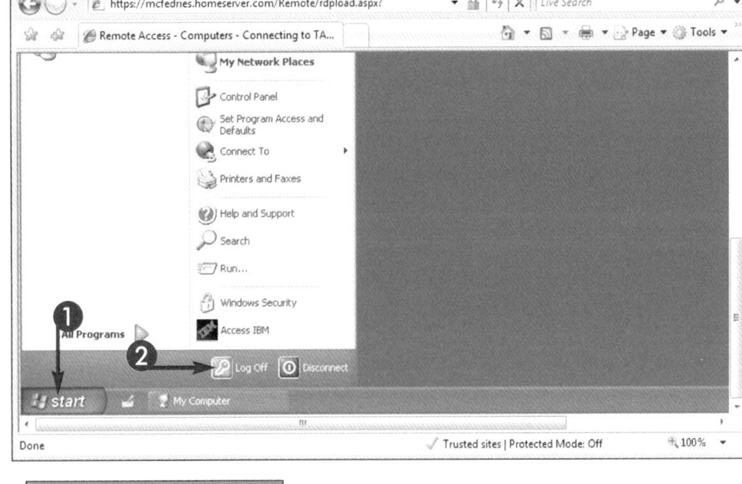


The Log Off Windows dialog box appears.

3. Click **Log Off**.

Windows Home Server closes the Remote Desktop session.

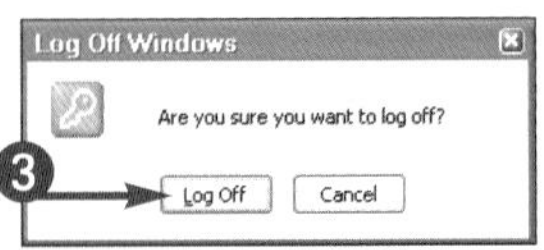

### Are there any other methods I can use to disconnect from a remote computer?

Yes, Windows Home Server offers another way to disconnect if you are running the remote computer desktop in full-screen mode instead of in the browser window. First, if you do not see the connection bar, move the mouse to the top of the screen, near the center. When the connection bar appears, click **Close** (☒). This closes the remote session, but leaves the session's programs running.

- The Close button

# Work with Shared Folders Over the Internet

You can use Remote Access to work with Windows Home Server's shared folders over the Internet. Within each shared folder, you can perform tasks such as uploading files from your computer to the server, downloading files from the server to your computer, creating subfolders, and renaming and deleting files.

**To perform certain actions on a Windows Home Server shared folder, you must have the necessary permissions. For more information about user permissions, see Chapter 7.**

## Work with Shared Folders Over the Internet

### DISPLAY A SHARED FOLDER

1. Use a Web browser to navigate to the Remote Access home page.

*Note: See the section "Display the Remote Access Home Page Over the Internet" earlier in this chapter.*

2. Click the **Shared Folders** tab.

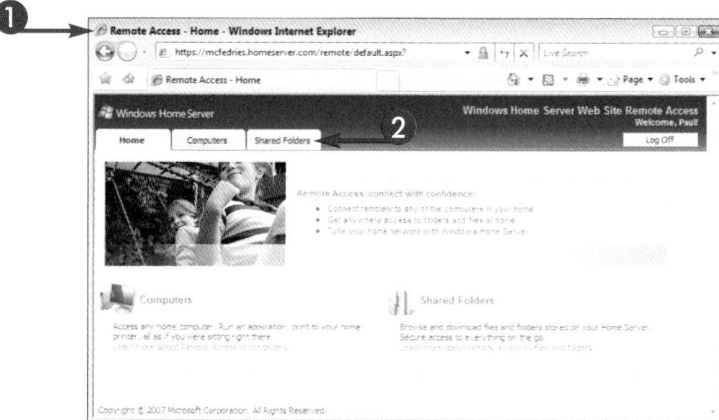


3. Click the shared folder you want to work with.

The shared folder appears.

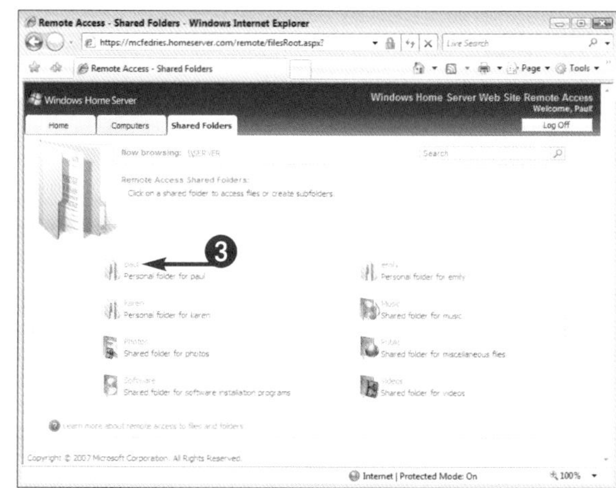

## NAVIGATE THE SHARED FOLDER

- Click **Next Page** (▷) to see the next group of files.
- Click **Previous Page** (◁) to see the previous group of files.
- Click **Last Page** (▷|) to see the last group of files.
- Click **First Page** (|◁) to see the first group of files.
- Click a Show link to change the number of displayed files.

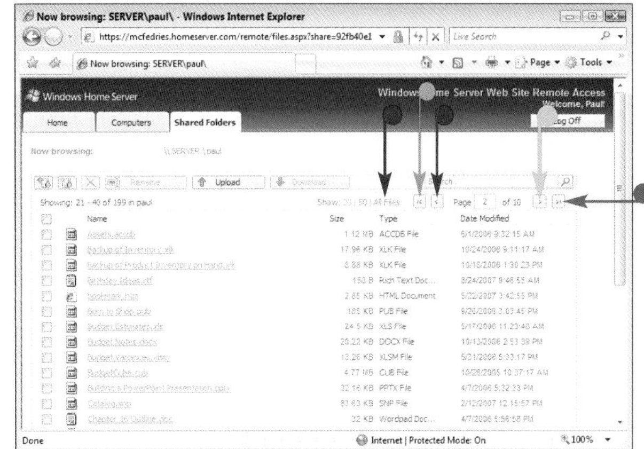


## PERFORM FILE TASKS

- Click a file and then click **Open** to view the file.
- Click a file's check box to select the file (☐ changes to ☑).
- To rename the selected file, click **Rename**, type the new name, and then click **OK**.
- To delete the selected file, click **Delete** (☒) and then click **OK**.

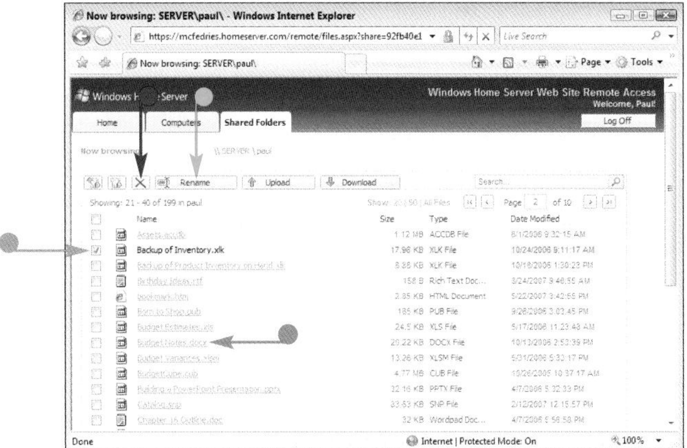

### How do I download a file from the shared folder?

Follow these steps:

1. Display the shared folder that contains the file you want to download.
2. Select the file (☐ changes to ☑).
3. Click **Download**.

   The File Download dialog box appears.
4. Click **Save**.

   The Save As dialog box appears.
5. Select the folder to which you want to download the file.
6. Click **Save**.

   The browser downloads the file to your computer.

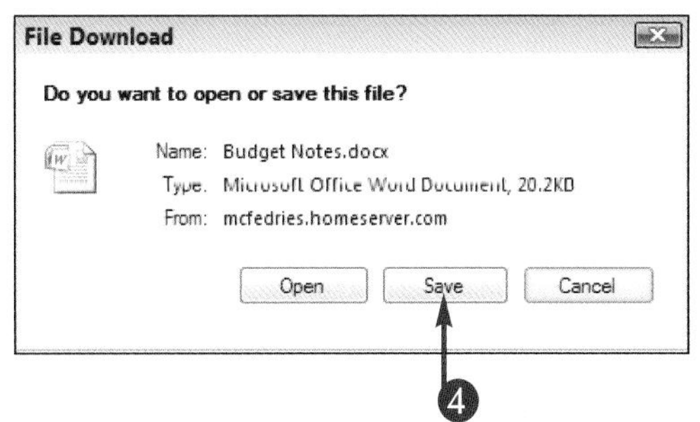

# Run the Windows Home Server Console Over the Internet

You can use Remote Access to run the Windows Home Server Console over the Internet. This means that you can change Windows Home Server settings, and work with backups, users, and storage, even when you are not connected to your network.

**To run the Windows Home Server Console over the Internet, you must know the password for the server's Administrator account. You must also first add the Windows Home Server Web site to your list of trusted sites.**

## Run the Windows Home Server Console Over the Internet

1. Use a Web browser to navigate to the Remote Access home page.

***Note:*** *See the section "Display the Remote Access Home Page Over the Internet" earlier in this chapter.*

2. Click the **Computers** tab.

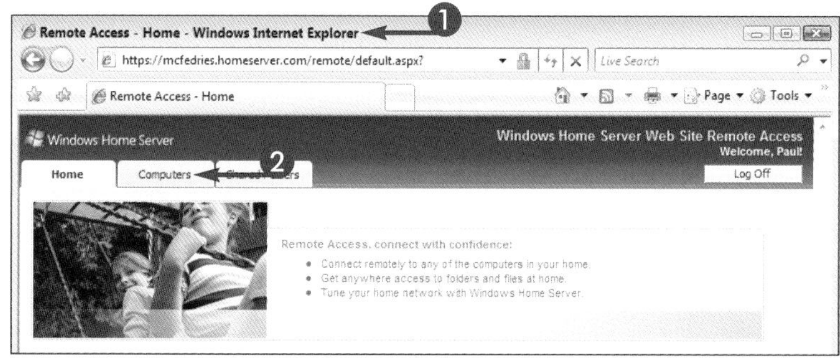


3. Click **Connect to your Home Server**.

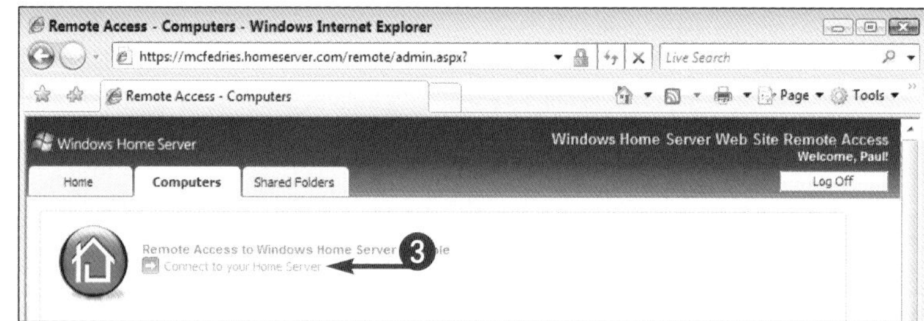

Windows Home Server prompts you for the server password.

4. Type the password for the Windows Home Server Administrator account.
5. Click **OK**.

Windows asks if you trust the computer you are connecting to.

6. Click **Yes**.
7. Press Spacebar or Enter to activate the window.

The Windows Home Server Console appears in the browser window.

- Click **Disconnect** when you are done.

The Windows Home Server Console closes.

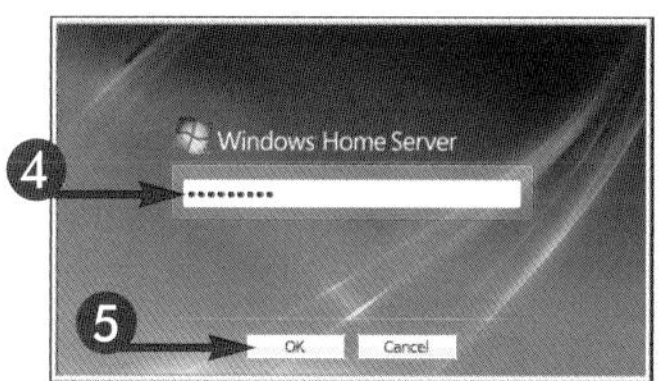


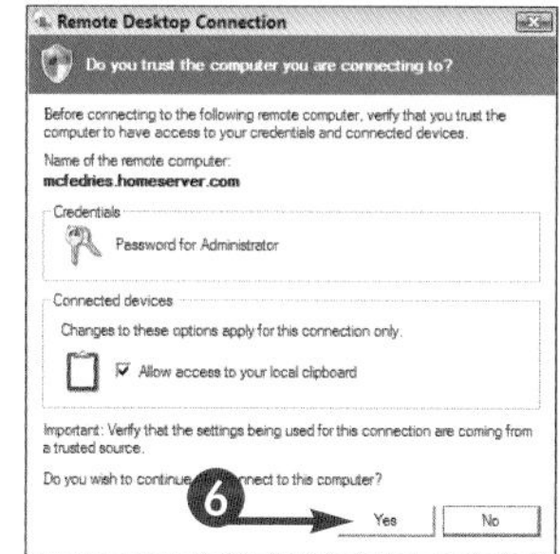


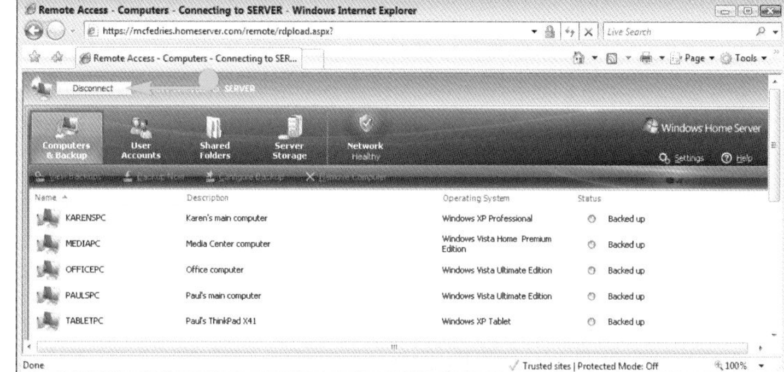

## How do I add my Windows Home Server Web site to Internet Explorer's list of trusted sites?

Here are the steps to follow:

1. In Internet Explorer, click **Tools**.
2. Click **Internet Options**.
3. In the Internet Options dialog box, click the **Security** tab.
4. Click **Trusted sites**.
5. Click **Sites**.
6. In the Trusted sites dialog box, type **https://*address***, where *address* is your Windows Home Server domain name or router Internet address.
7. Click **Add**.
8. Click **Close**.
9. In the Internet Options dialog box, click **OK**.

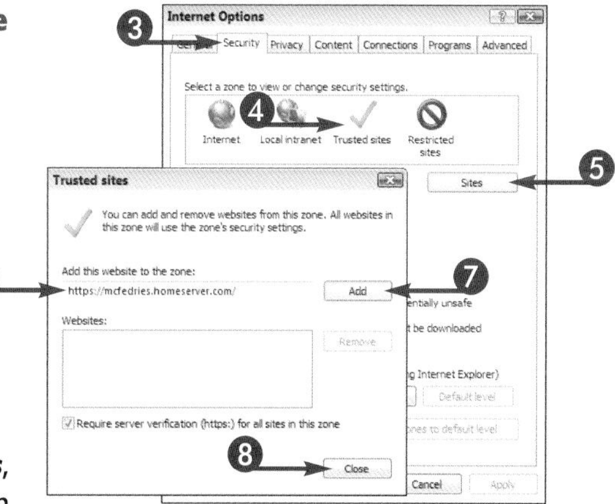

CHAPTER

14

# Maintaining and Troubleshooting Windows Home Server

To keep Windows Home Server running smoothly, maintain top performance, and reduce the risk of computer problems, you need to perform some routine maintenance chores. This chapter shows you how to perform tasks such as viewing network health, deleting unnecessary files, checking for hard drive errors, and repairing problems.

View Network Health ........................................290

Understanding the Network Health Notifications ........................................292

Check System Drive Free Space ........................................294

Delete Unnecessary Files from the System Drive ........................................296

Defragment the System Drive ........................................298

Check the System Drive for Errors ........................................300

Repair a Networking Problem ........................................302

Reinstall Windows Home Server ........................................304

# View Network Health

You can use Windows Home Server to view the health of your home network. Using either the Windows Home Server icon or Console, you can get information about the network status and security problems on your home computers.

**To view network health using the Windows Home Server Console, you must know the password of the Administrator account.**

## View Network Health

### USE THE WINDOWS HOME SERVER ICON

❶ Examine the color of the Windows Home Server icon in the taskbar's notification area.

***Note:*** *See the Tip on the following page to understand what the different icon colors represent.*

### USE THE WINDOWS HOME SERVER CONSOLE

❶ Start the Windows Home Server Console.

***Note:*** *See Chapter 3 for more information.*

❷ Examine the color of the Network icon.

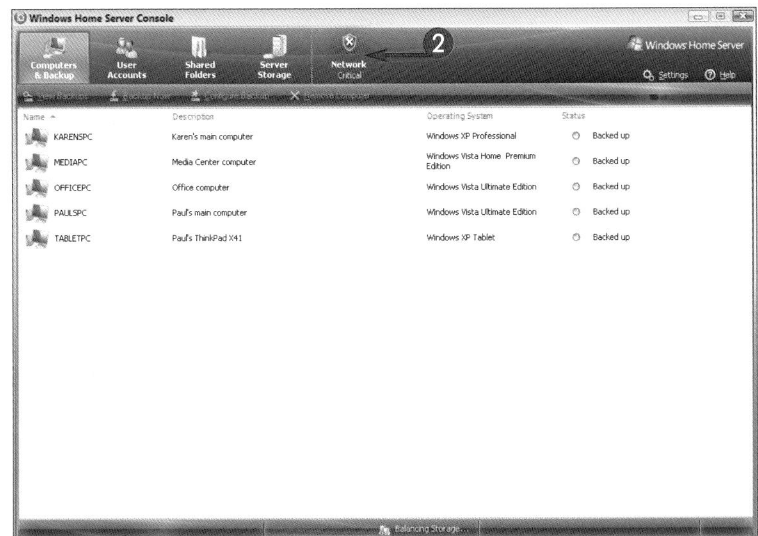

3 If the icon is a color other than green, click **Network**.

The Home Network Health dialog box appears.

- The network health notification appears here.
- If you do not want Windows Home Server to warn you about this problem on this computer in the future, you can click **Ignore this issue** (☐ changes to ☑).

4 Click **Close**.

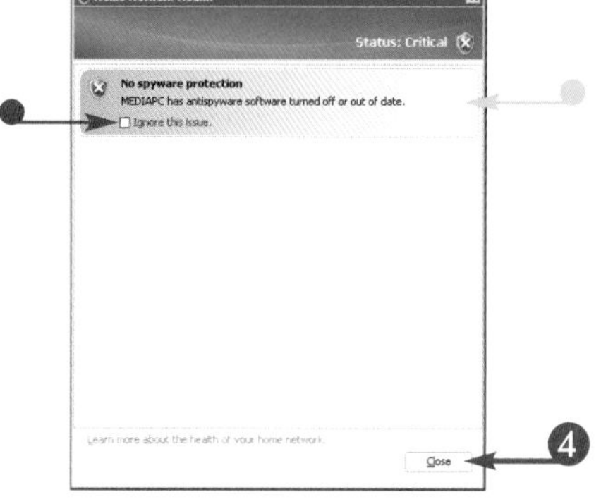

### What do the different icon colors mean?

- The green icon means that the network is healthy.
- The orange icon means that the network has a problem. For example, the most recent backup for a home computer may have failed.
- The red icon means that the network has a critical problem. This is most often a security issue, such as a home computer not having Windows Defender turned on.
- The blue icon means that Windows Home Server is currently backing up the home computer.
- The gray icon means that the home computer cannot locate Windows Home Server.

# Understanding the Network Health Notifications

Besides changing color, the Windows Home Server icon in the taskbar's notification area also displays network health notifications. Understanding the most common notifications will help you to monitor your network.

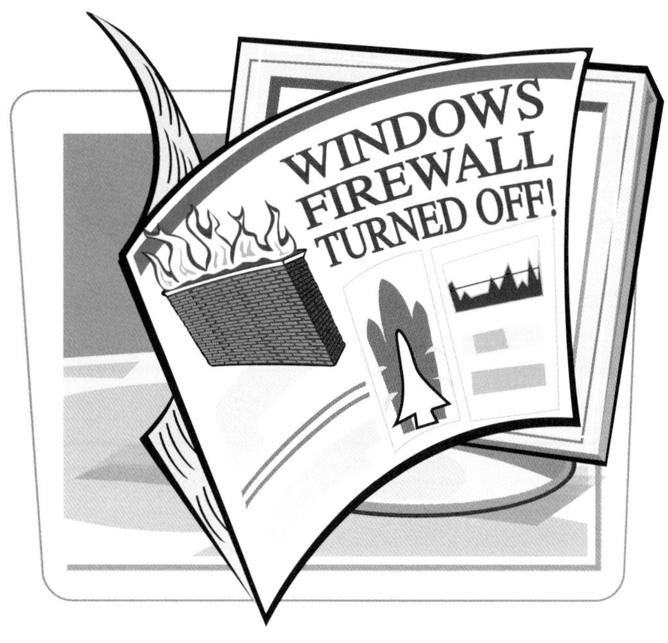


### Backup Is Starting

This notification means that Windows Home Server is starting to back up the computer, so your computer may be a bit slow while the backup proceeds. Click the notification to open the Backup Status dialog box and watch the progress of the backup.

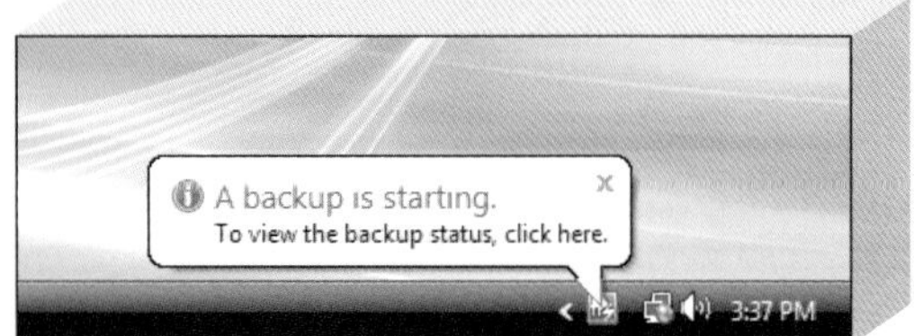


### Backup Error

This notification means that Windows Home Server was not able to back up the specified computer because of an error. To view the error, you can open the backup using Windows Home Server Console. For more information, see Chapter 10.

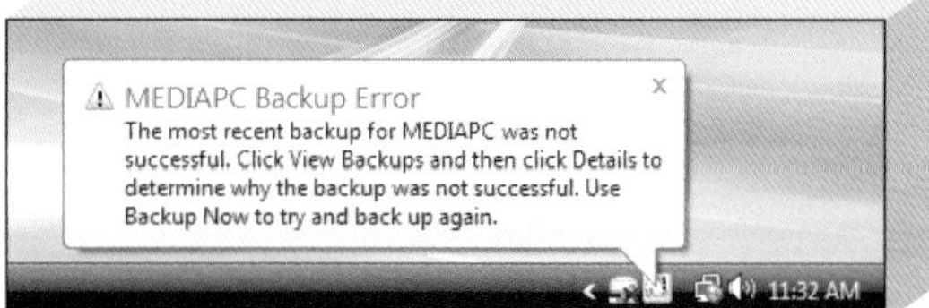

### Network Health Is Critical

This notification means that Windows Home Server is currently experiencing a serious error. You should open Windows Home Server Console to see what the problem is. For more information, see the section "View Network Health."

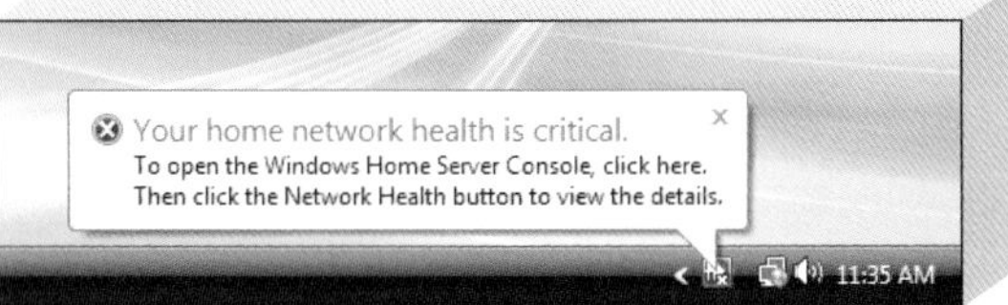


### Updates Are Ready

This notification means that Windows Home Server has detected that one or more updates are ready to install. You should review the updates that are available and then install them. For more information, see Chapter 5.

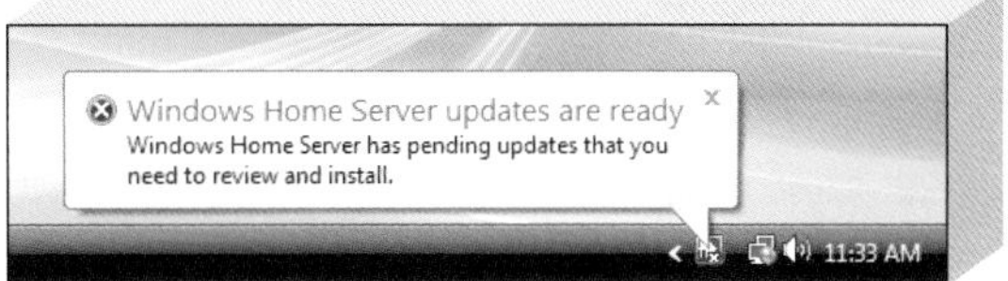


### Windows Firewall Is Off

This notification means that Windows Home Server has detected that one of your home computers has its Windows Firewall turned off. You should access that computer and turn the firewall back on. Note that you only see this notification for Windows Vista computers.

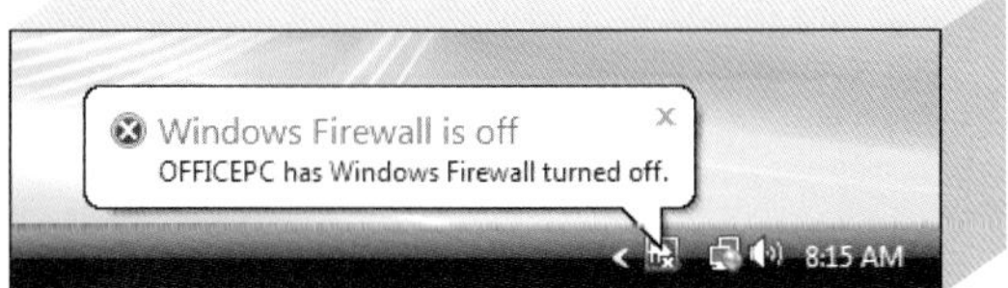


### No Spyware Protection

This notification means that Windows Home Server has detected that one of your home computers has its Windows Defender spyware protection turned off. You should access that computer and turn Windows Defender back on. Note that you only see this notification for Windows Vista computers.

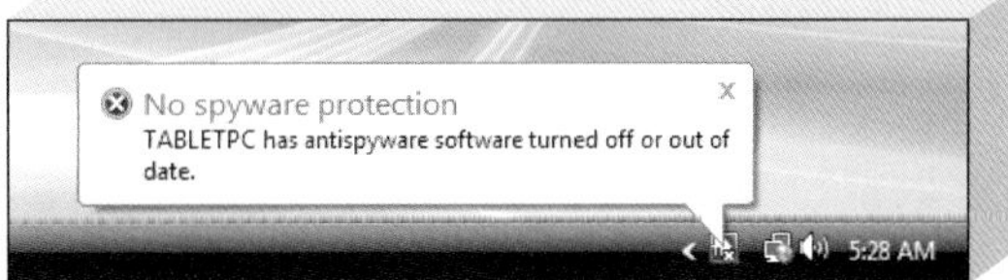

# Check System Drive Free Space

If you run out of space on your Windows Home Server system drive — drive C — you will not be able to install more programs or create more documents. To ensure that this does not happen, you can check how much free space your system drive has.

**Free space on the system drive is only a concern if you use Windows Home Server to install and run other programs and to create documents.**

## Check System Drive Free Space

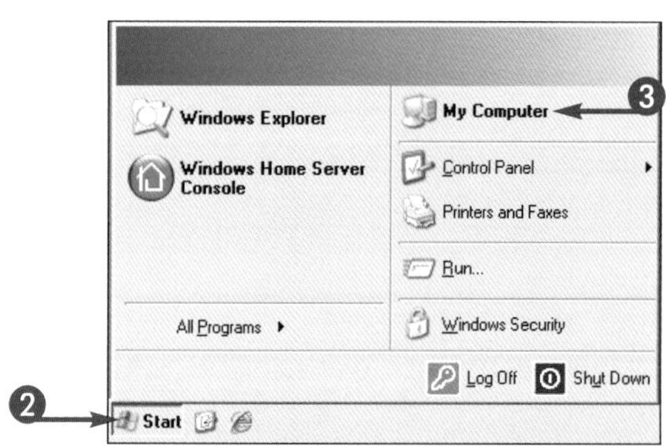


1. Connect to the Windows Home Server desktop.

***Note:*** *For more information about how to connect to the server desktop remotely, see Chapter 11.*

2. Click **Start**.
3. Click **My Computer**.

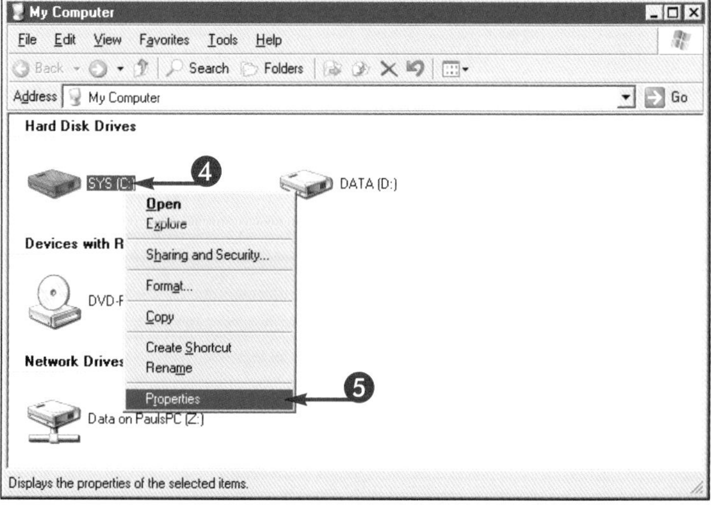


The My Computer window appears.

4. Right-click **drive C:**.
5. Click **Properties**.

- This value tells you the amount of free space on the drive.
- This value tells you the total amount of space on the drive.
- This pie slice shows you graphically how much free space is left.

6 Click **OK**.

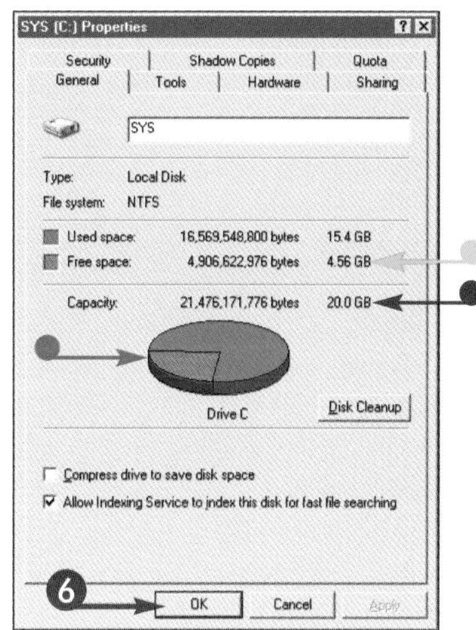


- When you select drive C:, My Computer also shows the free space in the status bar.

7 Click [X] to close the My Computer window.

8 Disconnect from Windows Home Server.

***Note:*** *For more information on how to disconnect, see Chapter 11.*

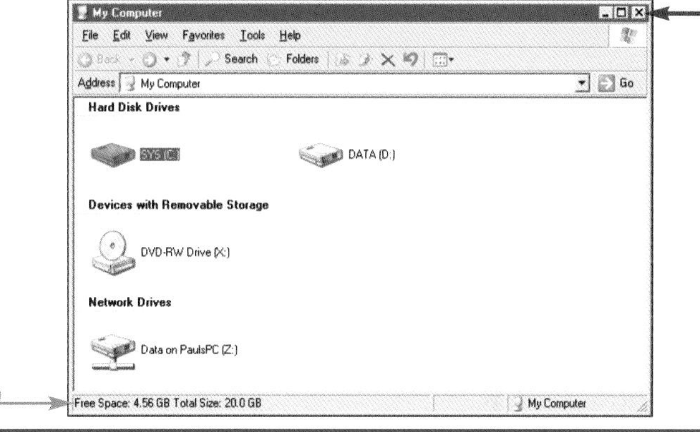

### How often should I check the free space on the system drive?

With normal computer use, you should check your Windows Home Server system drive's free space about once a month. If you install programs, create large files, or download media frequently, you should probably check your free space every couple of weeks.

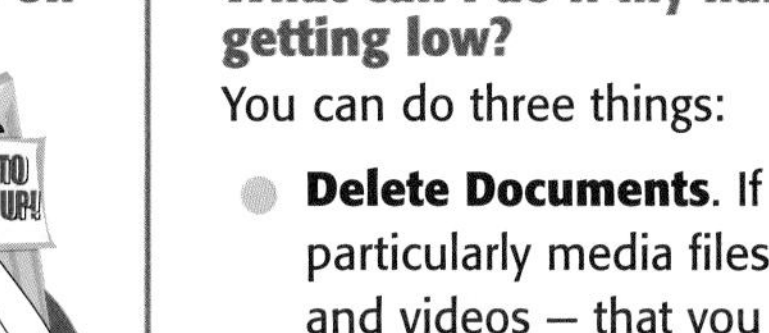


### What can I do if my hard drive space is getting low?

You can do three things:

- **Delete Documents**. If you have documents – particularly media files such as images, music, and videos – that you are sure you no longer need, delete them.
- **Remove Programs**. If you have programs that you no longer use, uninstall them.
- **Run Disk Cleanup**. Use the Disk Cleanup program to delete files that Windows Vista no longer uses. For more information, see the next section "Delete Unnecessary Files from the System Drive."

# Delete Unnecessary Files from the System Drive

To free up hard drive space on the Windows Home Server system drive and keep the server running efficiently, you can use the Disk Cleanup program to delete files that the server no longer needs.

**Run Disk Cleanup whenever your hard drive free space becomes too low. If hard drive space is not a problem, then run Disk Cleanup every two or three months.**

## Delete Unnecessary Files from the System Drive

1. Connect to the Windows Home Server desktop.

*Note: For more information about how to connect to the server desktop remotely, see Chapter 11.*

2. Click **Start**.
3. Click **All Programs**.
4. Click **Accessories**.
5. Click **System Tools**.
6. Click **Disk Cleanup**.

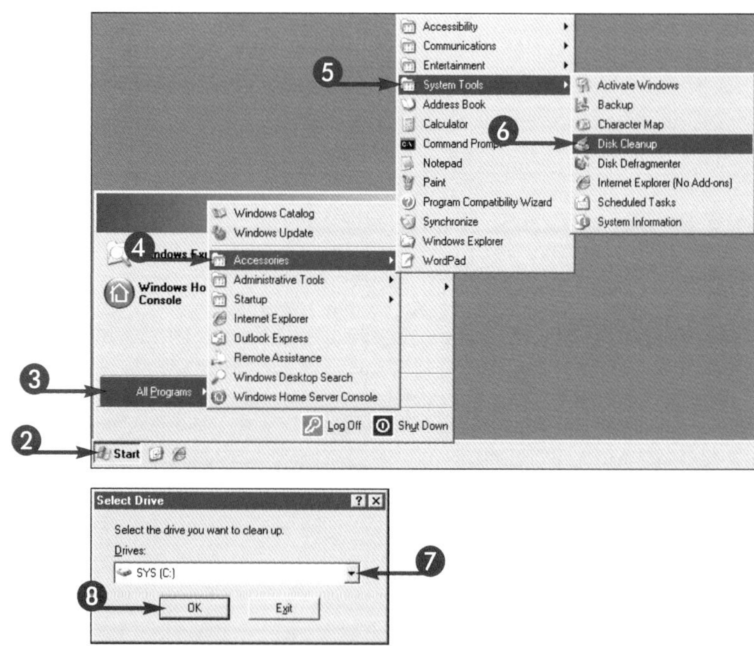


The Select Drive dialog box appears.

7. Click ▾ in the Drives list and then click **SYS (C:)**.
8. Click **OK**.

The Disk Cleanup dialog box appears.

- This area displays the total amount of drive space you can free up.
- This area displays the amount of drive space the activated options will free up.

9 Click the check box for each file type that you want to delete (☐ changes to ☑).

- This area displays a description of the highlighted file type.

10 Click **OK**.

Disk Cleanup asks you to confirm that you want to delete the file types.

11 Click **Yes**.

Disk Cleanup deletes the files.

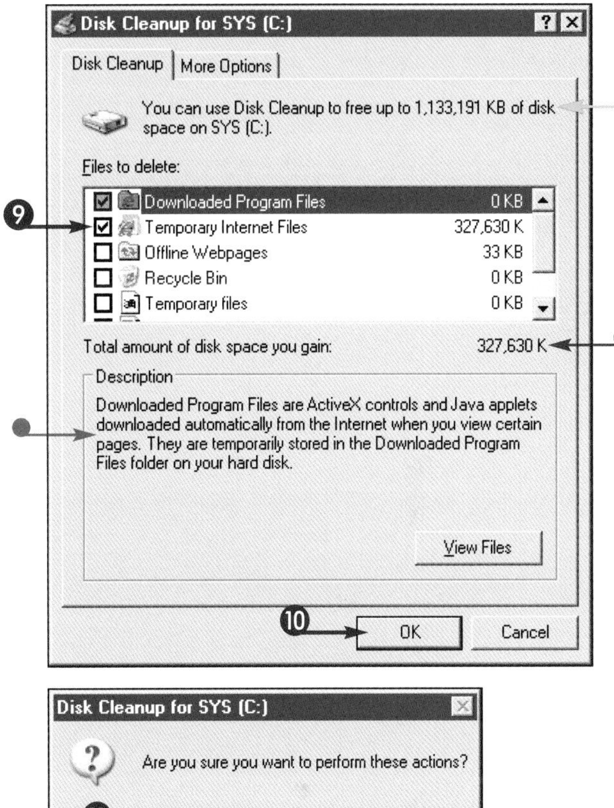

### What types of files does Disk Cleanup delete?

**Downloaded Program Files** – Small Web page programs that are downloaded onto your hard drive.

**Temporary Internet files** – Web page copies stored on your hard drive for faster viewing.

**Offline Web pages** – Web page copies stored on your hard drive for offline viewing.

**Recycle Bin** – Files that you have deleted recently.

**Temporary files** – Files used by programs to store temporary data.

**Compress old files** – Uses file compression to reduce the size of files that the server has not used for a while.

**Catalog files for the Content Indexer** – Old files that were once used to speed up file searches.

# Defragment the System Drive

You can make Windows Home Server and your server programs run faster, and your server documents open more quickly, by defragmenting the server's system drive.

**Most files are stored on the server's system drive in several pieces, and over time those pieces often become scattered around your hard drive. Defragmenting improves performance by bringing all of those pieces together, which makes it faster to find and open each file.**

## Defragment the System Drive

1. Connect to the Windows Home Server desktop.

*Note: For more information about how to connect to the server desktop remotely, see Chapter 11.*

2. Click **Start**.
3. Click **All Programs**.
4. Click **Accessories**.
5. Click **System Tools**.
6. Click **Disk Defragmenter**.

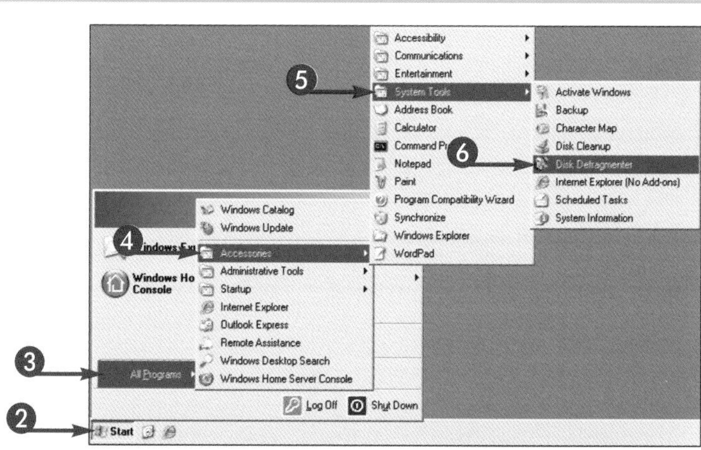


The Disk Defragmenter window appears.

7. Click **SYS (C:)**.
8. Click **Analyze**.

Disk Defragmenter checks the hard drive to see if you need to defragment it.

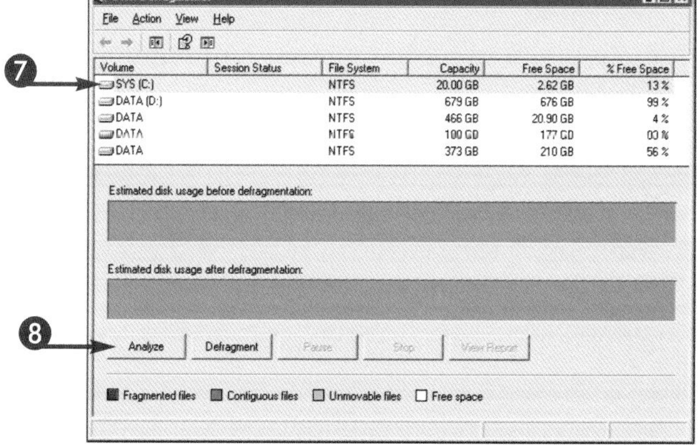

Disk Defragmenter displays a summary dialog box when it completes the analysis.

9 Click **Defragment** if you want to defragment your hard drive.

- You can click **Close** if you do not want to defragment your hard drive.

A dialog box appears when the defragmentation is complete.

10 Click **Close**.

11 Click **Close** (☒) to close Disk Defragmenter.

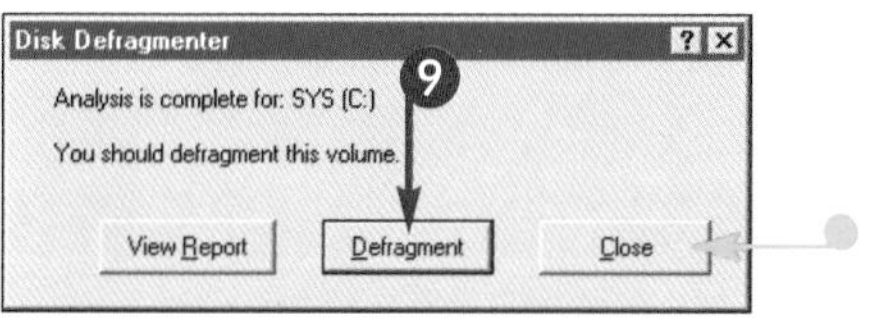


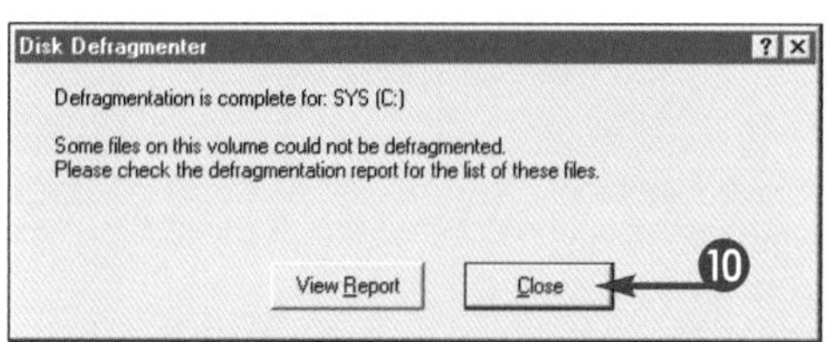


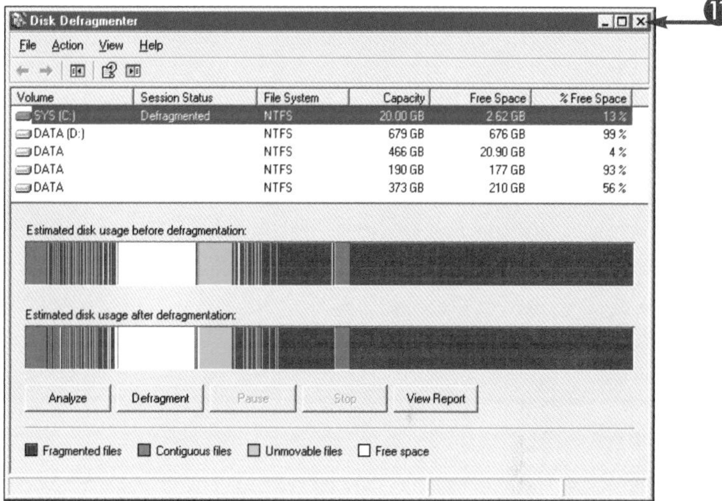

### How often should I defragment my hard drive?

This usually depends on how often you use the computer that you are defragmenting. For example, on a computer that you use only occasionally, you should defragment your hard drive every couple of months. However, your network uses Windows Home Server daily, so you should defragment the server's system drive once a week.

### How long does it take to defragment my hard drive?

It depends on the size of the hard drive, the amount of data that it contains, and the extent of the defragmentation. You should allow at least 15 minutes for the defragmentation, although it could take over an hour.

# Check the System Drive for Errors

Hard drive errors can cause files to become corrupted, which may prevent you from running a program or opening a document. To prevent this, you can use the Check Disk program to look for and fix errors on the Windows Home Server system drive.

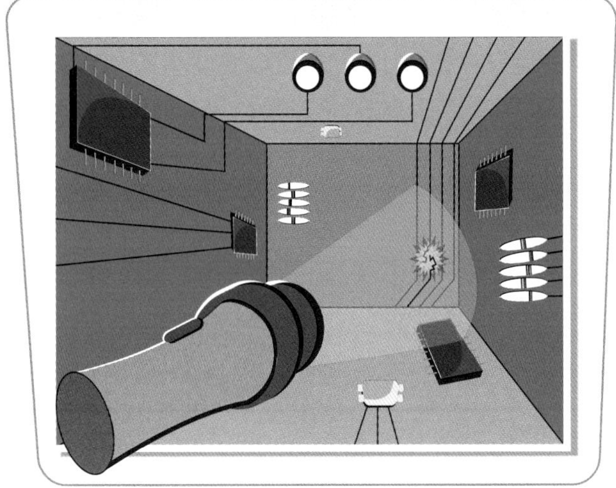

## Check the System Drive for Errors

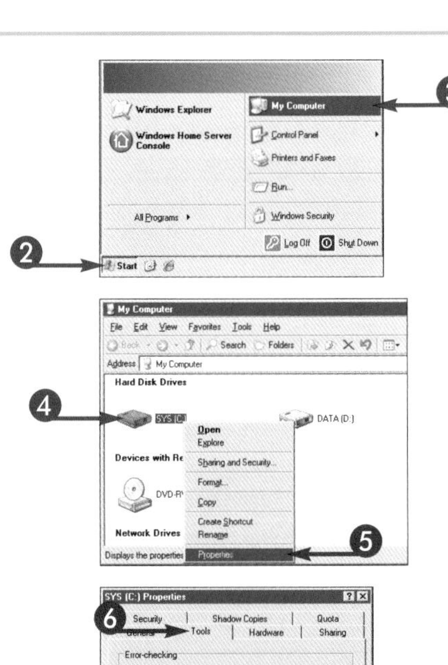

1. Connect to the Windows Home Server desktop.

*Note: For more information about how to connect to the server desktop remotely, see Chapter 11.*

2. Click **Start**.
3. Click **My Computer**.

   The My Computer window appears.

4. Right-click the **SYS (C:)** drive.
5. Click **Properties**.

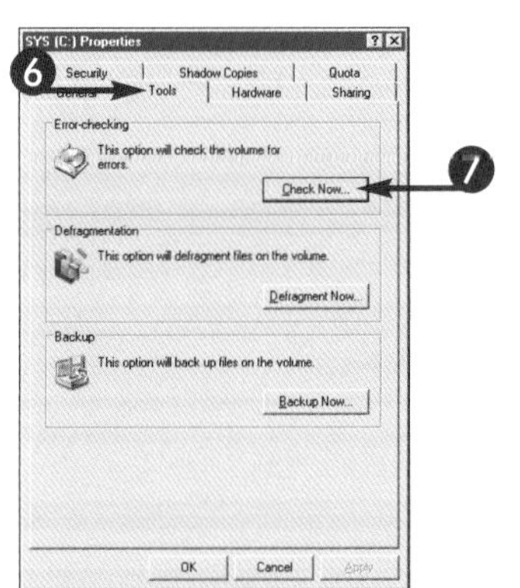

The hard drive's Properties dialog box appears.

6. Click the **Tools** tab.
7. Click **Check Now**.

The Check Disk dialog box appears.

8 If you want Check Disk to fix any errors it finds, click **Automatically fix file system errors** ( changes to ).

9 If you want Check Disk to look for bad sectors, click **Scan for and attempt recovery of bad sectors** ( changes to ).

10 Click **Start**.

The hard drive check begins.

If Check Disk finds any errors and you did not click the "Automatically fix file system errors" option, follow the instructions provided by the program.

A dialog box appears when the drive check is over.

11 Click **OK** to return to the hard drive's Properties dialog box.

12 Click **OK**.

The Properties dialog box closes.

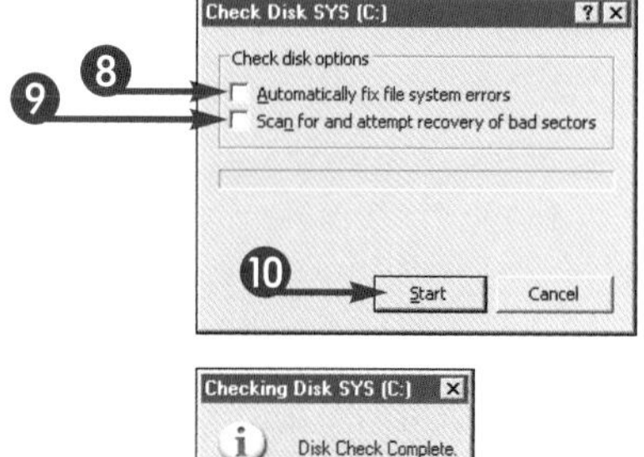


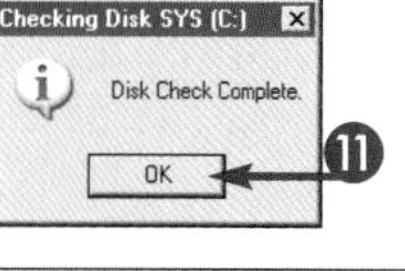


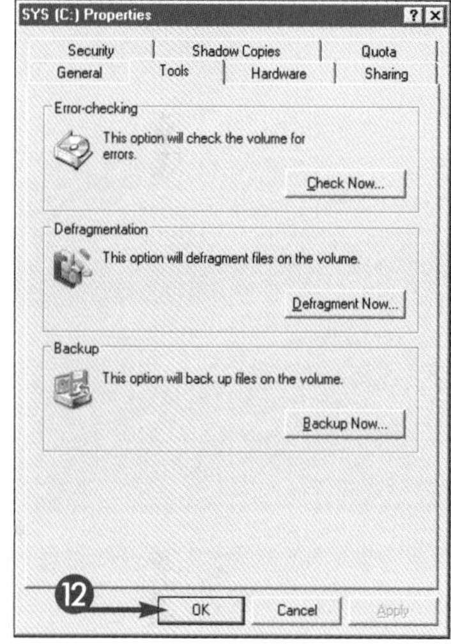

### What is a "bad sector"?

A *sector* is a small storage location on a hard drive. When Windows Home Server saves a file on the drive, it divides the file into pieces and stores each piece in a separate sector. A bad sector is one that, through physical damage or some other cause, can no longer be used to reliably store data.

### How often should I check for hard drive errors?

You should perform the basic hard drive check about once a week. Perform the more thorough bad sector check once a month. Note that the bad sector check can take several hours, so you should only perform this check when it is less likely that people will be using Windows Home Server.

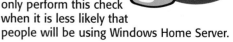

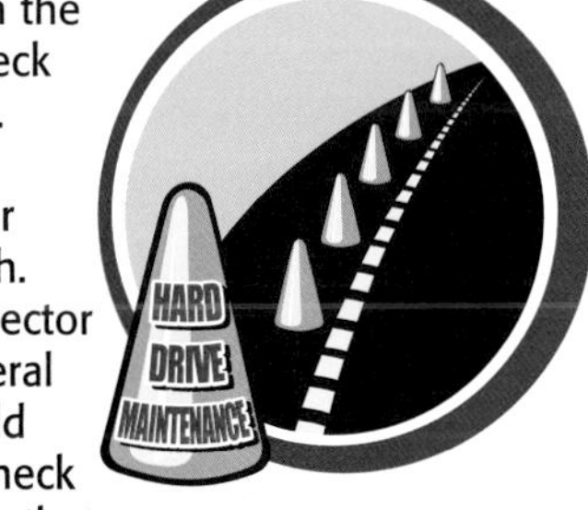

# Repair a Networking Problem

If you find that Windows Home Server can no longer see your home computers, or that none of your home computers can see or access Windows Home Server, then you may have a networking problem. Windows Home Server comes with a Repair feature that can fix most networking problems.

## Repair a Networking Problem

1. Connect to the Windows Home Server desktop.

*Note: For more information about how to connect to the server desktop remotely, see Chapter 11.*

2. Click **Start**.
3. Click **All Programs**.
4. Click **Accessories**.
5. Click **Communications**.
6. Click **Network Connections**.

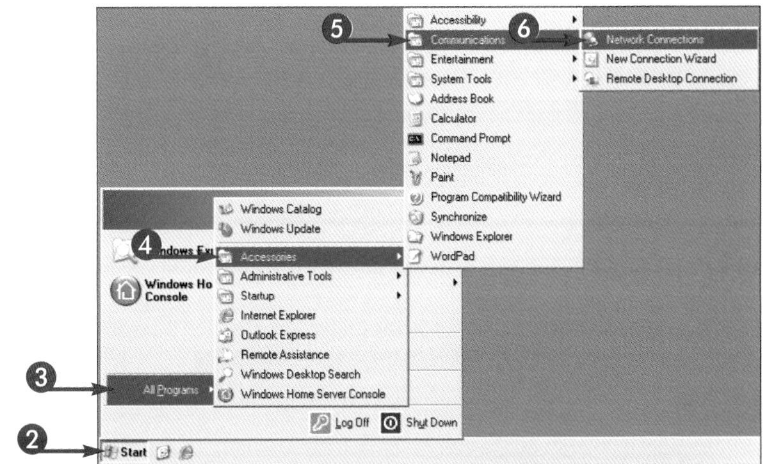

The Network Connections window appears.

7. Right-click **Local Area Connection**.
8. Click **Repair**.

Windows Home Server performs several tasks designed to fix most networking problems.

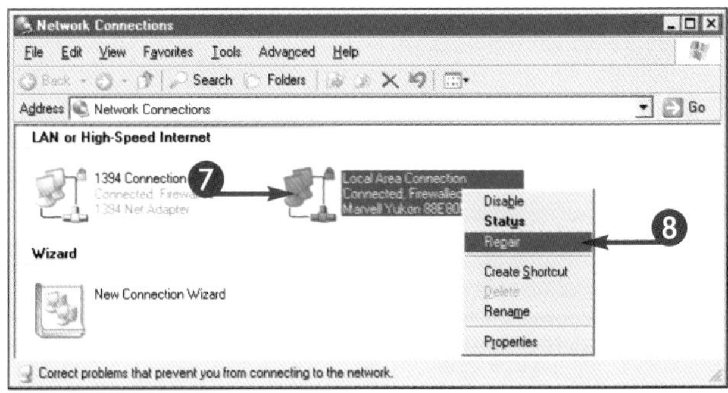

The Repair Local Area Connection dialog box appears.

9 Click **Close**.

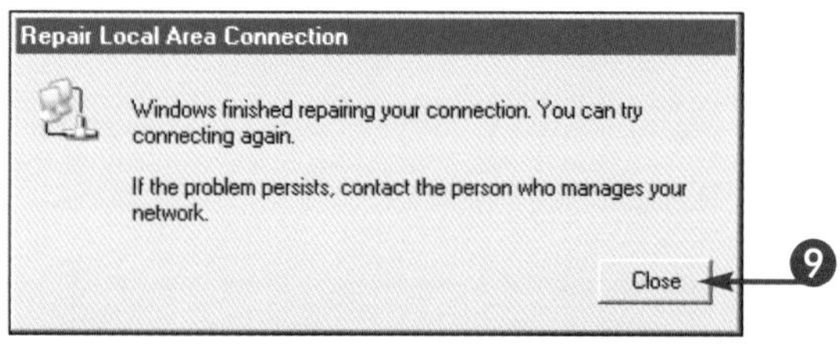


10 Click  to close the Network Connections window.

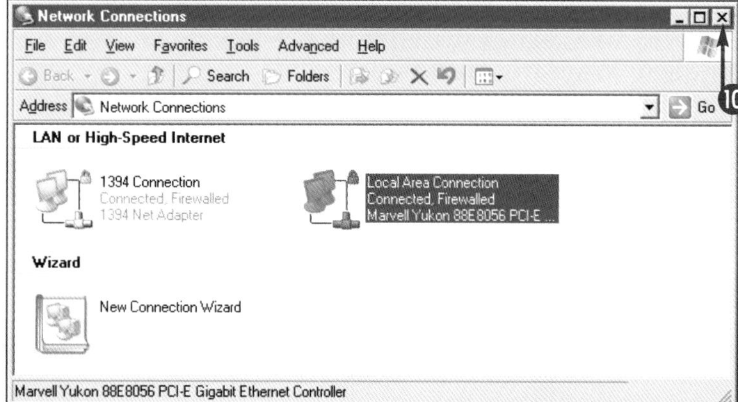


TIPS

### My Windows Vista computer cannot see Windows Home Server. How do I fix this problem?

If your Windows Vista computer cannot see Windows Home Server, then the likely cause is a networking problem on the Vista computer. To run Vista's network repair tool, follow these steps:

1 Right-click the **Network** icon.

2 Click **Diagnose and repair**.

Windows Vista runs the network repair tool.

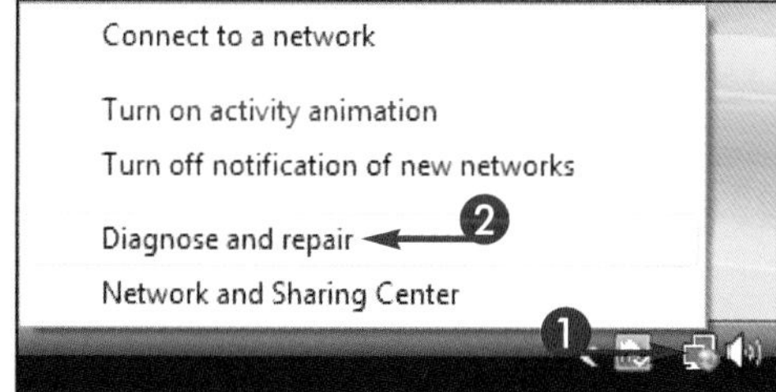


### My Windows XP computer cannot see Windows Home Server. How do I fix this problem?

Windows XP comes with the same networking repair tool that is found in Windows Home Server. Therefore, you can fix most Windows XP networking problems by following steps **2** to **10** in this section. Note that if your Windows XP computer uses a wireless connection, then in step **7** you should right-click the **Wireless Network Connection** icon, as shown here (●).

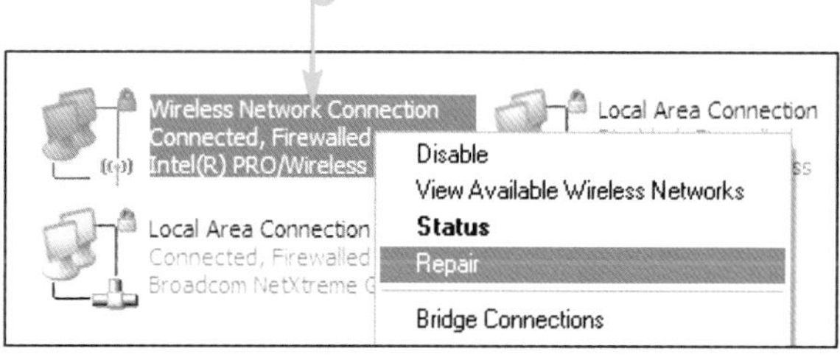

# Reinstall Windows Home Server

If you find that Windows Home Server will not start or is crashing regularly, the problem may be a corrupted system file. You can usually fix this type of problem by reinstalling Windows Home Server.

## Reinstall Windows Home Server

1. Attach a keyboard, mouse, and monitor to the home server computer.
2. Insert the Windows Home Server installation disc.
3. Start the home server computer.
4. Follow the instructions on the computer screen to boot from the disc.

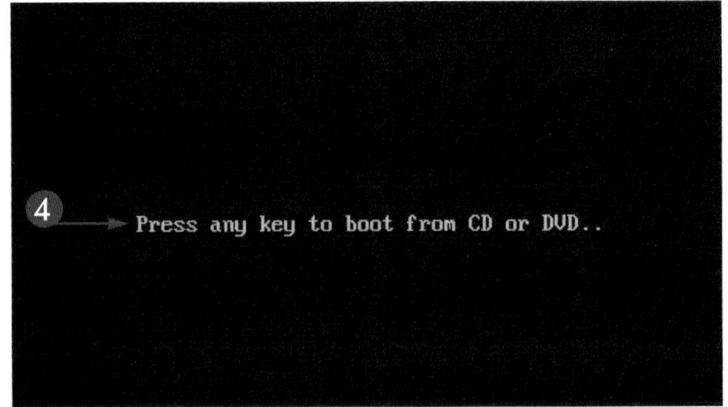


The Windows Home Server Setup Wizard appears.

5. Click **Next**.

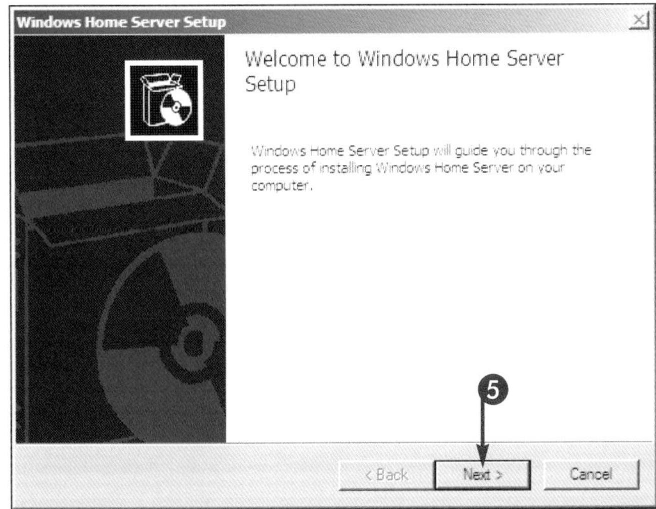

The Windows Home Server Setup Wizard displays a list of hard drives.

6 Click **Next**.

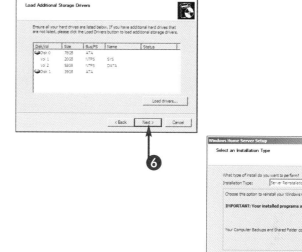

The Select an Installation Type dialog box appears.

7 In the Installation Type list, click ▾ and then click **Server Reinstallation**.

8 Click **Next**.

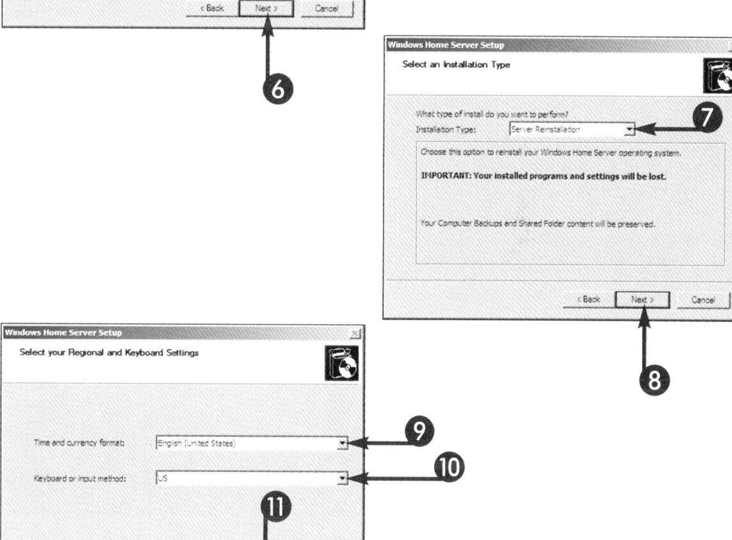

The Select your Regional and Keyboard Settings dialog box appears.

9 Click ▾ and then click your language and country.

10 Click ▾ and then click your keyboard type.

11 Click **Next**.

**When I replace my main hard drive, does Windows Home Server keep my user accounts and other settings?**

No, Windows Home Server does not preserve your user accounts or any options that you may have set in the Windows Home Server Settings dialog box. That data is stored on the home server's system drive, and part of the reinstall procedure involves formatting the system drive, which wipes out your user accounts and settings. Also note that any programs you installed on Windows Home Server will also be deleted during the reinstallation. After the reinstall is complete, you need to use the Windows Home Server Console to re-create your user accounts and reconfigure your Windows Home Server settings.

# Reinstall Windows Home Server *(continued)*

When you select Server Reinstallation as the installation type, you are telling Windows Home Server Setup not to format the other hard drives on the home server. This means that the data in the Windows Home Server shared folders will be preserved.

## Reinstall Windows Home Server *(continued)*

The End-User License Agreement dialog box appears.

12 Click **I accept this agreement** (◯ changes to ◉).

13 Click **Next**.

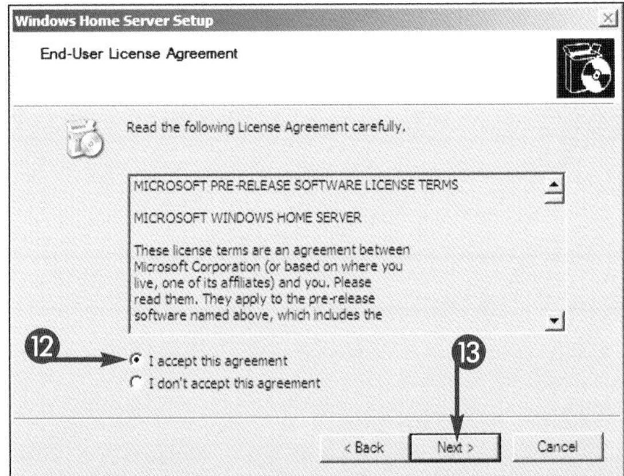


The Enter your Windows Home Server Product Key dialog box appears.

14 In the Product key text boxes, type your 25-digit Windows Home Server product key.

15 Click **Next**.

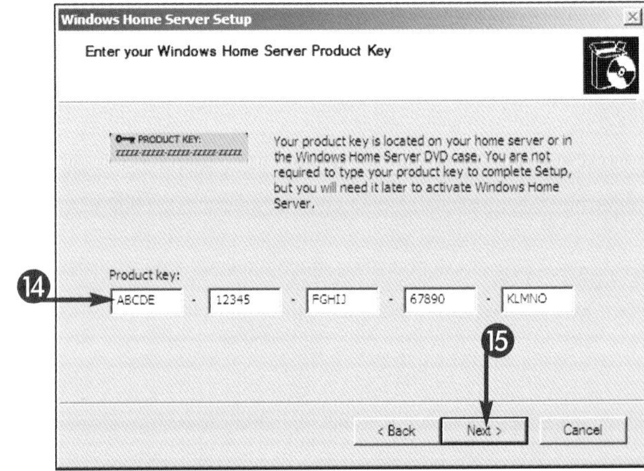

The Name Your Home Server dialog box appears.

16 Type the name you want to use for your home server.

***Note:*** *To avoid problems, you should keep the home server name the same. If you are not sure, use the default name of SERVER.*

17 Click **Next**.

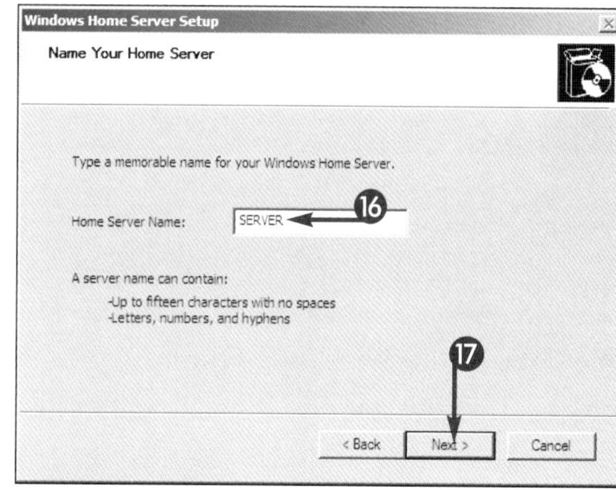


The Ready to install Windows Home Server dialog box appears.

18 Click **Start**.

The Setup Wizard begins installing Windows Home Server.

***Note:*** *The installation may take an hour or more, depending on the configuration of the server computer.*

***Note:*** *As part of the server reinstallation process, the Setup Wizard reinstalls Windows Home Server on the system hard drive. This means that you must run through all of the initial configuration steps, such as specifying the Administrator password.*

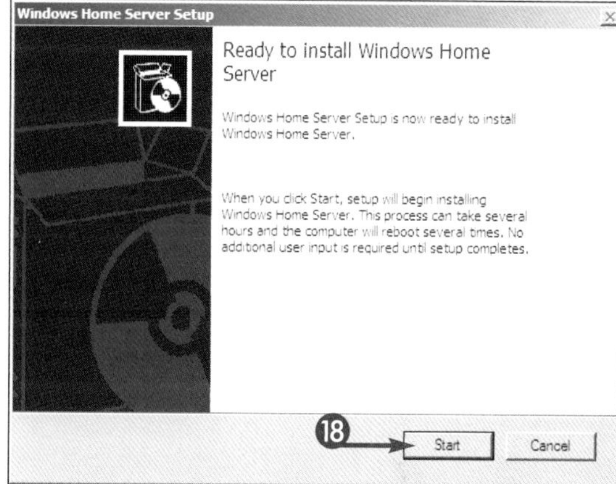


TIP

**After I have reinstalled the home server, the Windows Home Server icon appears gray instead of green. How can I fix this?**

During the reinstallation, your home computers may lose their connection to Windows Home Server. Unfortunately, when you reinstall the server as described in this section, some of your home computers may not be able to reconnect to Windows Home Server, so the icon appears gray. To fix this, you need to run the Discovery program. For more information, see Chapter 3.

# Index


## A

access points (APs), 24, 27, 33
ad hoc wireless networks, 24–26
adapters, network, 18, 26, 215
add-ins, 12, 102–105
addresses
    dynamic IP, 29
    gateway, 51
    Internet Protocol (IP), 29, 50–51, 264–265
    router, 51, 261, 274–275
    static IP, 29, 50–51
Advanced Technology Attachment (ATA) hard drives, 111
Always Available Offline feature, 149
APs (access points), 24, 27, 33
ATA (Advanced Technology Attachment) hard drives, 111
audio, 152, 168–169. *See also* digital media
Audio Video Interleave (AVI) format, 153
automatic backup management, 180–181. *See also* backups
automatic router configuration, 262–263
automatic updates, 95, 179, 293
Automatic Windows Error Reporting service, 100–101
automatically starting programs, 232–233
AVI (Audio Video Interleave) format, 153

## B

Backup Details dialog box, 198–199
Backup Error notification, 292
Backup Is Starting notification, 292
backups
    automatic management, 180–181
    complete, 194
    configuring time of, 178–179
    deletion of
        manual, 204–205
        preventing, 200–201
        scheduling, 195, 202–203
    disk drive, 182–183
    duration of, 199
    excluding folders from, 184–187
    icons, 197
    manual, 188–189
    overview, 6, 10, 17, 176–177
    replacing main hard drive, 121
    restoring
        backed up files, 195, 210–213
        previous computer configurations, 214–219
        previous file versions, 208–209
    saving, 195
    turning off, 190–191
    viewing, 196–199, 206–207
bad sectors, 301
Belkin routers, 269, 275
bit rate, 169
Bluetooth, 25–26
broadband modems, 19, 21, 28
broadcasting, 33. *See also* streaming media
browser, Firefox, 251

## C

cables, network, 18, 28, 36–37
centralized storage, 6
Check Disk program, 300
Check Point ZoneAlarm firewall program, 23
cleanup process, backup, 195, 204–205
clients, 5, 21, 223
client/server networks, 21
Command Prompt window, 264–265
complex passwords, 53, 71
computer names, 48–49
configuration
    network, 20–21, 36–39
    router, 262–263, 266–269
    Start menu, 58–59
    taskbar, 60–61
connection bar, 226–227
Connection Options dialog box, 253
connections
    networks. *See also* Remote Access Web page
        client/server, 21
        configuration of, 20–21, 36–39
        hardware requirements, 18–19
        monitoring health of, 11, 290–293
        overview, 4, 16–17
        problems with, 302–303
        security, 22–23
        wired, 36–37
        wireless, 24–31
    Remote Desktop Connection feature
        activating Windows Home Server Web site, 248–249
        clients, 223
        connecting to remote computers, 224–225, 244–245, 252–253
        connection bar, 226–227

customizing, 228–231, 256–257
disconnecting from remote computers, 254–255
displaying home page, 250–251
giving users permission, 246–247
hosts, 223, 238–241
installing on Windows XP, 242–243
optimizing performance, 234–235
overview, 222–223
saving settings, 229
starting programs automatically, 232–233
customizing
Remote Access site settings, 256–257
Remote Desktop Connection, 228–231
Start menu, 58–59
taskbar, 60–61


## D


date settings, 92–93
defragmentation, 298–299
deletion
backup
manual, 204–205
preventing, 200–201
scheduling, 195, 202–203
shared folder, 87, 146–147
unnecessary system drive file, 296–297
user account, 86–87
DHCP (Dynamic Host Configuration Protocol), 29
digital media
adding folders to Media Center, 170–171
adding folders to Media Player, 166–167
overview, 9, 152–153
ripping music, 168–169
slide shows, 162–165
streaming
overview, 7, 9, 154–155
playing in Media Center, 160–161
playing in Media Player, 158–159
shared folders, 159–160
Shared media icon, 39
turning off media sharing, 172–173
turning on media sharing, 156–157
types of, 152–153
digital media receivers (DMRs), 154
digital subscriber line (DSL) Internet connections, 21
disabling user accounts, 78–79
disconnecting
from remote computers, 254–255, 282–283
from wireless networks, 31
Discovery program, 56–57, 123, 307
Disk Cleanup program, 296–297
disk drives. *See also* system drives
adding to backups, 182–183
adding to storage pool, 114–115
drivers, 215
making shared folders appear as, 130–131
removing from backups, 183
removing from storage pool, 116–117
replacing, 118–123, 305
restoring, 219
storage in, 108
types of, 110–111
unsupported, 115
display names, 74–75
D-Link routers, 267, 274
DMRs (digital media receivers), 154
DNS (Domain Name Servers), 29, 51
DNS (dynamic domain name system) services, 274–277
Domain Name Details dialog box, 277
Domain Name Servers (DNS), 29, 51
domain names, 13, 261, 272–278
drive letters, 109, 130–131
drives
hard
adding to backups, 182–183
adding to storage pool, 114–115
Advanced Technology Attachment (ATA), 111
Advanced Technology Attachment (eSATA), 111
drivers, 215
external, 110–113
failed, 118–123
FireWire, 111
making shared folders appear as, 130–131
removing from backups, 183
removing from storage pool, 116–117
replacing, 118–123, 305
restoring, 219
storage in, 108
types of, 110–111
unsupported, 115
system
checking free space, 294–295
defragmenting, 298–299

# Index


deleting unnecessary files, 296–297
error checking, 300–301
DSL (digital subscriber line) Internet connections, 21
duplication
folder, 7, 109
shared folder, 127, 136–137
dynamic domain name system (DNS) services, 274–277
Dynamic Host Configuration Protocol (DHCP), 29
dynamic IP addresses, 29

## E

effects, graphics, 235
Enable files to be transferred from remote computer to this computer option, Connection Options dialog box, 253
Enable Guest Account Wizard, 83
enabling user accounts, 80–81
error checking, 300–301
Error Reporting service, 100–101
eSATA (external Serial Advanced Technology Attachment) hard drives, 111
Ethernet, 20
external hard drives, 110–113
external Serial Advanced Technology Attachment (eSATA) hard drives, 111

## F

failed hard drives, 118–123
Failing status, 117
family user accounts, 8
Fast Ethernet, 20, 223, 235
features
Always Available Offline, 149
media sharing, 39, 156–157, 159–160, 172–173
Remote Access
activating Windows Home Server Web site, 248–249
connecting to remote computers, 244–245, 252–253
customizing settings, 256–257
disconnecting from remote computers, 254–255
displaying home page, 250–251
giving users permission, 246–247
installing Remote Desktop Connection on Windows XP, 242–243
overview, 7, 13, 65, 245
Windows Vista as host, 238–239
Windows XP as host, 240–241
Remote Desktop Connection
activating Windows Home Server Web site, 248–249
clients, 223
connecting to remote computers, 224–225, 244–245, 252–253
connection bar, 226–227
customizing, 228–231, 256–257
disconnecting from remote computers, 254–255
displaying home page, 250–251
giving users permission, 246–247
hosts, 223, 238–241
installing on Windows XP, 242–243
optimizing performance, 234–235
overview, 222–223
saving settings, 229
starting programs automatically, 232–233
remote Internet access
connecting to remote computers, 280–281
connection speed, 260
disconnecting from remote computers, 282–283
displaying Remote Access home page, 278–279
domain names, 272–277
IP addresses, 264–265
overview, 260–261
routers, 262–263, 266–271
running Windows Home Server Console, 286–287
security, 261
shared folders, 284–285
Repair, 37, 117, 302–303
shared media, 39, 156–157, 159–160, 172–173
View Backups, 194, 196–197
files
deleting, 296–297
digital video, 153
downloading from shared folders, 285
protecting, 181
restoring, 195, 208–213
sharing
accessing shared folders, 128–129
applying user access permissions, 138–141
in Console, 132–133
creating shared folders, 8, 144–145
deleting shared folders, 146–147
digital media, 155
duplication settings, 136–137
offline, 148–149
overview, 6, 11, 16, 126–127

Photos shared folder, 162
remote Internet access, 284–285
renaming shared folders, 134–135
security, 12
shared folders as disk drives, 130–131
storage, 9
Users shared folder, 127
viewing history, 142–143
storage, 9
synchronizing, 149
system, 113
transferring over Internet, 281
viewing backup, 206–207
Firefox Web browser, 251
firewalls, 23, 293
FireWire hard drives, 111
firmware, 263
folders
digital media, 166–167, 170–171
duplicating, 7, 109
excluding from backups, 184–187
shared
accessing, 128–129
applying user access permissions, 138–141
in Console, 132–133
creating, 8, 144–145
deleting, 146–147
digital media, 155
as disk drives, 130–131
duplication settings, 136–137
offline, 148–149
overview, 6, 11, 16, 126–127
Photos shared folder, 162
remote Internet access, 284–285
renaming, 134–135
security, 12
storing, 9
Users shared folder, 127
viewing history, 142–143
user access permissions
applying to shared folders, 138–141
defined, 23, 65, 127
Full user permission
applying to shared folders, 138–141
defined, 23, 65, 127
Guest accounts, 84

## G

gateway addresses, 51
gateways, wireless, 28–29
Gigabit Ethernet, 20, 223, 235
graphics effects, 235
Guest accounts, 82–85

## H

hard drives. *See also* system drives
adding to backups, 182–183
adding to storage pool, 114–115
Advanced Technology Attachment (ATA), 111
Advanced Technology Attachment (eSATA), 111
drivers, 215
external, 110–113
failed, 118–123
FireWire, 111
making shared folders appear as, 130–131
removing from backups, 183
removing from storage pool, 116–117
replacing, 118–123, 305
restoring, 219
storage in, 108
types of, 110–111
unsupported, 115
hardware requirements, 5, 18–19
headless operation, 5, 13, 37, 222
health, network, 11, 290–293
hints, password, 53
history, shared folder, 142–143
Home Computer Restore CD, 10
home page, Remote Access, 257
Home Server
activating Web site, 248–249
advanced uses, 12–13
benefits of, 10–11
common tasks, 8–9
features, 6–7
getting IP address, 264–265
network configurations, 20–21
overview, 4–5
Home Server Connector, 40–41, 55
Home Server Console program
network health, 290–291
overview, 7

# Index


running, 42–43, 286–287
shared folders, 132–133
hosts, 223

## I

icons
backup, 197
Start menu, 58–59
Windows Home Server
color of, 97, 123, 307
number of, 39, 157
viewing network health via, 290–291
IEEE 1394 ports, 111
images, 153, 162–165. *See also* digital media
infrastructure wireless networks, 24
installing
Remote Desktop Connection, 242–243
Windows Home Server, 304–307
Windows Home Server Connector, 40–41
internal hard drives
adding to backups, 182–183
adding to storage pool, 114–115
Advanced Technology Attachment (ATA), 111
Advanced Technology Attachment (eSATA), 111
drivers, 215
failed, 118–123
making shared folders appear as, 130–131
removing from backups, 183
removing from storage pool, 116–117
replacing, 118–123, 305
restoring, 219
storage in, 108
types of, 110–111
unsupported, 115
Internet access feature, remote
connecting to remote computers, 280–281
connection speed, 260
disconnecting from remote computers, 282–283
displaying Remote Access home page, 278–279
domain names, 272–277
IP addresses, 264–265
overview, 260–261
routers
automatic configuration, 262–263
manual configuration, 266–269
viewing details, 270–271
running Windows Home Server Console, 286–287
security, 261
shared folders, 284–285
Internet Explorer trusted sites, 287
Internet Protocol (IP) addresses
configuring server with, 50–51
defined, 29
getting, 264–265
router, 274–275
Internet service providers (ISPs), 19, 29
IP (Internet Protocol) addresses
configuring server with, 50–51
defined, 29
getting, 264–265
router, 274–275
ISPs (Internet service providers), 19, 29

## K

Kbps (kilobits per second), 169
keyboard shortcuts, 45
keystrokes, Remote Desktop Connection, 230–231
kilobits per second (Kbps), 169

## L

language settings, 94
LANs (local area networks), 20, 28
Library, Media Player, 159, 167
license agreement, 40
Linksys routers, 274
Live Custom Domains service, Microsoft Windows, 277
Live OneCare firewall program, 23
load balancing, 109
local area networks (LANs), 20, 28
logging off, 23
logging on, 22, 279
logon names, 64

## M

maintenance
network health, 290–293
reinstalling Windows Home Server, 304–307
repairing networking problems, 302–303
system drives
checking free space, 294–295
defragmenting, 298–299

deleting unnecessary files, 296–297
error checking, 300–301
manual backups, 188–189. *See also* backups
manual router configuration, 266–269
Media Center, 160–161, 170–171
media, digital
adding folders to Media Center, 170–171
adding folders to Media Player, 166–167
overview, 9, 152–153
ripping music, 168–169
slide shows, 162–165
streaming
overview, 7, 9, 154–155
playing in Media Center, 160–161
playing in Media Player, 158–159
shared folders, 159–160
Shared media icon, 159–160
turning off media sharing, 172–173
turning on media sharing, 156–157
types of, 152–153
Media Player, 158–159, 166–167, 173
media sharing feature, 39, 156–157, 159–160, 172–173
media stream, 154–155
Medium password policy, 67, 71
Microsoft Media Center, 160–161, 170–171
Microsoft Media Player, 158–159, 166–167, 173
Microsoft PlaysForSure logo, 155
Microsoft Windows Home Server
activating Web site, 248–249
advanced uses, 12–13
benefits of, 10–11
common tasks, 8–9
features, 6–7
getting IP address, 264–265
network configurations, 20–21
overview, 4–5
Microsoft Windows Home Server Connector, 40–41, 55
Microsoft Windows Home Server Console program
network health, 290–291
overview, 7
running, 42–43, 286–287
shared folders, 132–133
Microsoft Windows Live Custom Domains service, 277
Microsoft Windows Live OneCare firewall program, 23
Microsoft Windows Media Video files, 153
Microsoft Windows Vista
allowing connections to computers running, 239
configuring as Remote Desktop Connection host, 238–239
networking problems, 303
Sidebar slide shows, 164–165
viewing network, 38
Microsoft Windows XP
networking problems, 303
Photos slide shows, 163
previous file versions, 209
Remote Desktop Connection
configuring as host, 240–243
finding, 225
viewing network, 39
Microsoft WMA format, 152, 161
modems, broadband, 19, 21, 28
Motion Picture Experts Group (MPEG) format, 153
MPEG (Motion Picture Experts Group) format, 153
MP3 format, 152
music, 152, 168–169. *See also* digital media


## N


names
computer, 48–49
display, 74–75
domain, 13, 261, 272–278
logon, 64
network, 29
shared folder, 135, 145
subdomain, 13
usernames, 22–23, 267
Netgear routers, 269, 275
network adapters, 18, 26, 215
network cables, 18, 28, 36–37
network cards, 18, 26, 215
Network Health Is Critical notification, 293
network interface cards (NICs), 18, 26, 215
network names, 29
networks
client/server, 21
configuration of, 20–21, 36–39
hardware requirements, 18–19
monitoring health of, 11, 290–293
overview, 4, 16–18
problems with, 302–303
Remote Access Web page
activating Windows Home Server Web site, 248–249
connecting with, 252–253
customizing settings, 256–257

# Index


displaying, 250–251
giving users remote access, 246–247
Remote Desktop Connection
connecting with, 244–245
disconnecting, 254–255
optimizing performance of, 234–235
Windows Vista, 238–239
Windows XP, 240–243
security, 22–23
wired, 36–37
wireless
connecting to, 30–31
devices, 26–27
disconnecting from, 31
gateways, 28–29
overview, 24–25
security, 32–33
NICs (network interface cards), 18, 26, 215
No Spyware Protection notification, 293
None user permission
Access Denied message, 129
applying to shared folders, 138–141
defined, 65, 127

## O

operating systems (OS), 4

## P

passwords
access point, 33
complex, 53, 71
configuring logon screen to remember, 43
forgotten, 41
on local computers, 68–69
Medium password policy, 67, 71
network security, 23
policies, 66–67, 71, 247
router, 267
strong, 247
Strong password policy, 67, 247
synchronizing local and server, 72–73, 77
user account, 64, 76–77
Weak password policy, 67
Windows Home Server, 52–53
PC cards, 26
peer-to-peer networks, 21
performance issues, 223, 234–235
permissions
Full
applying to shared folders, 138–141
defined, 23, 65, 127
Guest accounts, 84
None
Access Denied message, 129
applying to shared folders, 138–141
defined, 65, 127
Read, 23, 65, 127, 138–141
Remote Desktop Connection, 223
user access
applying to shared folders, 138–141
defined, 23, 65, 127
personalization
Remote Access site settings, 256–257
Remote Desktop Connection, 228–231
Start menu, 58–59
taskbar, 60–61
photos, 153, 162–165. *See also* digital media
Photos shared folder, 162
Photos slide shows, 163
picture frames, digital, 155
PlaysForSure logo, 155
Point-to-Point Protocol over Ethernet (PPPoE), 29
port forwarding, 261
ports, 6, 36
forwarding, 261
IEEE 1394, 111
Remote Desktop Protocol (RDP), 268
WAN, 28
PPPoE (Point-to-Point Protocol over Ethernet), 29
Previous Versions tab, 209
print servers, wireless, 27
privacy, 23, 30, 139
programs
Check Disk, 300
Check Point ZoneAlarm firewall, 23
Discovery, 56–57, 123, 307
Disk Cleanup, 296–297
Live OneCare firewall, 23
Microsoft Windows Home Server Console
network health, 290–291
overview, 7

running, 42–43, 286–287
shared folders, 132–133
Microsoft Windows Live OneCare firewall, 23
starting automatically, 232–233
Properties dialog boxes, 75, 135


## R


radio signals, 24, 32
radio transceivers, 24
range extenders, wireless, 27
ranges, wireless, 25
RDP (Remote Desktop Protocol) port, 268
Read user permission, 23, 65, 127, 138–141
recovering. *See also* restoring
deleted shared folders, 147
PCs, 10
rediscovering Windows Home Server, 56–57
region settings, 94
reinstalling Windows Home Server, 304–307
Remember my credentials check box, 245
Remote Access feature
activating Windows Home Server Web site, 248–249
connecting to remote computers, 244–245, 252–253
customizing settings, 256–257
disconnecting from remote computers, 254–255
displaying home page, 250–251
giving users permission, 246–247
installing Remote Desktop Connection on Windows XP, 242–243
overview, 7, 13, 65, 245
Windows Vista as host, 238–239
Windows XP as host, 240–241
Remote Desktop Connection feature
activating Windows Home Server Web site, 248–249
clients, 223
connecting to remote computers, 224–225, 244–245, 252–253
connection bar, 226–227
customizing
Remote Access site settings, 256–257
sounds and keystrokes, 230–231
window, 228–229
disconnecting from remote computers, 254–255
displaying home page, 250–251
giving users permission, 246–247
hosts
defined, 223
Windows Vista as, 238–239
Windows XP as, 240–241
installing on Windows XP, 242–243
optimizing performance, 234–235
overview, 222–223
saving settings, 229
starting programs automatically, 232–233
Remote Desktop Protocol (RDP) port, 268
remote Internet access feature
connecting to remote computers, 280–281
connection speed, 260
disconnecting from remote computers, 282–283
displaying Remote Access home page, 278–279
domain names, 272–277
IP addresses, 264–265
overview, 260–261
routers
automatic configuration, 262–263
manual configuration, 266–269
viewing details, 270–271
running Windows Home Server Console, 286–287
security, 261
shared folders, 284–285
Remove button, 147
renaming shared folders, 134–135
Repair feature, 37, 117, 302–303
requirements, hardware, 5, 18–19
residential gateways, 19
Resources tab, Windows Home Server Settings dialog box, 91
restart settings, 96–97
restoring
backed up files, 195, 210–213
overview, 10
previous computer configurations, 195, 214–219
previous file versions, 195, 208–209
ripping music, 152, 168–169
Router Configuration Details dialog box, 271
routers
addresses, 51, 261, 274–275
Belkin, 269, 275
configuration of
automatic, 262–263
manual, 266–269
overview, 21

# Index


defined, 19
displaying Remote Access home page, 278
D-Link, 267, 274
as firewalls, 23
Linksys, 274
Netgear, 269, 275
port forwarding, 261
viewing details of, 270–271

## S

SATA (Serial Advanced Technology Attachment) hard drives, 111
saving backups, 195
scheduling backup deletion, 195, 202–203
sectors, 301
Secure Sockets Layer (SSL), 268
security
- components of, 22–23
- implementing, 32–33
- Network Level Authentication, 239
- overview, 12, 261
- passwords
  - access point, 33
  - complex, 53, 71
  - configuring logon screen to remember, 43
  - forgotten, 41
  - on local computers, 68–69
  - Medium password policy, 67, 71
  - network security, 23
  - policies, 66–67, 71, 247
  - router, 267
  - strong, 247
  - Strong password policy, 67, 247
  - synchronizing local and server, 72–73, 77
  - user account, 64, 76–77
  - Weak password policy, 67
  - Windows Home Server, 52–53
- permissions
  - Full, 23, 65, 84, 127, 138–141
  - None, 65, 127, 129, 138–141
  - Read, 23, 65, 127, 138–141
  - Remote Desktop Connection, 223
  - unsecured networks, 30

security keys, 32
Serial Advanced Technology Attachment (SATA) hard drives, 111
servers, 5, 21
Service Set Identifiers (SSIDs), 29, 33
services
- Automatic Windows Error Reporting, 100–101
- dynamic domain name system (DNS), 274–277
- Error Reporting, 100–101
- Microsoft Windows Live Custom Domains, 277

settings
- add-ins, 102–105
- Automatic Windows Error Reporting, 100–101
- date and time, 92–93
- displaying, 90–91
- region and language, 94
- Remote Access site, 256–257
- Remote Desktop Connection feature, 228–231
- restart, 96–97
- shared folder duplication, 136–137
- shut down, 98–99
- Windows Update, 95

shadow copies, 209
shared equipment, 16–17
shared folders
- accessing, 128–129
- applying user access permissions, 138–141
- in Console, 132–133
- creating, 8, 144–145
- deleting, 146–147
- digital media, 155
- as disk drives, 130–131
- duplication settings, 136–137
- offline, 148–149
- overview, 6, 11, 16, 126–127
- Photos shared folder, 162
- remote Internet access, 284–285
- renaming, 134–135
- security, 12
- storing, 9
- Users shared folder, 127
- viewing history, 142–143

shared media feature, 39, 156–157, 159–160, 172–173
shortcuts, 44–45, 47
shut down settings, 98–99
Sidebar, 164–165

signal strength, wireless, 31
slide shows, 162–165
sounds, 230–231
speeds, wireless, 25
spyware, 293
SSIDs (Service Set Identifiers), 29, 33
SSL (Secure Sockets Layer), 268
Start menu, 44–45, 58–59
static IP addresses, 29, 50–51
stopping backups, 190–191
storage
  adding, 114–115
  capacity, 9, 108, 115
  centralized, 6
  hard drive types, 110–111
  overview, 9, 108–109
  removing, 116–117
  replacing main hard drives, 118–123
  viewing, 112–113
storage pool, 108–109
streaming media
  in Media Center, 160–161
  in Media Player, 158–159
  media sharing
    folders, 159–160
    icon, 39
    turning off, 172–173
    turning on, 156–157
  overview, 7, 9, 154–155
Strong password policy, 67, 247
subdomain names, 13
switches, 19
synchronizing
  files, 149
  local and server passwords, 72–73, 77
  user accounts with Windows, 65
system drives
  checking free space, 294–295
  defragmenting, 298–299
  deleting unnecessary files, 296–297
  error checking, 300–301
system files, 113
System Properties dialog box, 47
System storage pie chart item, 113

# T

taskbar, 60–61
time settings, 92–93
time zones, 93
timing, backup, 178–179
transceivers, 24
transferring files, 281
troubleshooting, 37. *See also* maintenance
trusted sites, 287
turning off backups, 190–191

# U

uninstalling
  add-ins, 104–105
  Windows Home Server Connector, 55
Universal Plug and Play (UPnP), 263, 271
Universal Serial Bus (USB)
  hard drives, 111
  ports, 26, 111
  wireless network adapters, 26
updates, 95, 179, 293
Updates Are Ready notification, 293
Updating Windows Live Custom Domains item, 277
UPnP (Universal Plug and Play), 263, 271
USB (Universal Serial Bus)
  hard drives, 111
  ports, 26, 111
  wireless network adapters, 26
user access permissions, 23, 65, 127, 138–141
user accounts
  adding, 70–71
  disabling, 78–79
  display names, 74–75
  enabling, 80–81
  family, 8
  Guest accounts, 82–85
  overview, 64–65
  passwords
    changing, 68–69, 76–77
    setting policies, 66–67
    synchronizing local and server, 72–73
  removing, 86–87
  replacing main hard drive, 119
User Accounts tab, 8

# Index


user permission
- Full
  - applying to shared folders, 138–141
  - defined, 23, 65, 127
  - Guest accounts, 84
- None
  - Access Denied message, 129
  - applying to shared folders, 138–141
  - defined, 65, 127
- Read, 23, 65, 127, 138–141

user subfolders, 65
usernames
- logon, 64
- network, 22–23
- router, 267

Users shared folder, 127

## V

video, 153. *See also* digital media
View Backups feature, 194, 196–197
Vista, Windows
- allowing connections to computers running, 239
- configuring as Remote Desktop Connection host, 238–239
- networking problems, 303
- Sidebar slide shows, 164–165
- viewing network, 38

## W

WAN ports, 28
wardriving, 32–33
Weak password policy, 67
Web browser, Firefox, 251
Wi-Fi (Wireless Fidelity), 25, 32
Wi-Fi Protected Access (WPA), 32
Windows Firewall Is Off notification, 293
Windows Home Server
- activating Web site, 248–249
- advanced uses, 12–13
- benefits of, 10–11
- common tasks, 8–9
- features, 6–7
- getting IP address, 264–265
- network configurations, 20–21
- overview, 4–5

Windows Home Server Connector, 40–41, 55
Windows Home Server Console program
- network health, 290–291
- overview, 7
- running, 42–43, 286–287
- viewing shared folders, 132–133

Windows Live Custom Domains item, 277
Windows Live OneCare firewall program, 23
Windows Media Audio (WMA) format, 152
Windows Media Center, 160–161, 170–171
Windows Media Player, 158–159, 166–167, 173
Windows Media Video (WMV) format, 153
Windows Update settings, 95
Windows Vista
- allowing connections to computers running, 239
- configuring as Remote Desktop Connection host, 238–239
- networking problems, 303
- Sidebar slide shows, 164–165
- viewing network, 38

Windows XP
- networking problems, 303
- Photos slide shows, 163
- previous file versions, 209
- Remote Desktop Connection, 225, 240–243
- viewing network, 39

wired networks, 36–37
wireless access points (APs), 24, 27, 33
wireless devices, 26
Wireless Fidelity (Wi-Fi), 25, 32
wireless gateways, 28–29
wireless networks
- connecting to, 30–31
- devices, 26–27
- disconnecting from, 31
- gateways, 28–29
- overview, 24–25
- range of, 25
- security, 32–33
- speed of, 25

wireless print servers, 27
wireless range extenders, 27
WMA (Windows Media Audio) format, 152
WMV (Windows Media Video) format, 153
workgroup names, 37, 46–47
WPA (Wi-Fi Protected Access), 32

## X

Xbox 360, 161
XP, Windows
- networking problems, 303
- Photos slide shows, 163
- previous file versions, 209
- Remote Desktop Connection
  - configuring as host, 240–243
  - finding, 225
- viewing network, 39

## Z

ZoneAlarm firewall program, 23

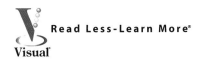